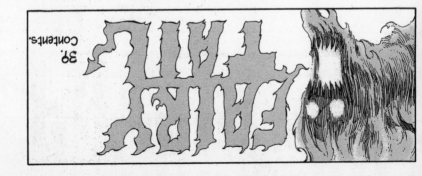

FAIRY TAIL

39.
Contents.

FAIRY TAIL

39

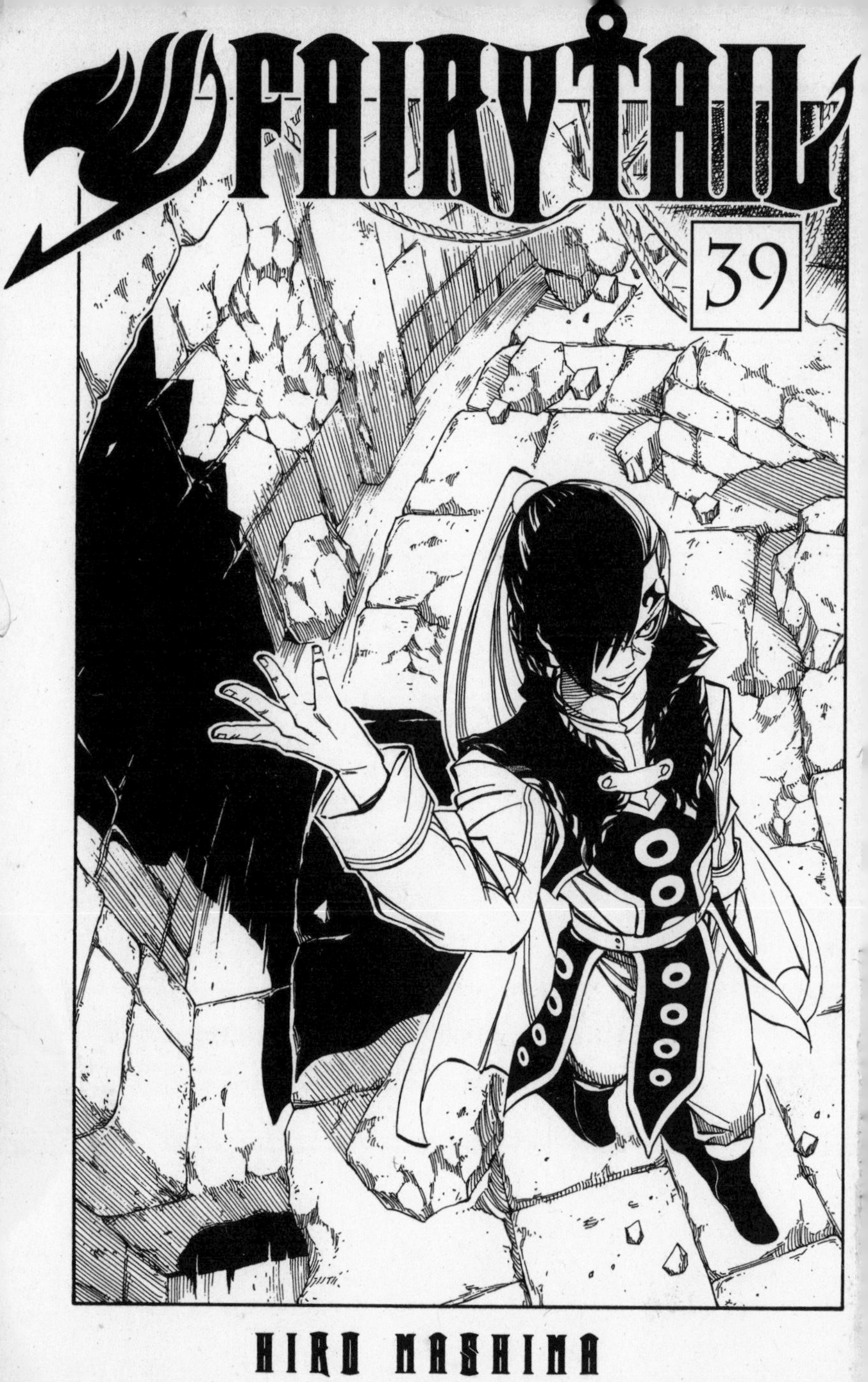

HIRO MASHIMA

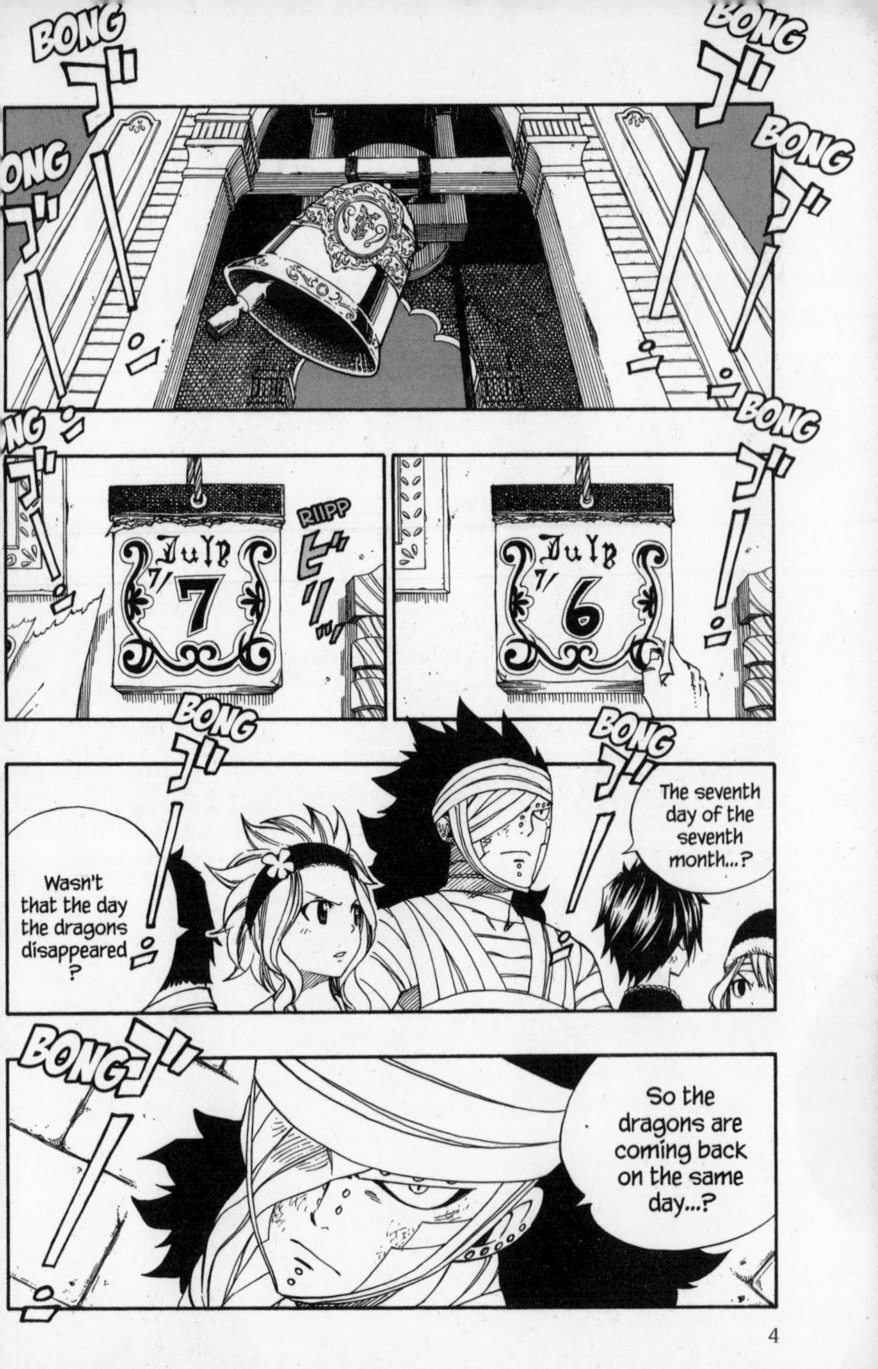
BONG
BONG
BONG
BONG
BONG
July
7/6
RIIPP
July
7/7
BONG
BONG
The seventh day of the seventh month...?
Wasn't that the day the dragons disappeared?
BONG
So the dragons are coming back on the same day...?

FAIRY TAIL

フェアリーテイル

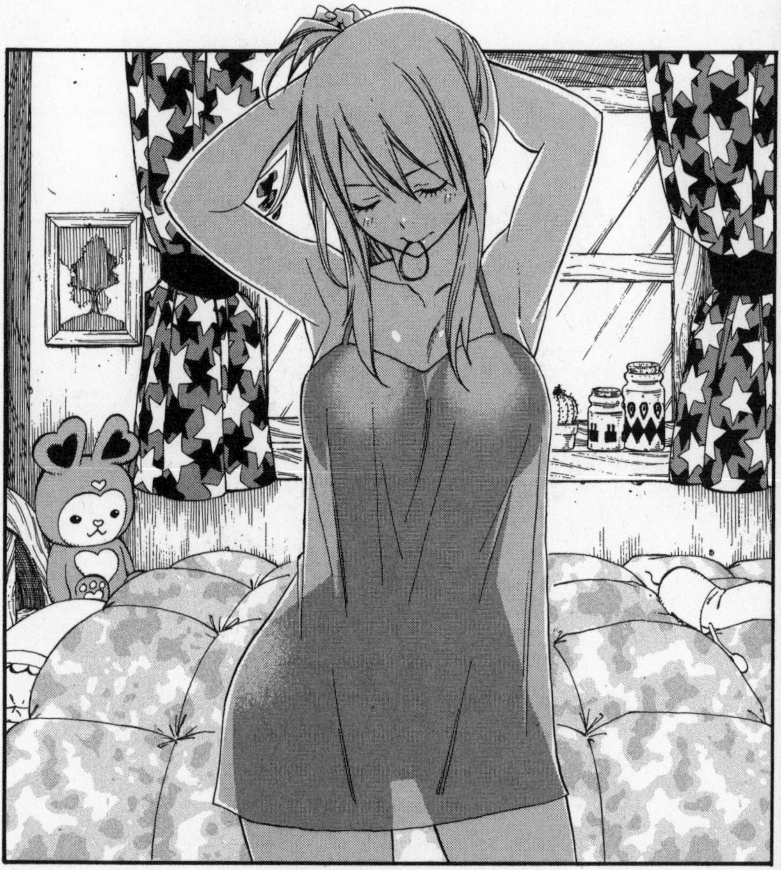

Chapter 326: Natsu vs. Rogue

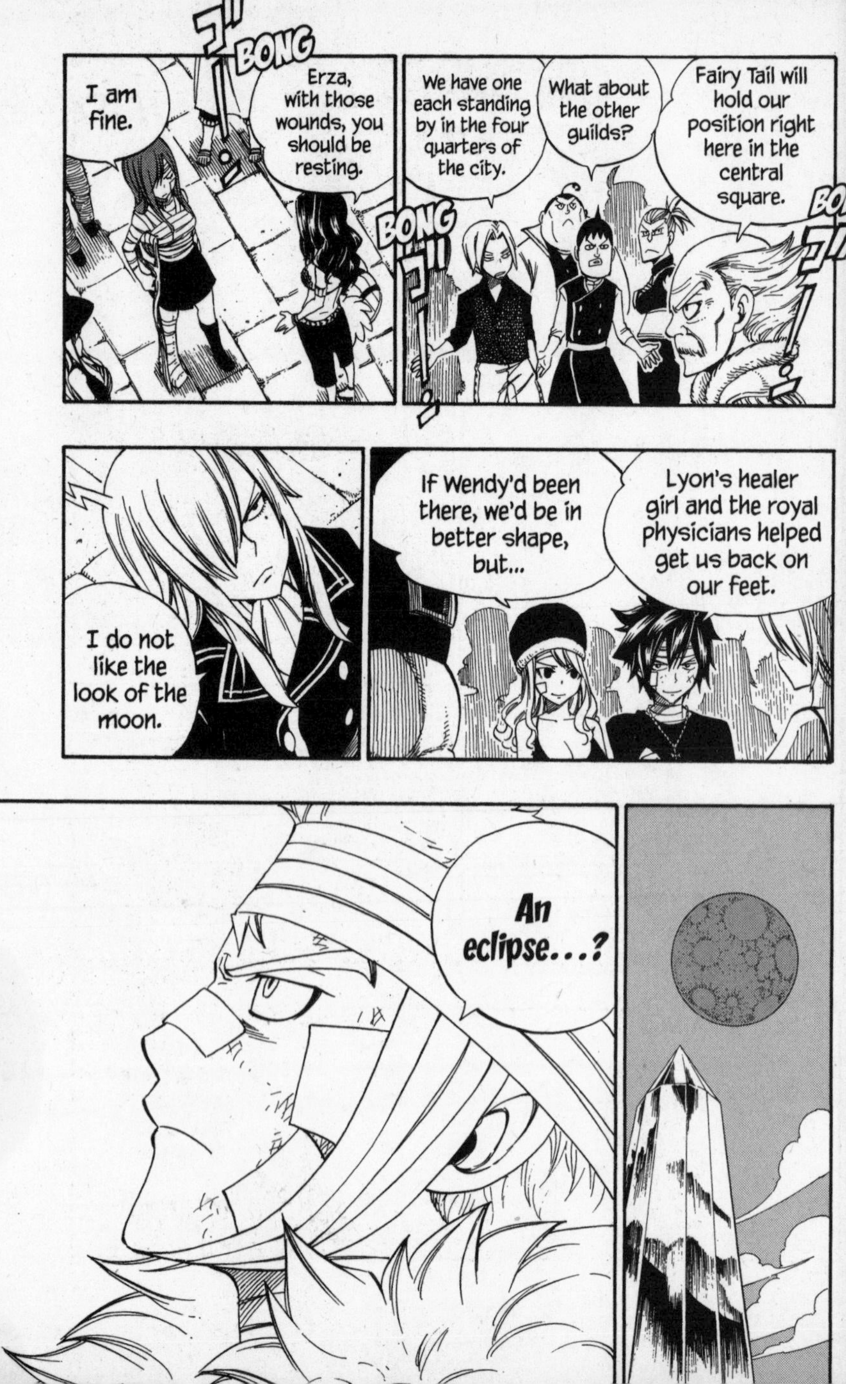
BONG
Fairy Tail will hold our position right here in the central square.
What about the other guilds?
We have one each standing by in the four quarters of the city.
BONG
BONG
Erza, with those wounds, you should be resting.
I am fine.
Lyon's healer girl and the royal physicians helped get us back on our feet.
If Wendy'd been there, we'd be in better shape, but...
I do not like the look of the moon.
An eclipse...?

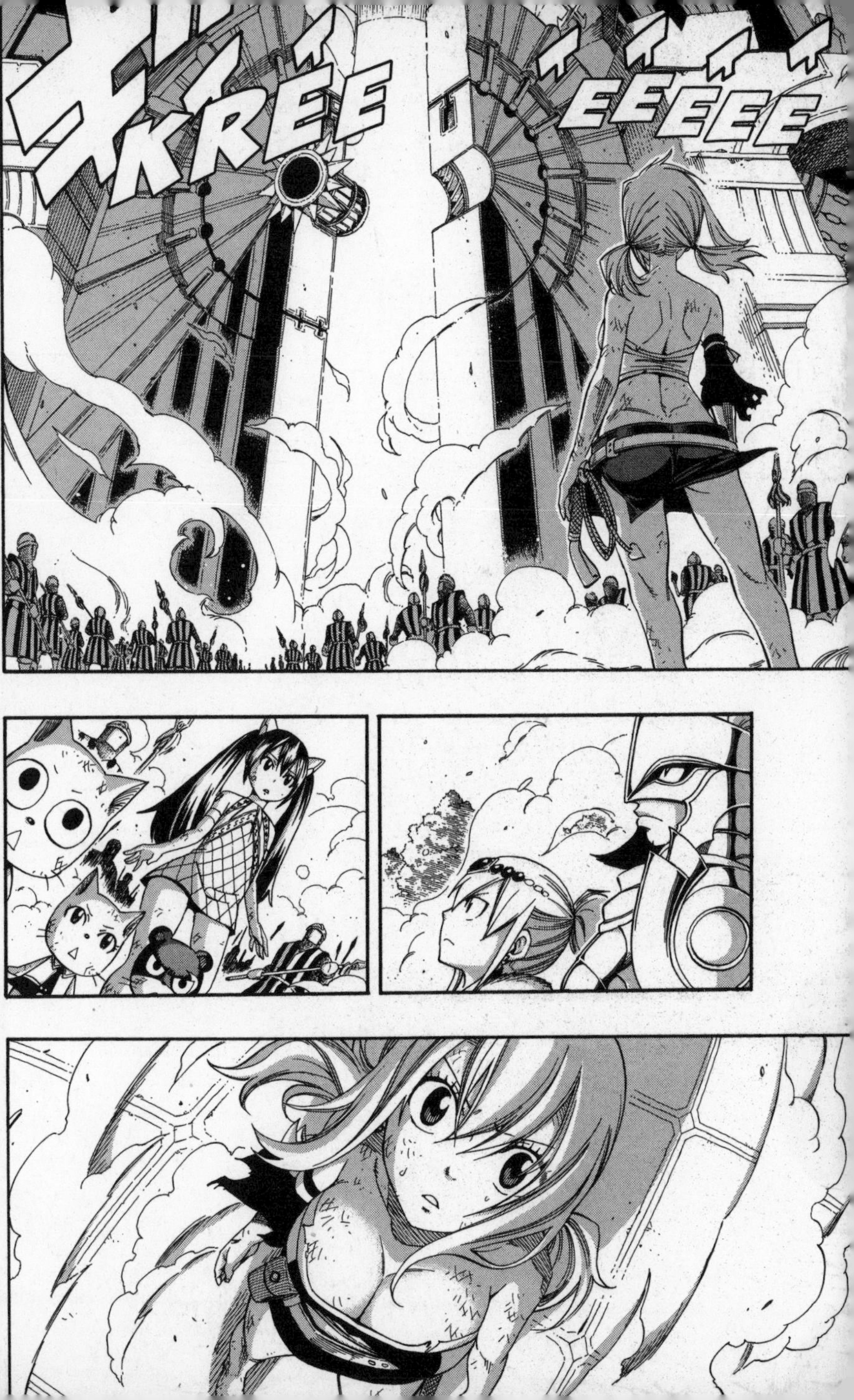
KREEEEEEEE

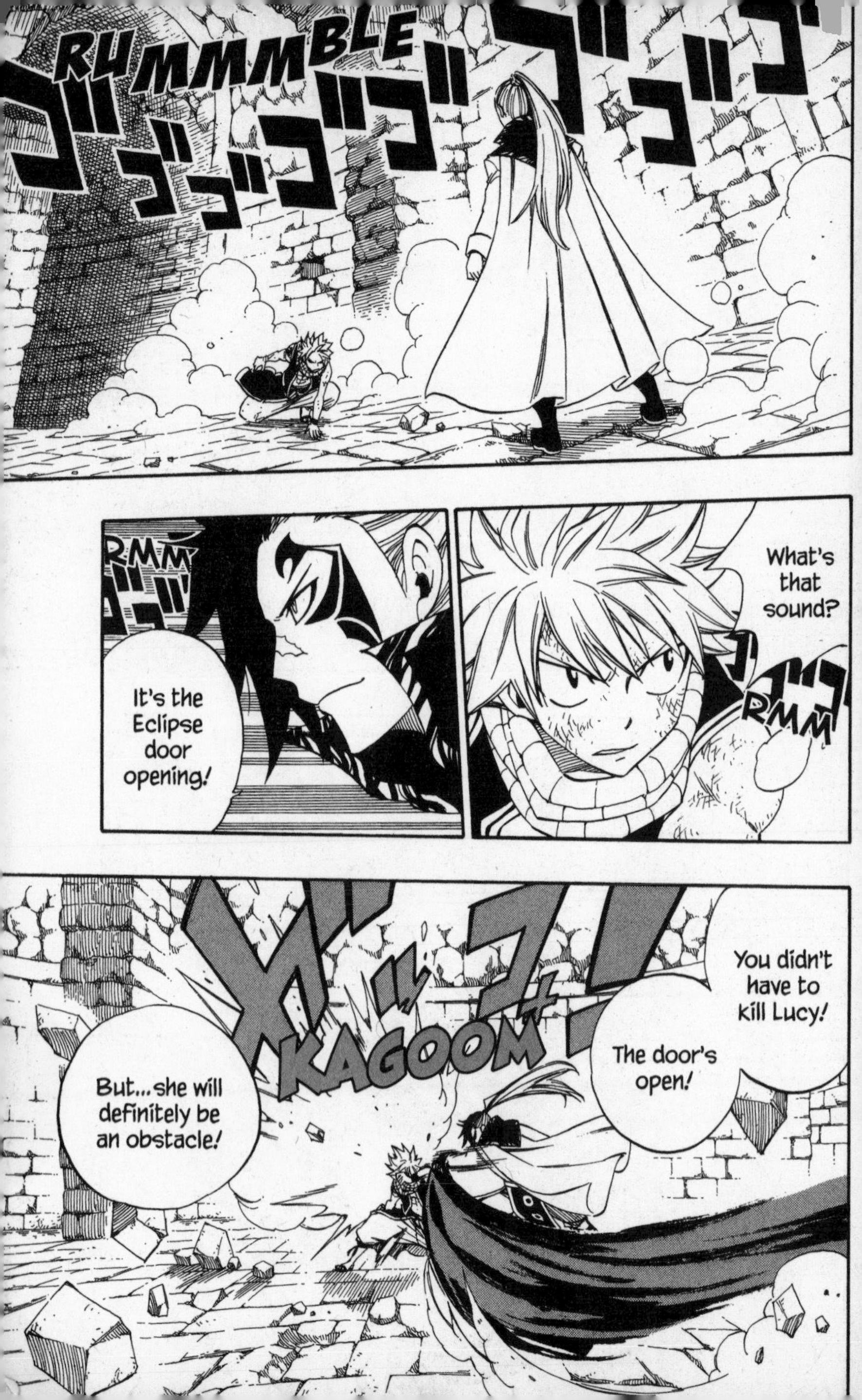
RUMMMBLE
What's that sound?
RMM
RMM
It's the Eclipse door opening!
You didn't have to kill Lucy!
The door's open!
KAGOOM
But...she will definitely be an obstacle!

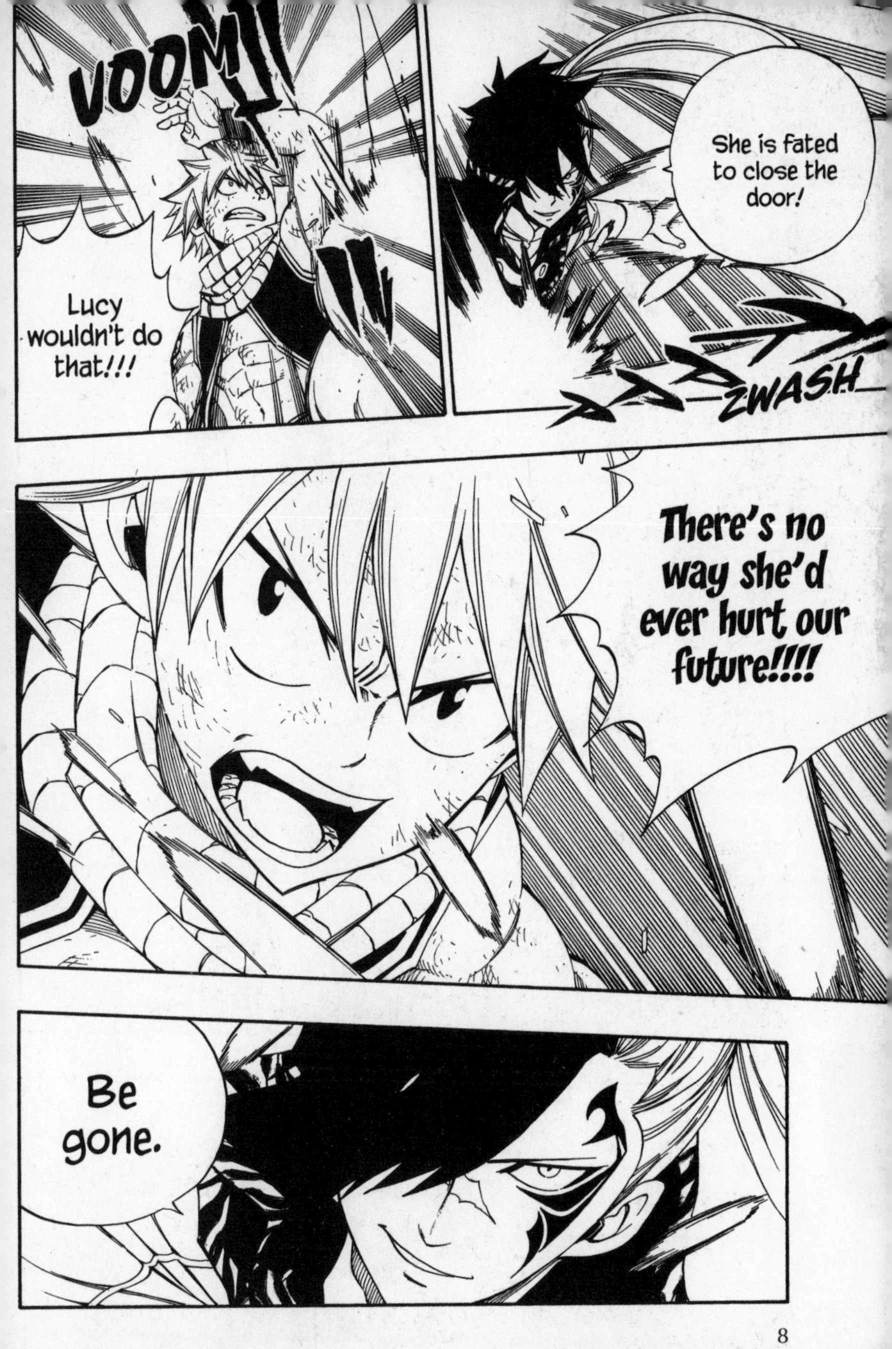
She is fated to close the door!
ZWASH
VOOM!!
Lucy wouldn't do that!!!
There's no way she'd ever hurt our future!!!!
Be gone.

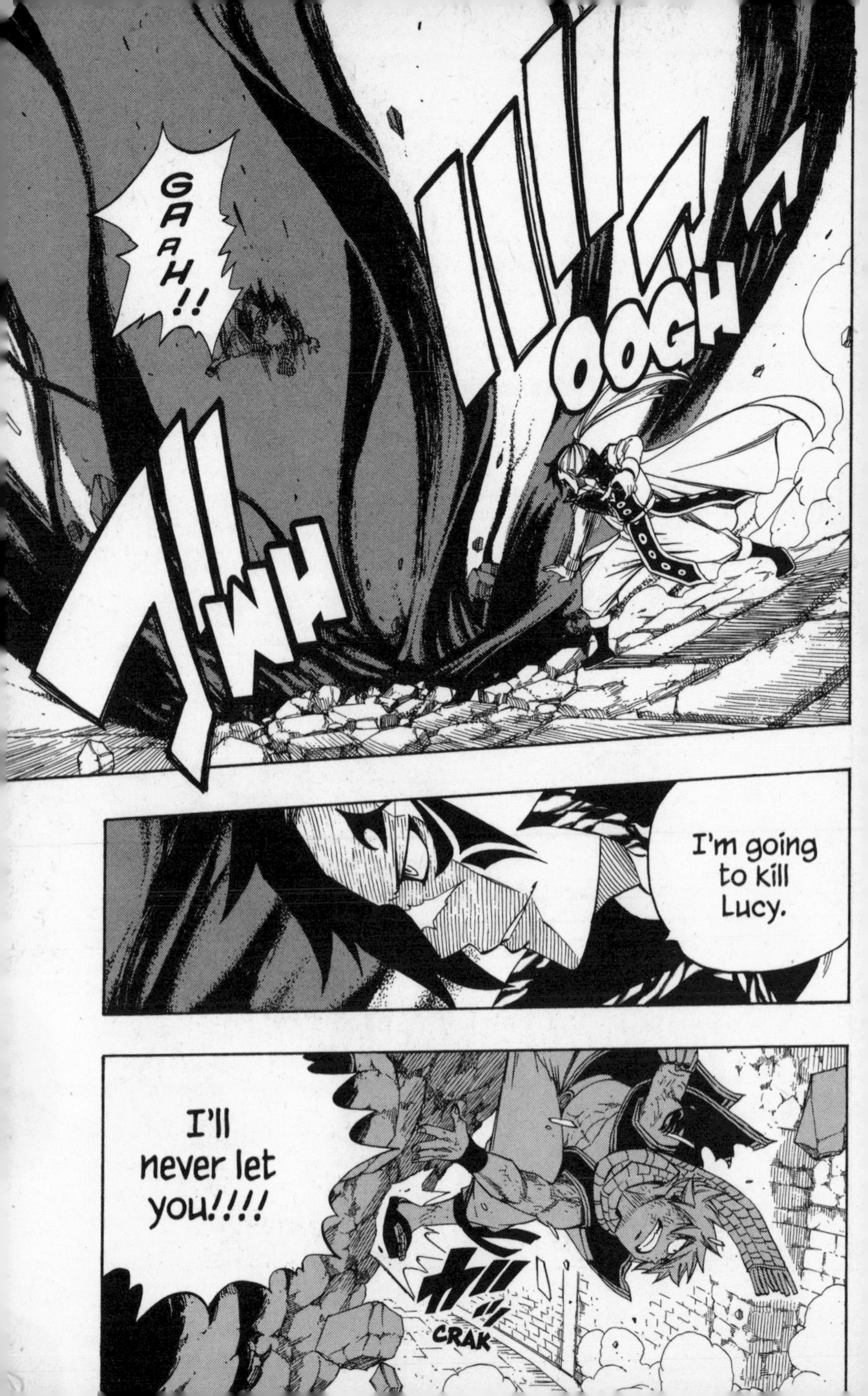
OOGH
GAAH!!
I'm going to kill Lucy.
I'll never let you!!!!
CRAK

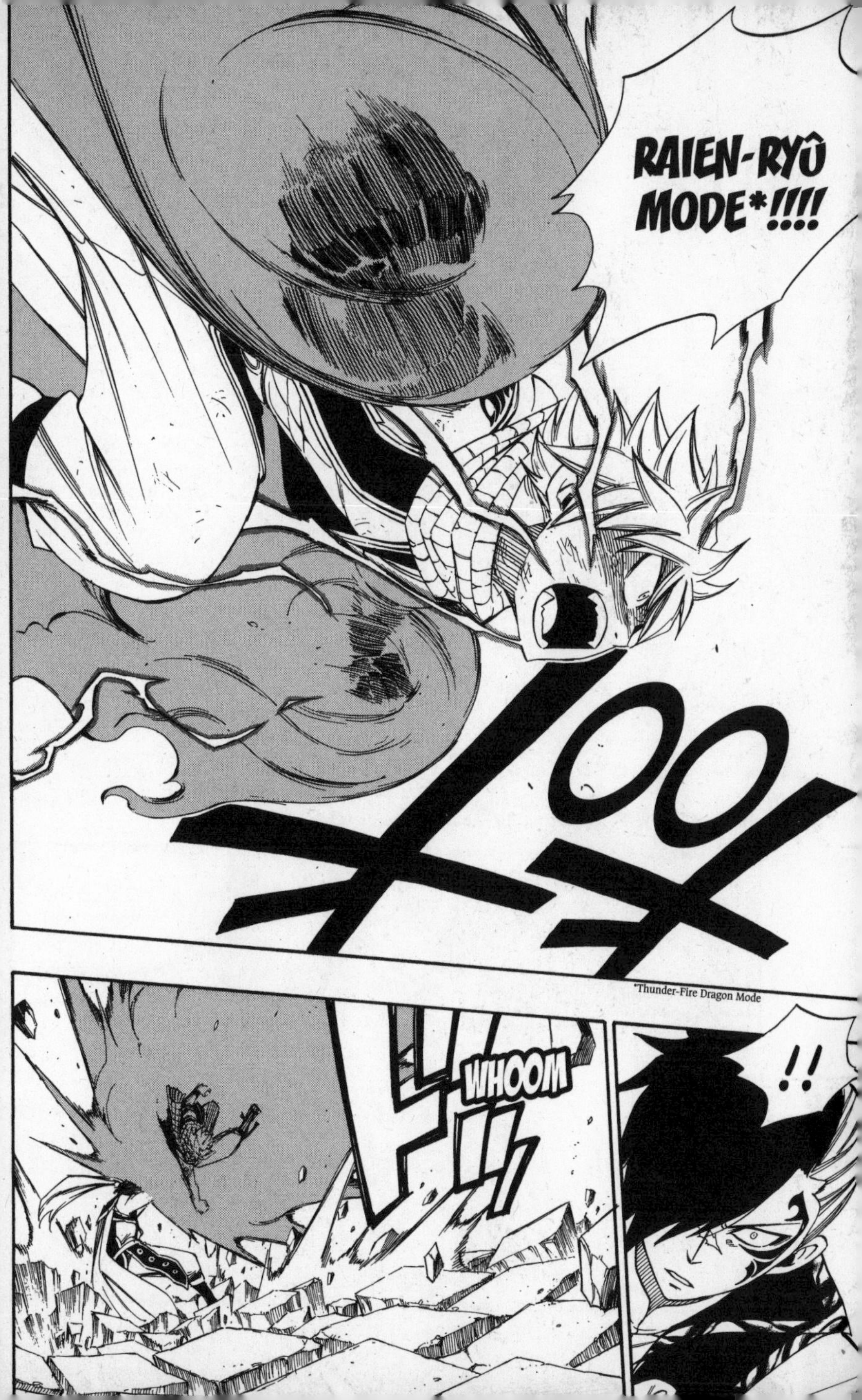
RAIEN-RYÛ MODE*!!!!
!!
WHOOM
*Thunder-Fire Dragon Mode

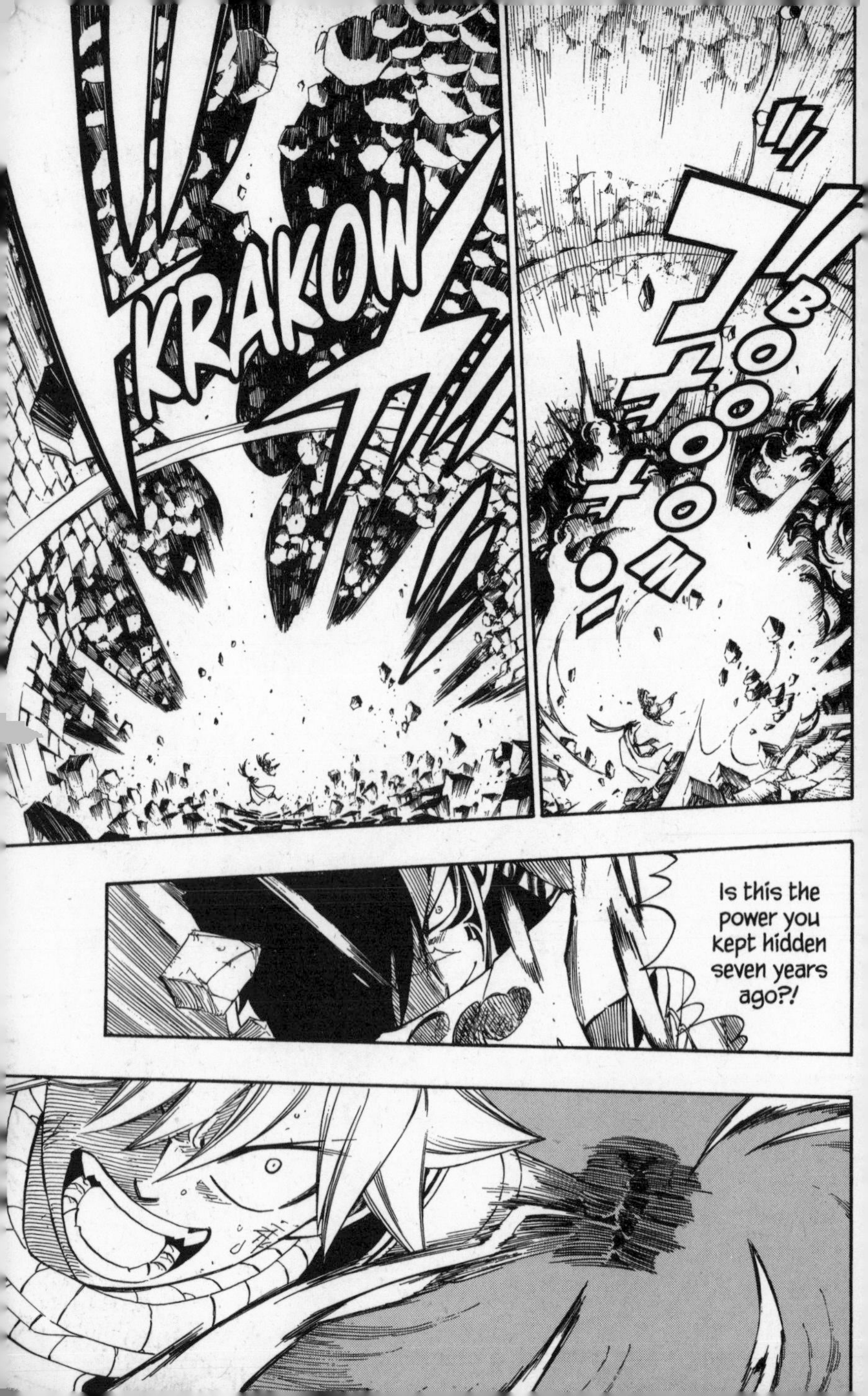
BOOOOOM
KRAKOW
Is this the power you kept hidden seven years ago?!

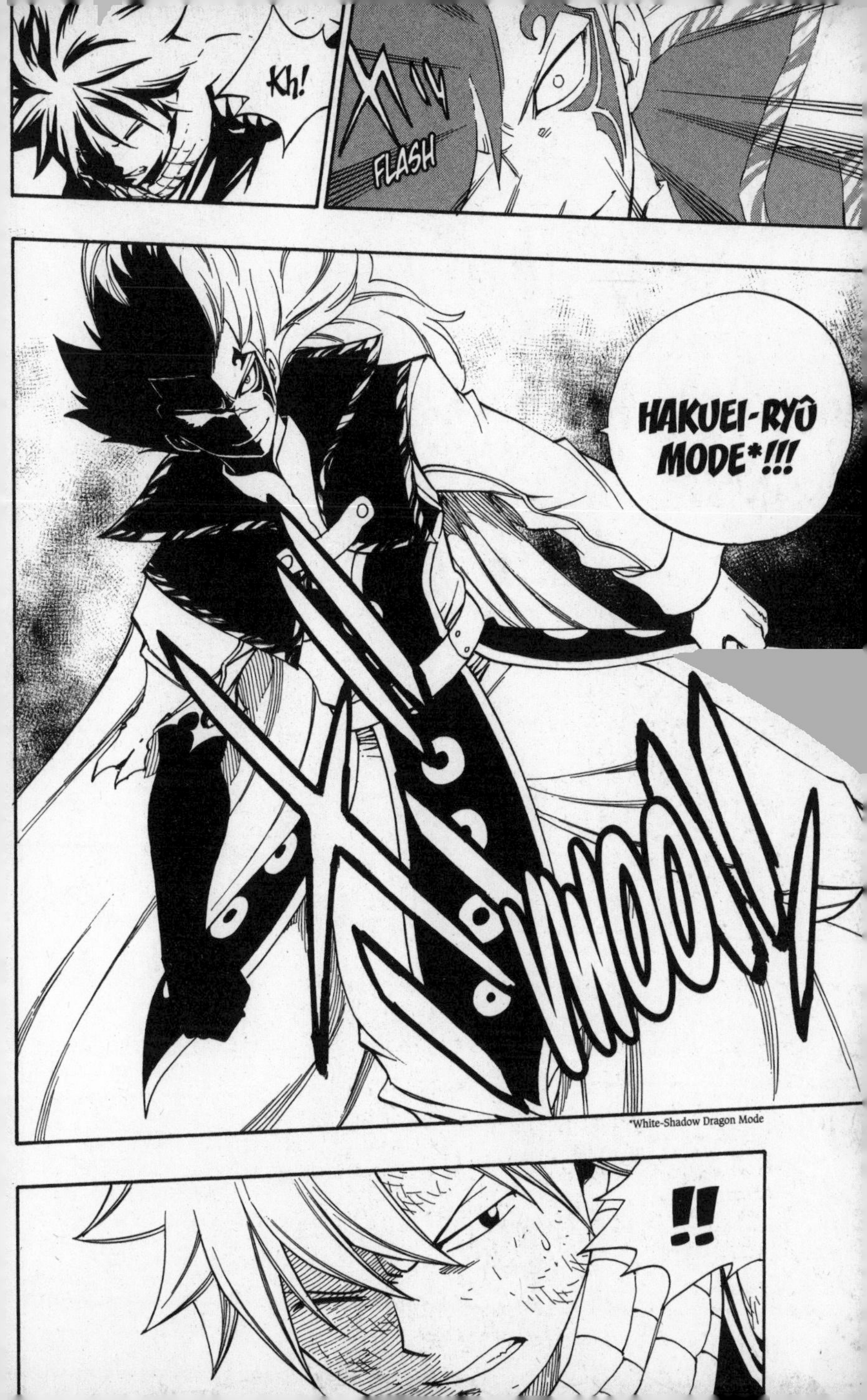
FLASH
Kh!
HAKUEI-RYÔ MODE*!!!
!!
*White-Shadow Dragon Mode

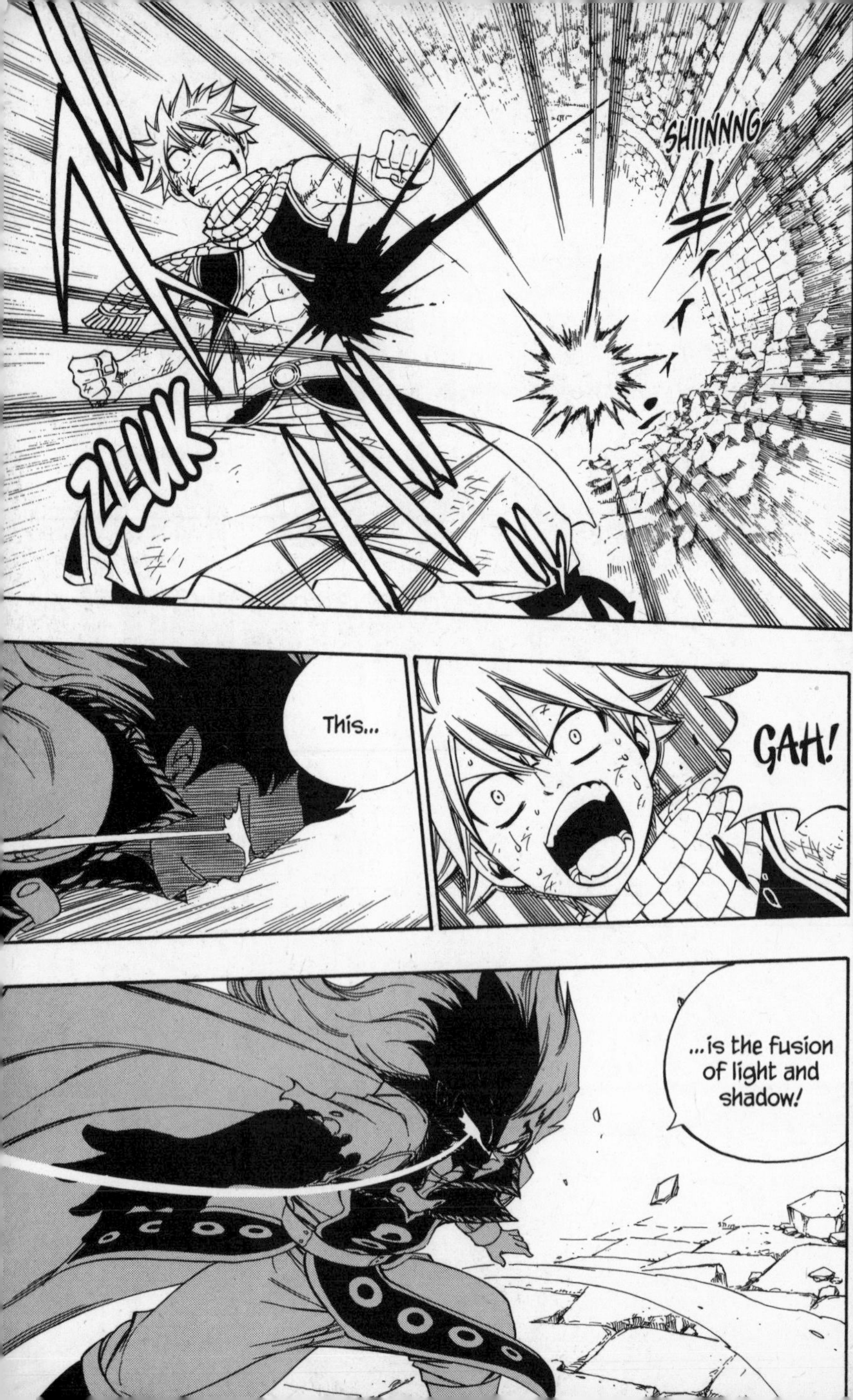
SHIIINNNG
ZLUK
GAH!
This...
...is the fusion of light and shadow!

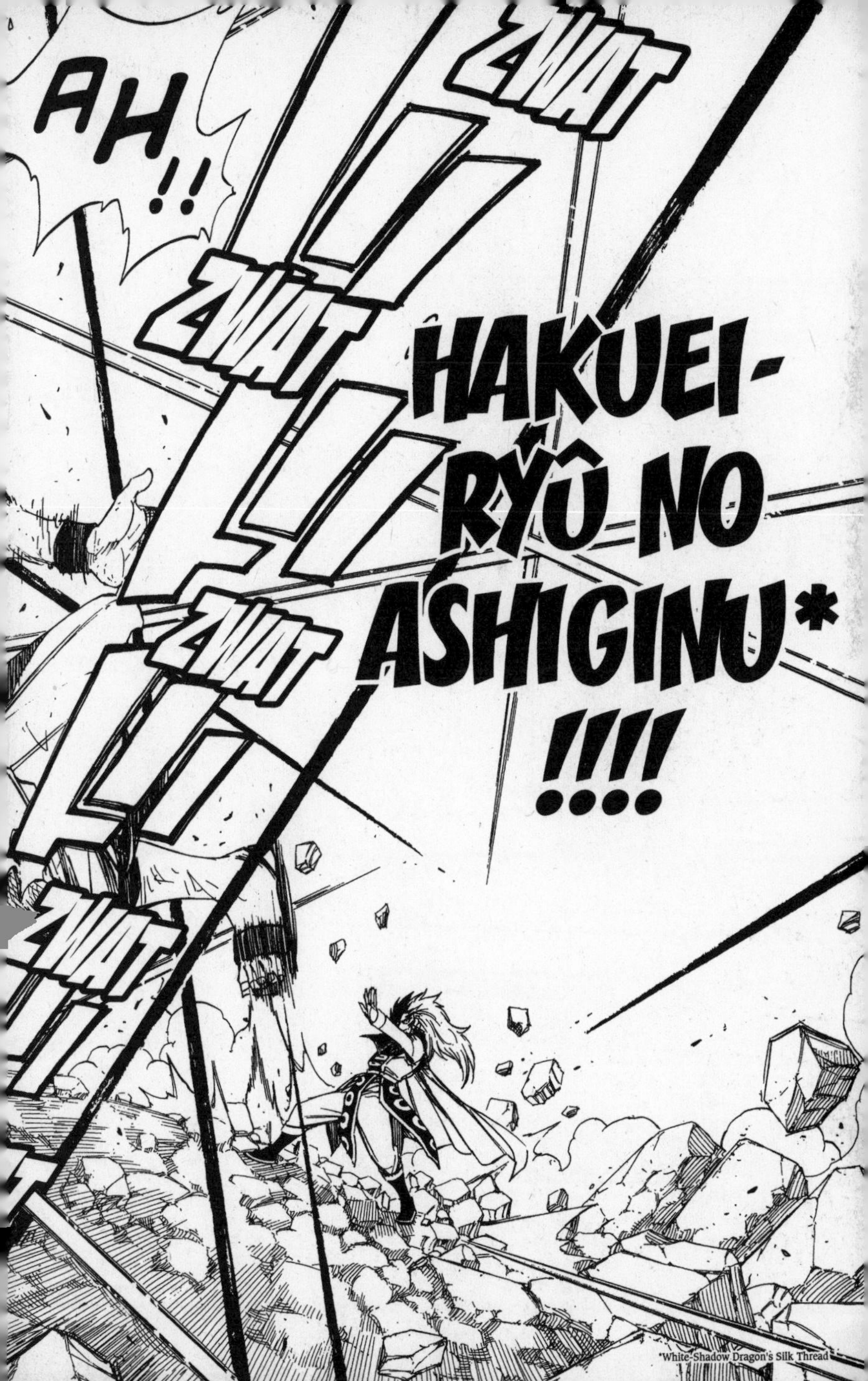
ZWAT
AH!!
ZWAT
HAKUEI-RYÛ NO ASHIGINU*!!!!
ZWAT
ZWAT
*White-Shadow Dragon's Silk Thread

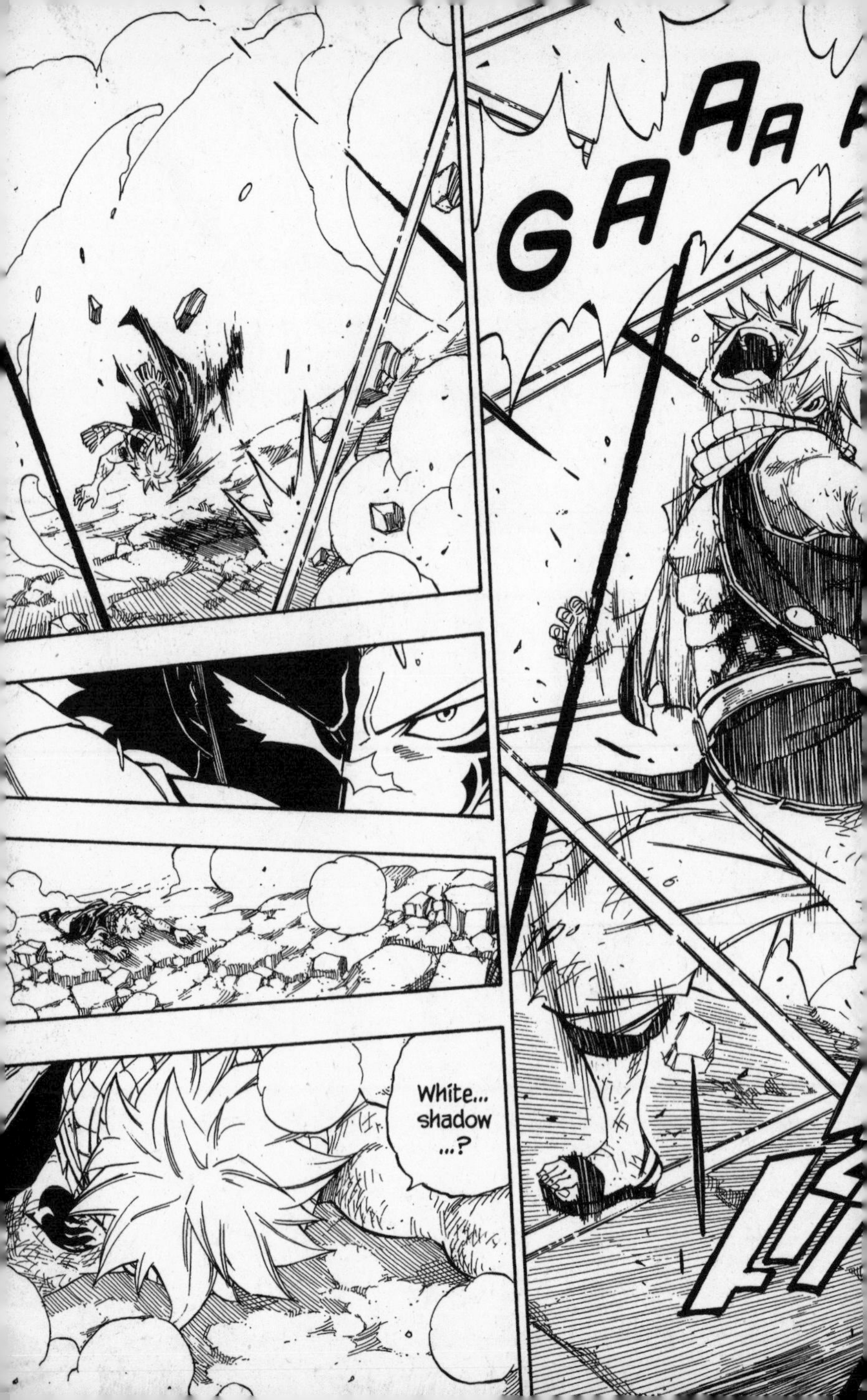
GAAA
White... shadow ...?

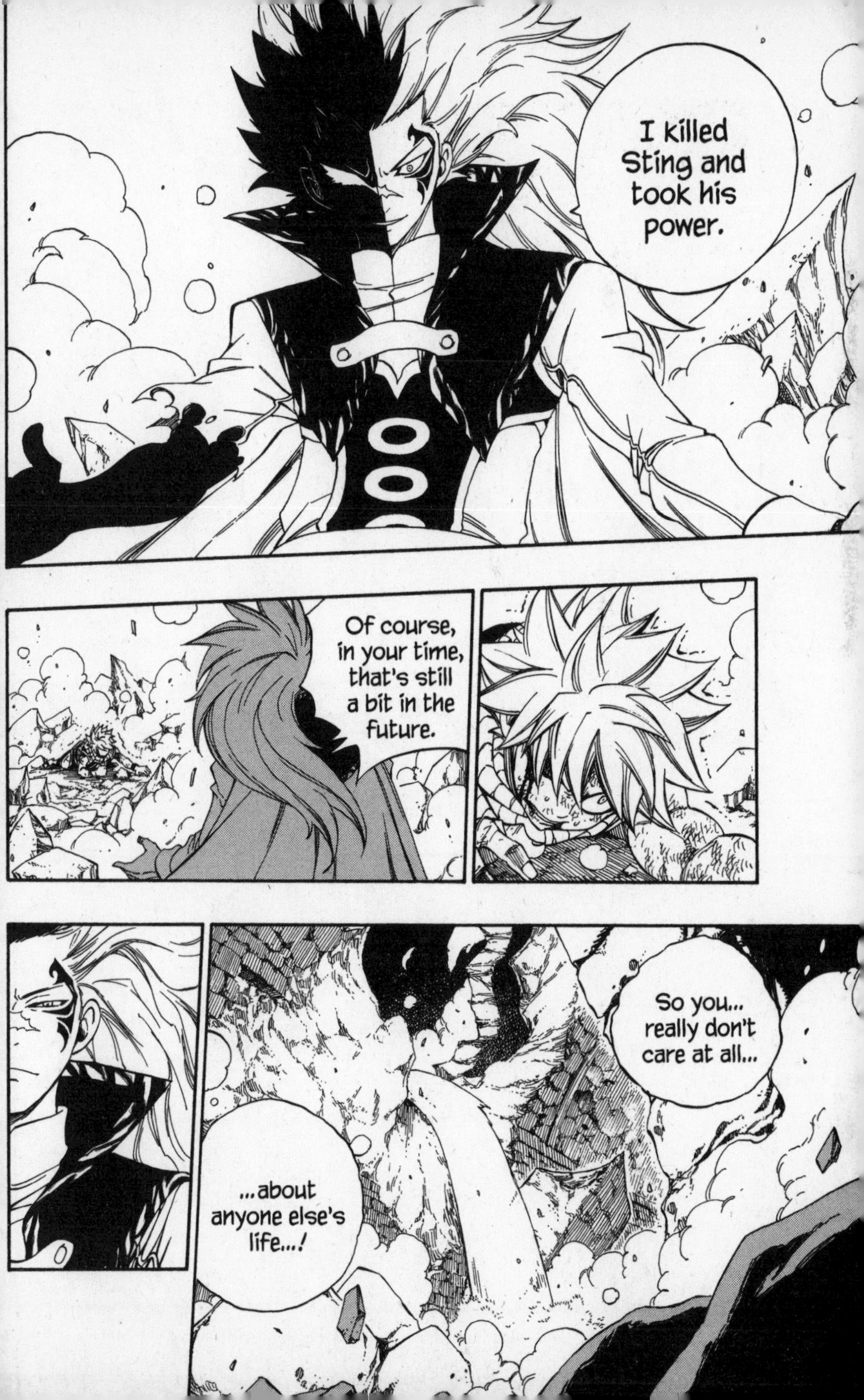
I killed Sting and took his power.
Of course, in your time, that's still a bit in the future.
So you... really don't care at all...
...about anyone else's life...!

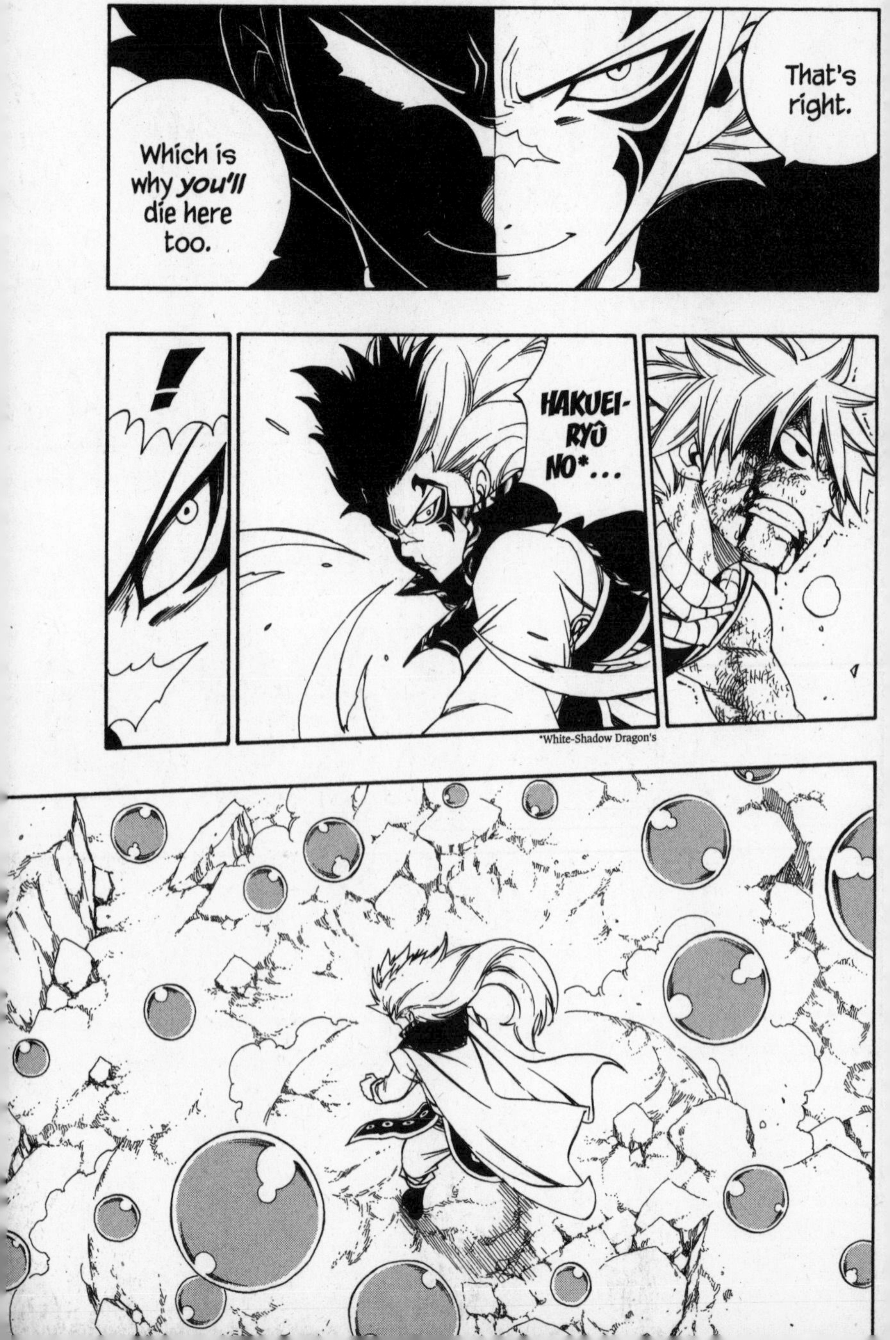
That's right.
Which is why *you'll* die here too.
HAKUEI-RYÛ NO*...
!
*White-Shadow Dragon's

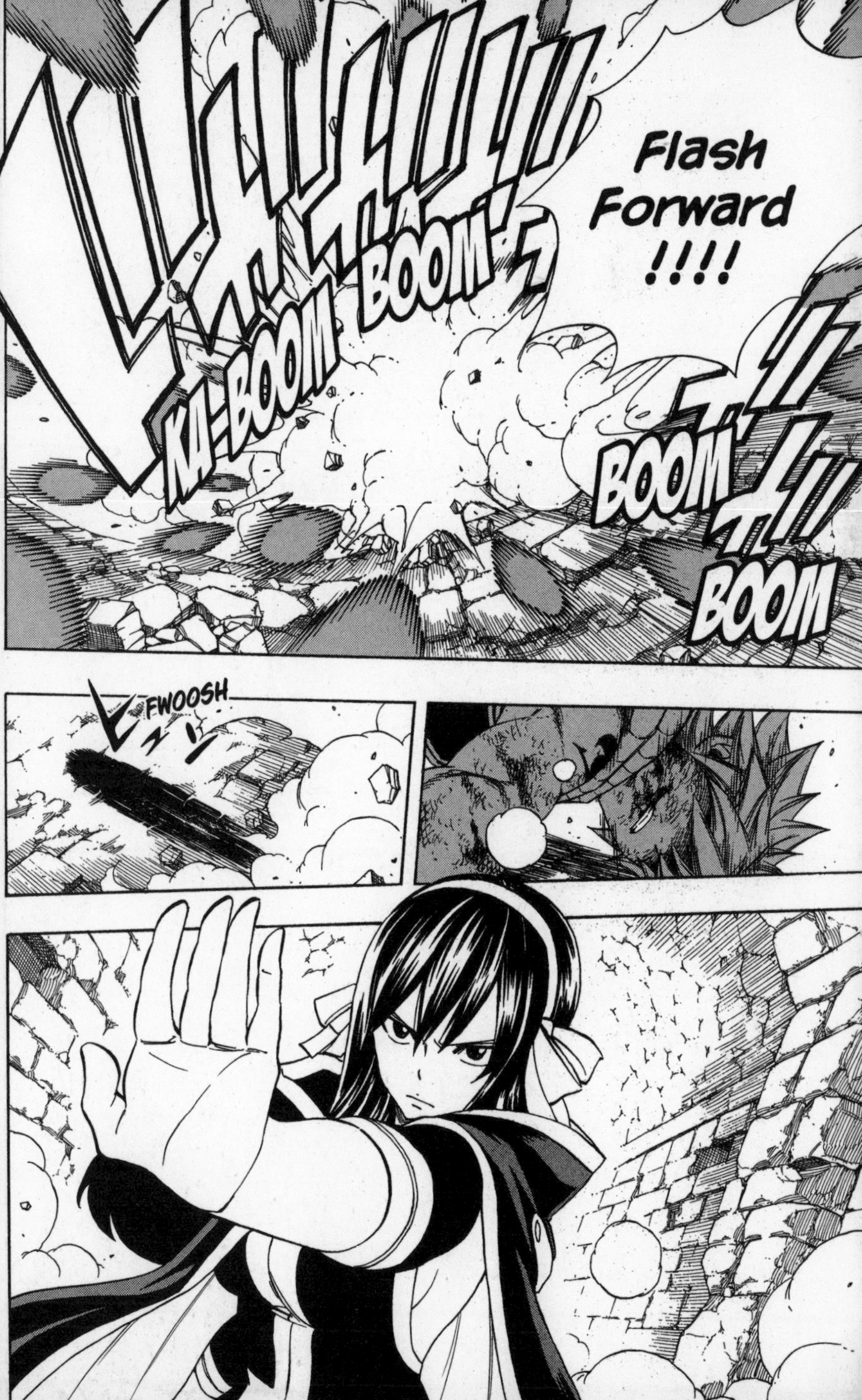
Flash Forward !!!!
BOOM BOOM
KA-BOOM BOOM
FWOOSH

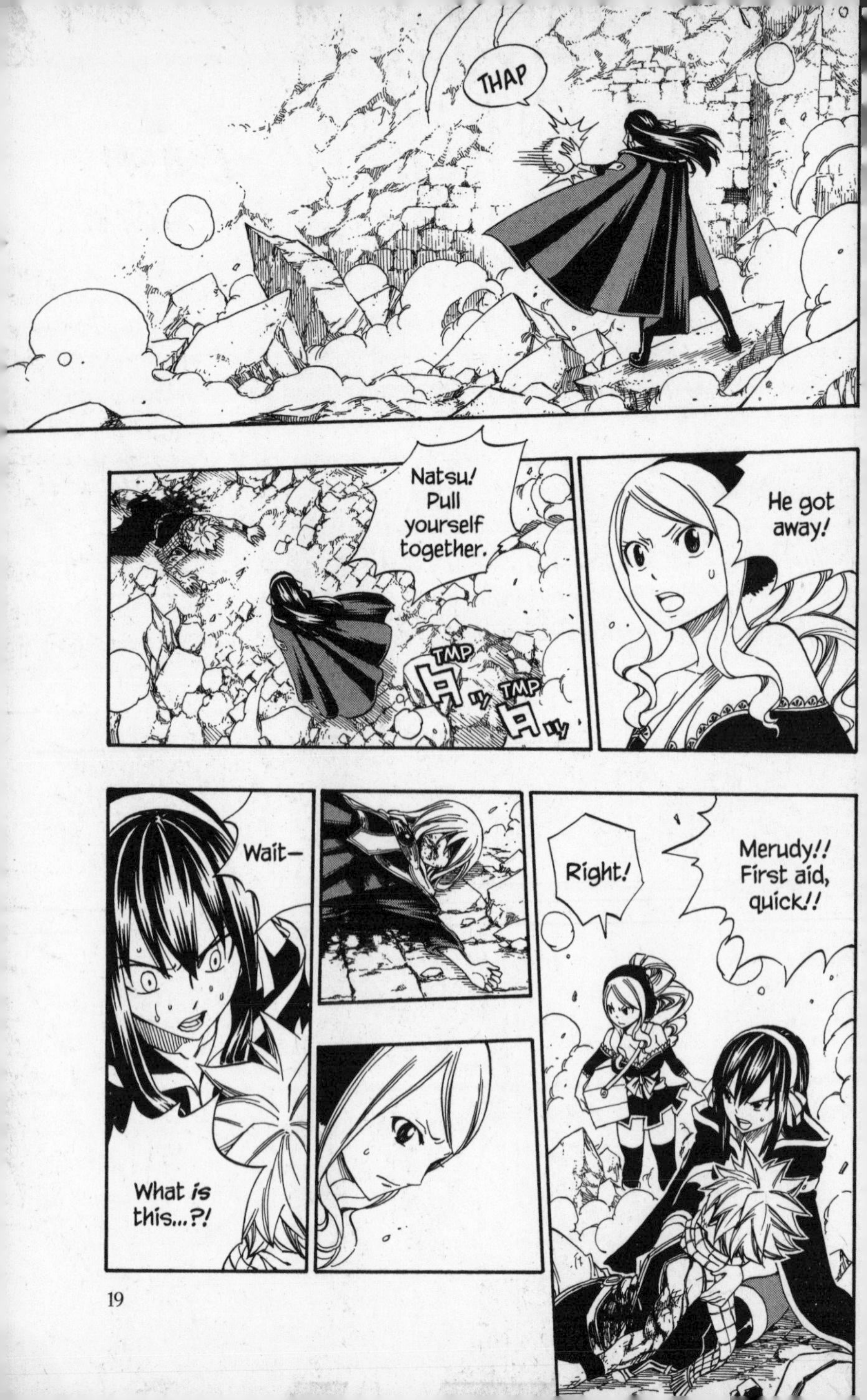
THAP
He got away!
Natsu! Pull yourself together.
TMP
TMP
Merudy!! First aid, quick!!
Right!
Wait—
What *is* this...?!

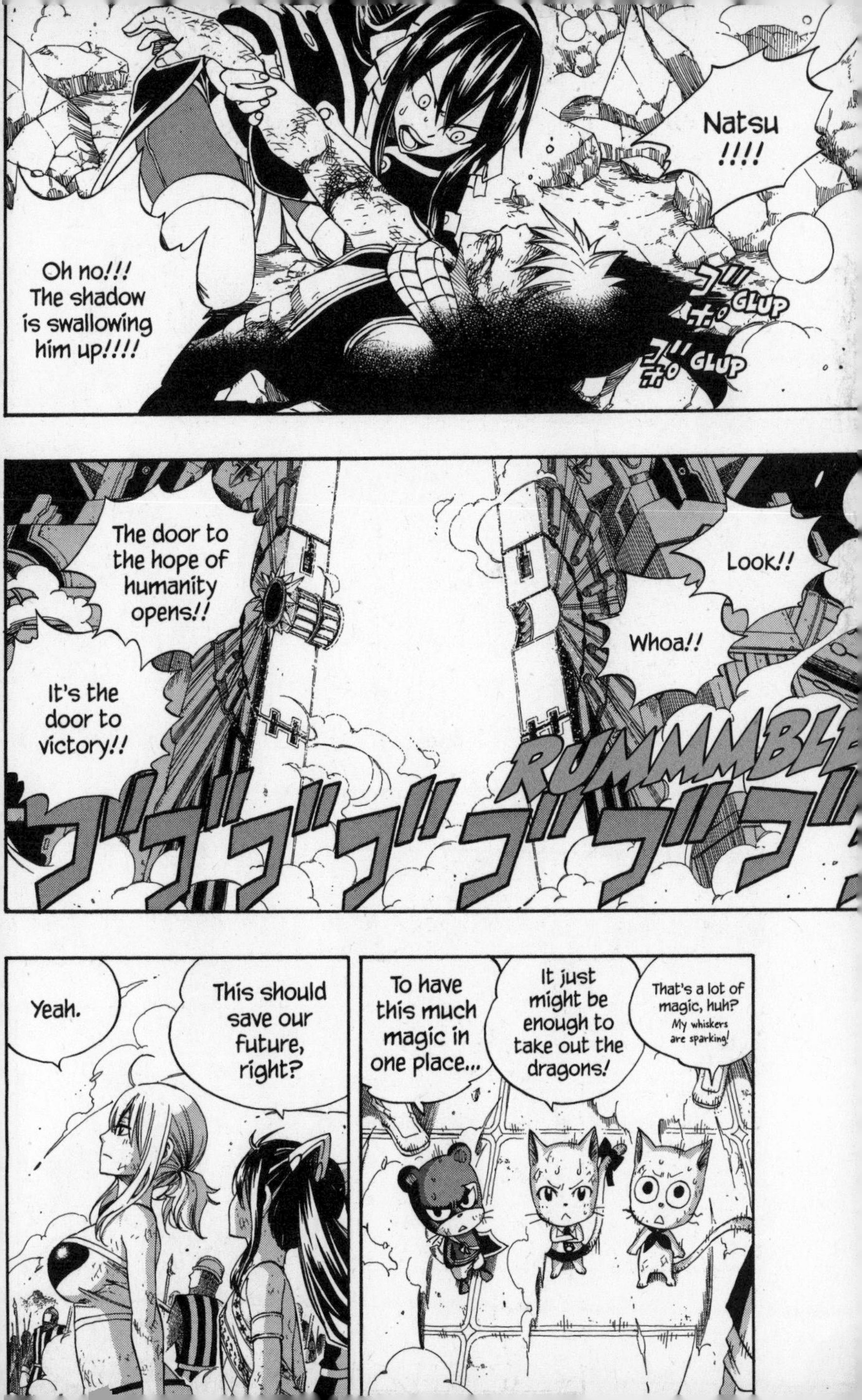
Natsu !!!!
GLUP
GLUP
Oh no!!! The shadow is swallowing him up!!!!
Look!!
Whoa!!
The door to the hope of humanity opens!!
It's the door to victory!!
RUMMMBLE
That's a lot of magic, huh? My whiskers are sparking!
It just might be enough to take out the dragons!
To have this much magic in one place...
This should save our future, right?
Yeah.

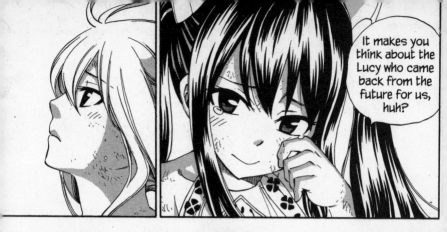

It makes you think about the Lucy who came back from the future for us, huh?

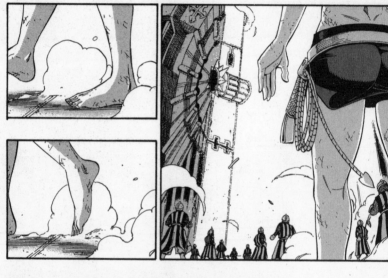

No...

Lucy-san?

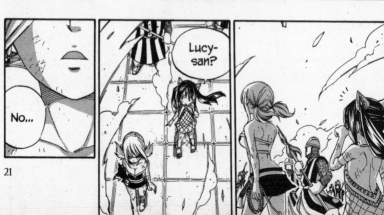

21

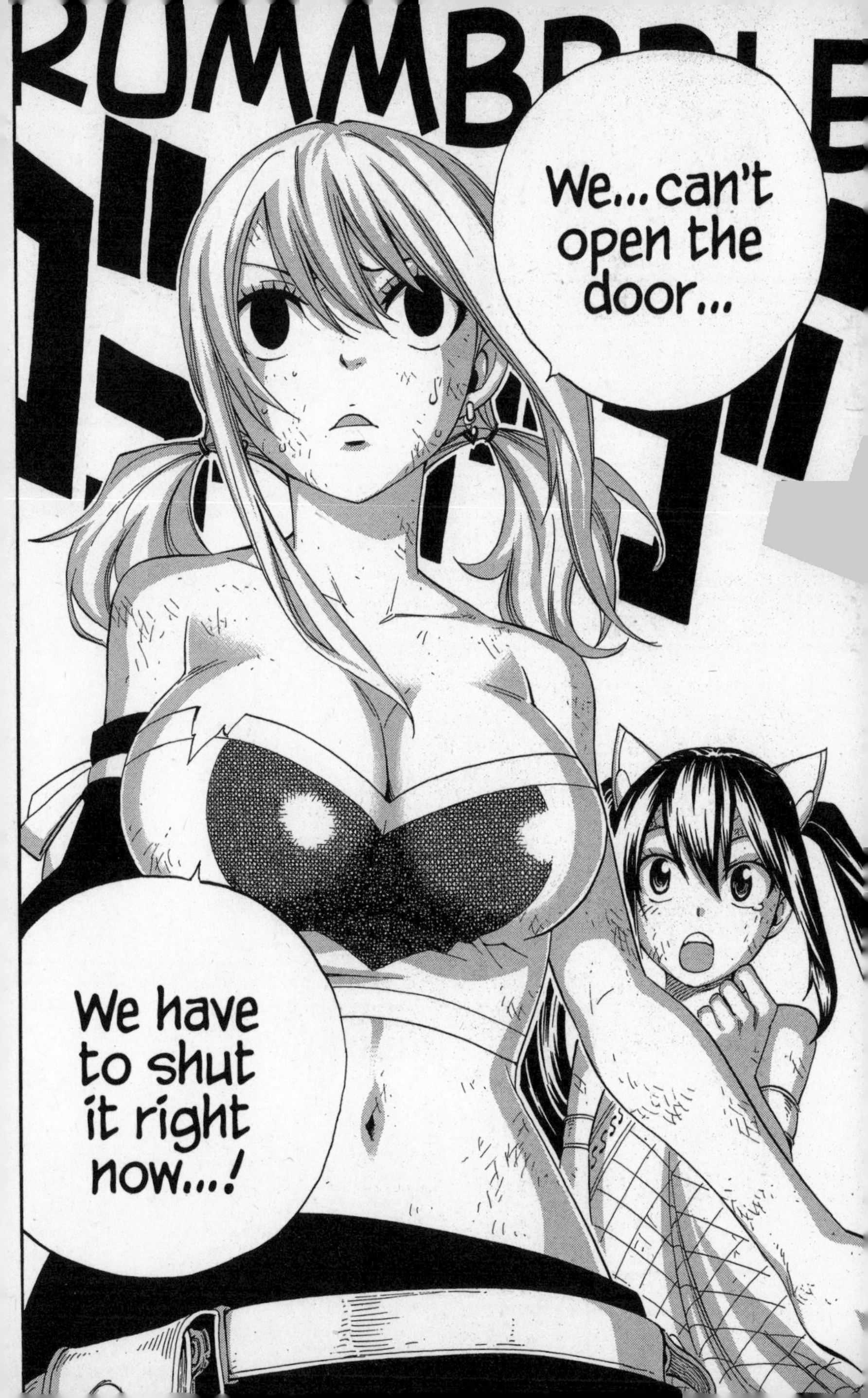
RUMMBBLE
We...can't open the door...
We have to shut it right now...!

FAIRY TAIL
フェアリーテイル

Chapter 327: Live On for Her

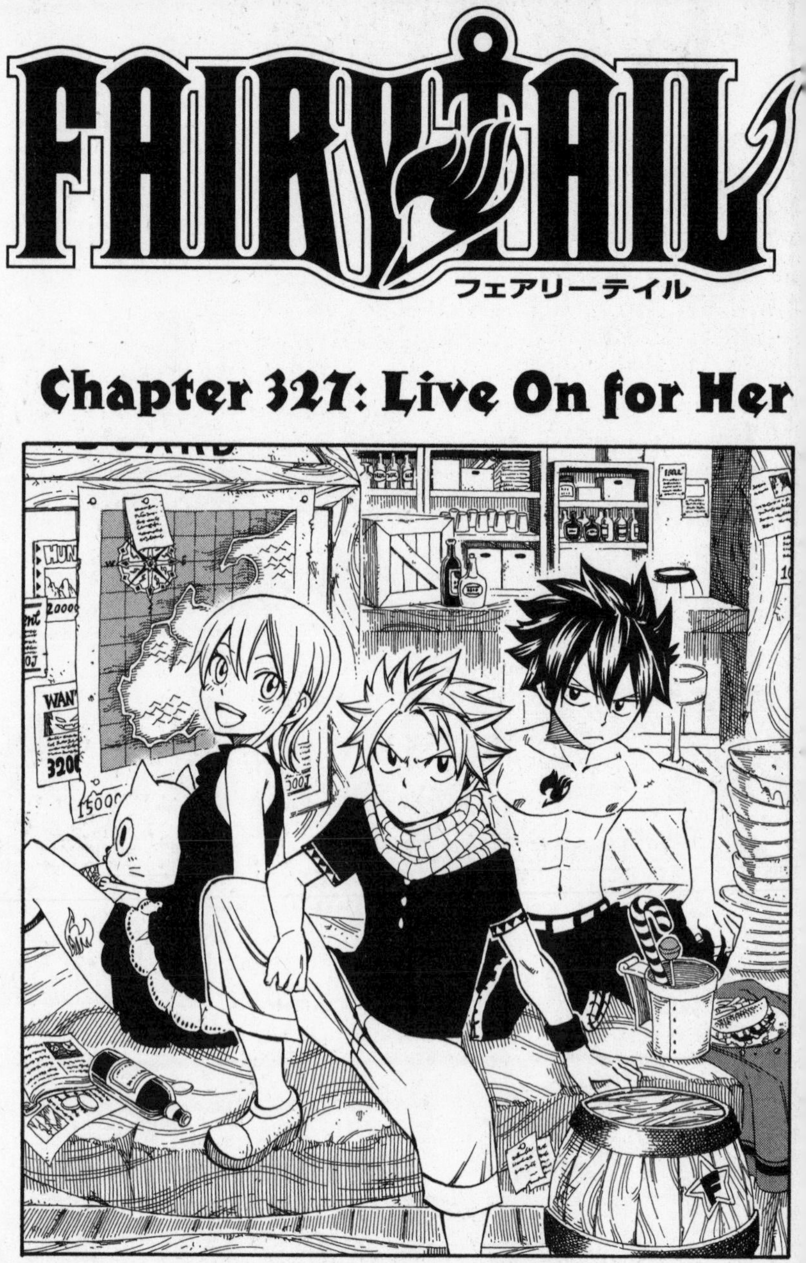

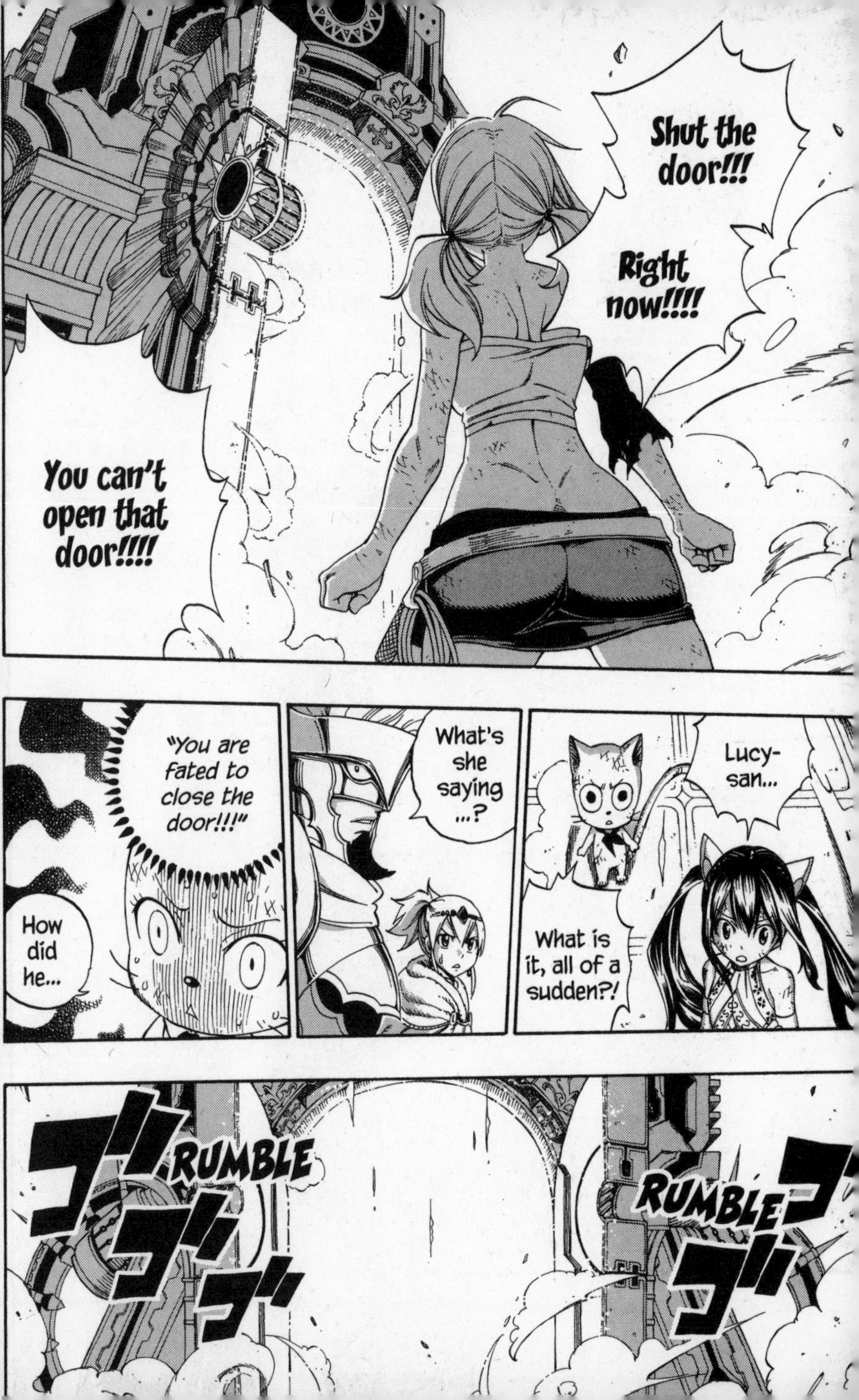
Shut the door!!!
Right now!!!!
You can't open that door!!!!
Lucy-san...
What is it, all of a sudden?!
What's she saying ...?
"You are fated to close the door!!!"
How did he...
RUMBLE
RUMBLE

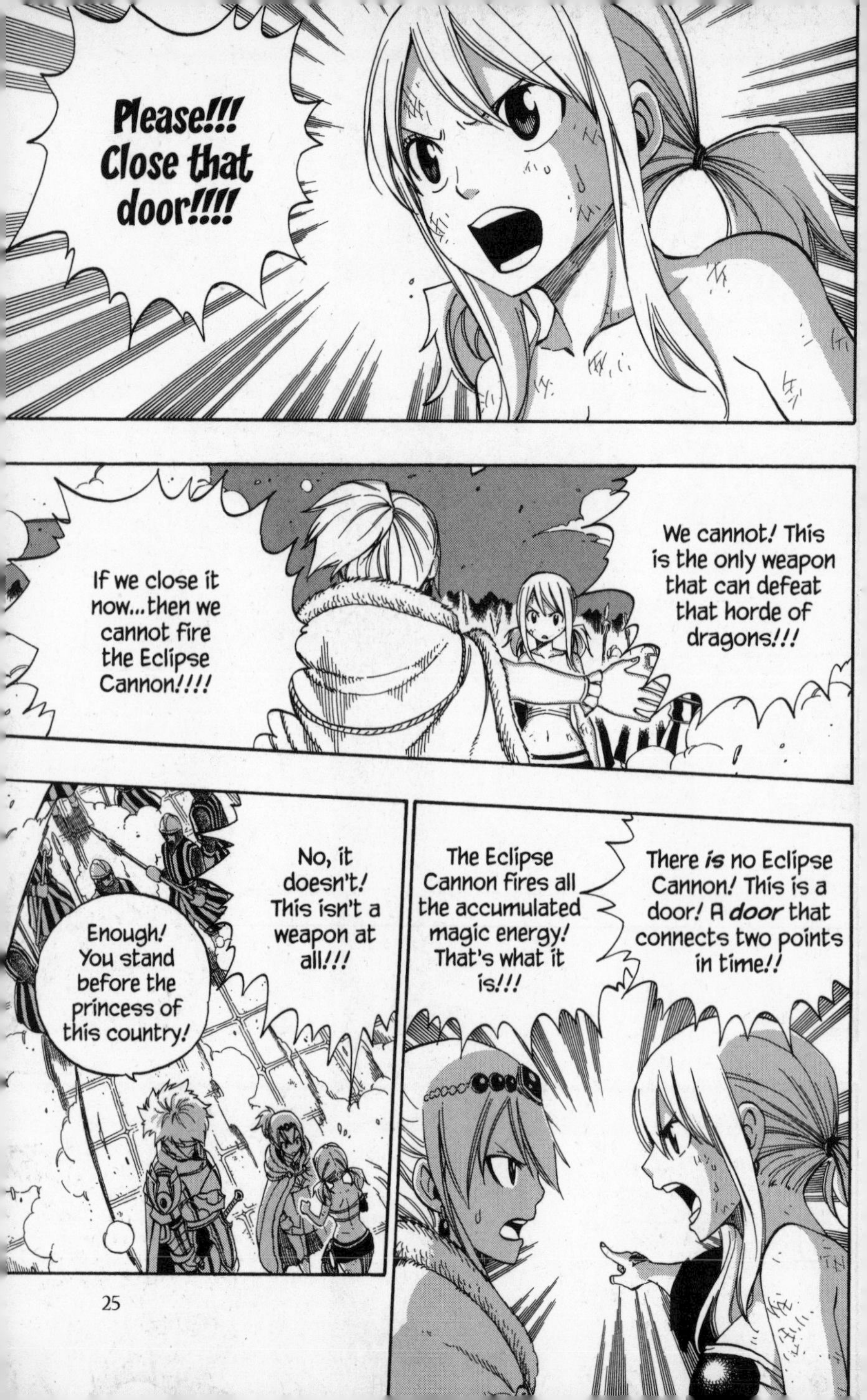
Please!!! Close that door!!!!
We cannot! This is the only weapon that can defeat that horde of dragons!!!
If we close it now...then we cannot fire the Eclipse Cannon!!!!
There *is* no Eclipse Cannon! This is a door! A *door* that connects two points in time!!
The Eclipse Cannon fires all the accumulated magic energy! That's what it is!!!
No, it doesn't! This isn't a weapon at all!!!
Enough! You stand before the princess of this country!

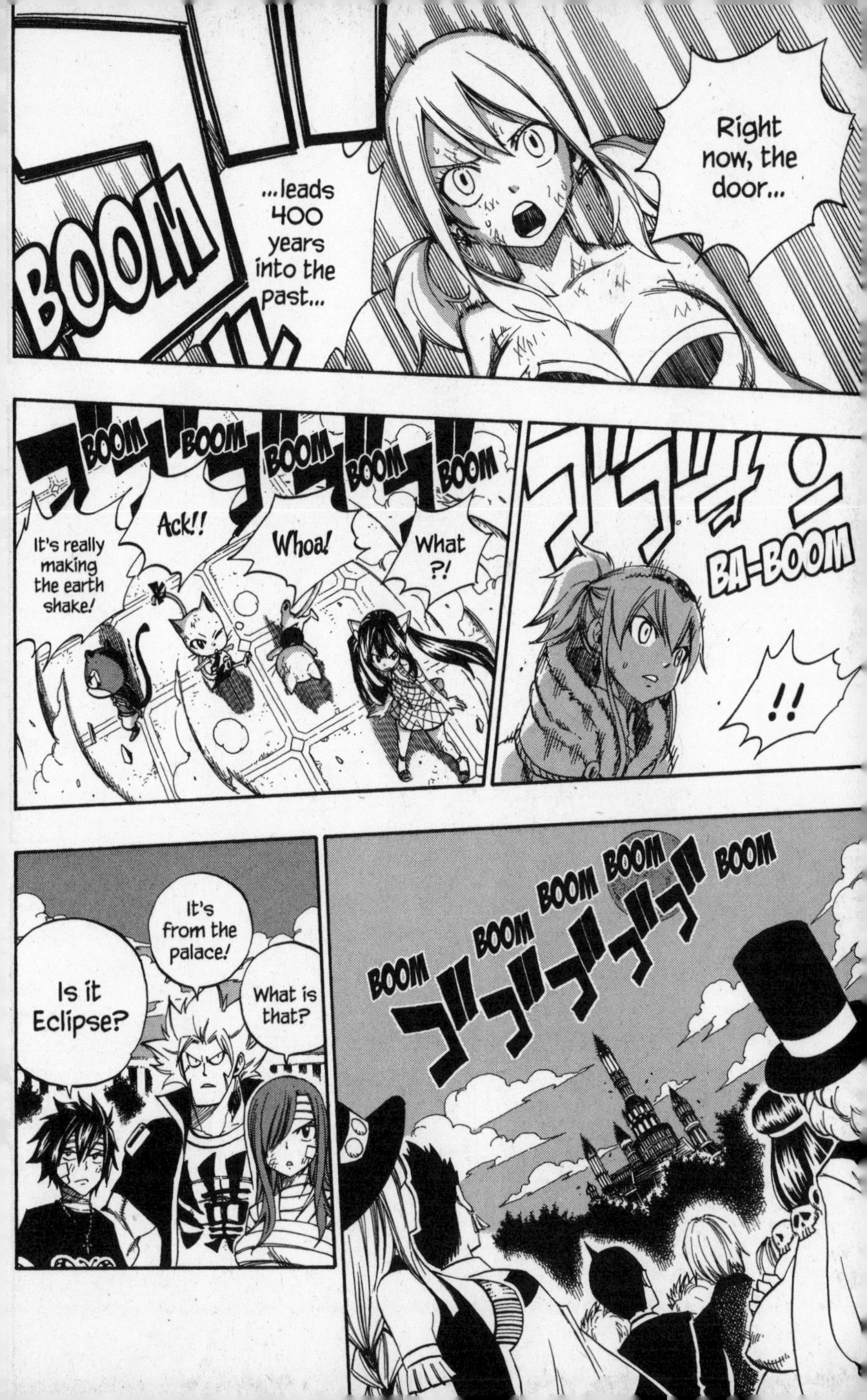
Right now, the door...
...leads 400 years into the past...
BOOM
BA-BOOM
!!
BOOM BOOM BOOM BOOM BOOM
What ?!
Whoa!
Ack!!
It's really making the earth shake!
BOOM BOOM BOOM BOOM BOOM BOOM
What is that?
It's from the palace!
Is it Eclipse?

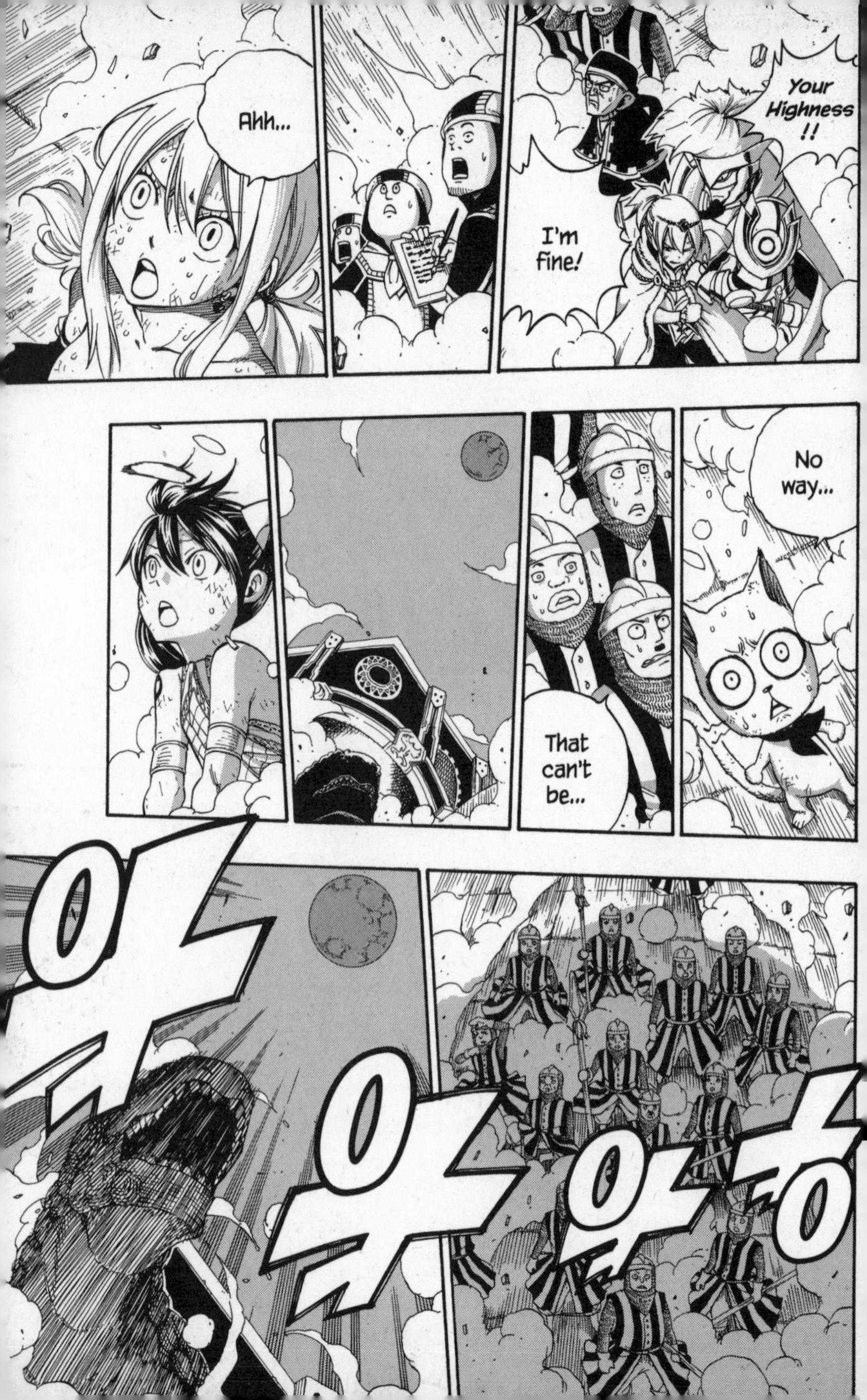
Your Highness !!
I'm fine!
Ahh...
No way...
That can't be...

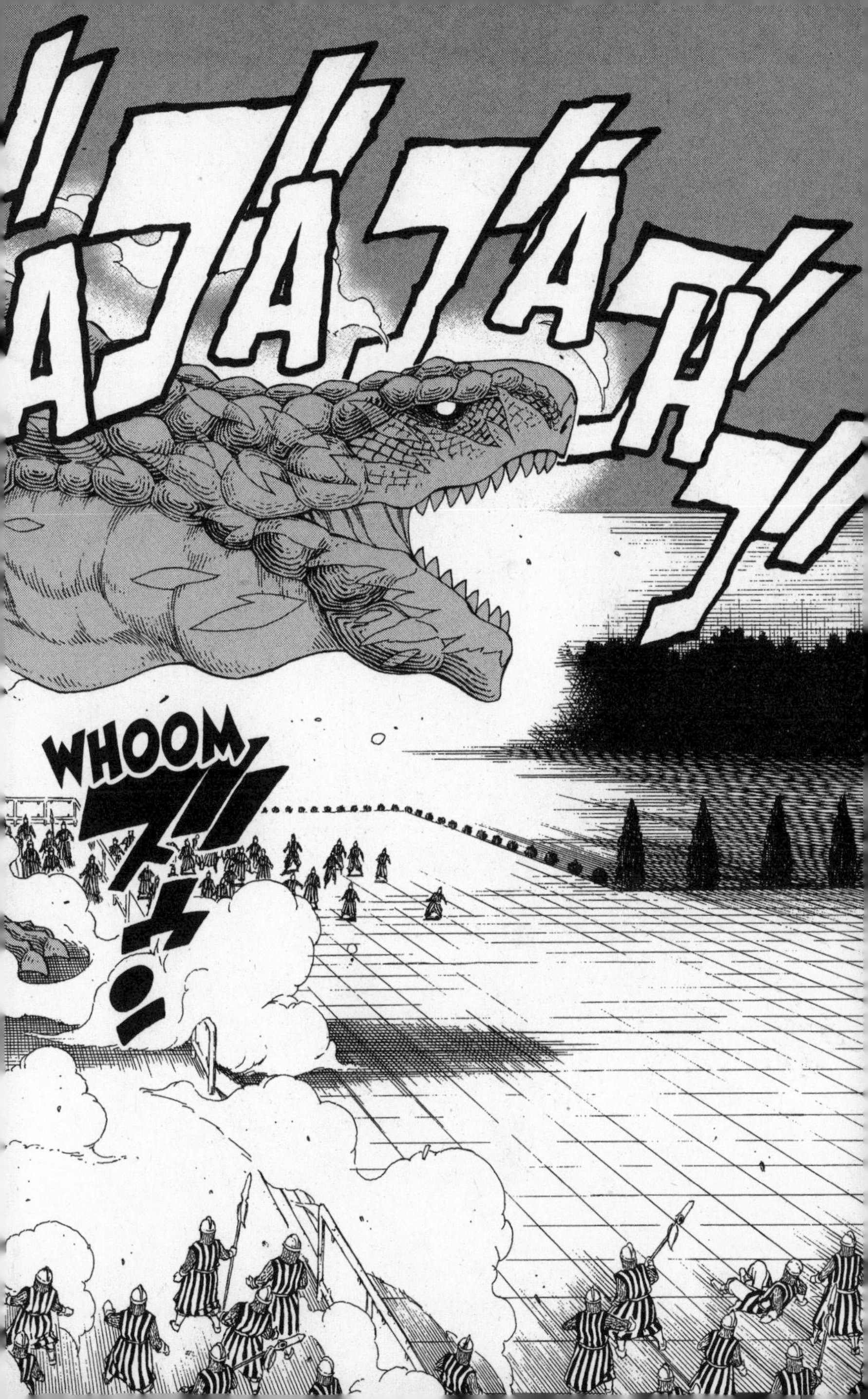
AAAAH!!
WHOOM

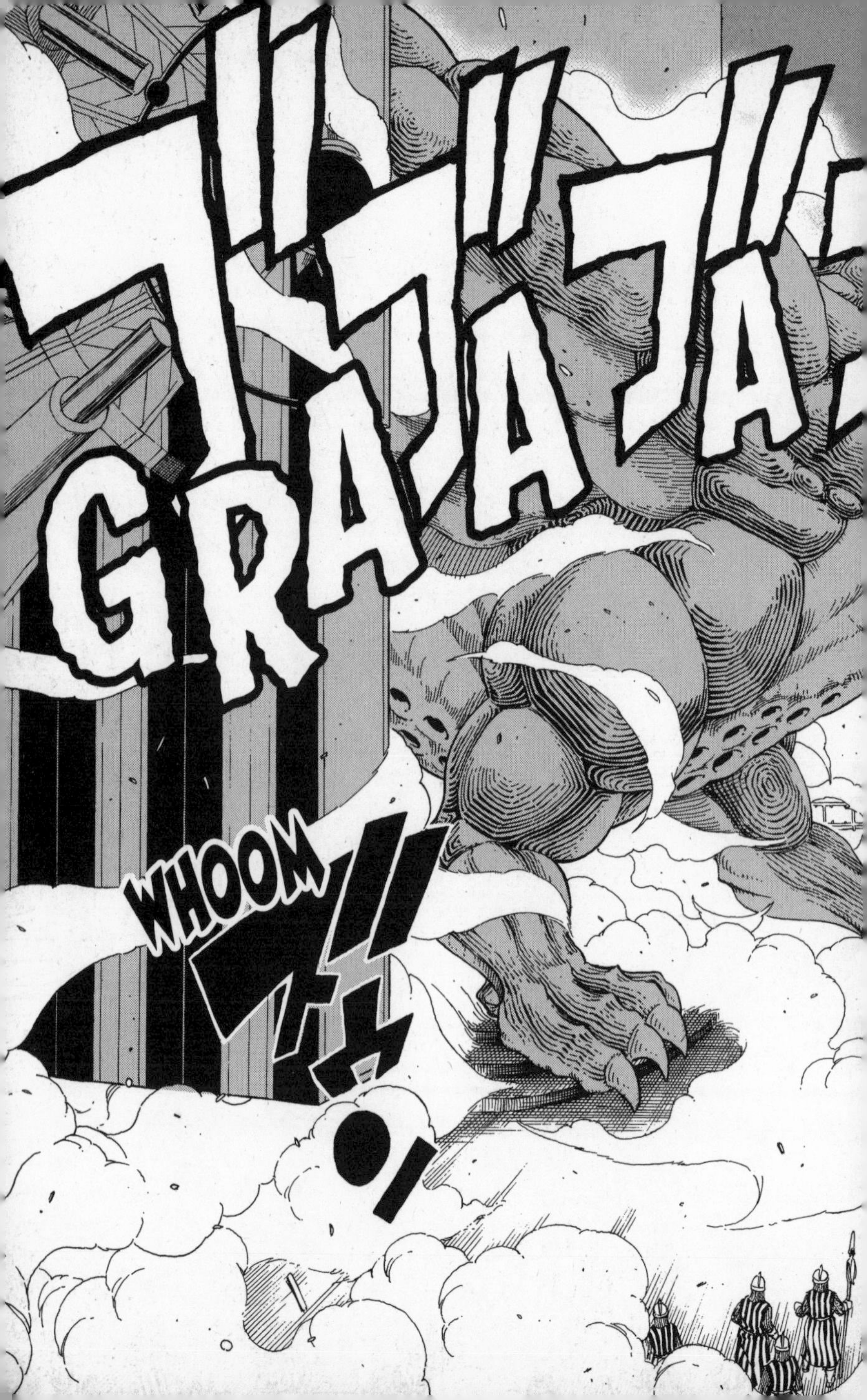
GRAAAA
WHOOM!!

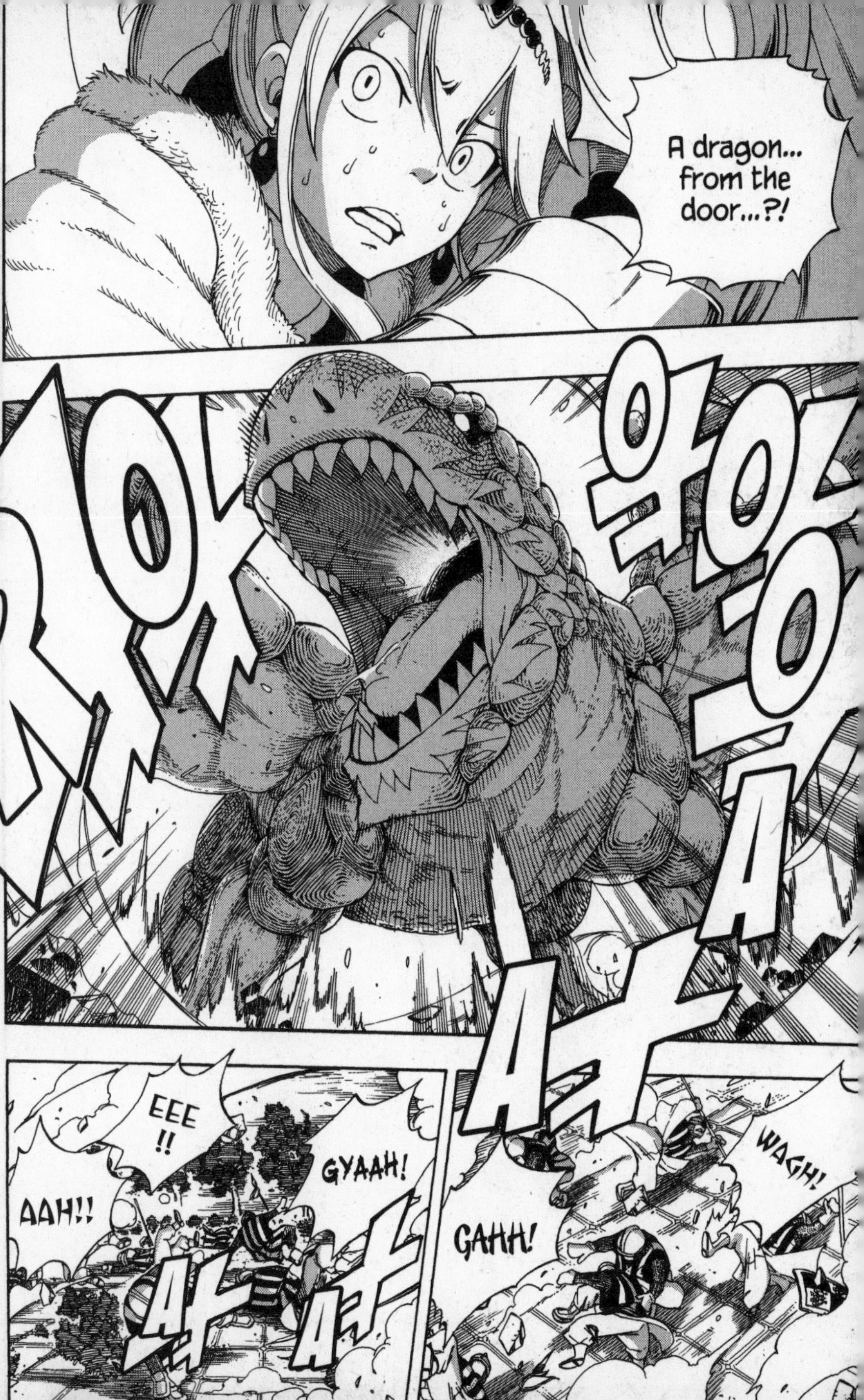
A dragon... from the door...?!
WAGH!
GAHH!
GYAAH!
EEE !!
AAH!!

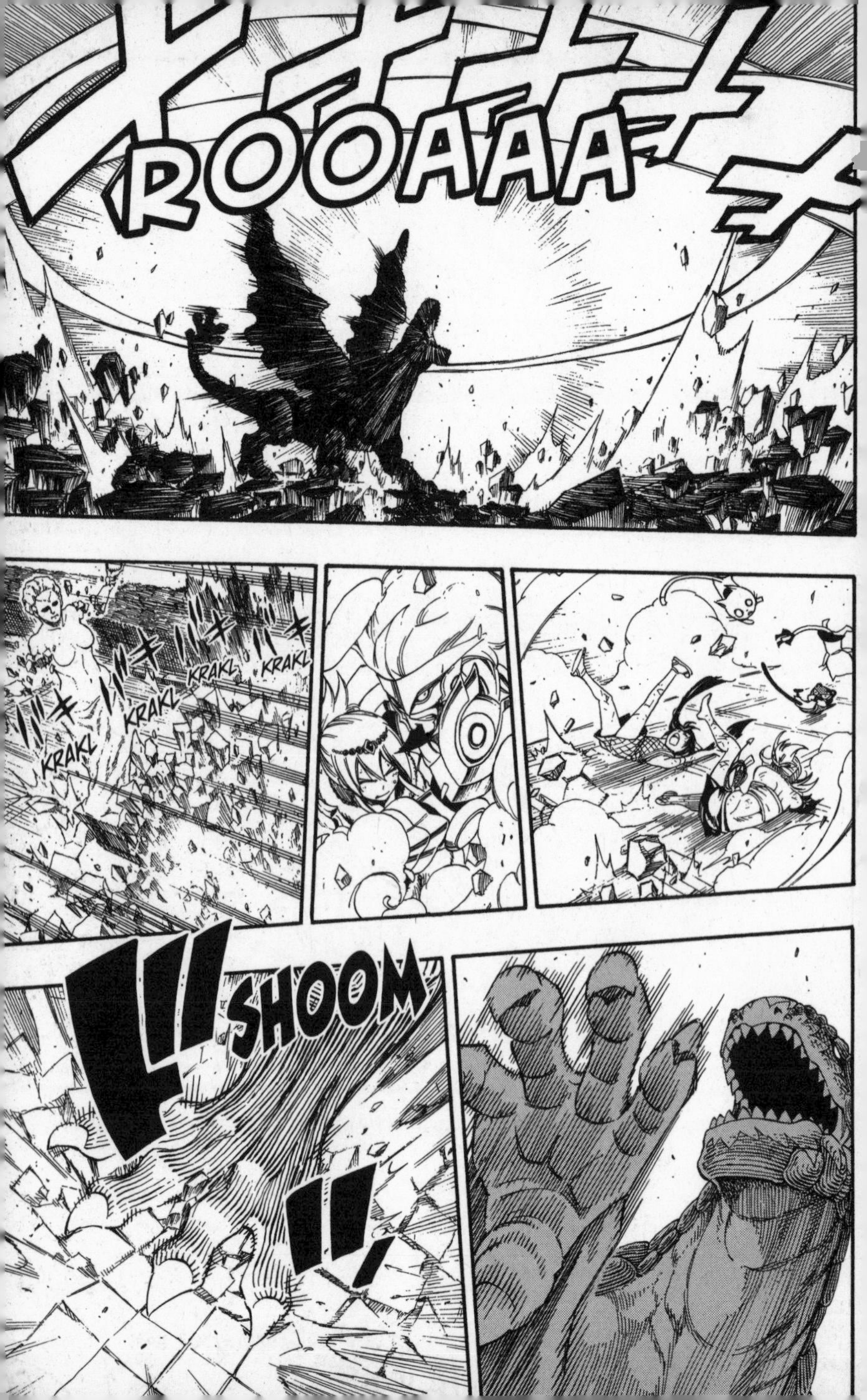
ROOAAA
KRAKL
KRAKL
KRAKL
KRAKL
SHOOM

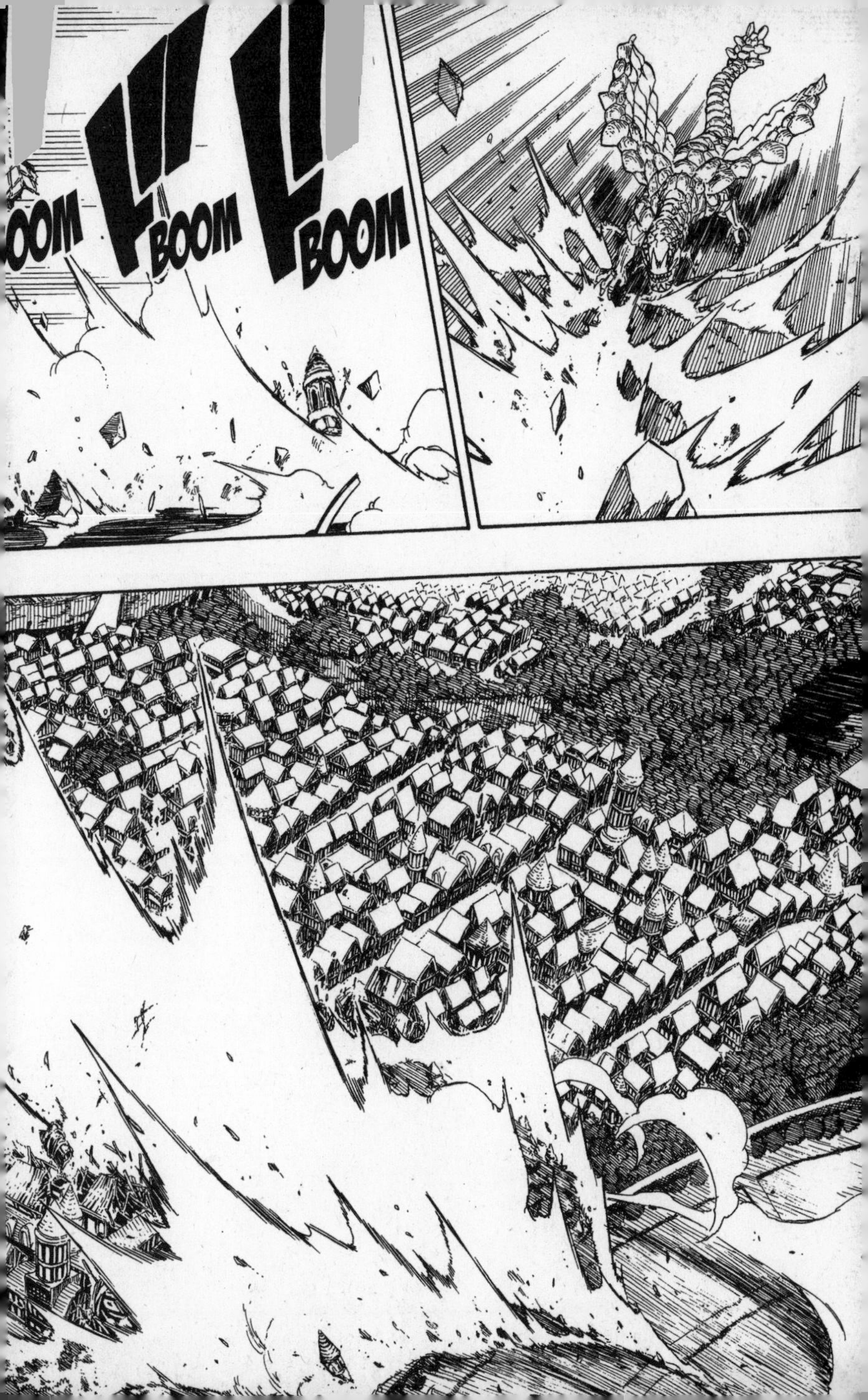
BOOM
BOOM
OOM

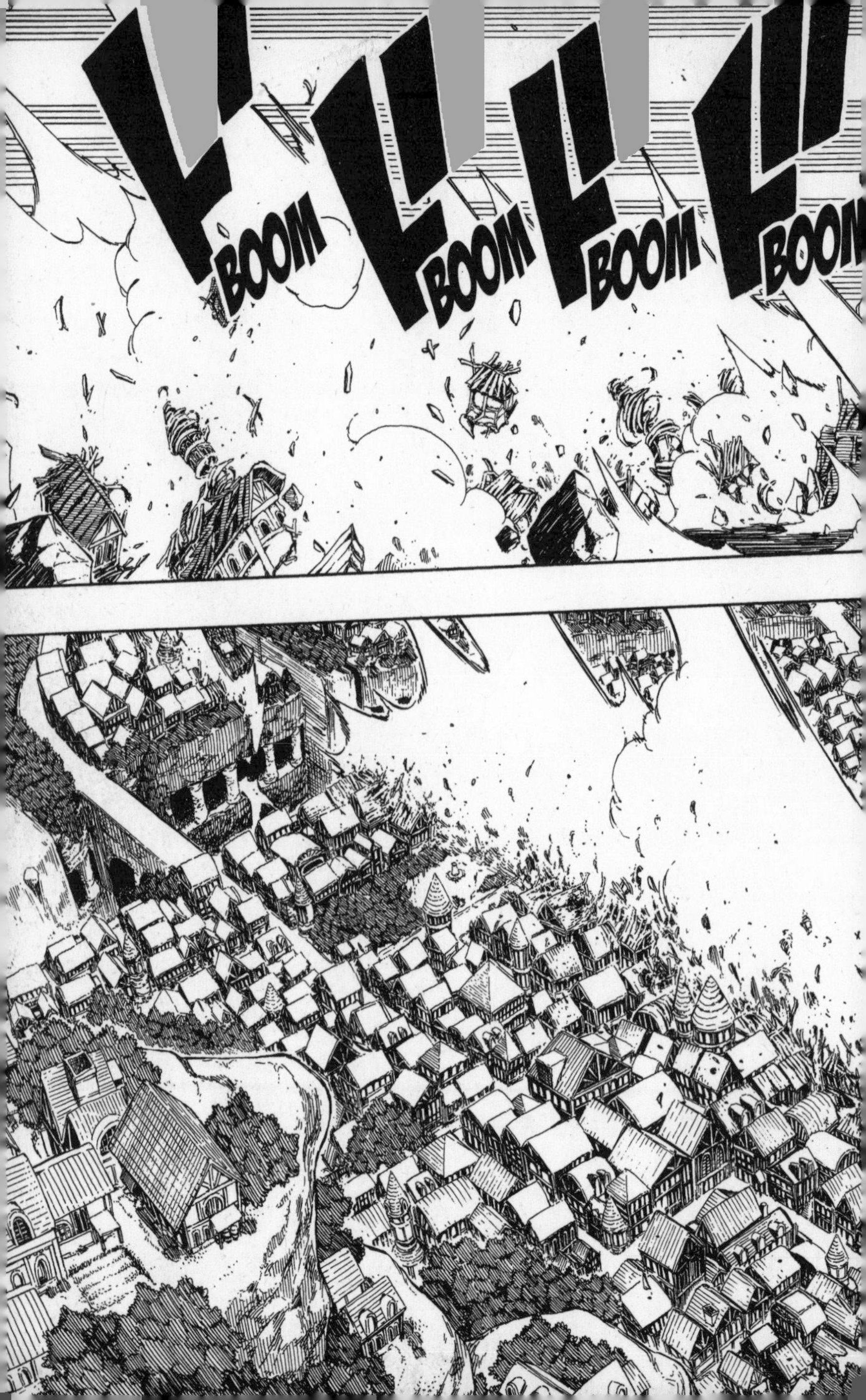
BOOM
BOOM
BOOM
BOOM

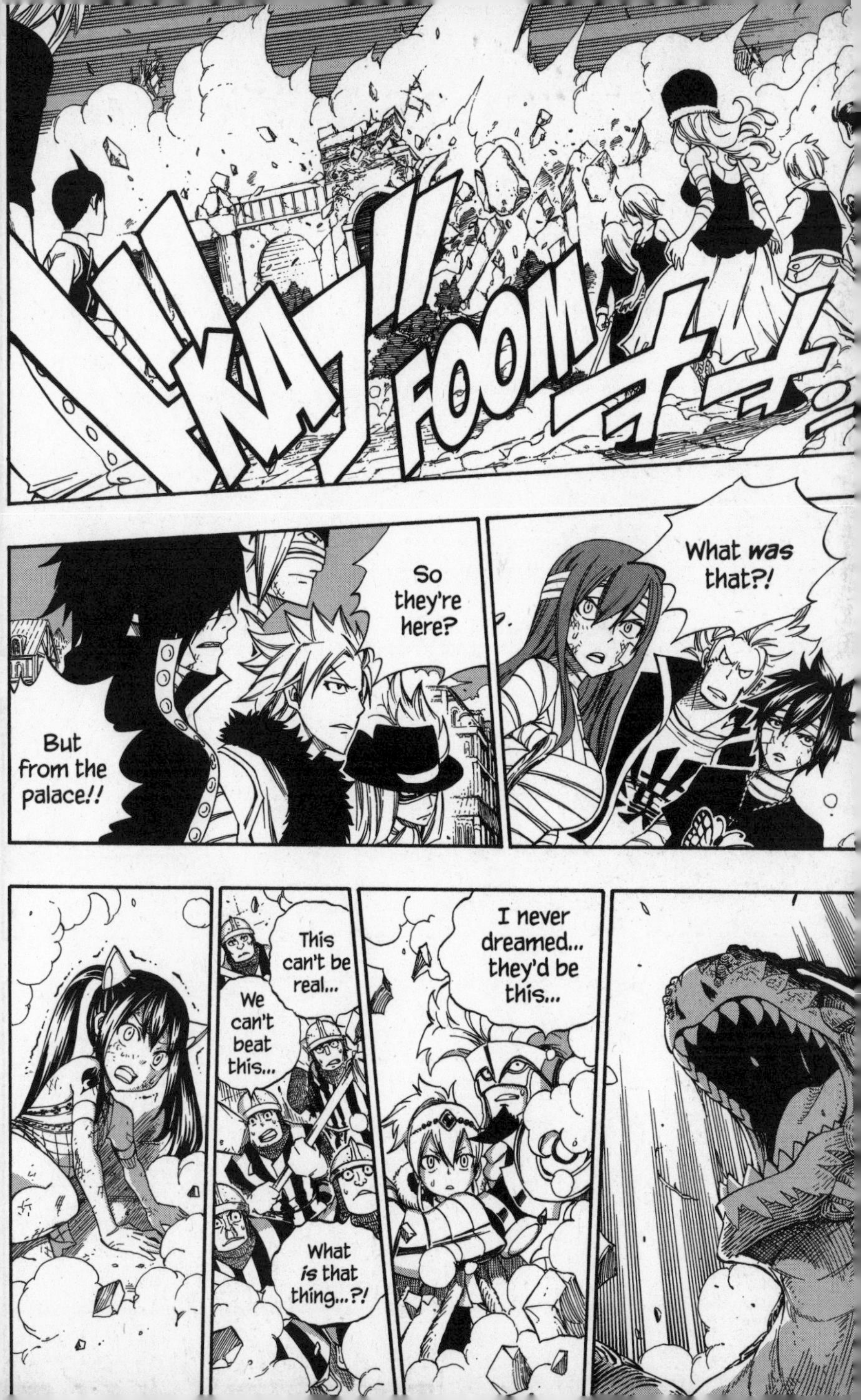
KA!!
FOOM
What *was* that?!
So they're here?
But from the palace!!
I never dreamed... they'd be this...
This can't be real...
We can't beat this...
What *is* that thing...?!

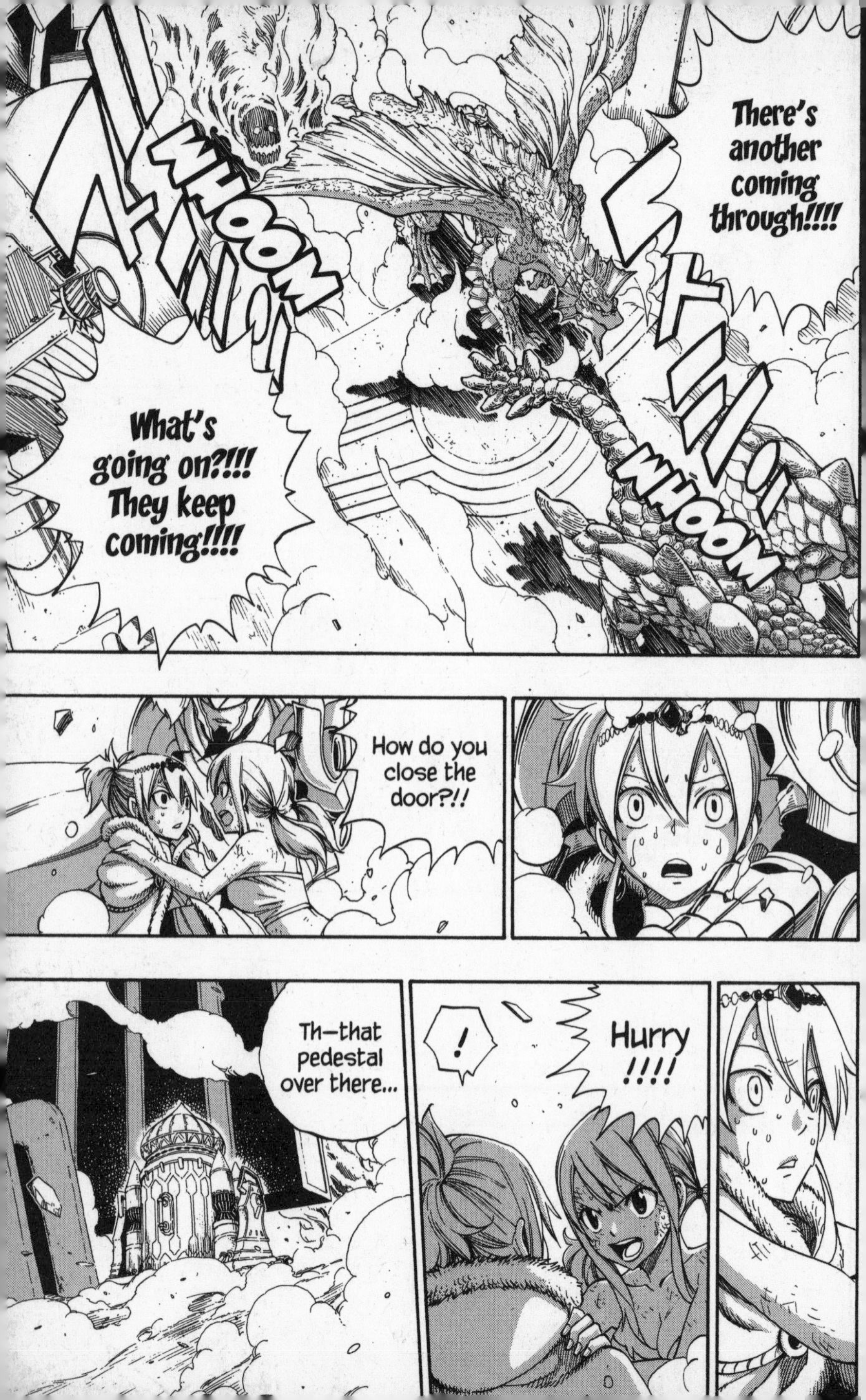
There's another coming through!!!!
WHOOM
WHOOM
What's going on?!!! They keep coming!!!!
How do you close the door?!!
Hurry !!!!
!
Th—that pedestal over there...

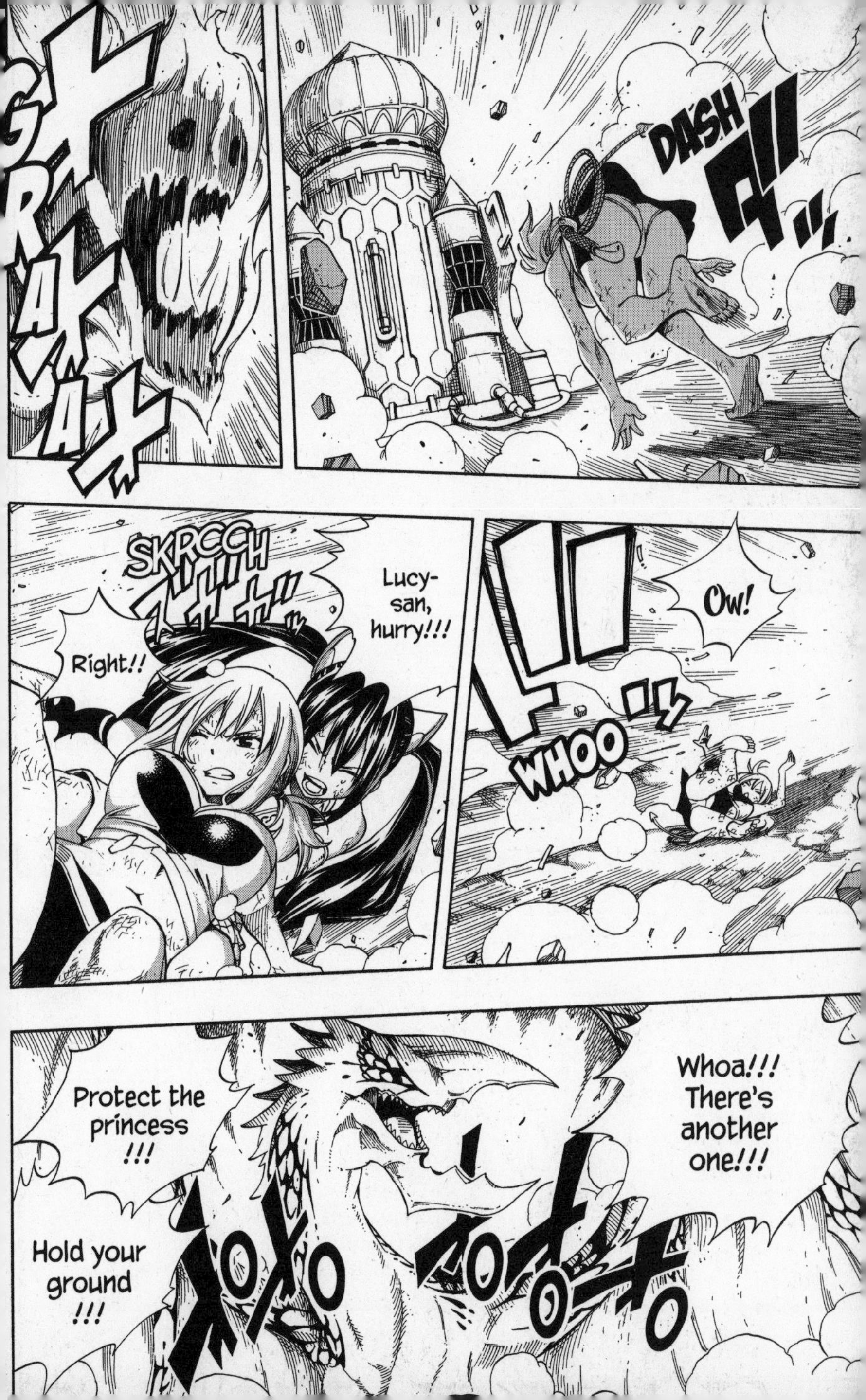
DASH
GRAA
Ow!
WHOO
Lucy-san, hurry!!!
Right!!
SKRCCH
Whoa!!! There's another one!!!
Protect the princess !!!
Hold your ground !!!

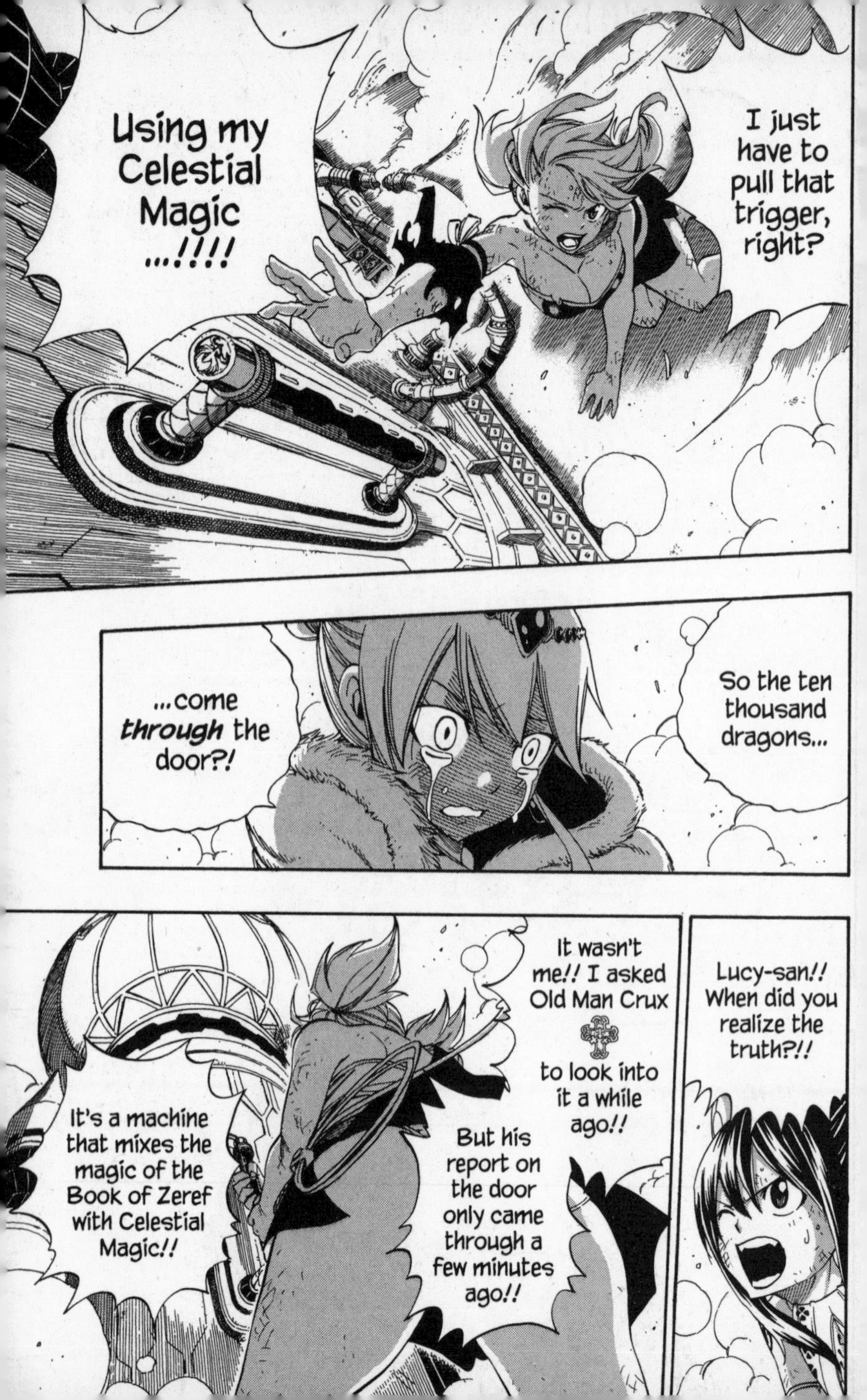
I just have to pull that trigger, right?
Using my Celestial Magic ...!!!!
So the ten thousand dragons...
...come *through* the door?!
Lucy-san!! When did you realize the truth?!!
It wasn't me!! I asked Old Man Crux to look into it a while ago!!
But his report on the door only came through a few minutes ago!!
It's a machine that mixes the magic of the Book of Zeref with Celestial Magic!!

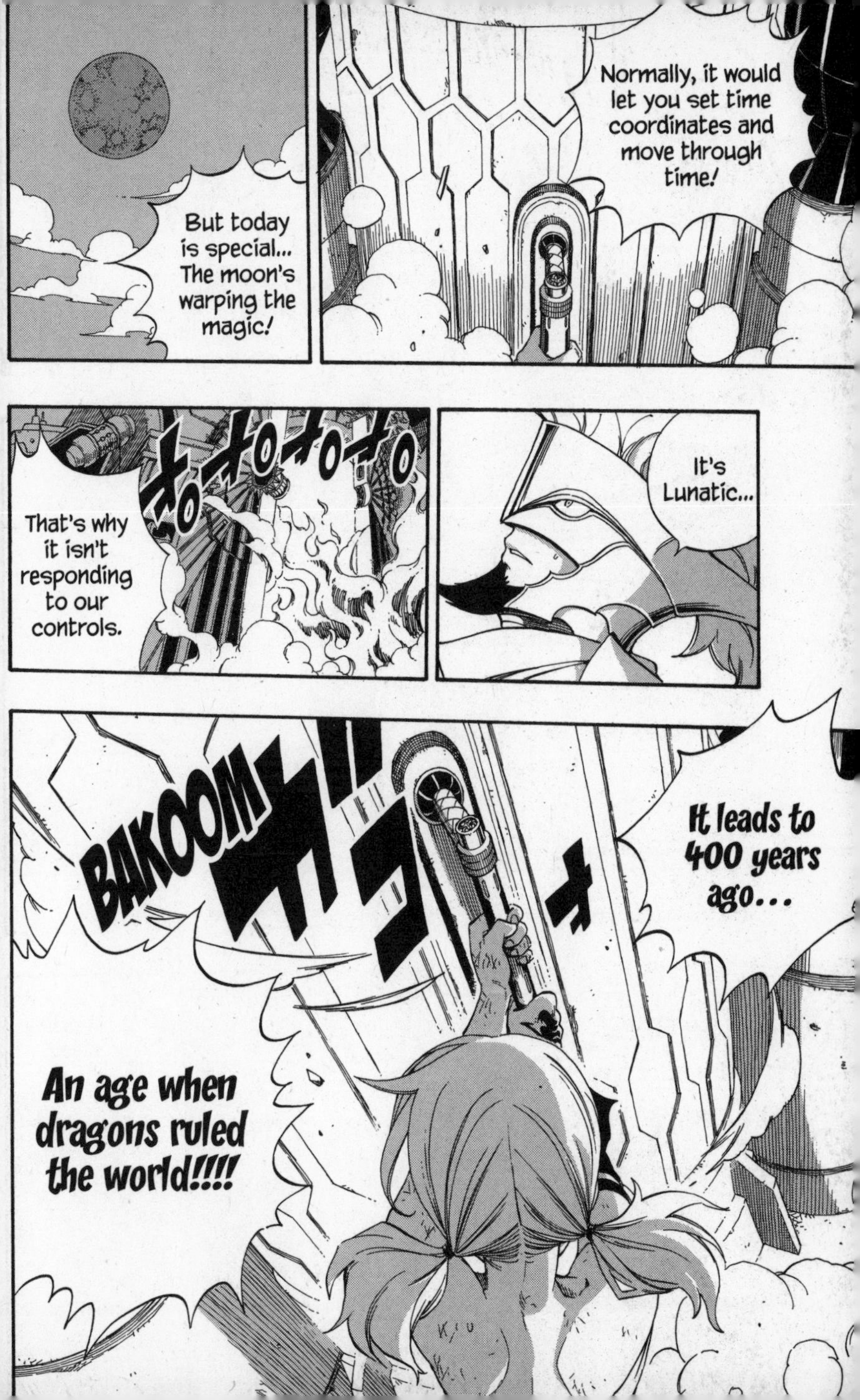
Normally, it would let you set time coordinates and move through time!
But today is special... The moon's warping the magic!
It's Lunatic...
That's why it isn't responding to our controls.
It leads to 400 years ago...
BAKOOM
An age when dragons ruled the world!!!!

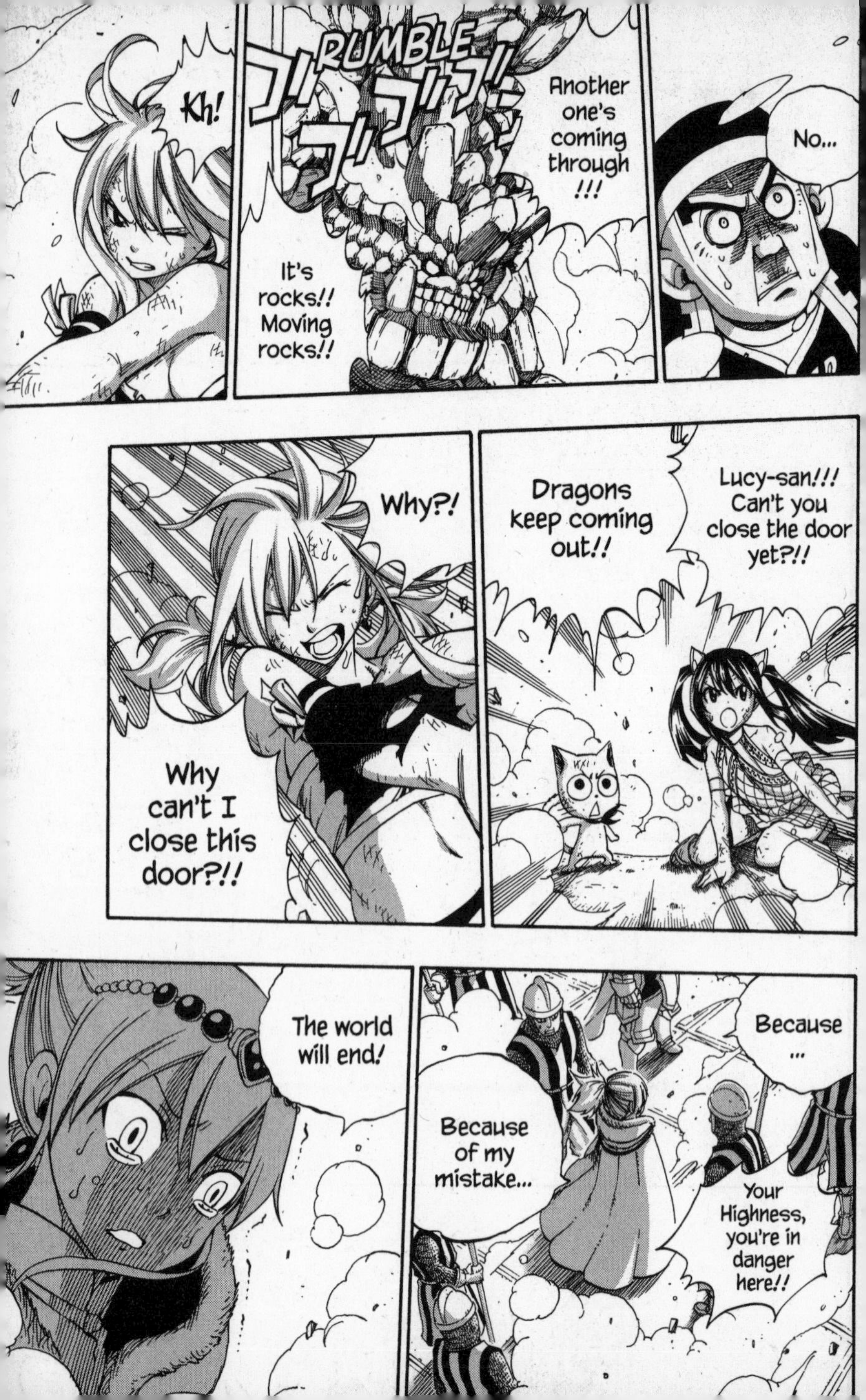
No...
RUMBLE
Another one's coming through!!!
It's rocks!! Moving rocks!!
Kh!
Lucy-san!!! Can't you close the door yet?!!
Dragons keep coming out!!
Why?!
Why can't I close this door?!!
Because ...
Your Highness, you're in danger here!!
Because of my mistake...
The world will end!

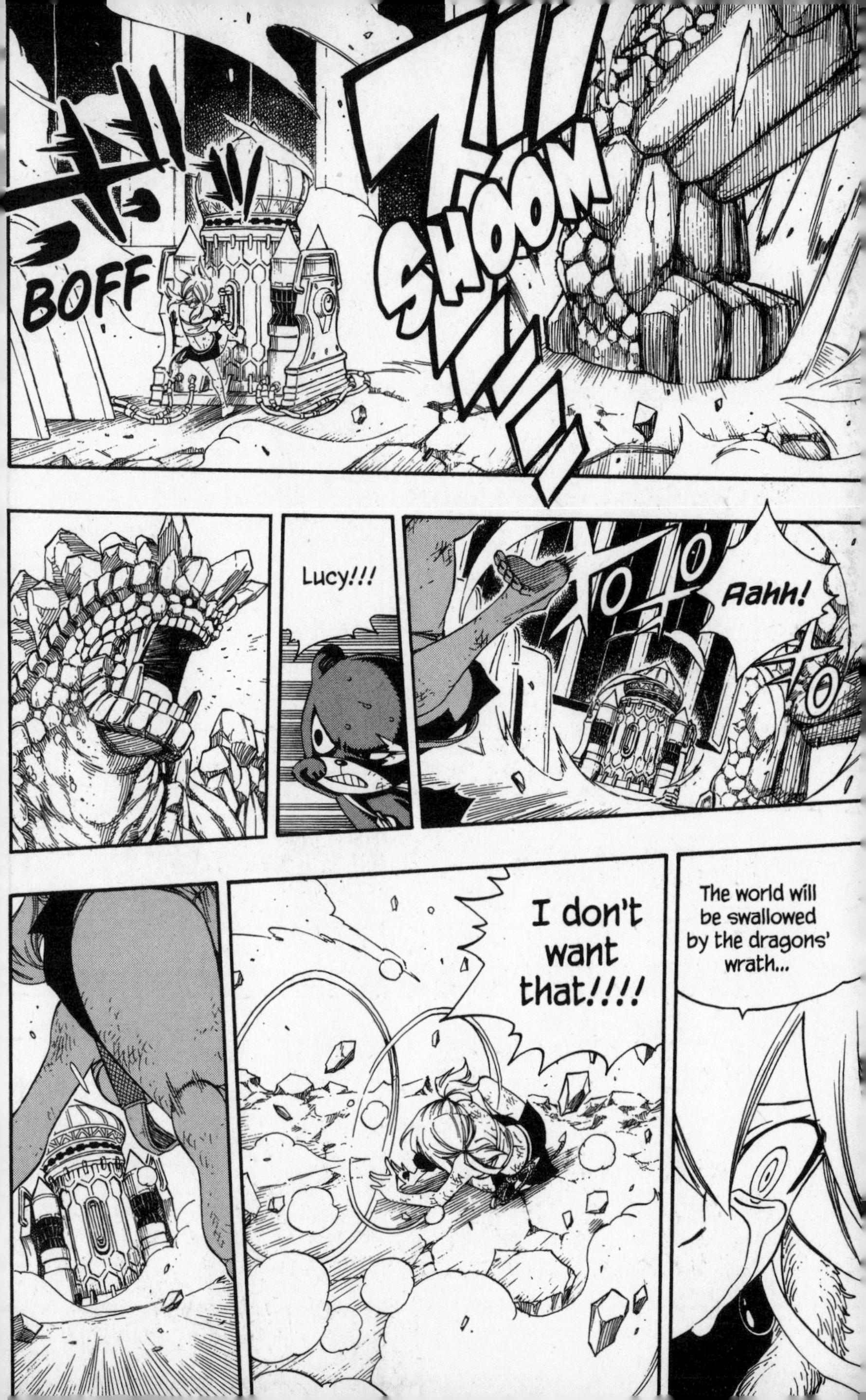
SHOOM
BOFF
Aahh!
Lucy!!!
The world will be swallowed by the dragons' wrath...
I don't want that!!!!

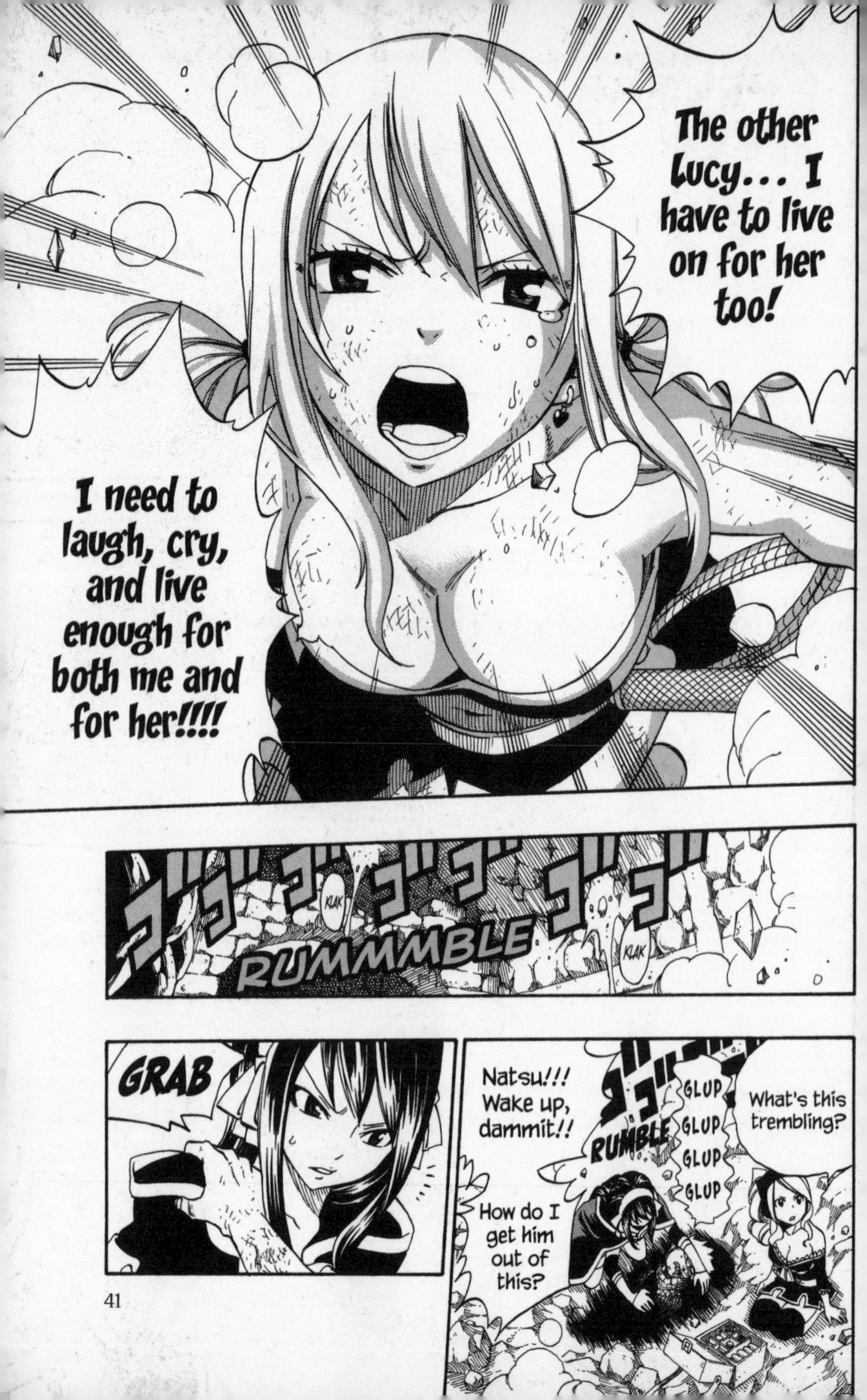
The other Lucy... I have to live on for her too!
I need to laugh, cry, and live enough for both me and for her!!!!
KLAK
RUMMMBLE
KLAK
What's this trembling?
GLUP GLUP GLUP GLUP GLUP
RUMBLE
Natsu!!! Wake up, dammit!!
How do I get him out of this?
GRAB

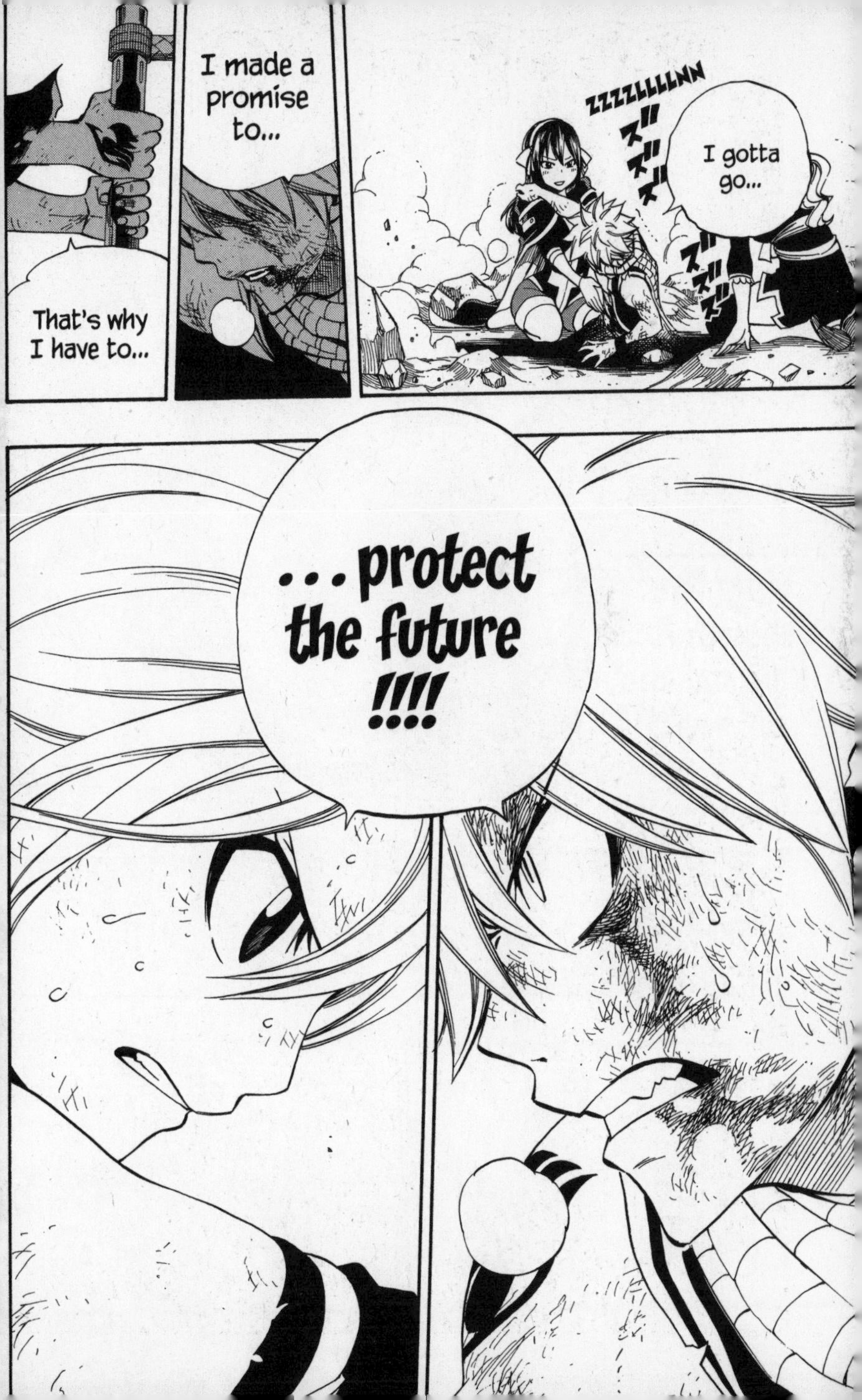
ZZZZLLLLNN
ズズズ
I gotta go...
ズズズ
I made a promise to...
That's why I have to...
...protect the future!!!!

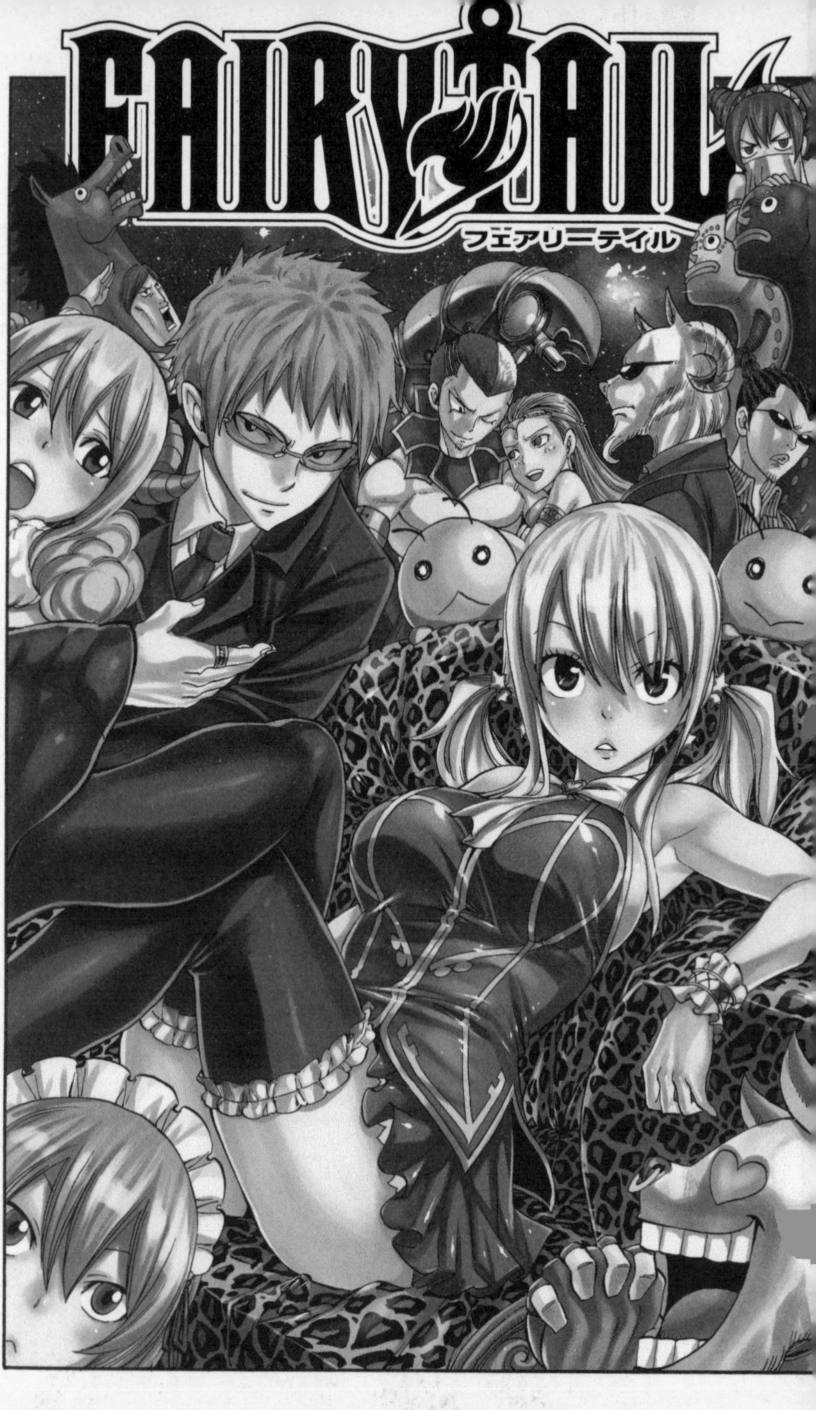
FAIRY TAIL
フェアリーテイル

KREE EEEEE

FAIRY TAIL

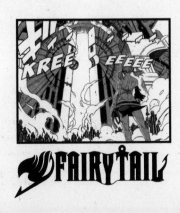

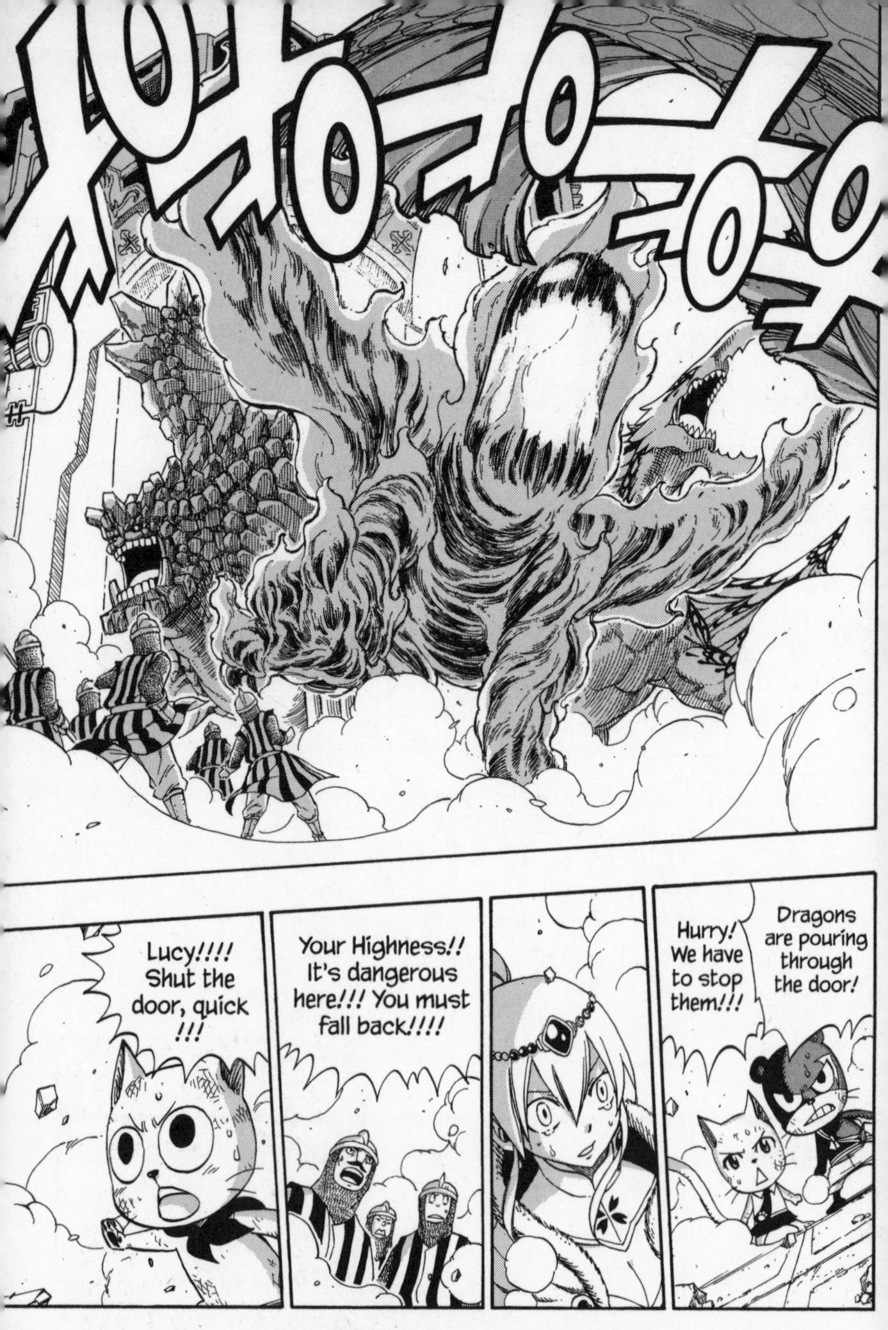
Dragons are pouring through the door!
Hurry! We have to stop them!!!
Your Highness!! It's dangerous here!!! You must fall back!!!!
Lucy!!!! Shut the door, quick !!!

Chapter 328: Zodiac

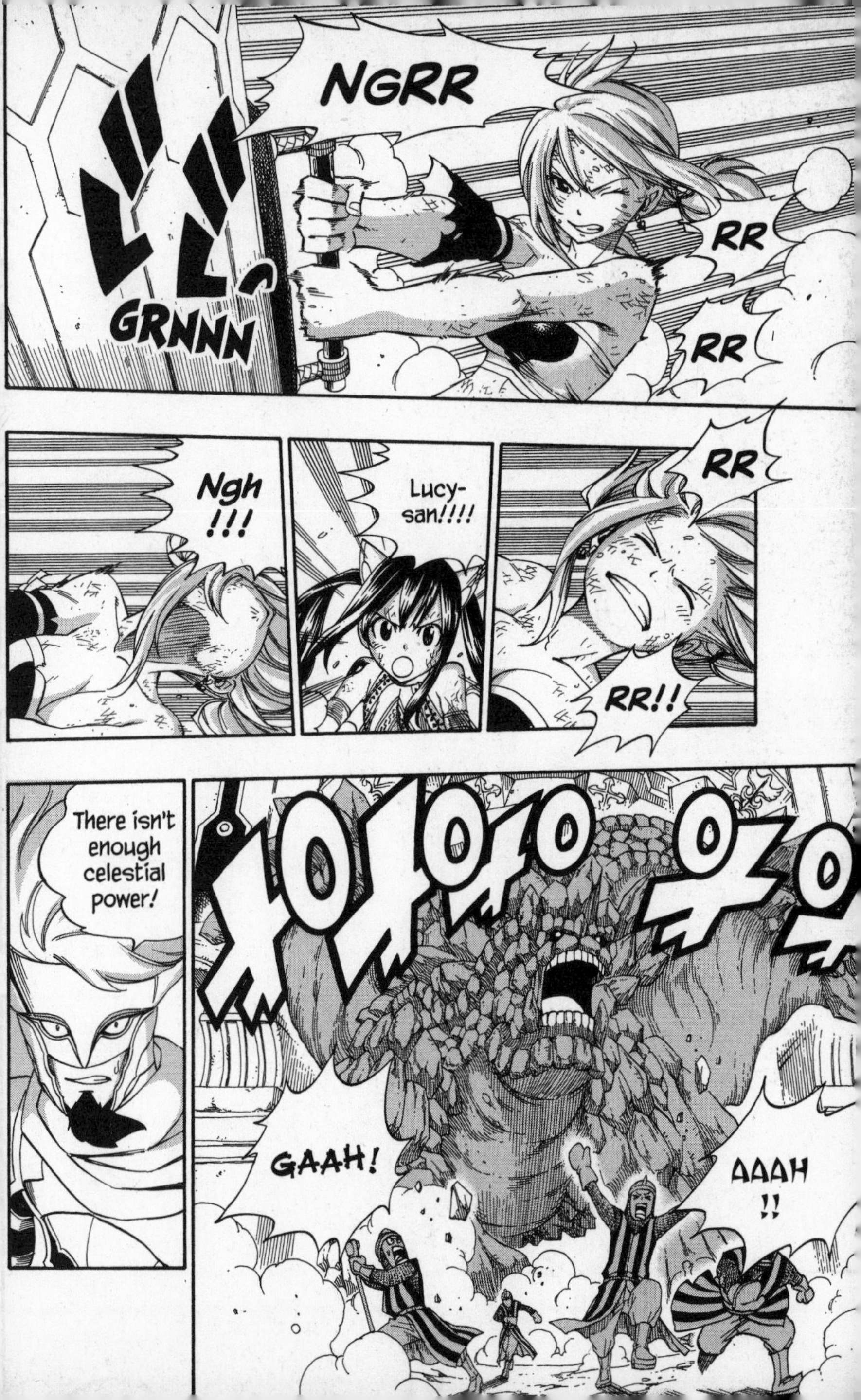
NGRR
RR
RR
GRNNN
RR
RR!!
Lucy-san!!!!
Ngh!!!
AAAH!!
GAAH!
There isn't enough celestial power!

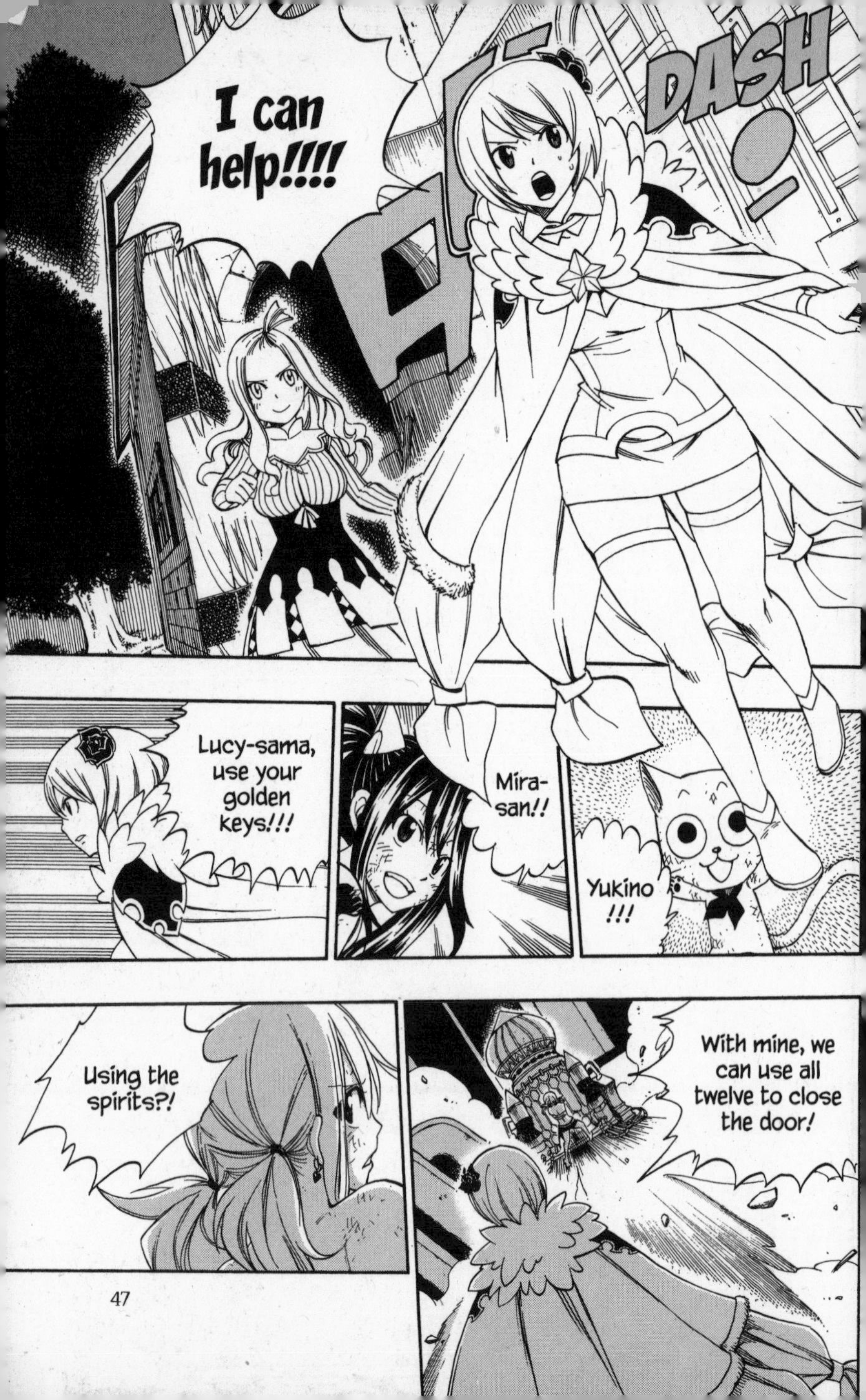
DASH
I can help!!!!
Yukino!!!
Mira-san!!
Lucy-sama, use your golden keys!!!
With mine, we can use all twelve to close the door!
Using the spirits?!

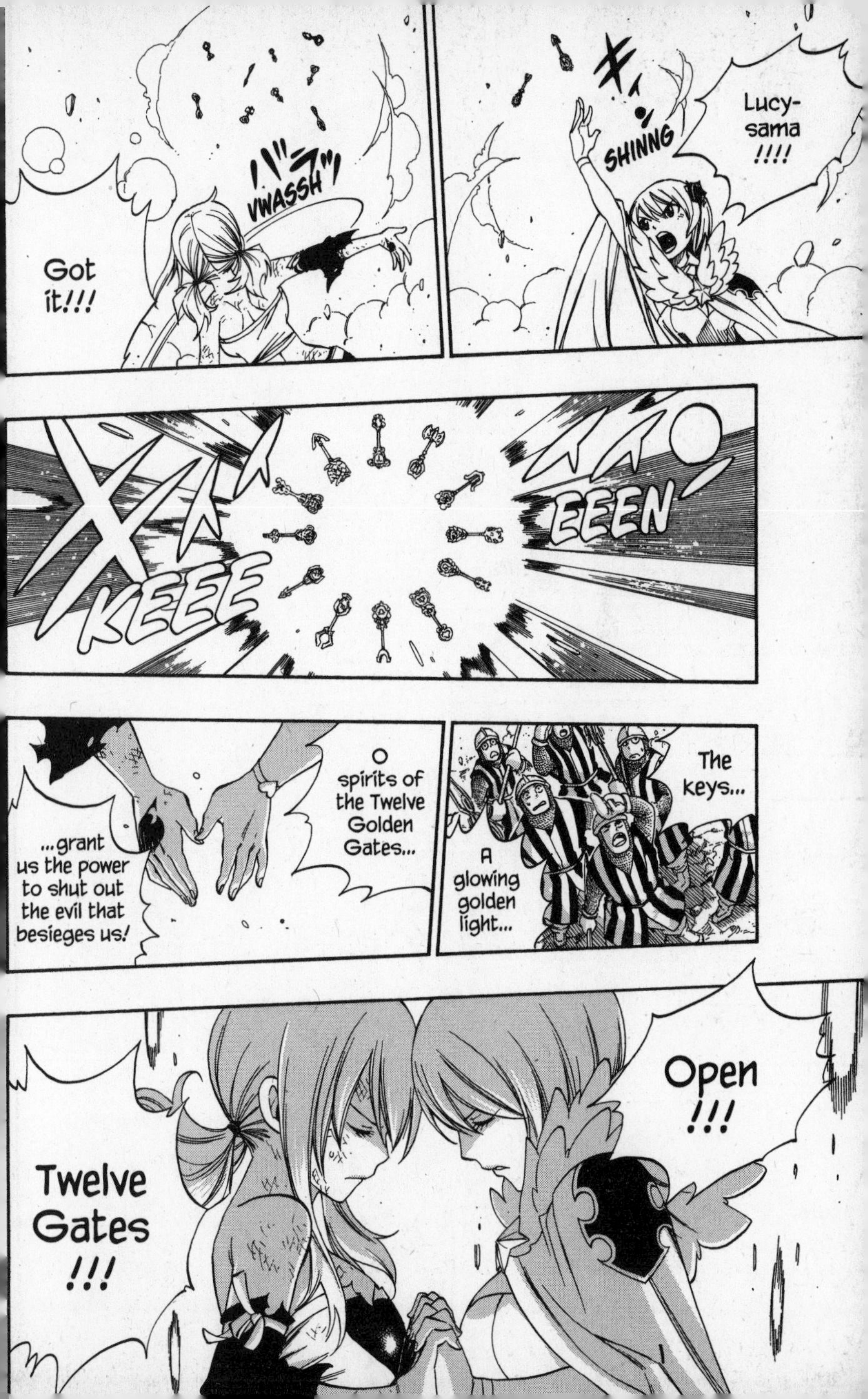

Lucy-sama!!!!
SHINNG
VWASSH
Got it!!!
KEEE
EEEN
The keys...
A glowing golden light...
O spirits of the Twelve Golden Gates...
...grant us the power to shut out the evil that besieges us!
Open!!!
Twelve Gates!!!

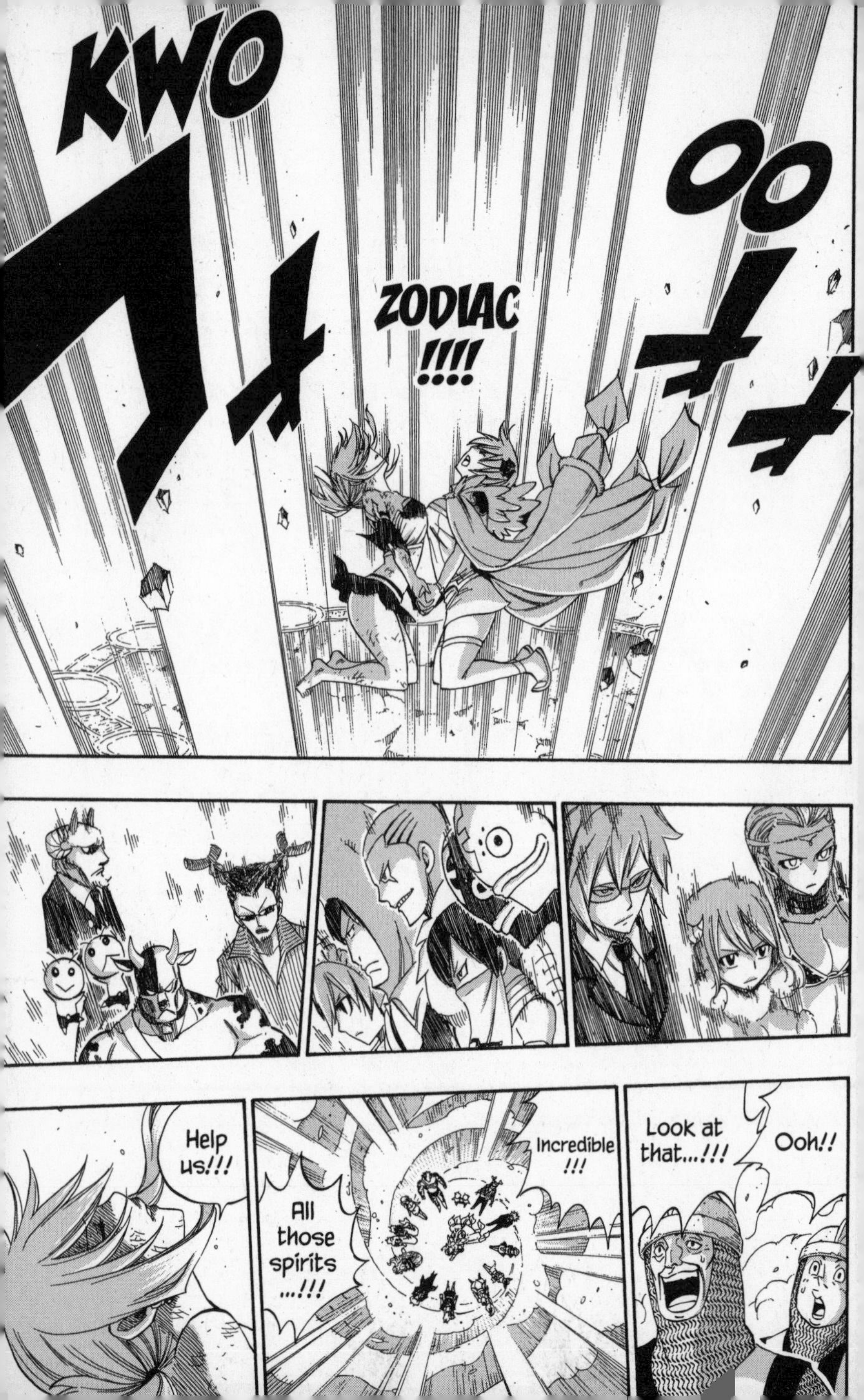
KWO
OO
ZODIAC !!!!
Ooh!!
Look at that...!!!
Incredible !!!
All those spirits ...!!!
Help us!!!

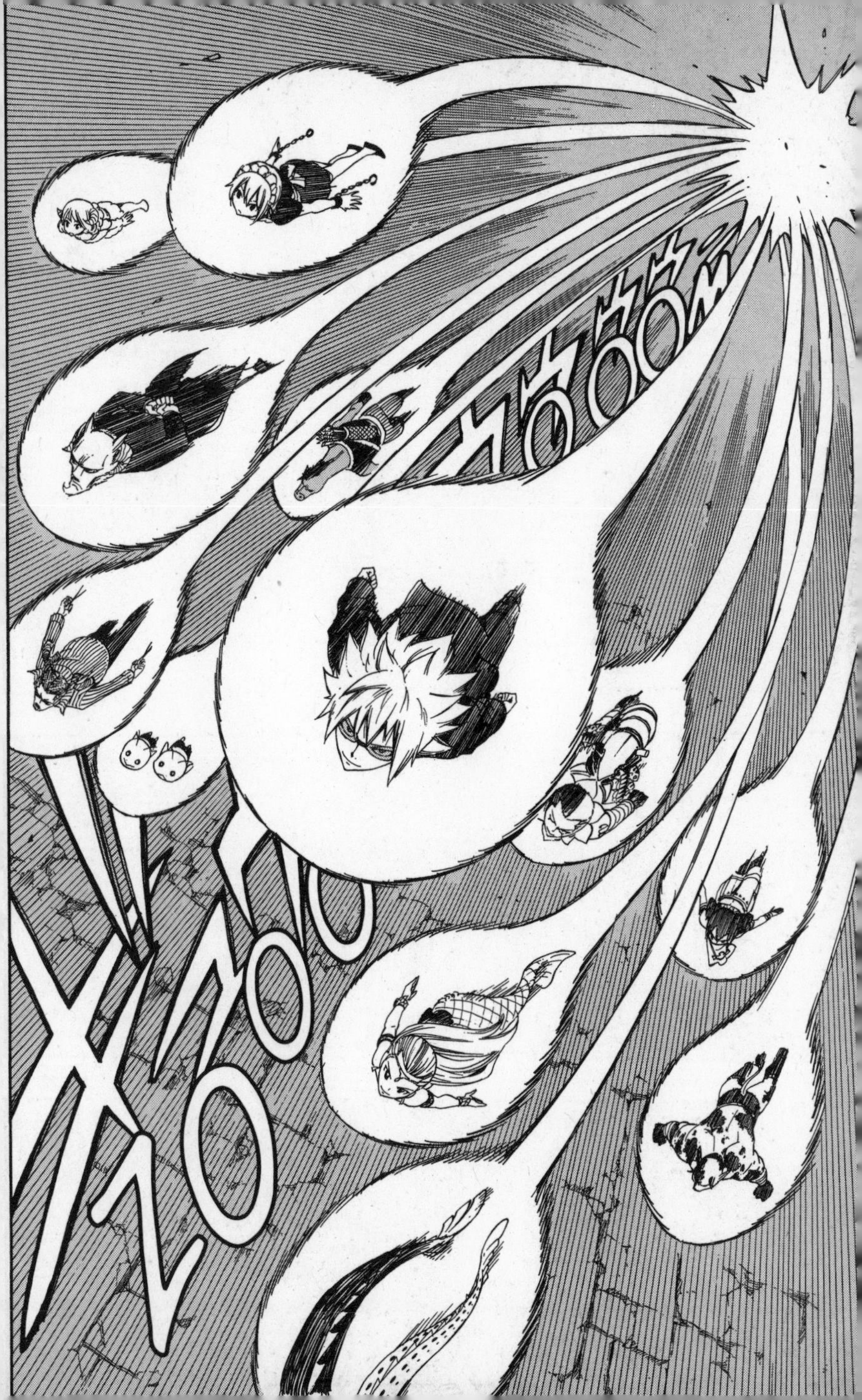
ZOOOOM
ZOOOO

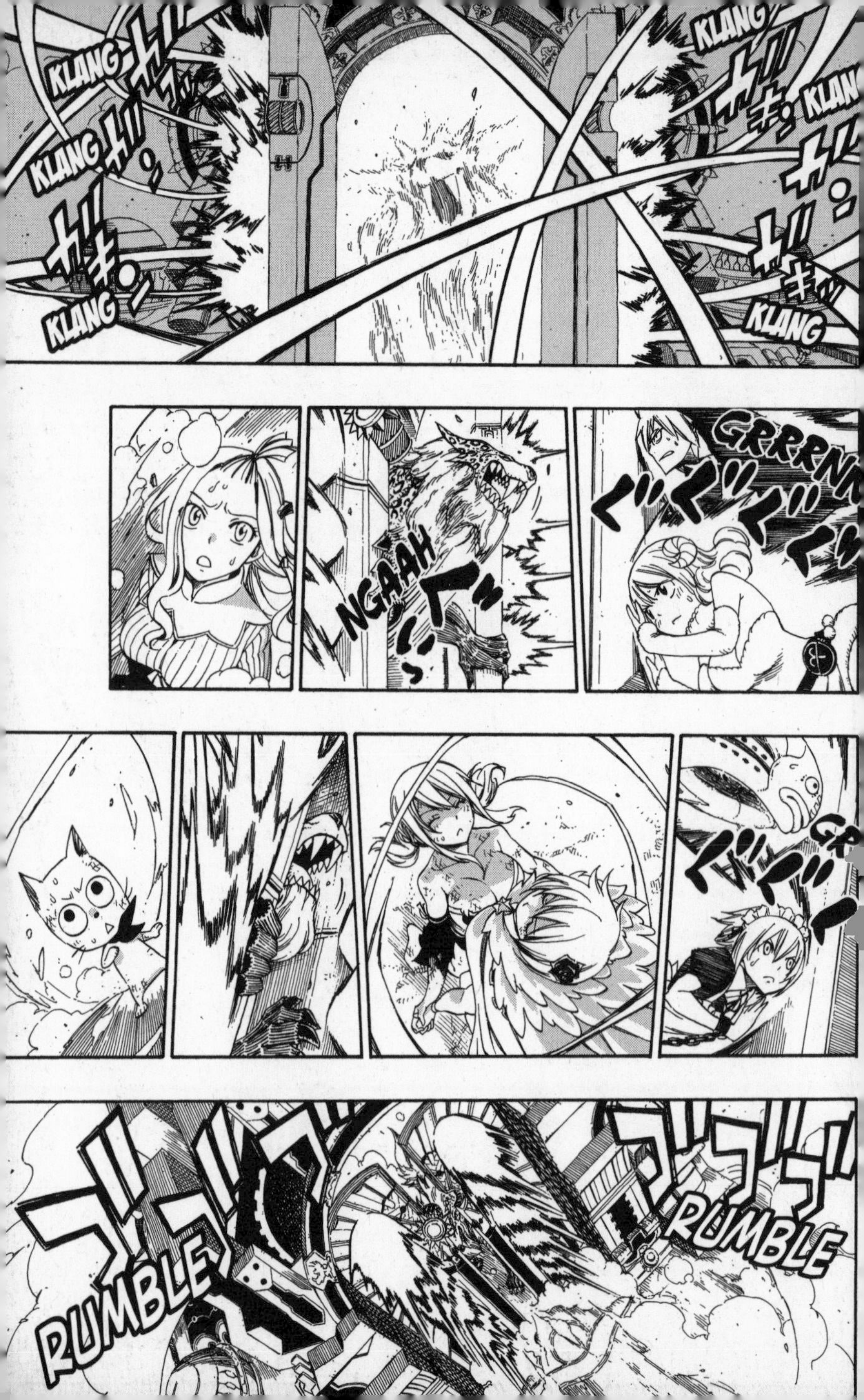
KLANG
KLAN
KLANG
KLANG
KLANG
KLANG
GRRRNN
NGAAH
GR
RUMBLE
RUMBLE

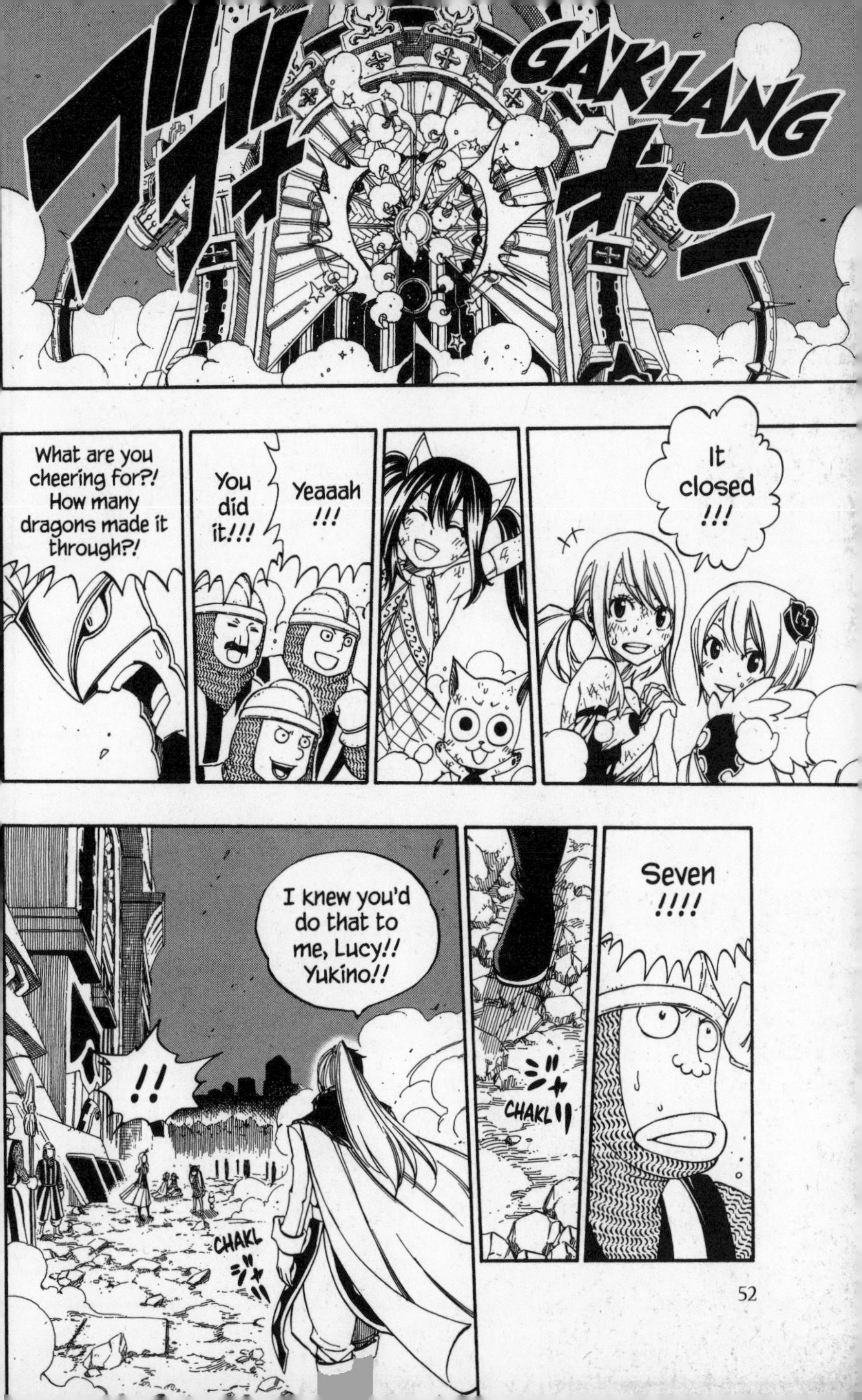
GARLANG
It closed !!!
Yeaaah !!!
You did it!!!
What are you cheering for?! How many dragons made it through?!
Seven !!!!
CHAKL
I knew you'd do that to me, Lucy!! Yukino!!
!!
CHAKL

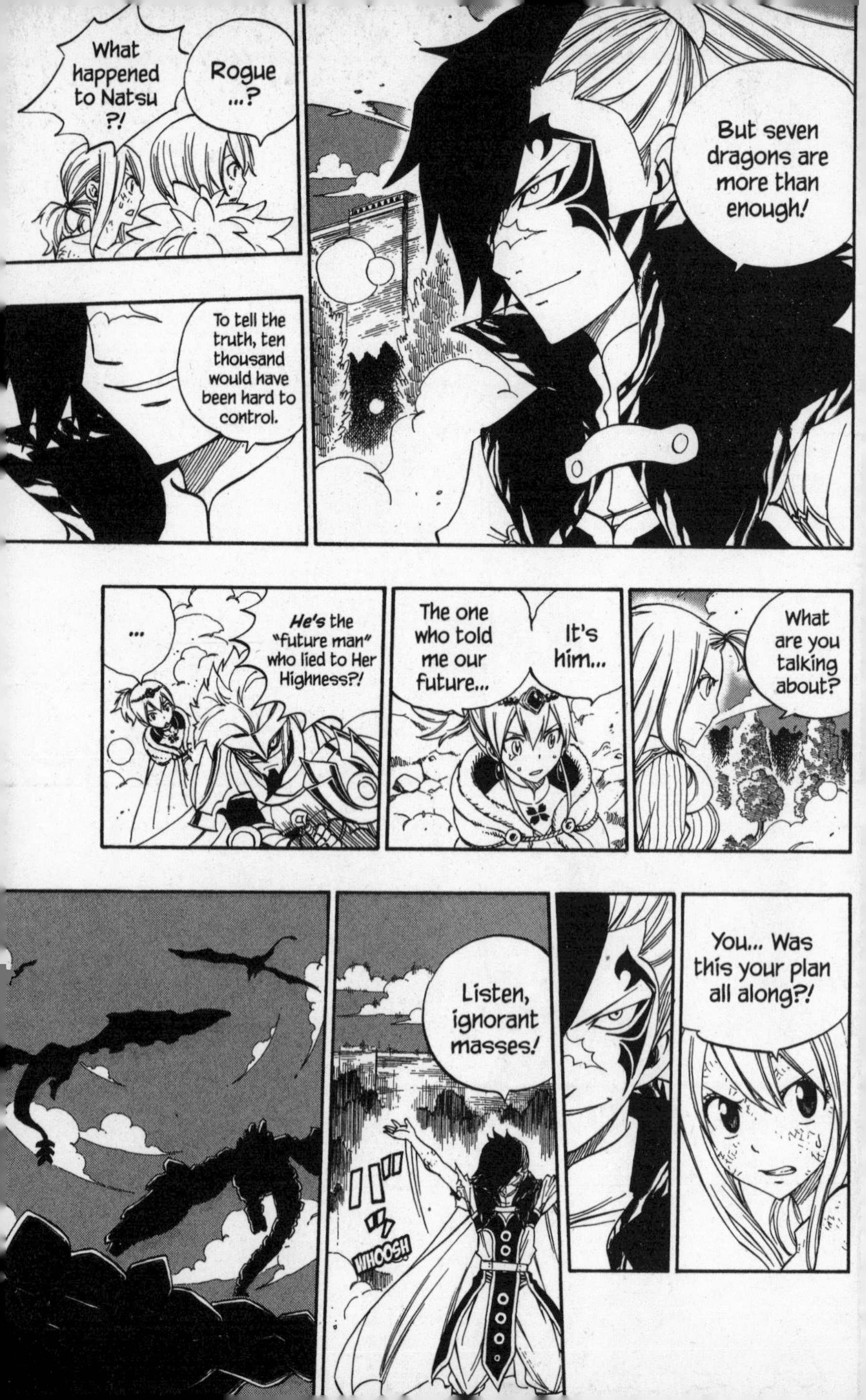

But seven dragons are more than enough!
Rogue ...?
What happened to Natsu ?!
To tell the truth, ten thousand would have been hard to control.
What are you talking about?
It's him...
The one who told me our future...
He's the "future man" who lied to Her Highness?!
...
You... Was this your plan all along?!
Listen, ignorant masses!
WHOOSH

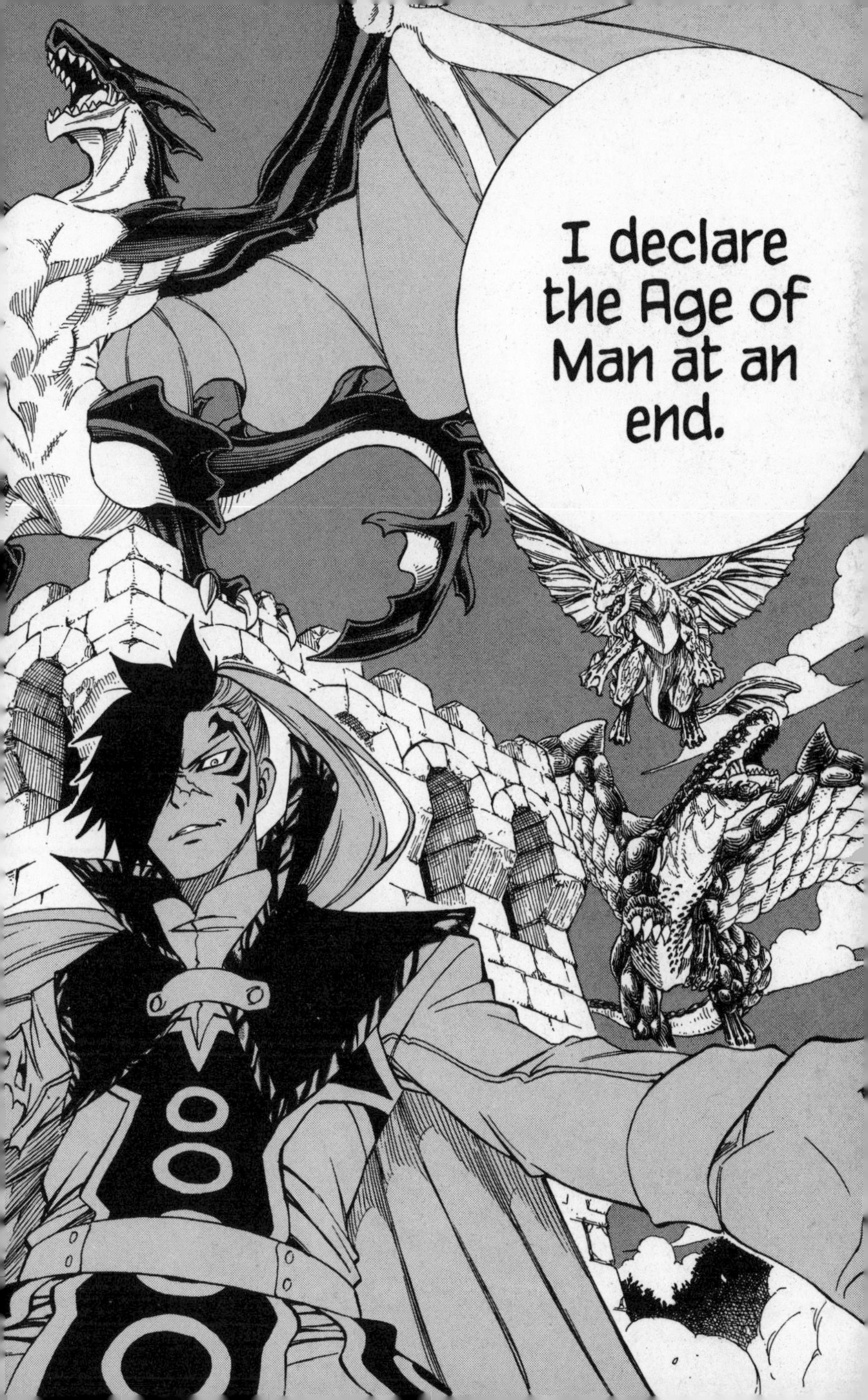
I declare the Age of Man at an end.

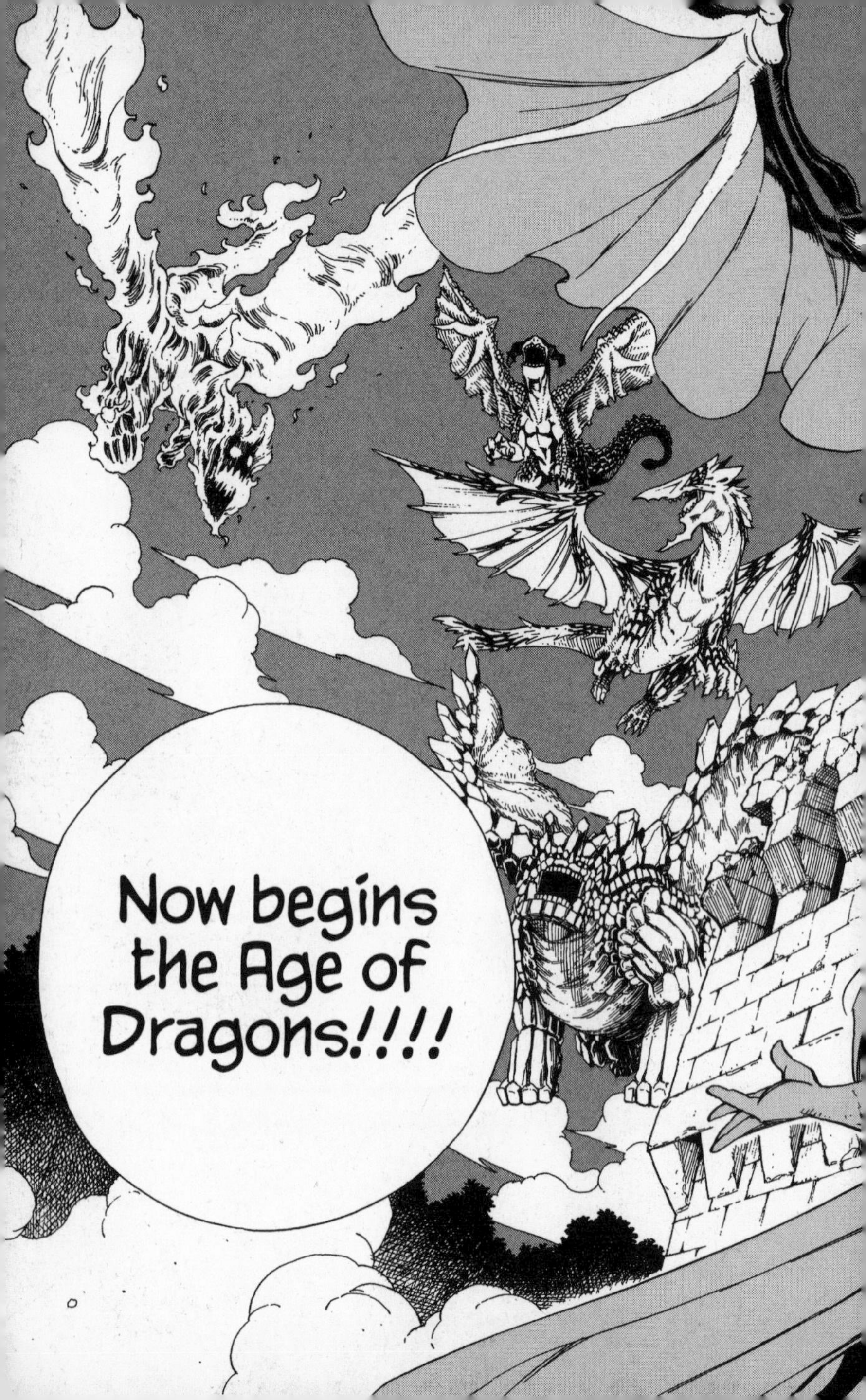
Now begins the Age of Dragons!!!!

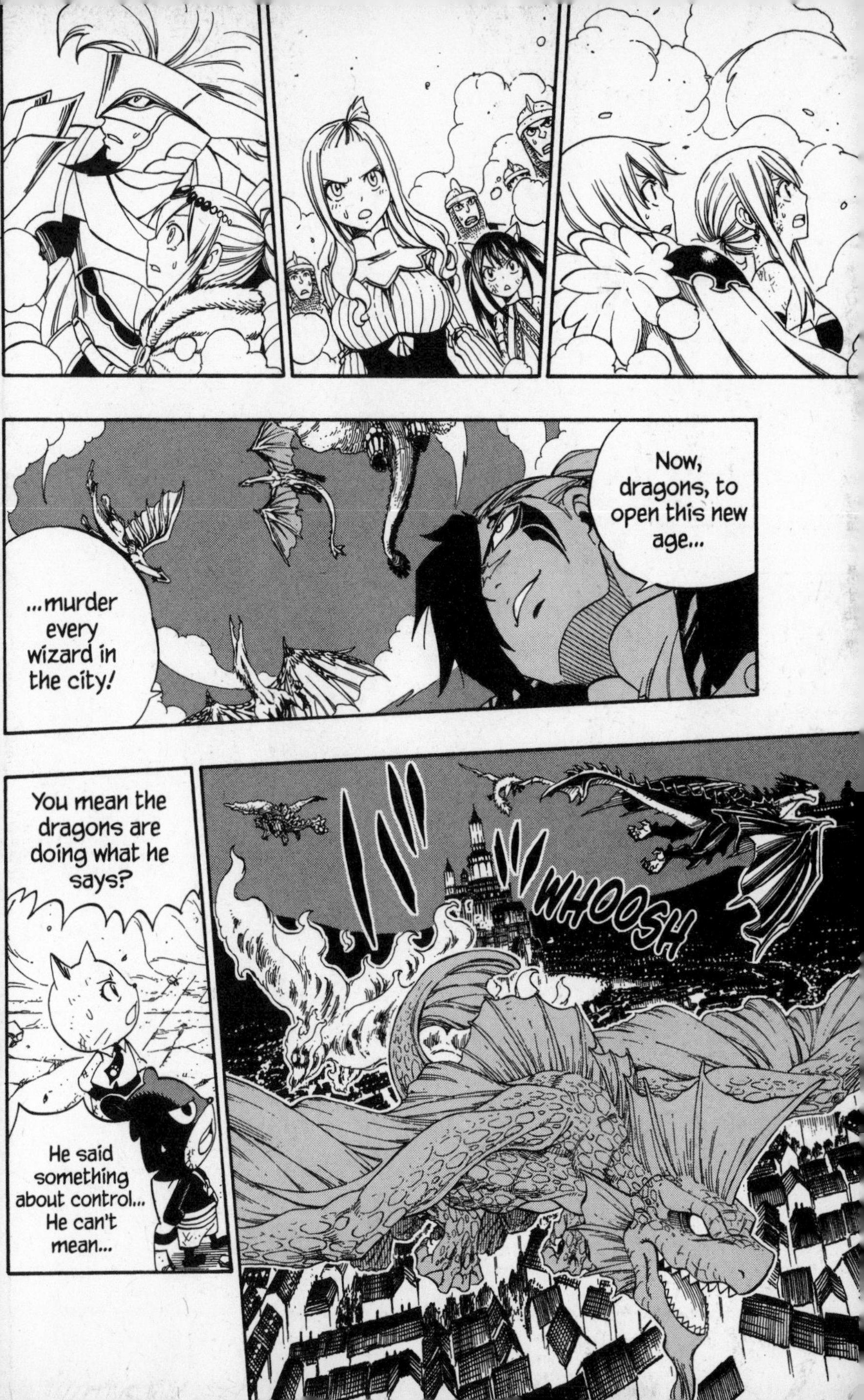
Now, dragons, to open this new age...
...murder every wizard in the city!
WHOOSH
You mean the dragons are doing what he says?
He said something about control... He can't mean...

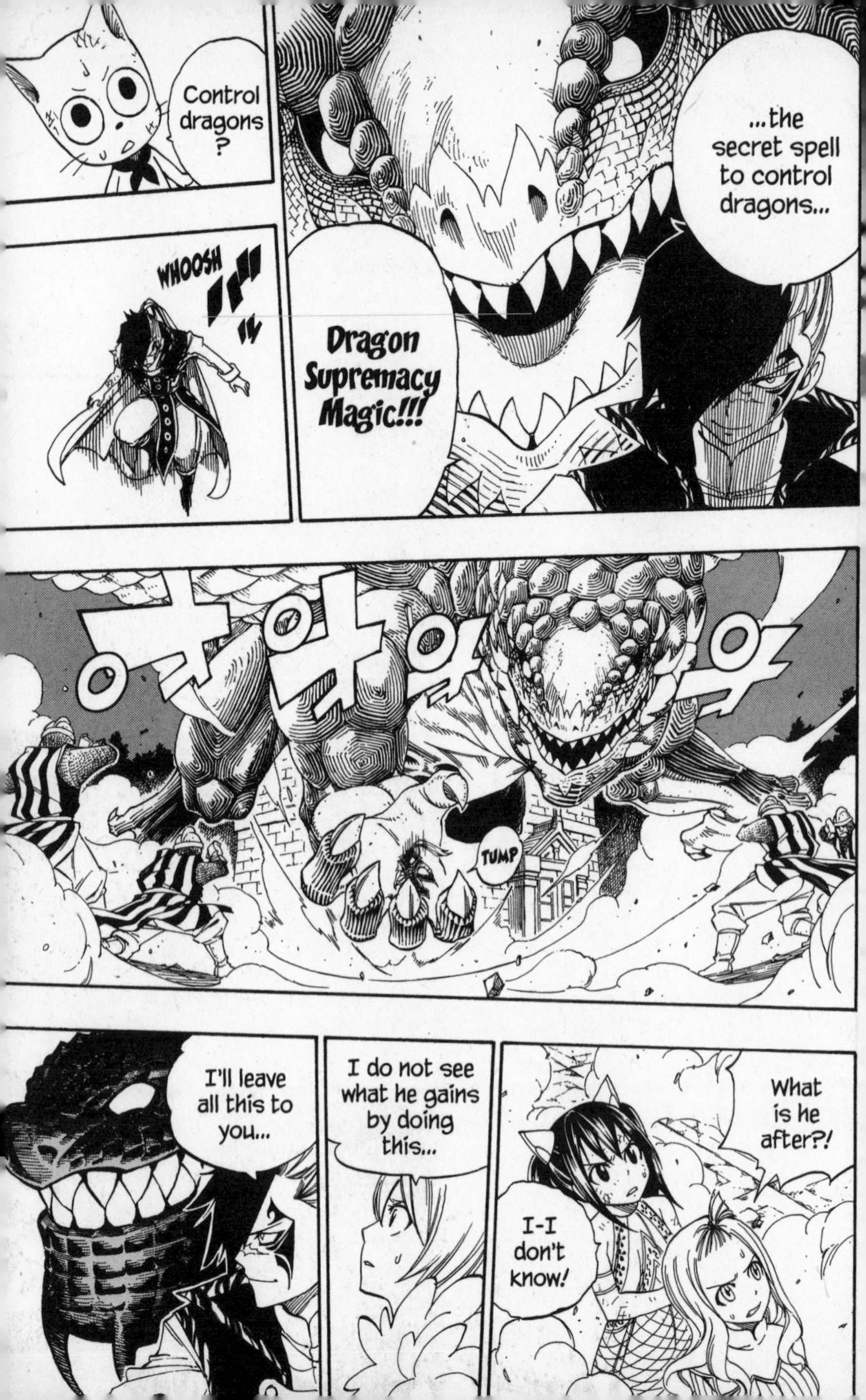
...the secret spell to control dragons...
Dragon Supremacy Magic!!!
Control dragons?
WHOOSH
TUMP
What is he after?!
I-I don't know!
I do not see what he gains by doing this...
I'll leave all this to you...

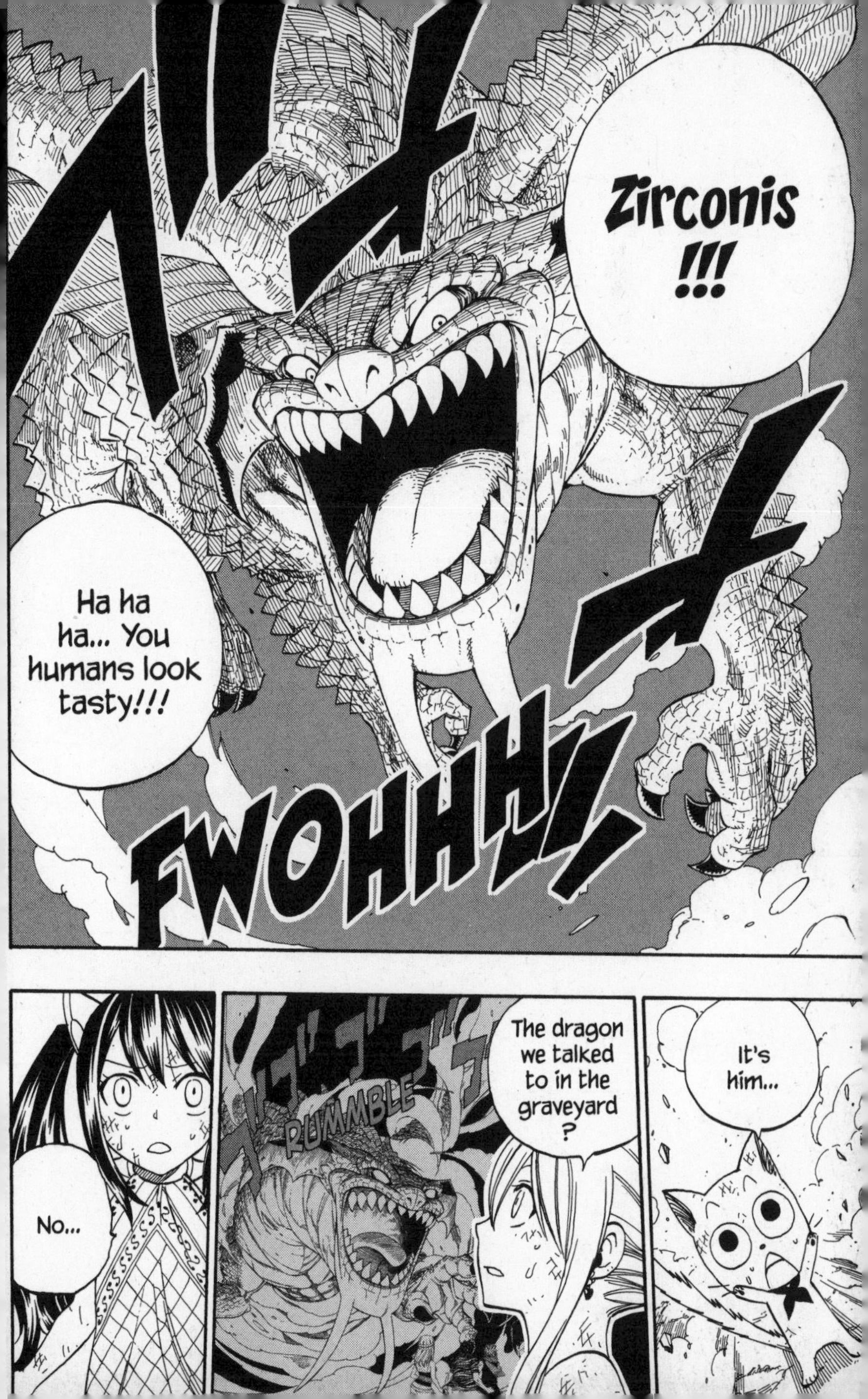
Zirconis !!!
Ha ha ha... You humans look tasty!!!
FWOHHH
It's him...
The dragon we talked to in the graveyard ?
RUMMBLE
No...

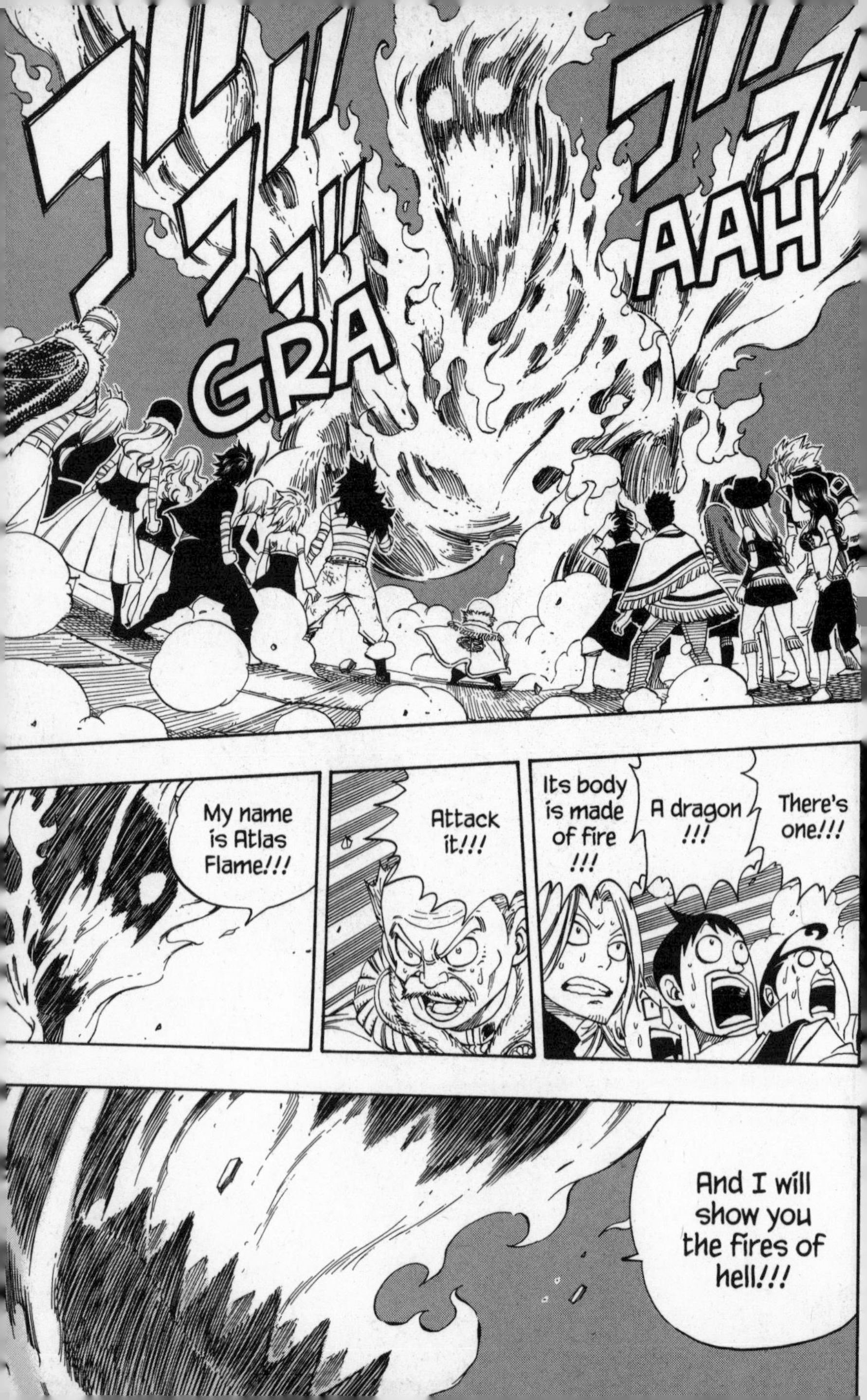
GRA
AAH
There's one!!!
A dragon!!!
Its body is made of fire!!!
Attack it!!!
My name is Atlas Flame!!!
And I will show you the fires of hell!!!

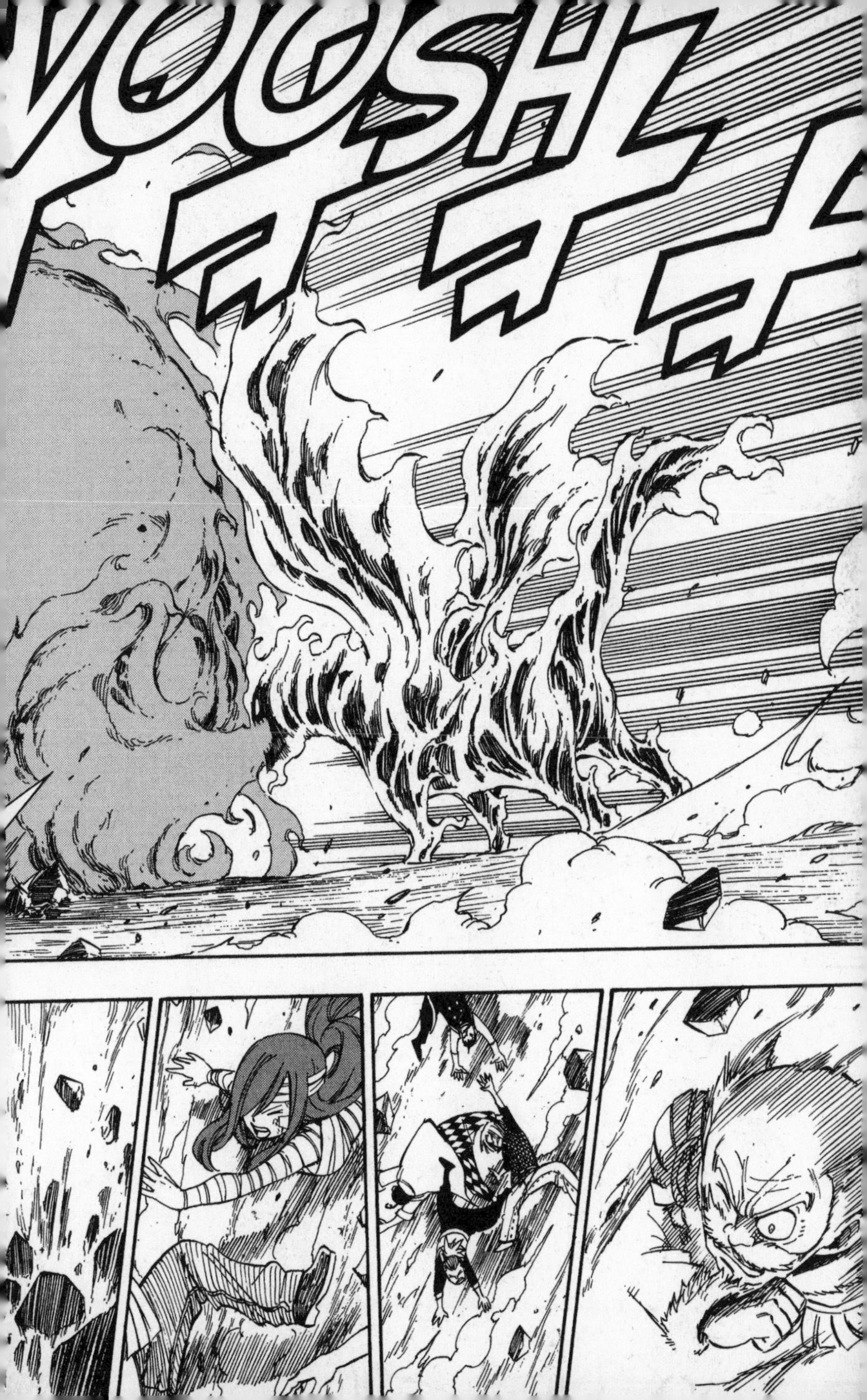
VOOSH

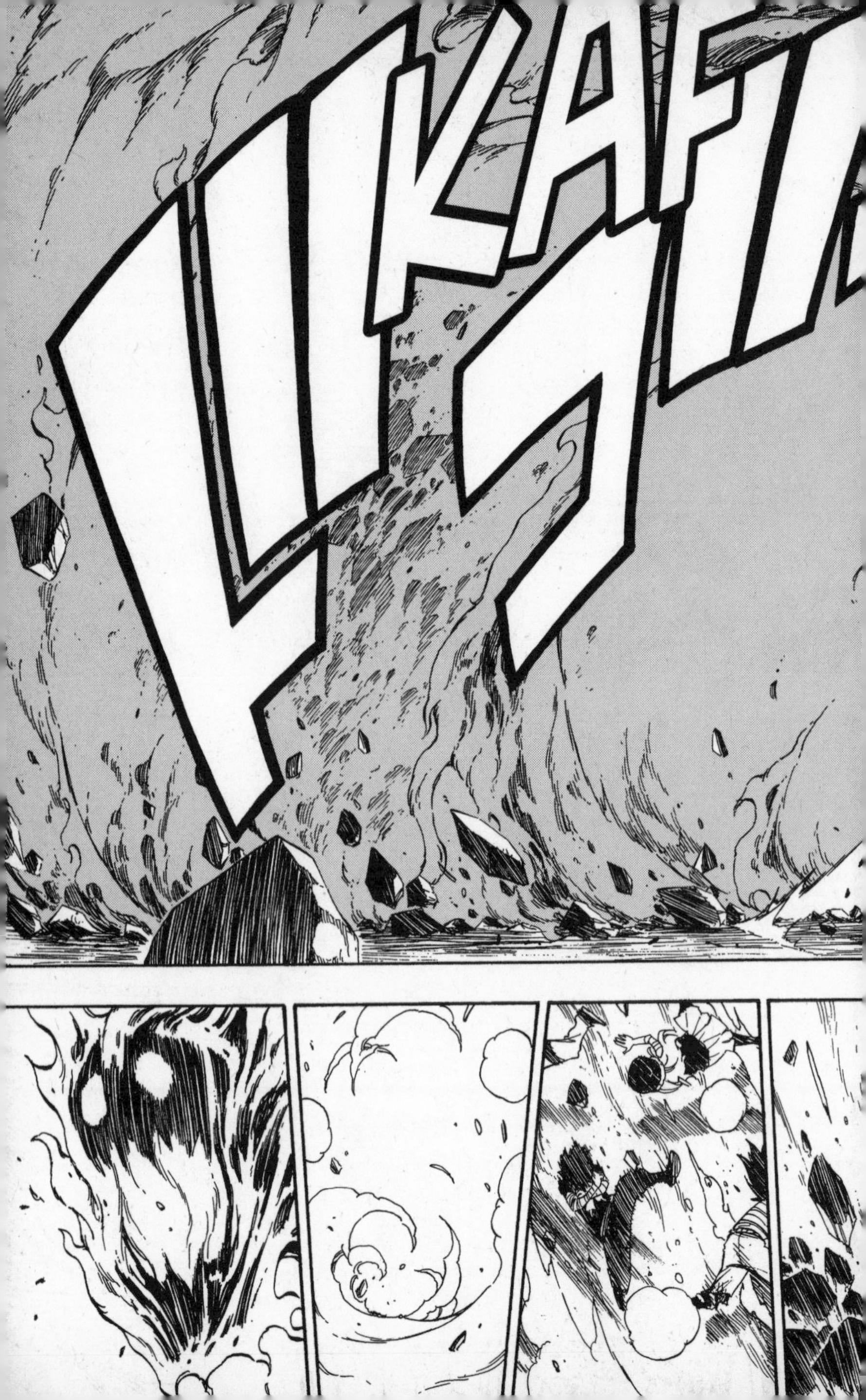

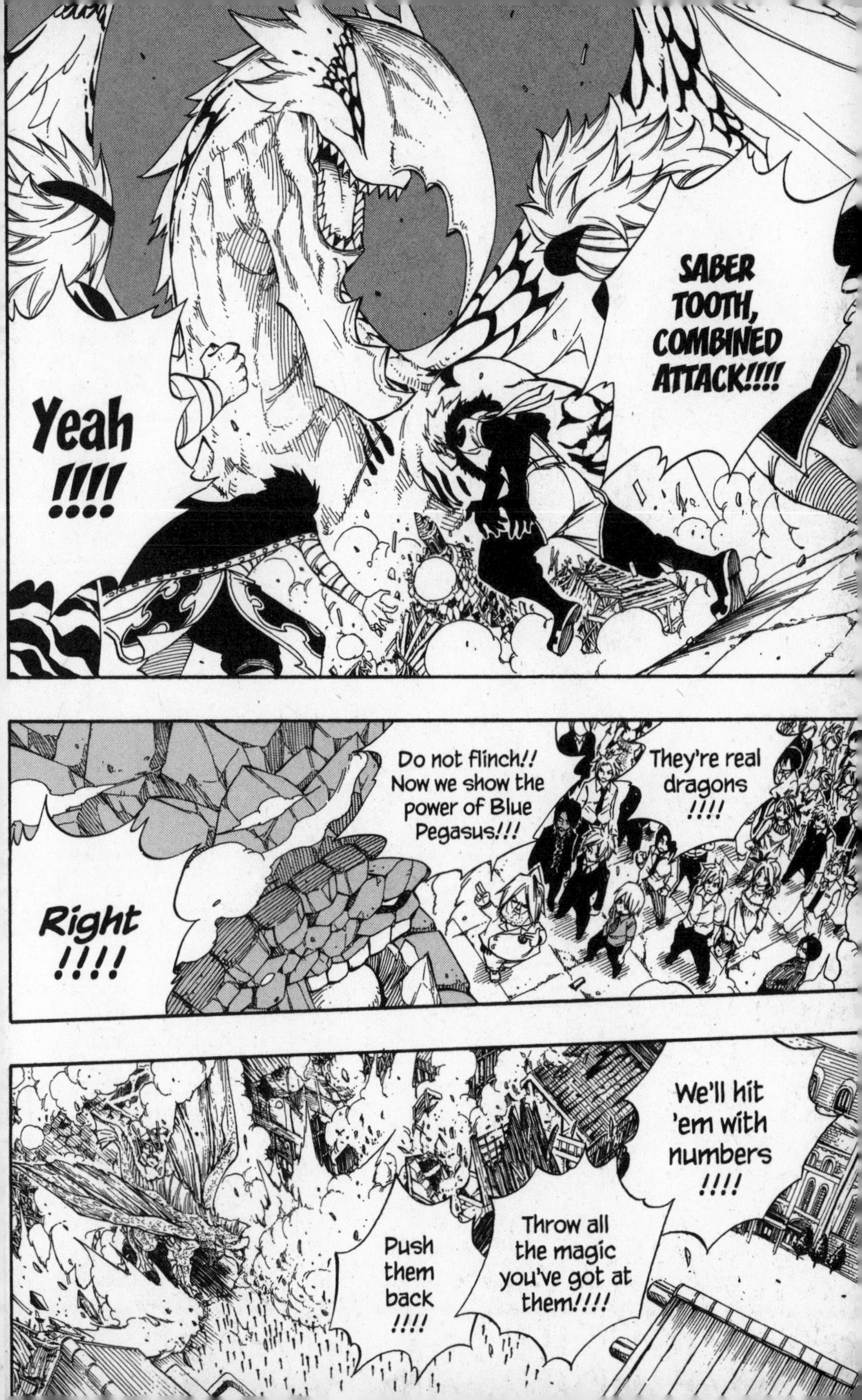
SABER TOOTH, COMBINED ATTACK!!!!
Yeah !!!!
They're real dragons !!!!
Do not flinch!! Now we show the power of Blue Pegasus!!!
Right !!!!
We'll hit 'em with numbers !!!!
Throw all the magic you've got at them!!!!
Push them back !!!!

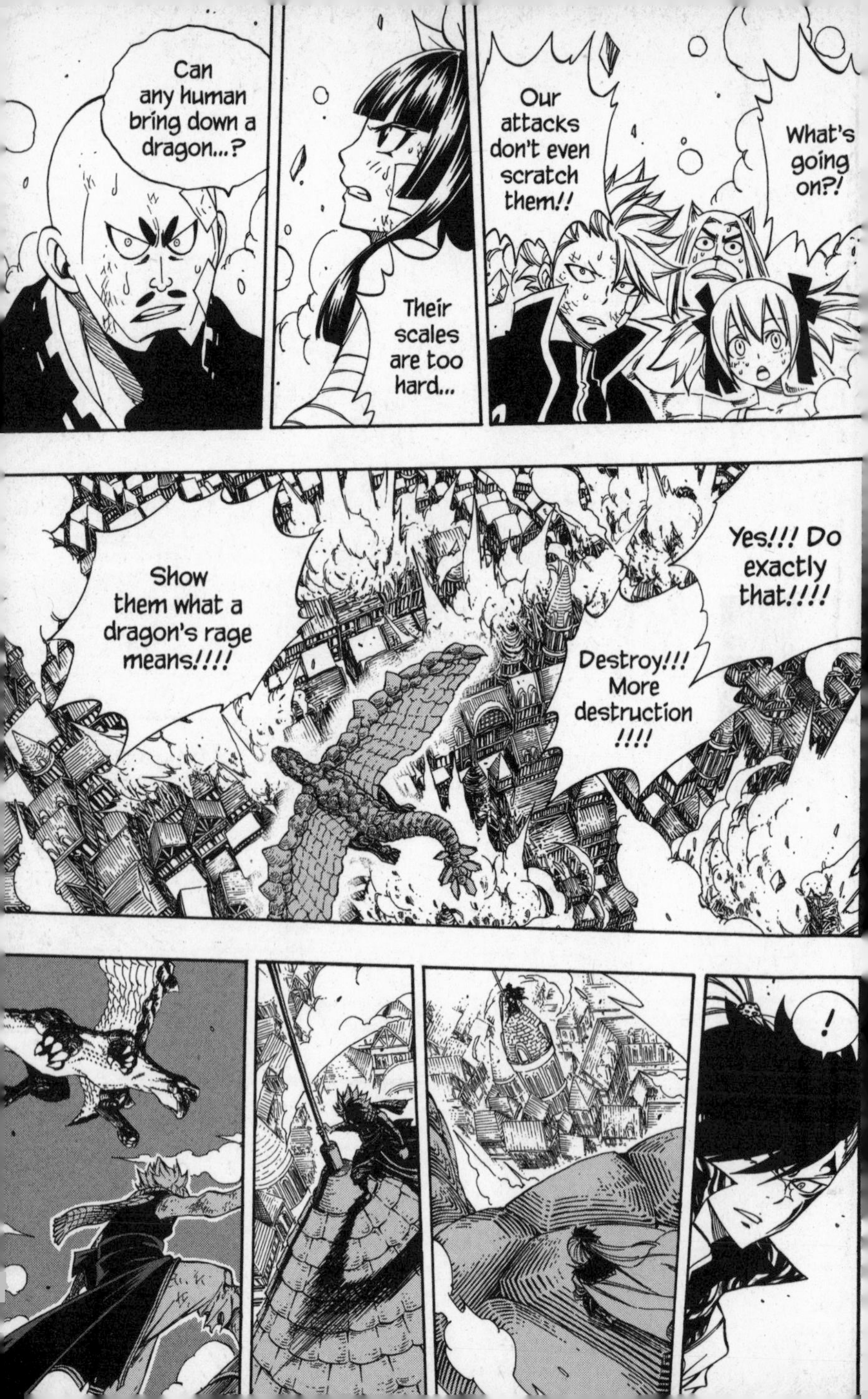
What's going on?!
Our attacks don't even scratch them!!
Their scales are too hard...
Can any human bring down a dragon...?
Yes!!! Do exactly that!!!!
Destroy!!! More destruction !!!!
Show them what a dragon's rage means!!!!
!

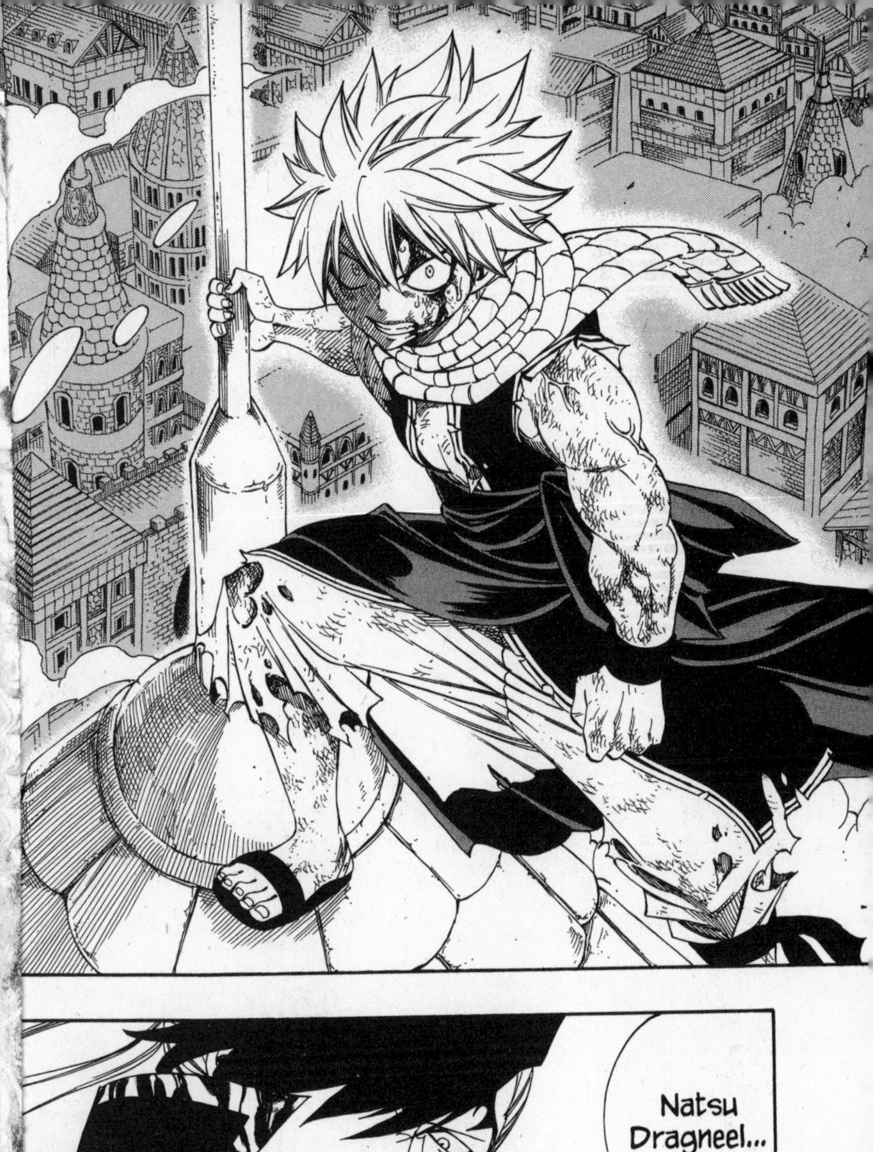

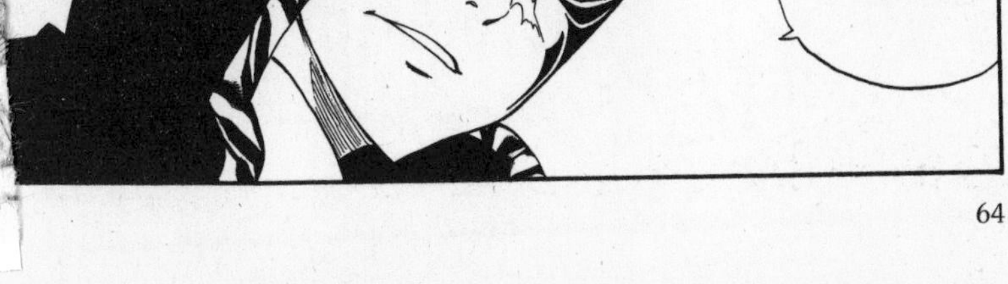
Natsu Dragneel...

FAIRY TAIL
フェアリーテイル

Chapter 329: Seven Dragons

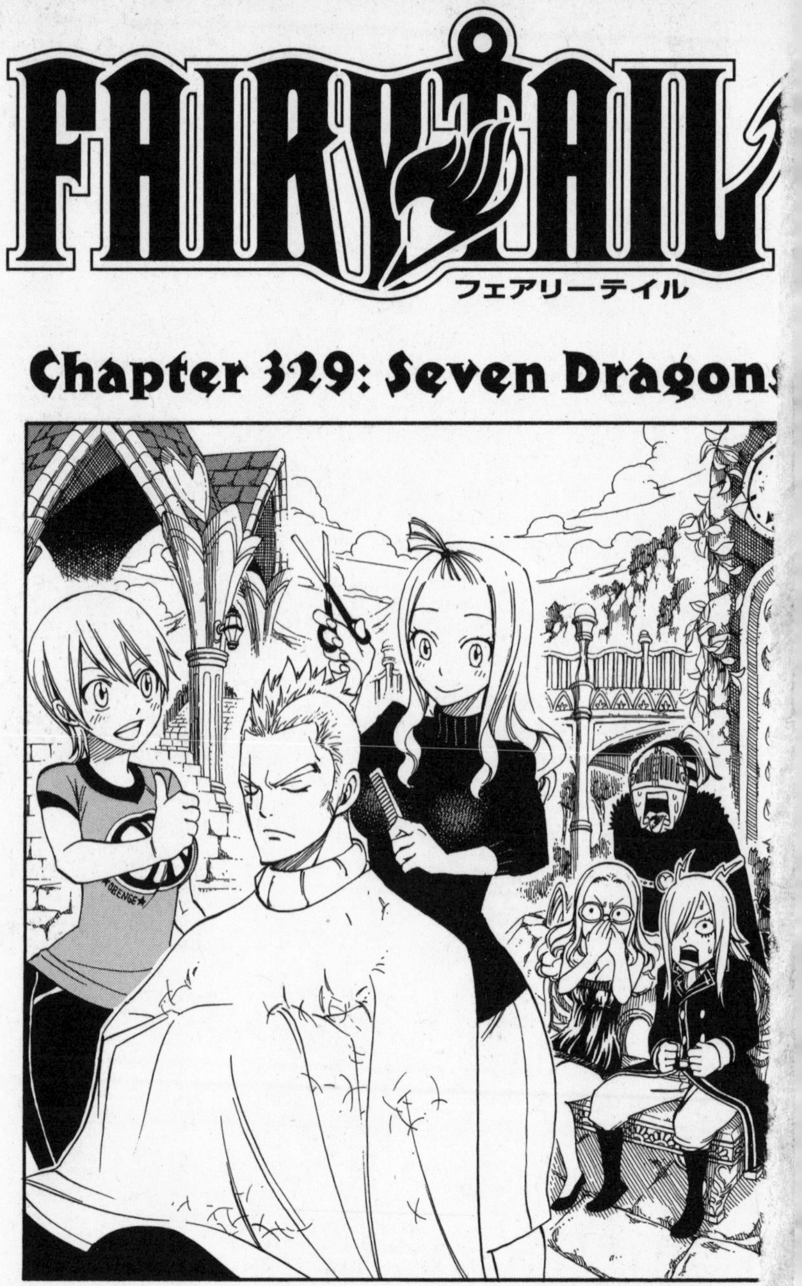

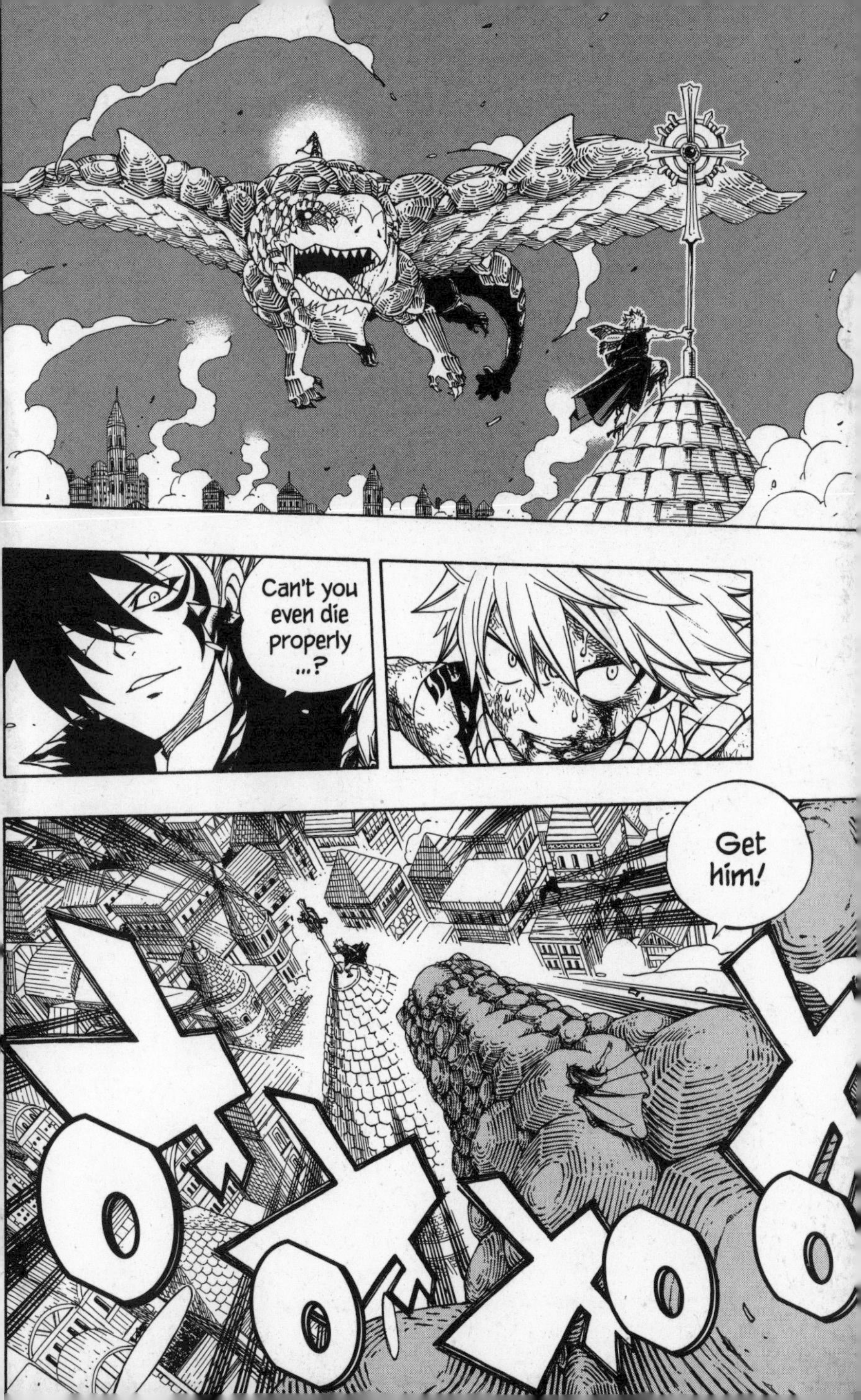
Can't you even die properly ...?
Get him!

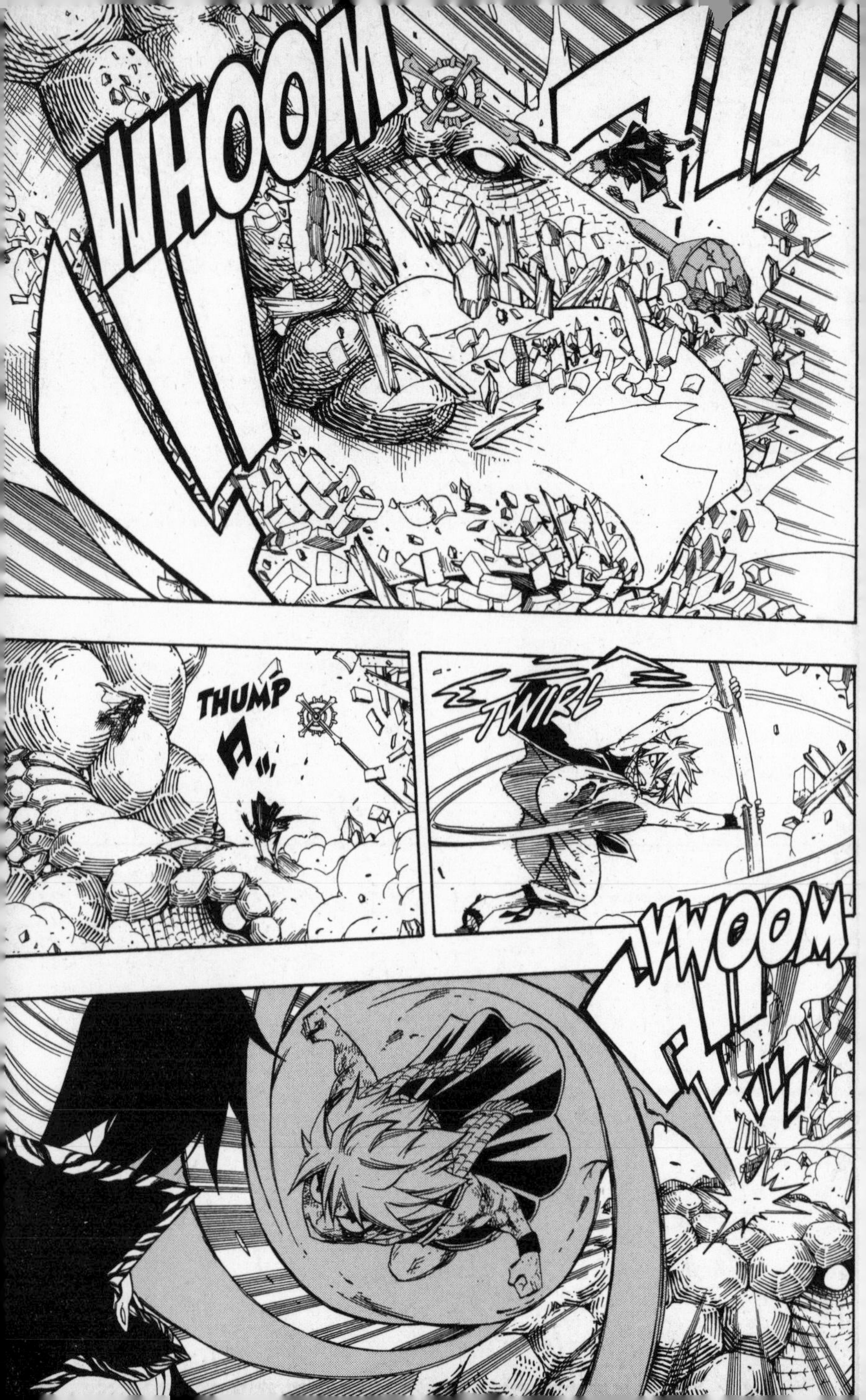
WHOOM
TWIRL
THUMP
VWOOM

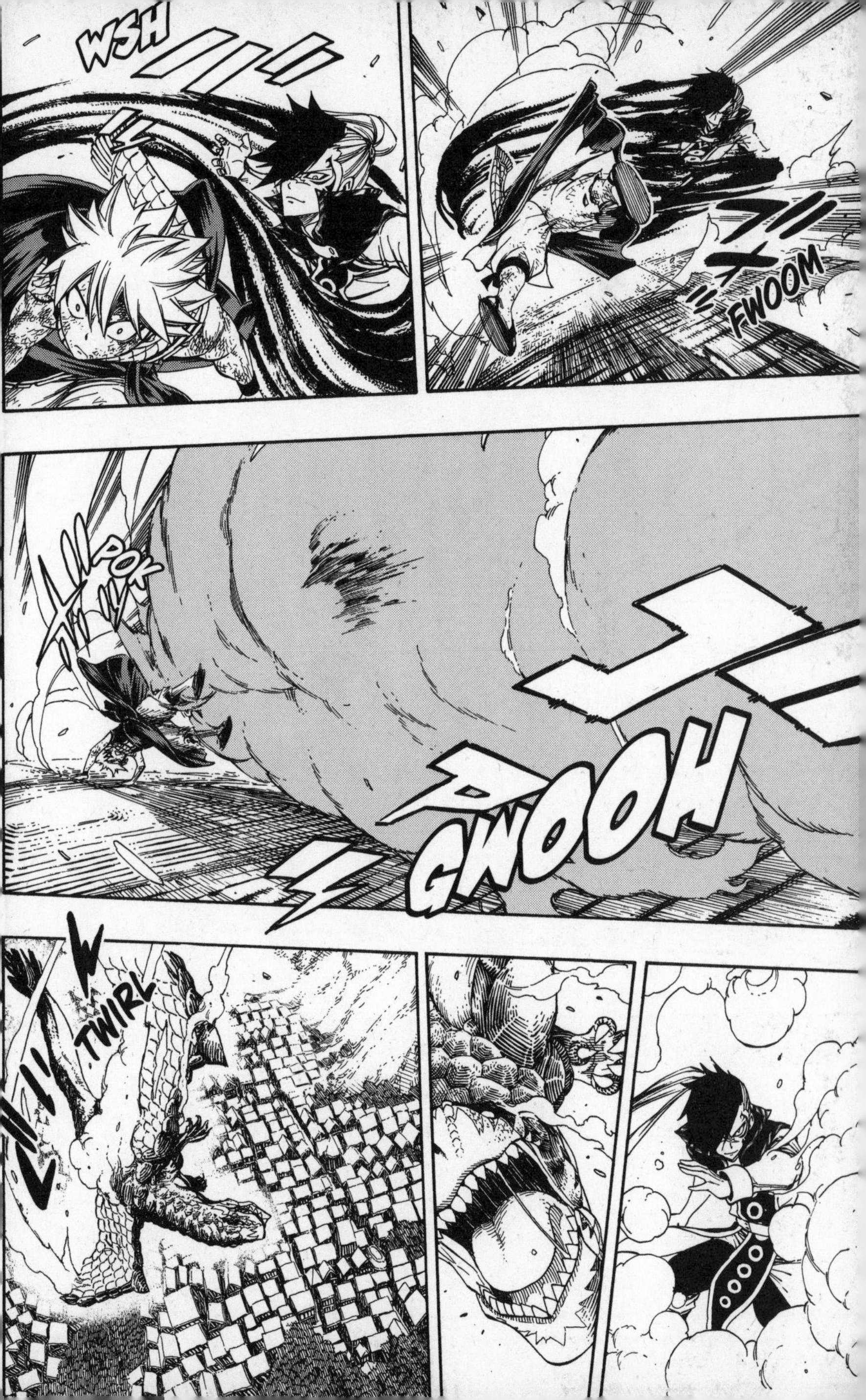
FWOOM
WSH
GWOOH
POK
TWIRL

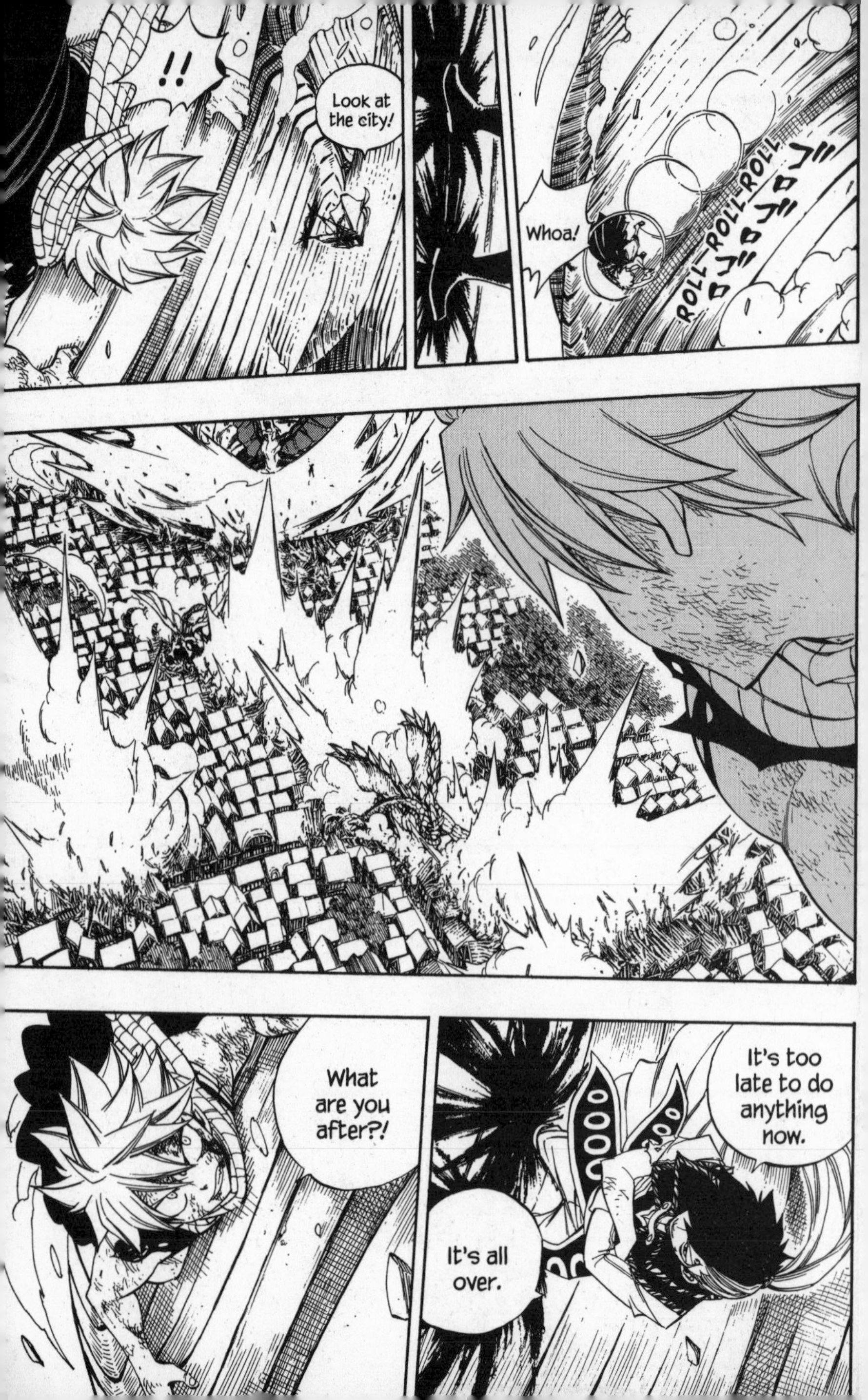
Whoa!
ROLL-ROLL-ROLL
ゴロゴロゴロ
Look at the city!
!!
It's too late to do anything now.
It's all over.
What are you after?!

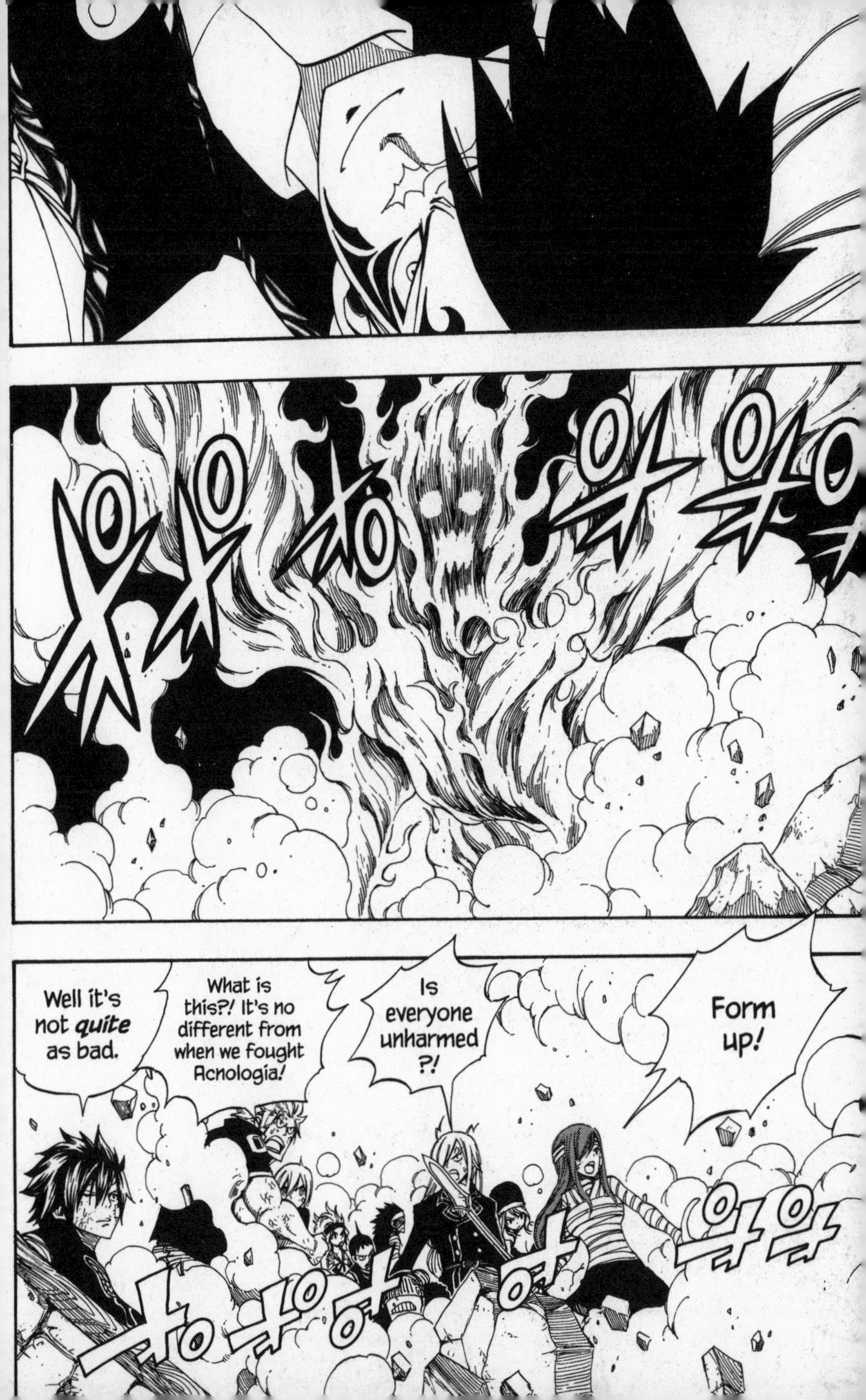
Form up!
Is everyone unharmed?!
What is this?! It's no different from when we fought Acnologia!
Well it's not *quite* as bad.

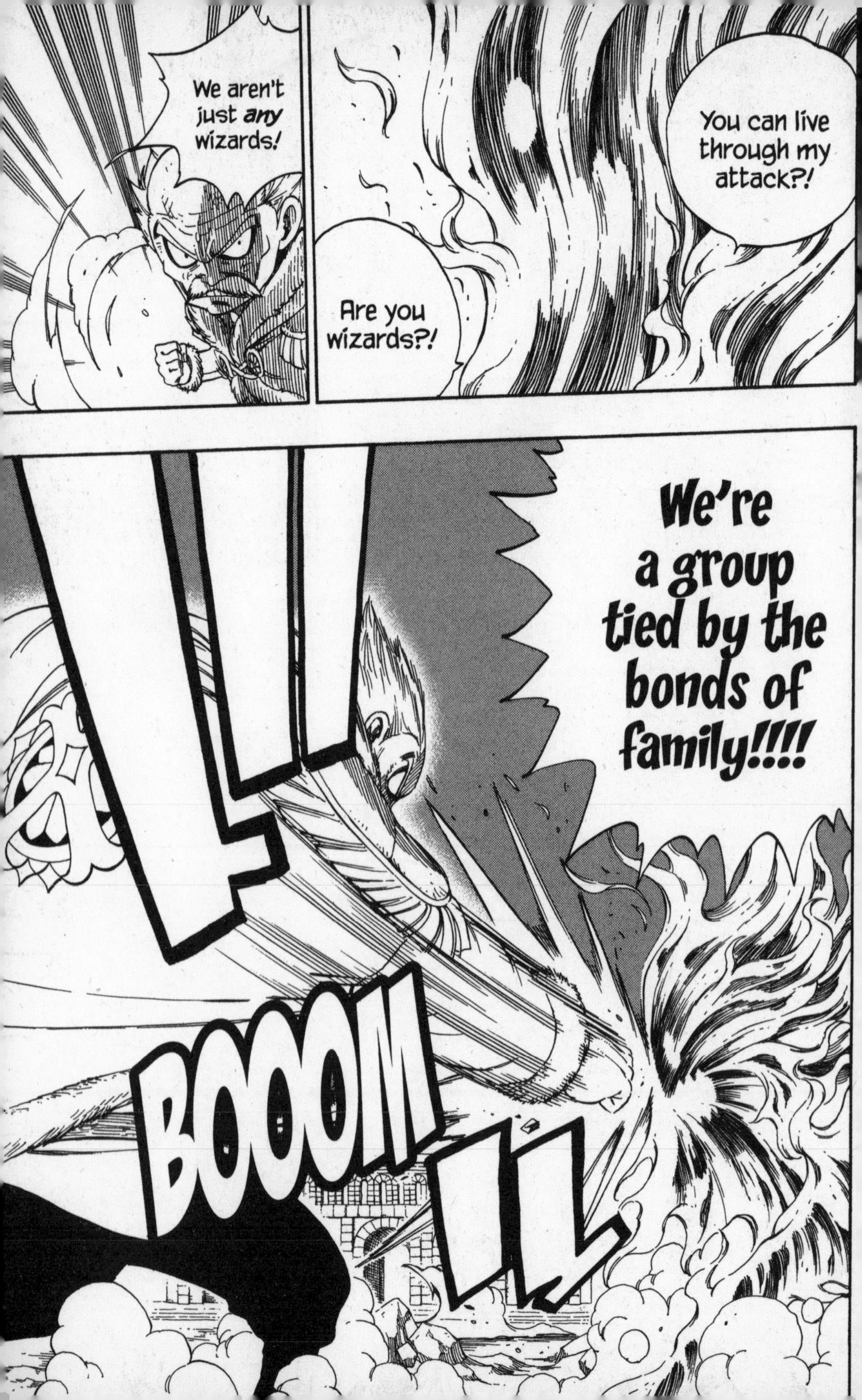
You can live through my attack?!
Are you wizards?!
We aren't just *any* wizards!
We're a group tied by the bonds of family!!!!
BOOOM

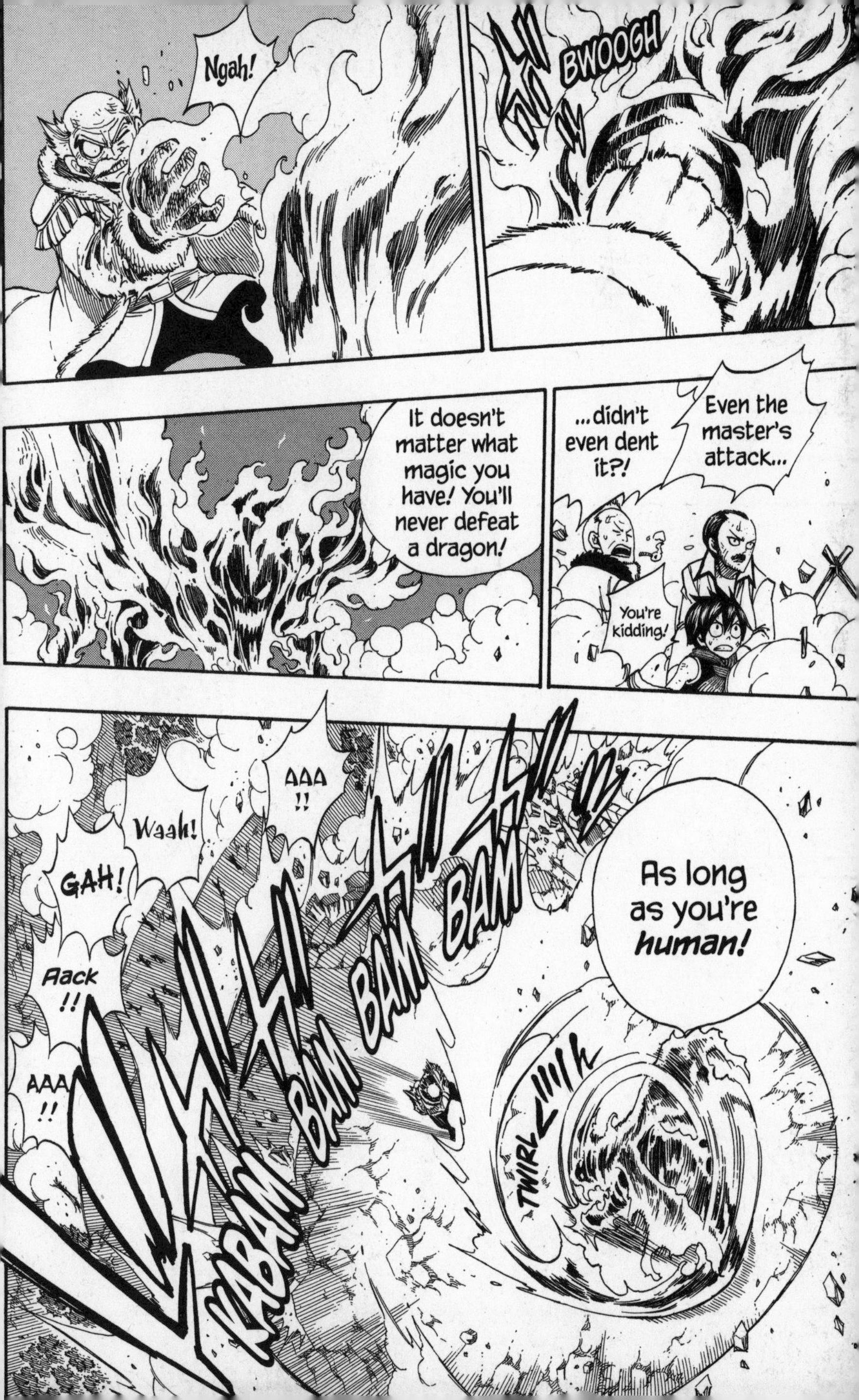
BWOOGH
Ngah!
Even the master's attack...
...didn't even dent it?!
You're kidding!
It doesn't matter what magic you have! You'll never defeat a dragon!
As long as you're *human!*
TWIRL
BAM BAM BAM
AAA !!
Waah!
GAH!
Aack !!
KABAM
AAA !!

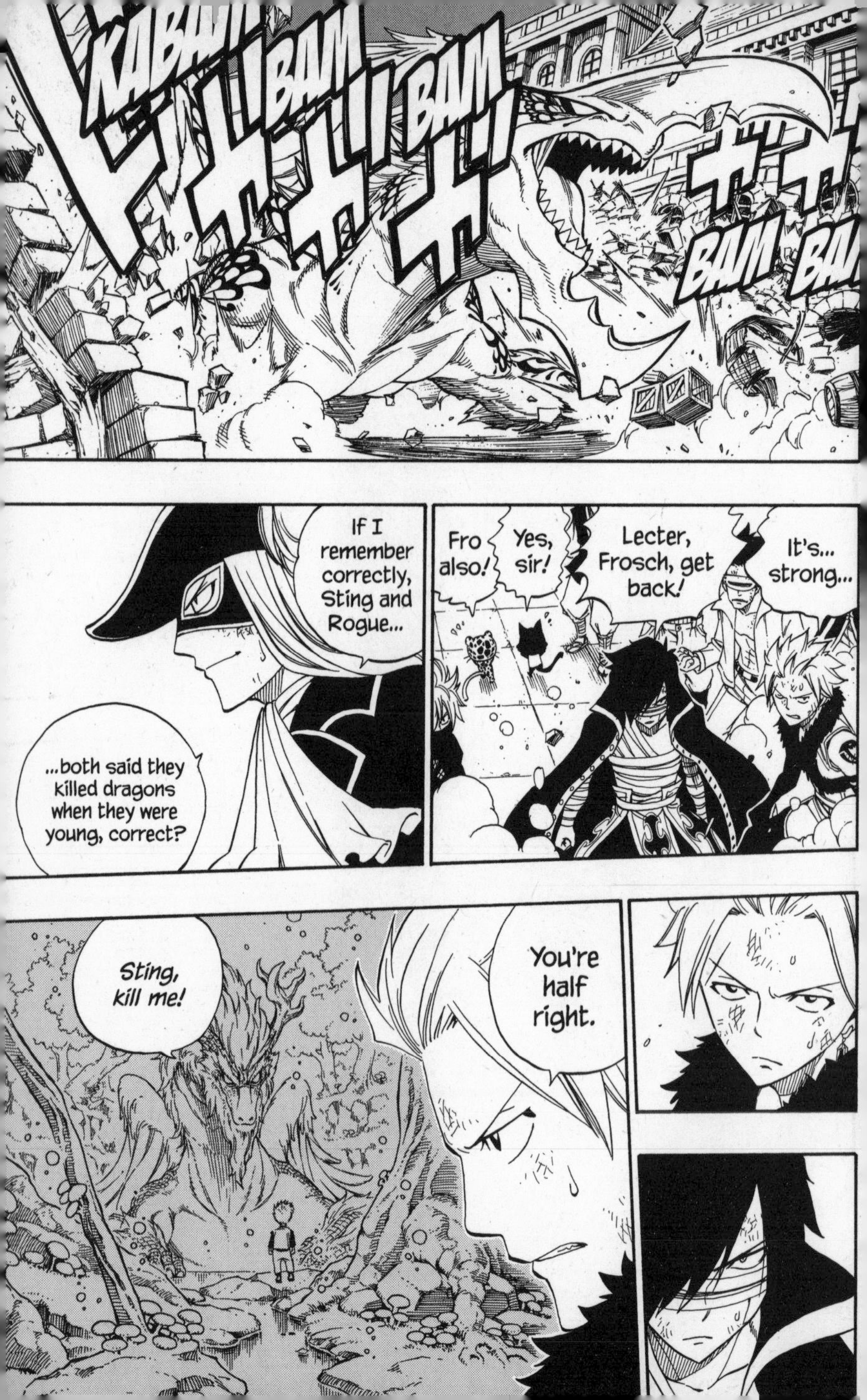
BAM
BAM
BAM
BAM
KABAM
It's... strong...
Lecter, Frosch, get back!
Yes, sir!
Fro also!
If I remember correctly, Sting and Rogue...
...both said they killed dragons when they were young, correct?
You're half right.
Sting, kill me!

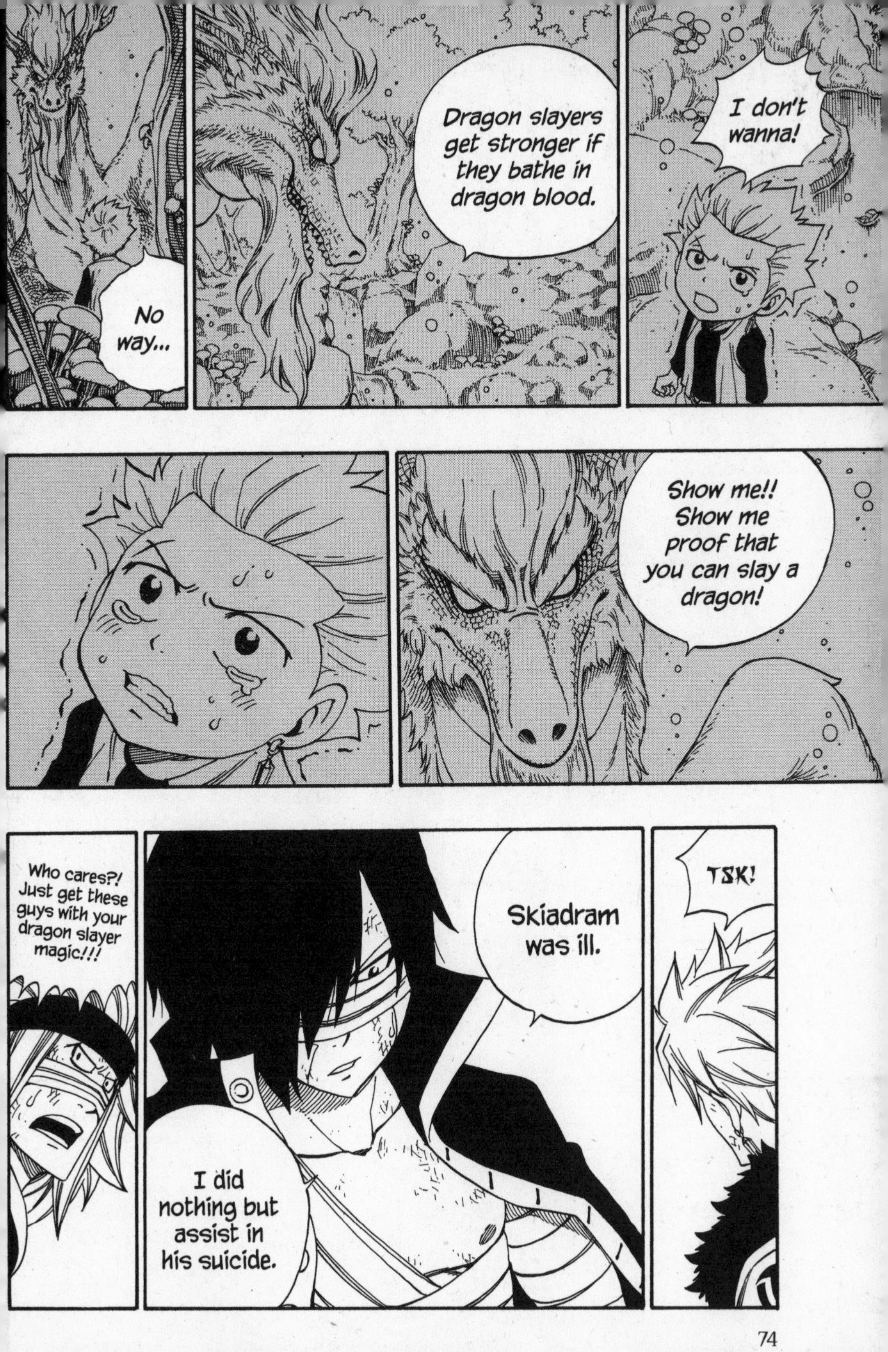
I don't wanna!
Dragon slayers get stronger if they bathe in dragon blood.
No way...
Show me!! Show me proof that you can slay a dragon!
TSK!
Skiadram was ill.
I did nothing but assist in his suicide.
Who cares?! Just get these guys with your dragon slayer magic!!!

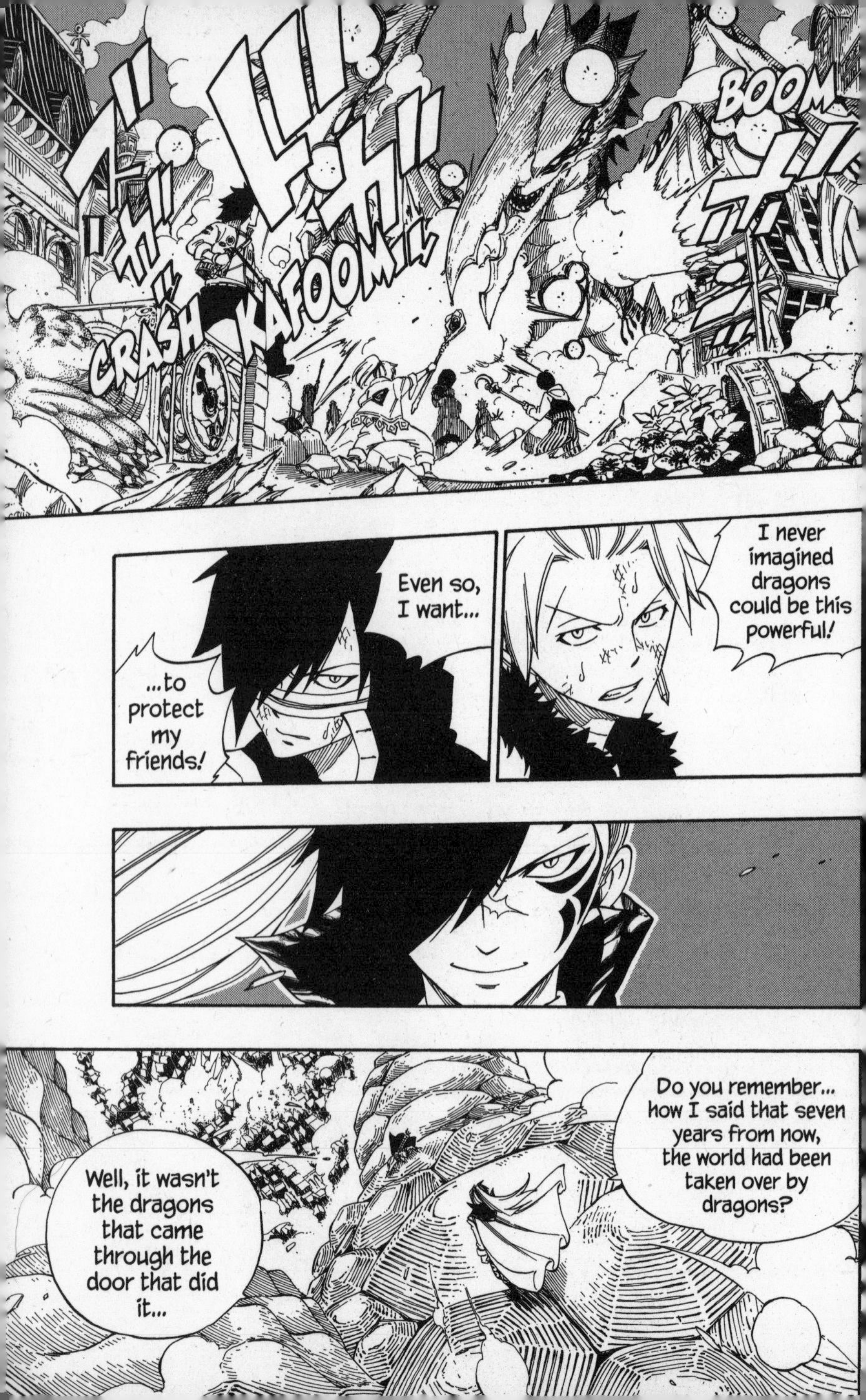
BOOM
KAFOOM
CRASH
I never imagined dragons could be this powerful!
Even so, I want...
...to protect my friends!
Do you remember... how I said that seven years from now, the world had been taken over by dragons?
Well, it wasn't the dragons that came through the door that did it...

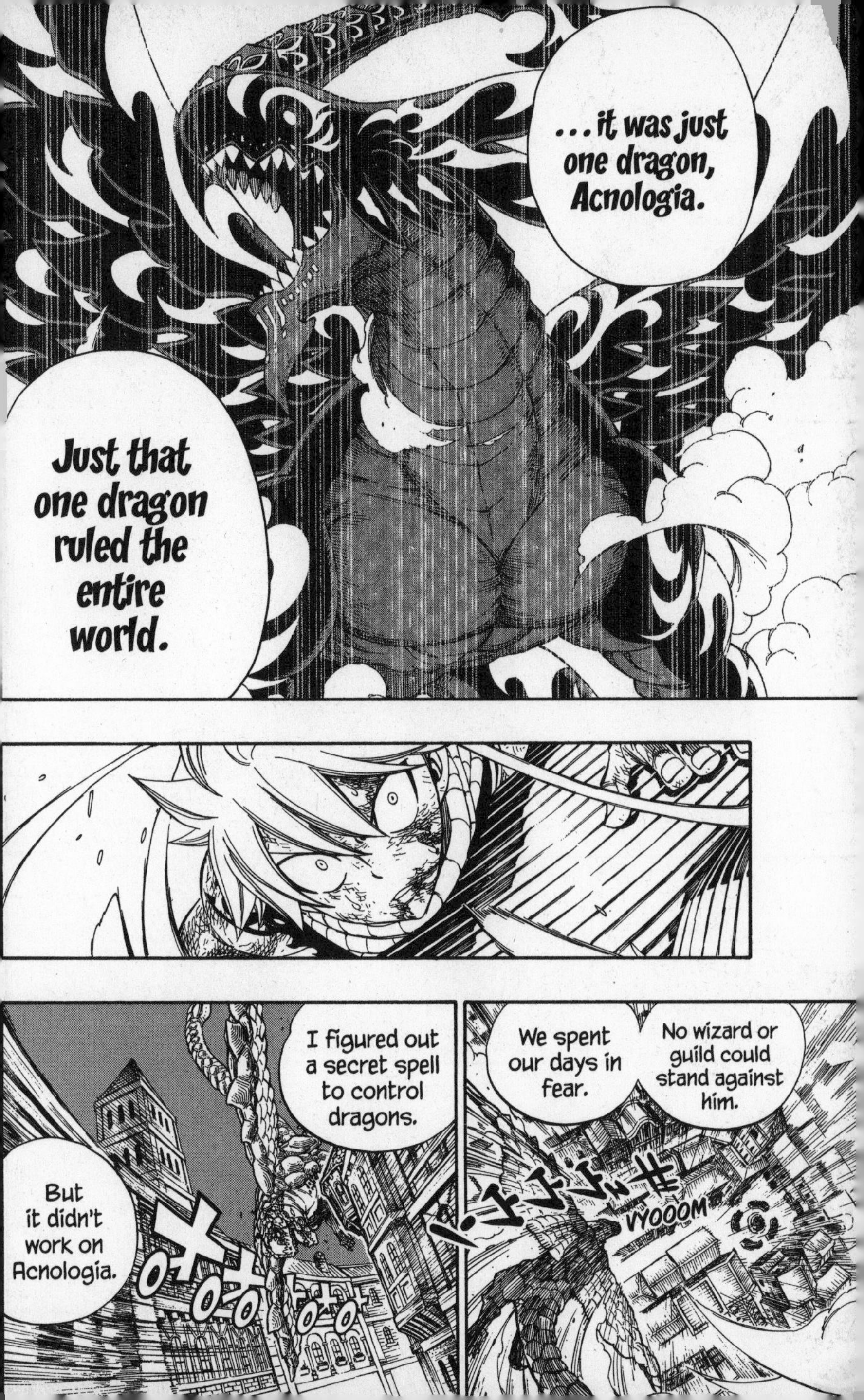
...it was just one dragon, Acnologia.
Just that one dragon ruled the entire world.
No wizard or guild could stand against him.
We spent our days in fear.
VYOOOM
I figured out a secret spell to control dragons.
But it didn't work on Acnologia.

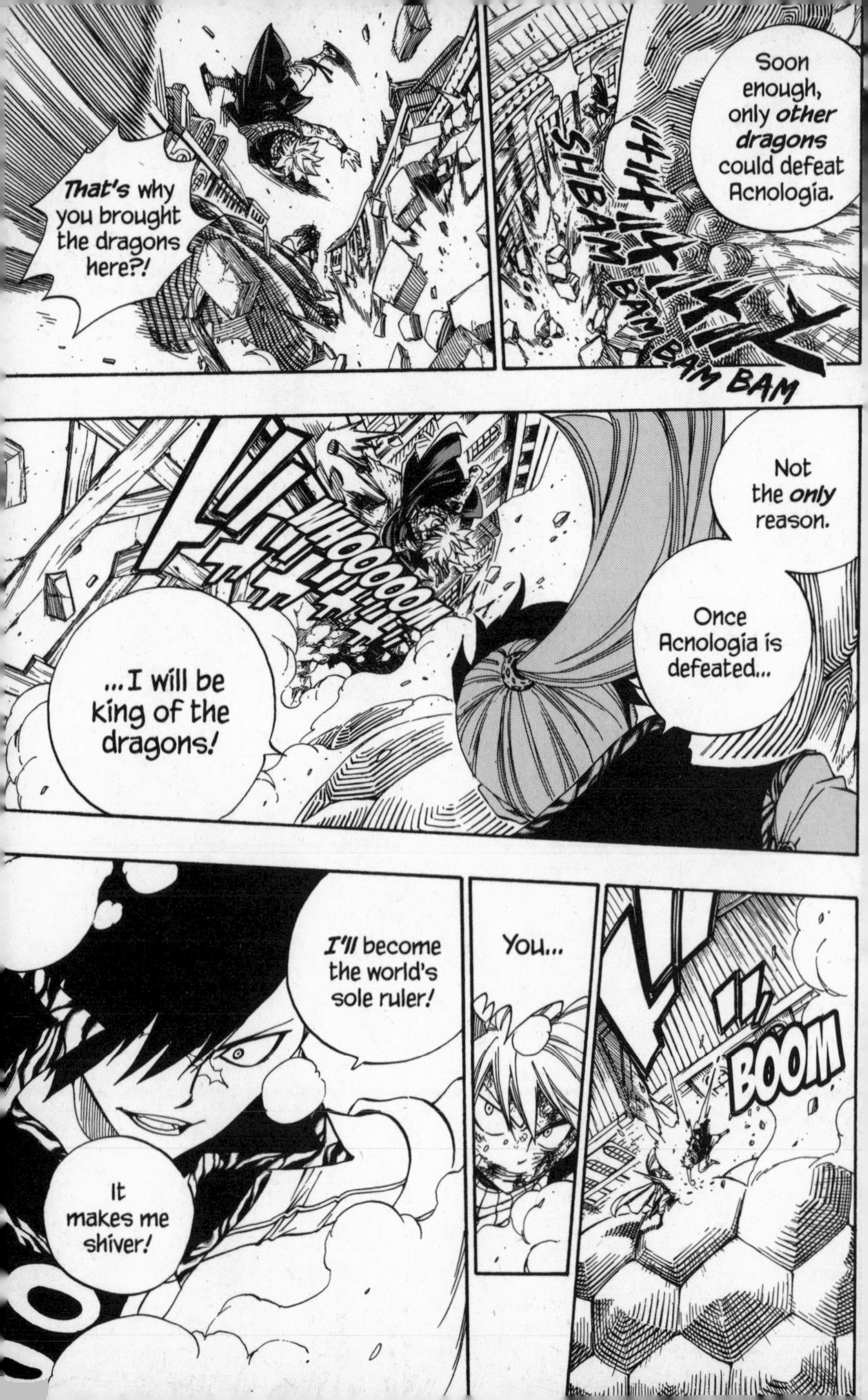
Soon enough, only *other dragons* could defeat Acnologia.
SHBAM BAM BAM BAM BAM
That's why you brought the dragons here?!
Not the *only* reason.
Once Acnologia is defeated...
...I will be king of the dragons!
WHOOOOOM
BOOM
You...
I'll become the world's sole ruler!
It makes me shiver!

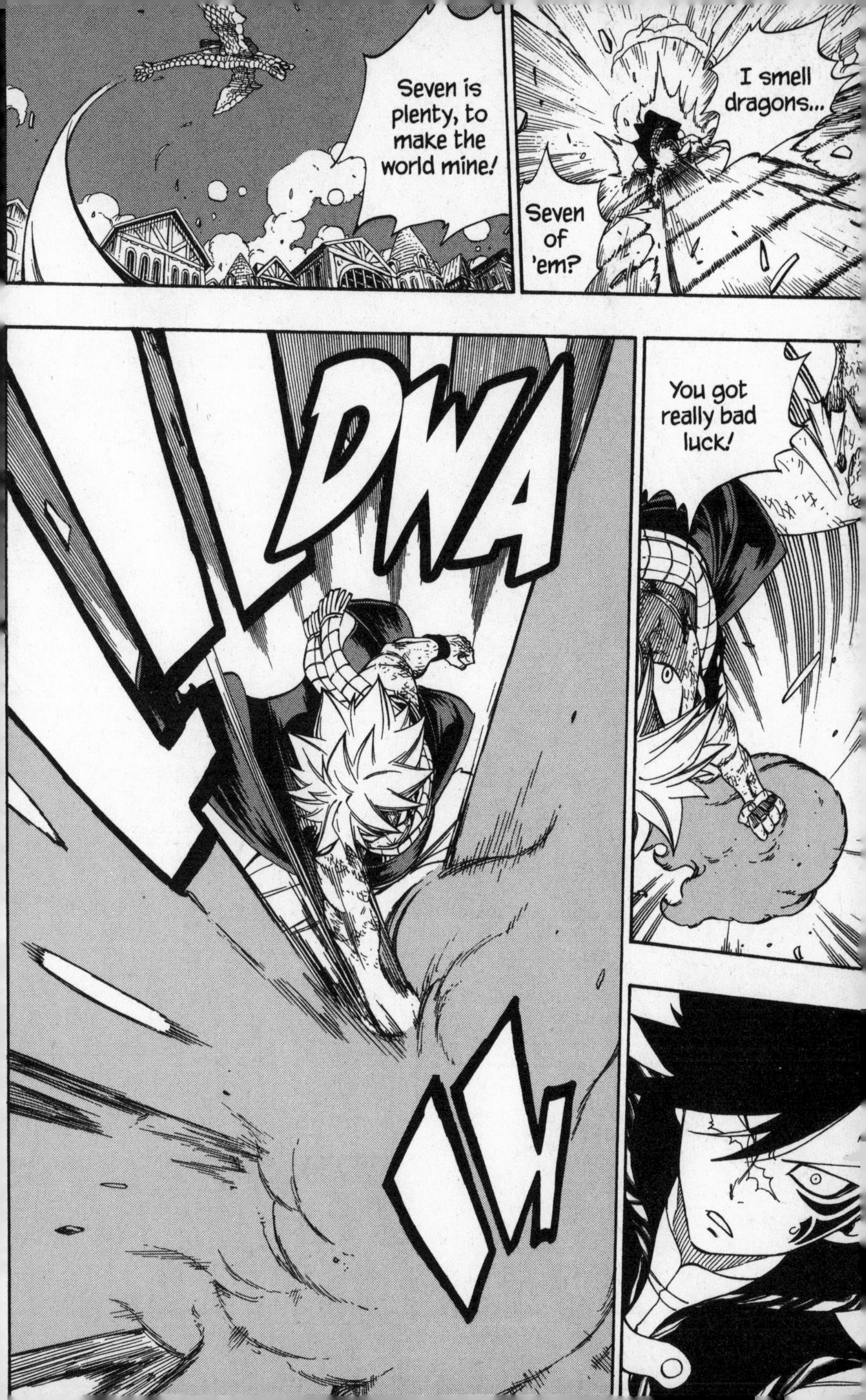
I smell dragons...
Seven of 'em?
Seven is plenty, to make the world mine!
You got really bad luck!
DWA

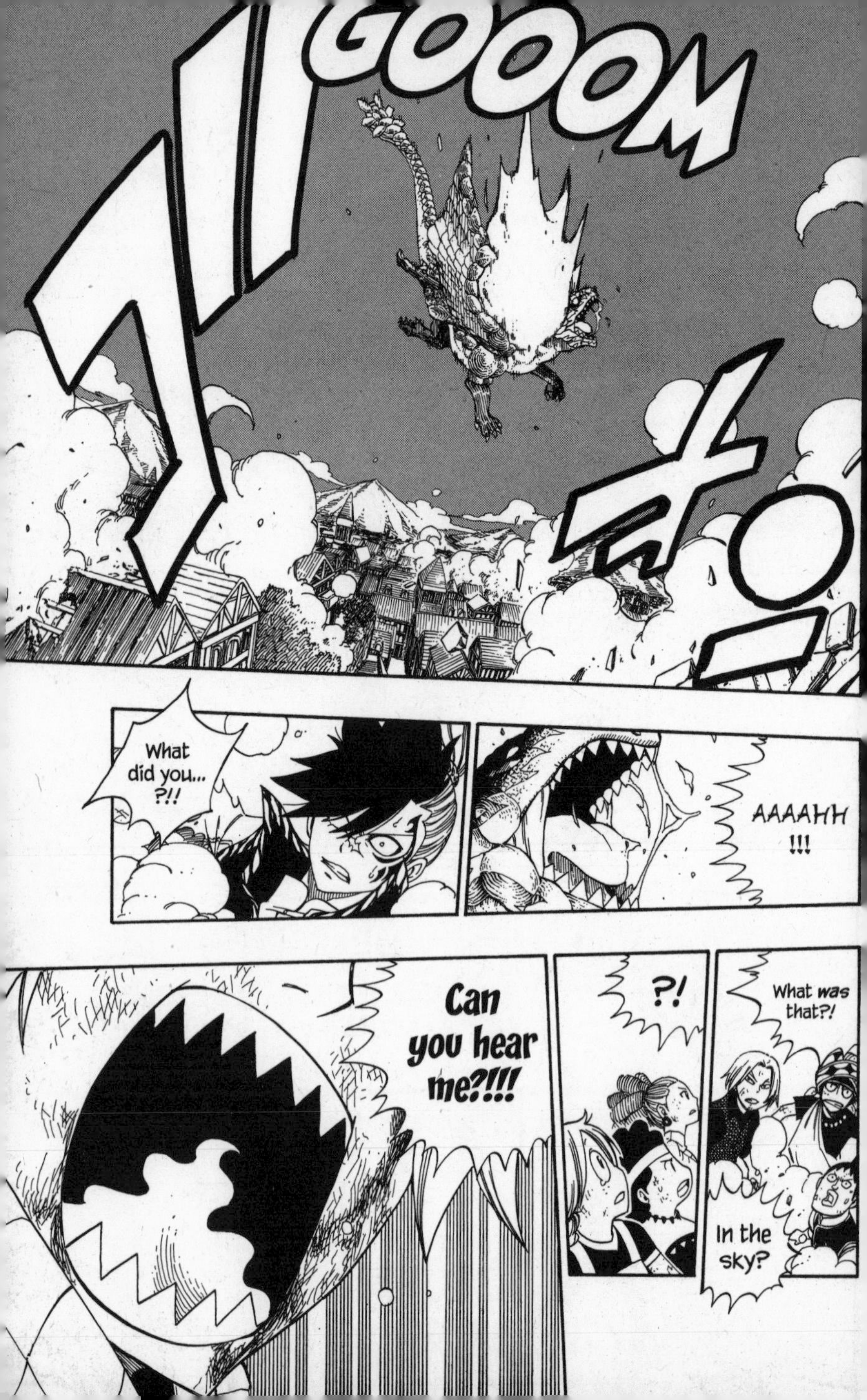
GOOOM
AAAAHH !!!
What did you...?!!
What was that?!
In the sky?
?!
Can you hear me?!!!

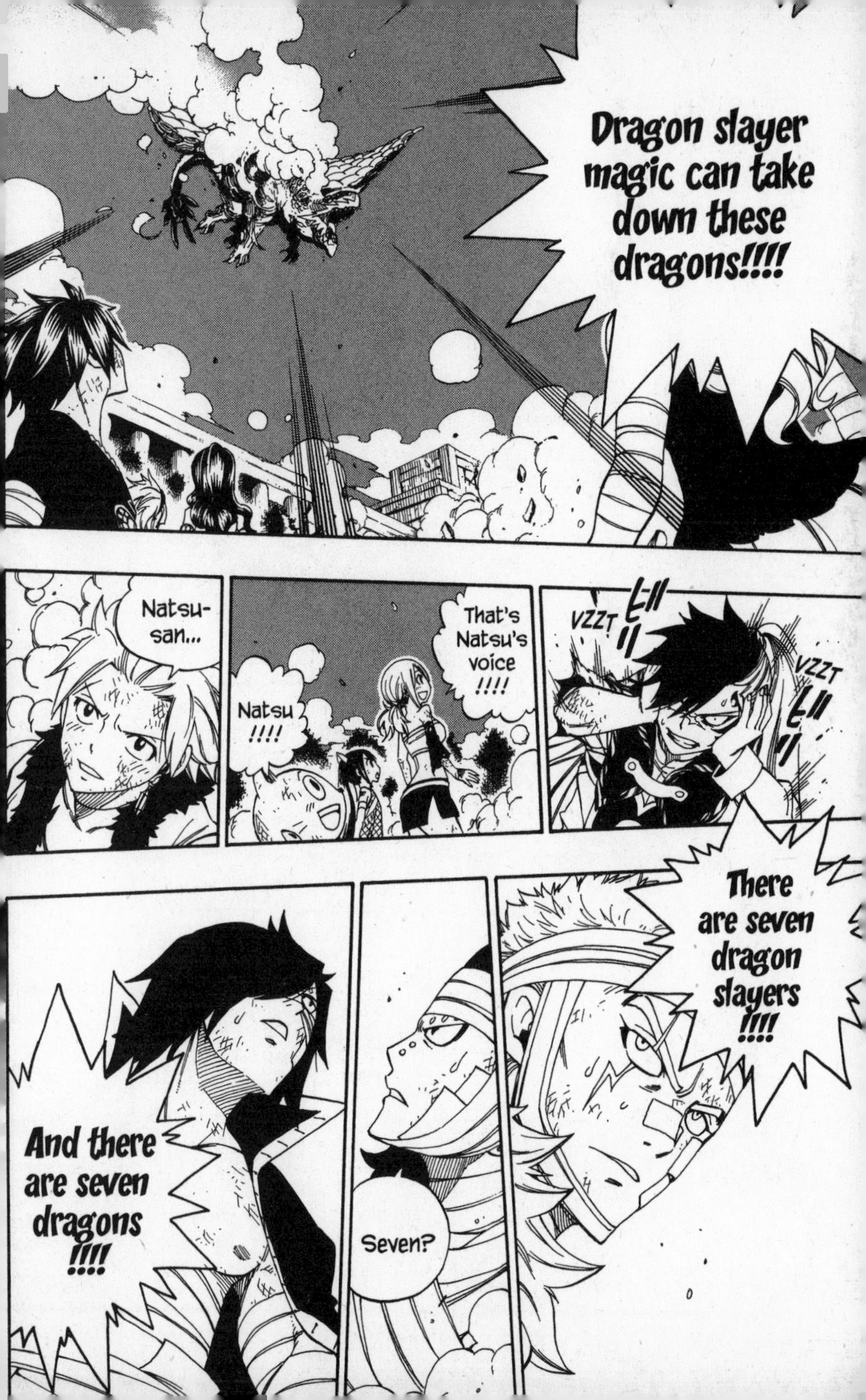
Dragon slayer magic can take down these dragons!!!!
VZZT
VZZT
That's Natsu's voice!!!!
Natsu!!!!
Natsu-san...
There are seven dragon slayers!!!!
Seven?
And there are seven dragons!!!!

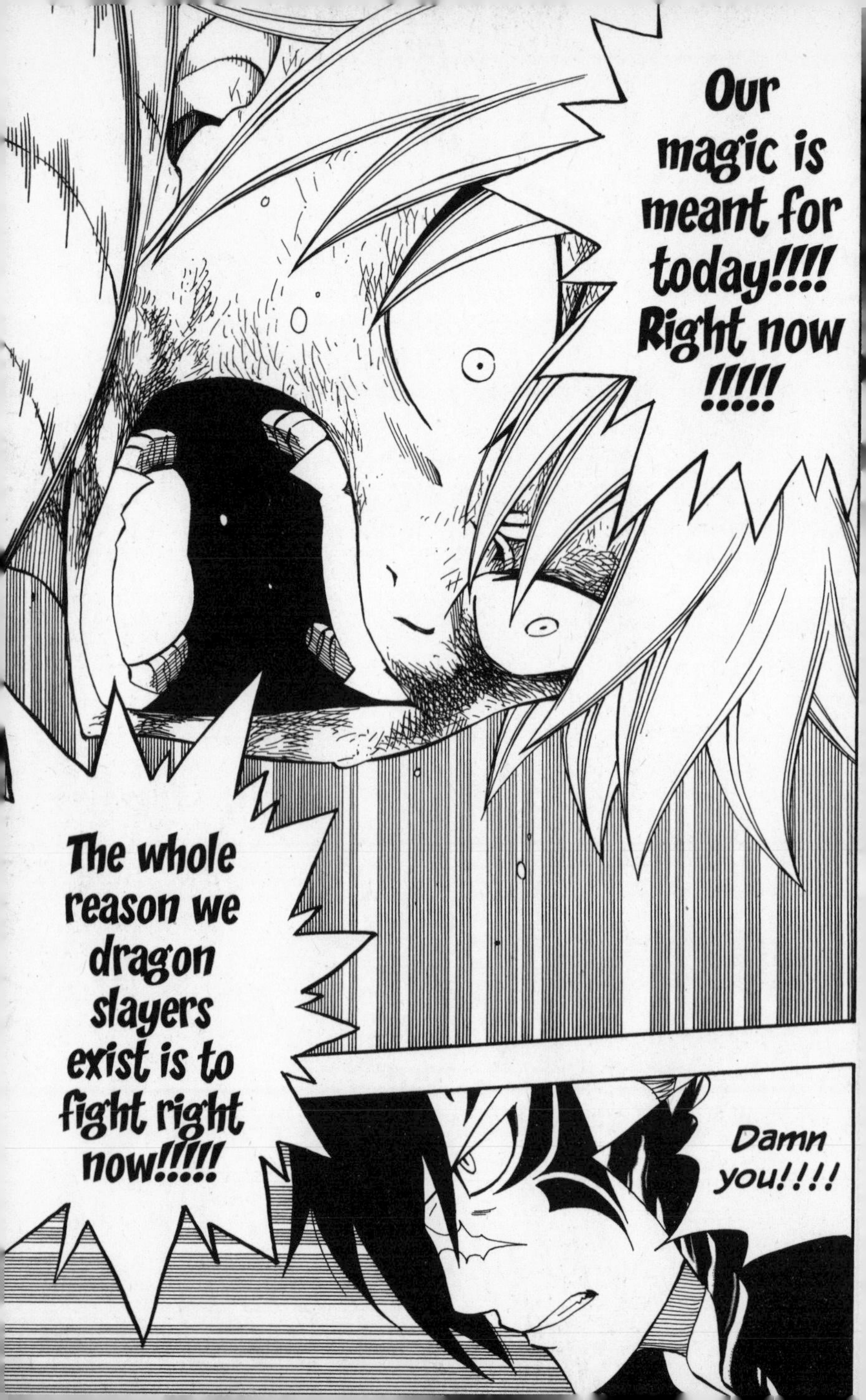
Our magic is meant for today!!!! Right now!!!!!
The whole reason we dragon slayers exist is to fight right now!!!!!
Damn you!!!!

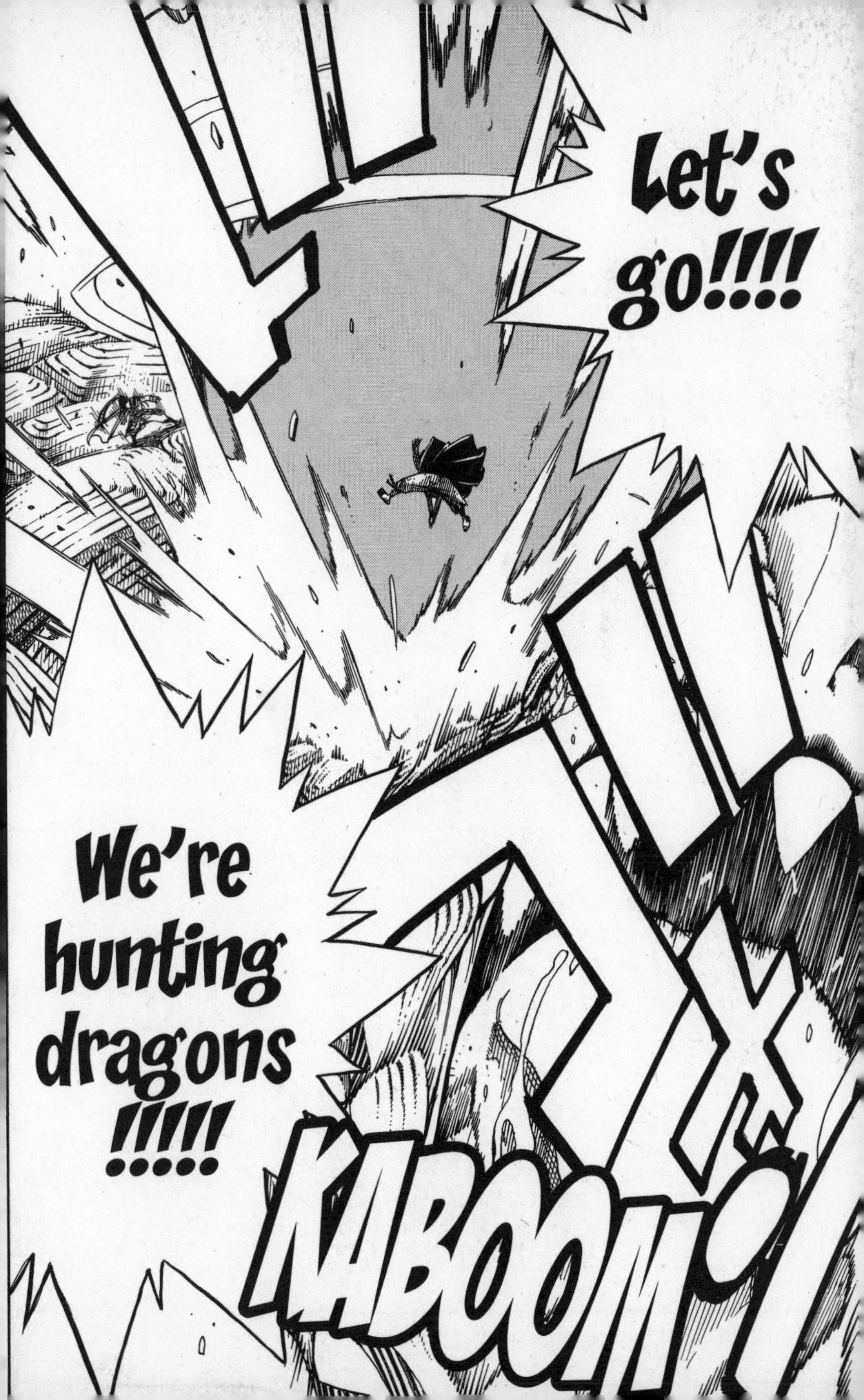
Let's go!!!!
We're hunting dragons!!!!!
KABOOM

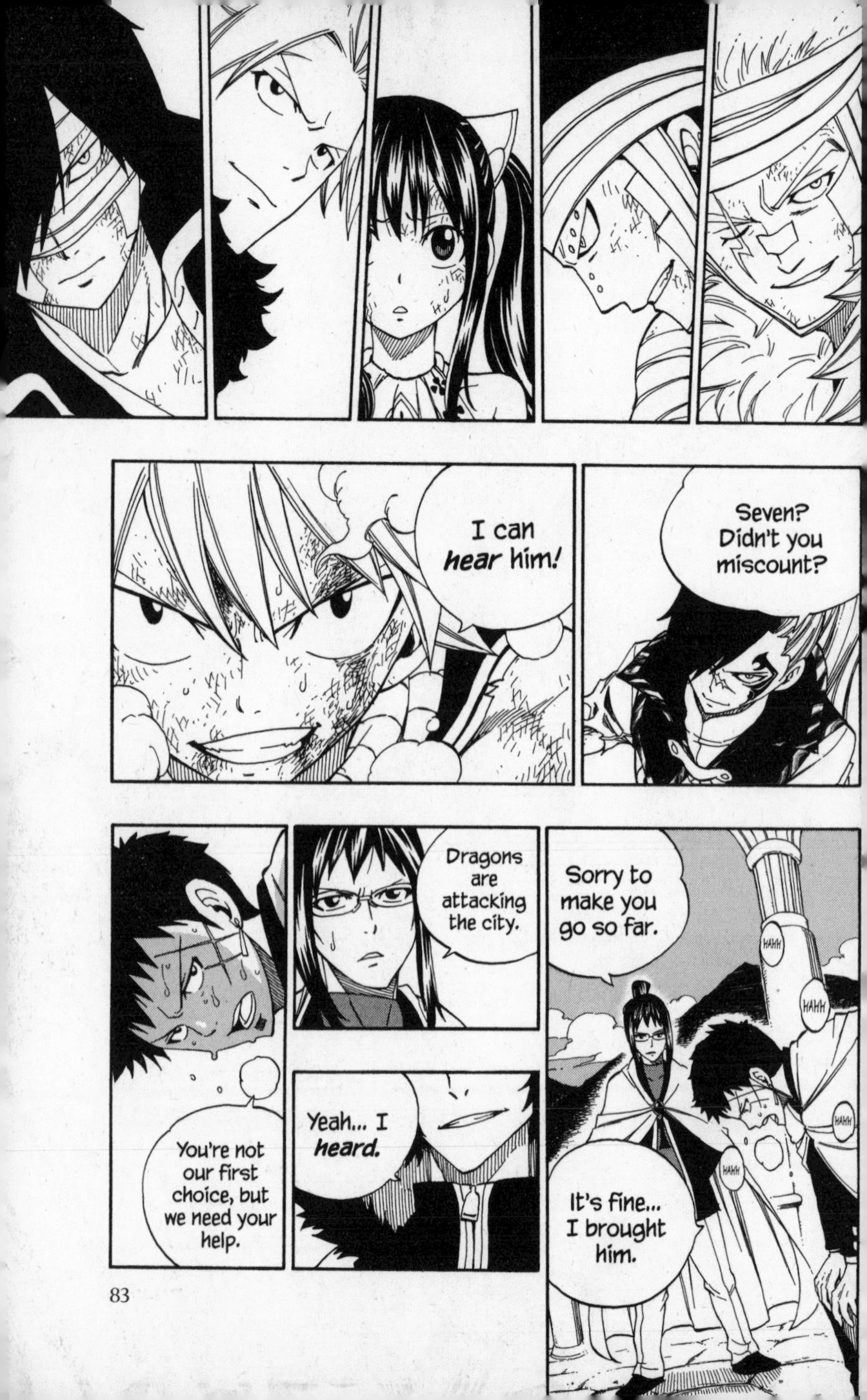
Seven? Didn't you miscount?
I can *hear* him!
Sorry to make you go so far.
HAHH
HAHH
HAHH
HAHH
It's fine... I brought him.
Dragons are attacking the city.
Yeah... I *heard.*
You're not our first choice, but we need your help.

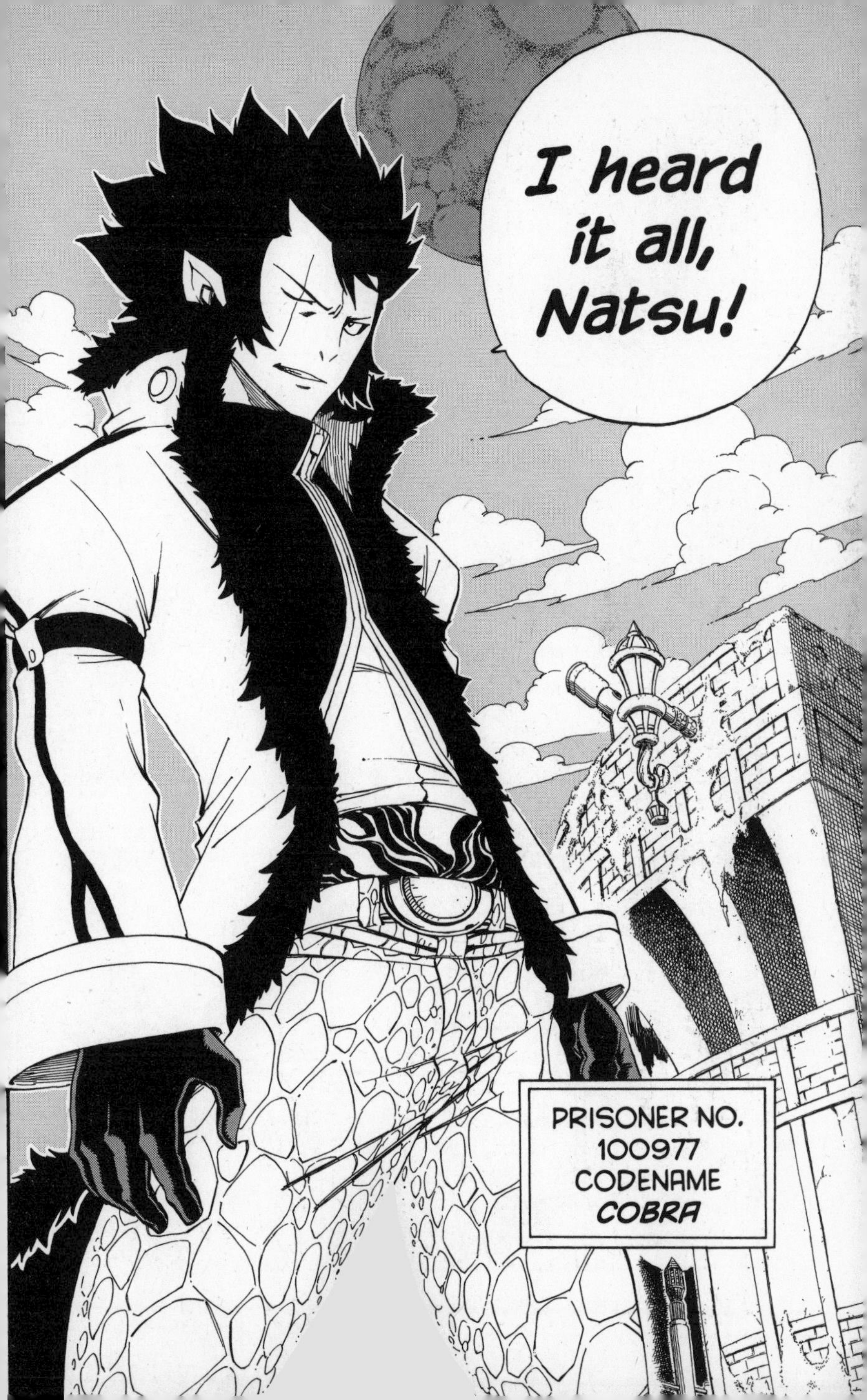
I heard it all, Natsu!
PRISONER NO. 100977 CODENAME COBRA

FAIRY TAIL

フェアリーテイル

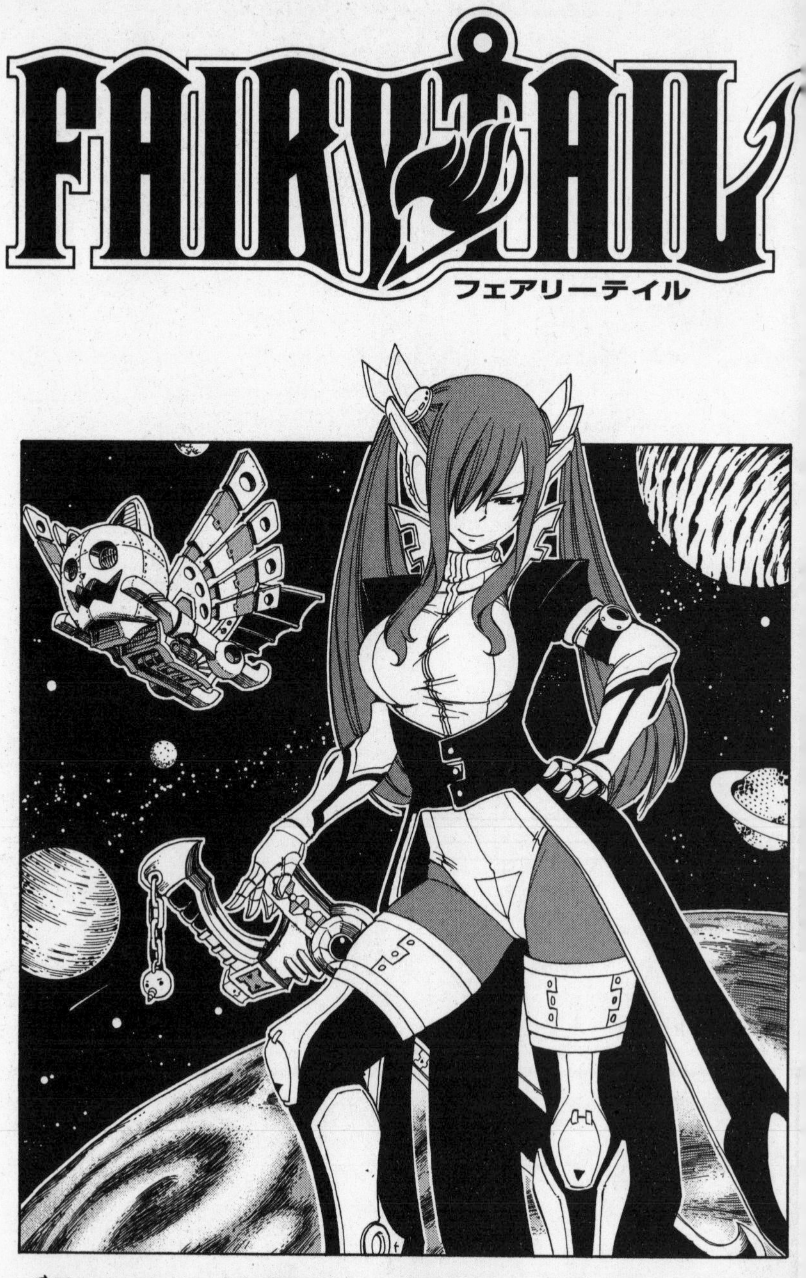

Chapter 330: The Magic of Zirconis

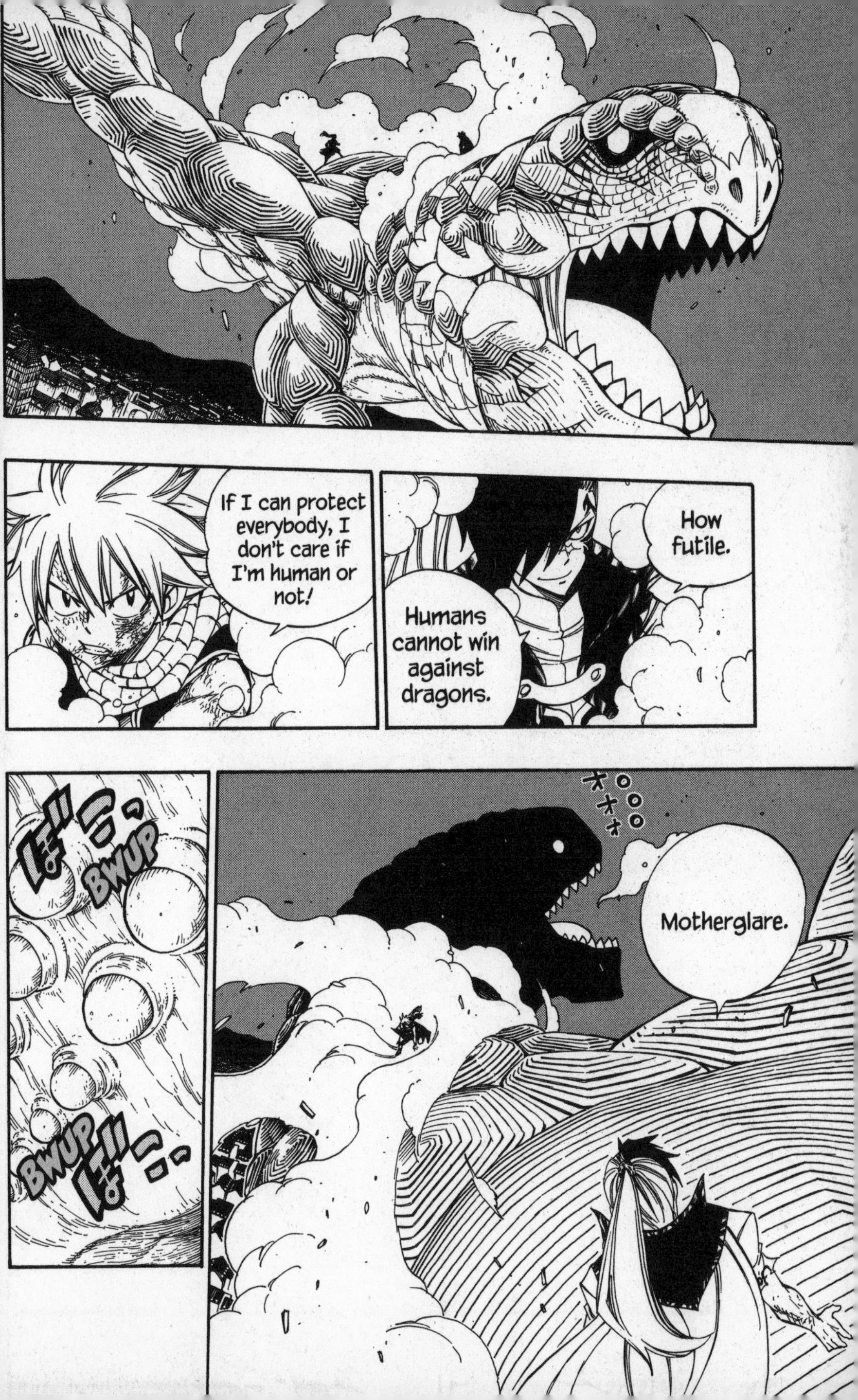
How futile.
Humans cannot win against dragons.
If I can protect everybody, I don't care if I'm human or not!
Motherglare.
BWUP
BWUP

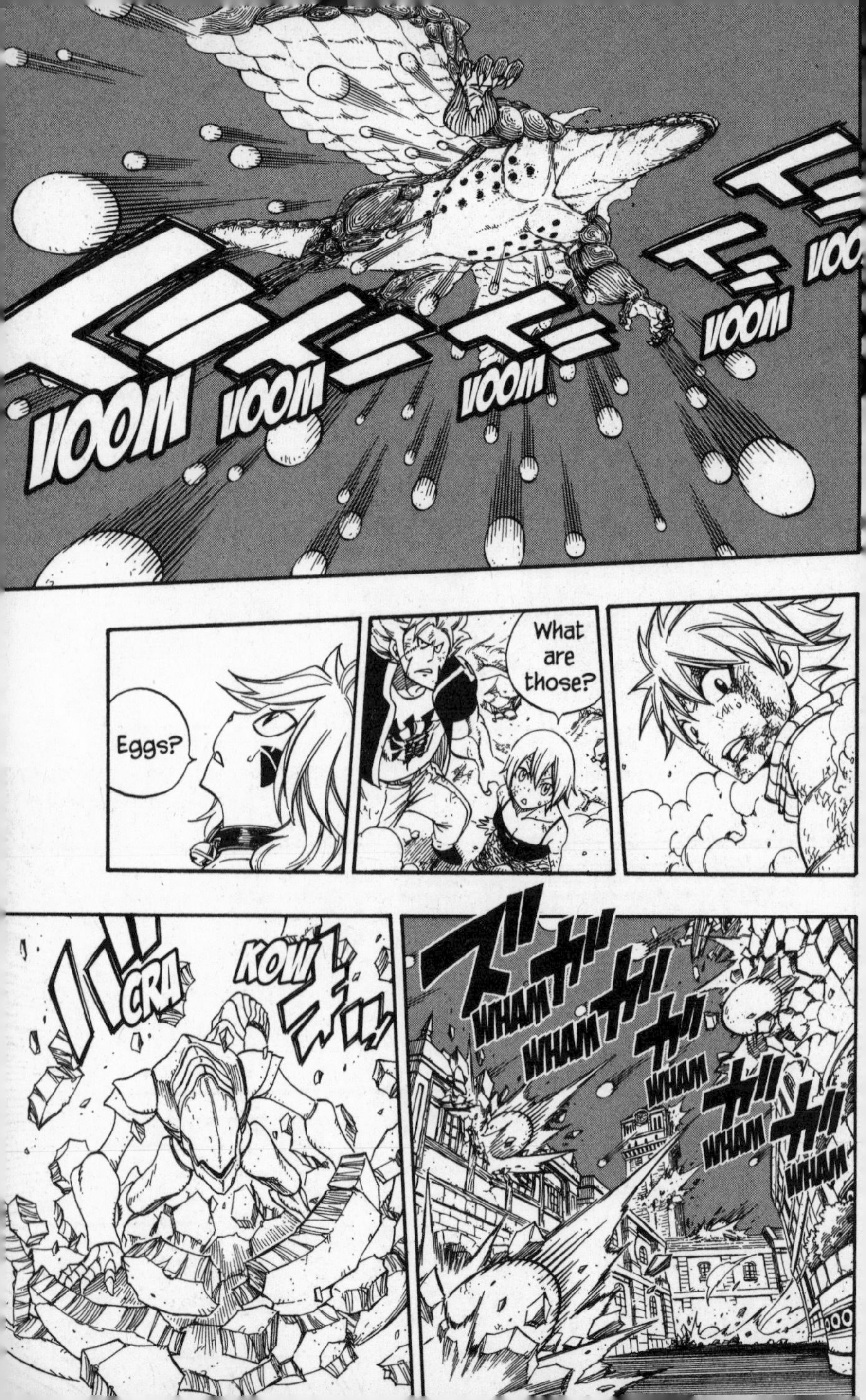
VOOM
VOOM
VOOM
VOOM
VOOM
What are those?
Eggs?
WHAM
WHAM
WHAM
WHAM
WHAM
CRA
KOW

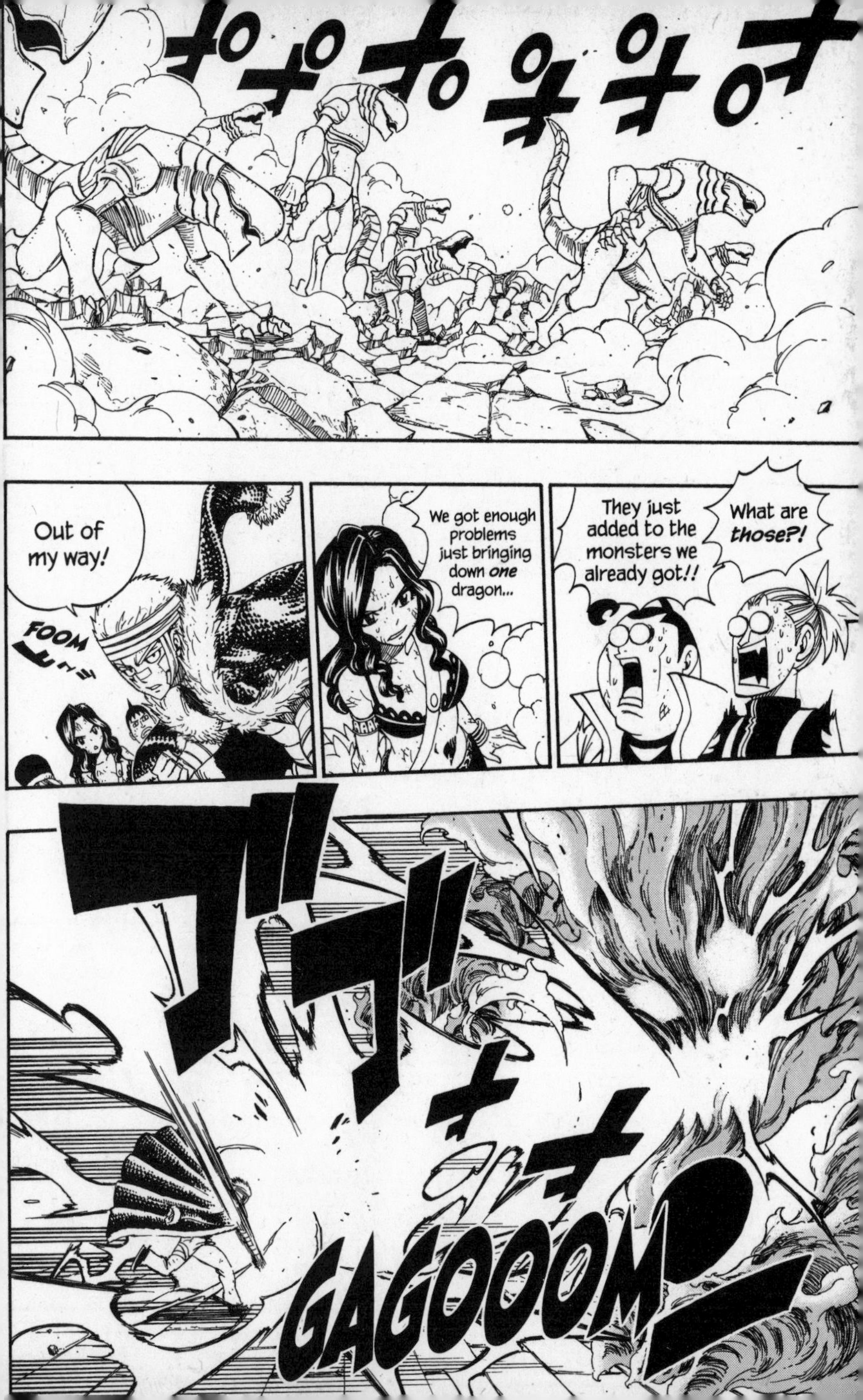
What are *those?!*
They just added to the monsters we already got!!
We got enough problems just bringing down *one* dragon...
Out of my way!
FOOM
GAGOOOM

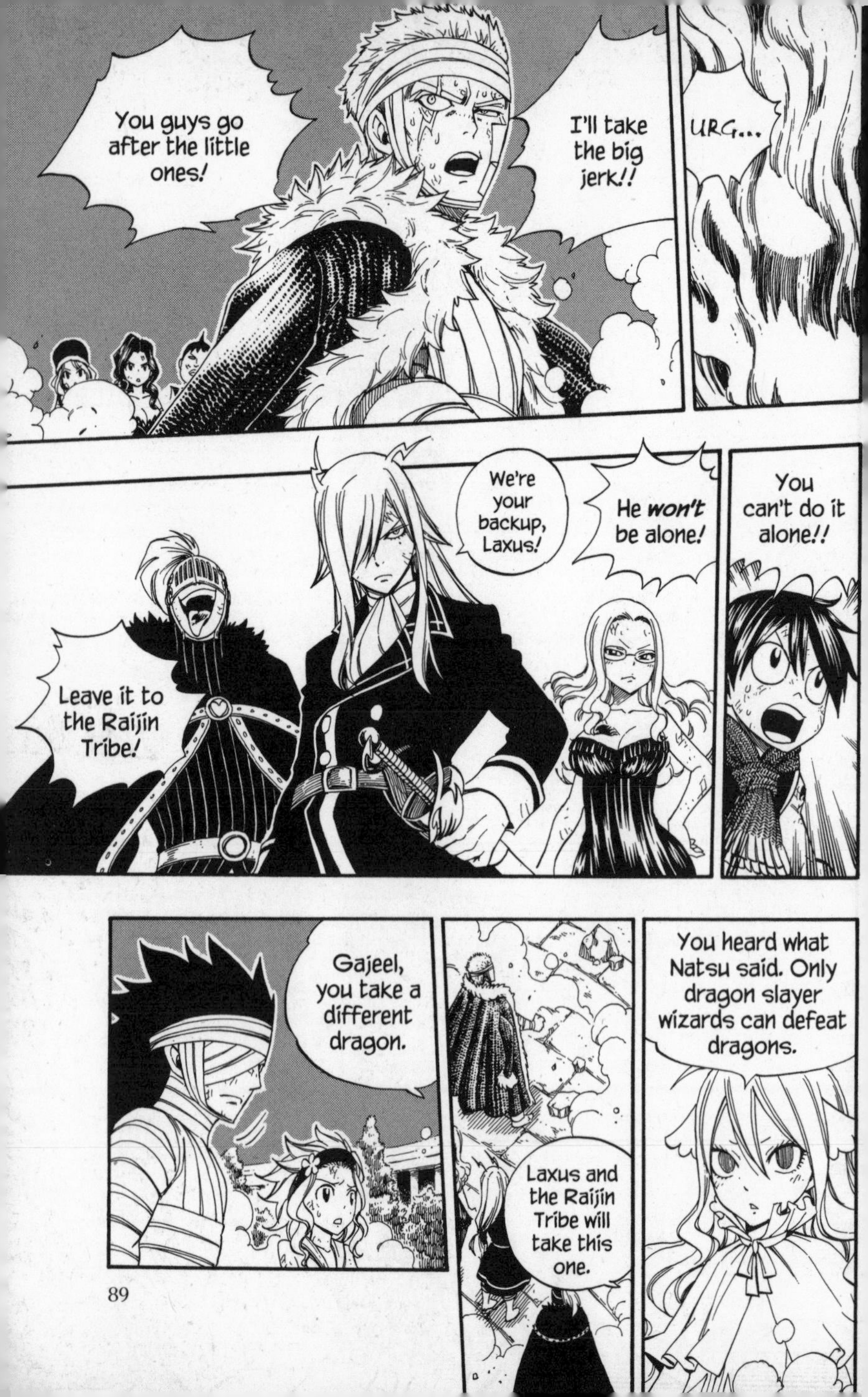
URG...
I'll take the big jerk!!
You guys go after the little ones!
You can't do it alone!!
He *won't* be alone!
We're your backup, Laxus!
Leave it to the Raijin Tribe!
You heard what Natsu said. Only dragon slayer wizards can defeat dragons.
Laxus and the Raijin Tribe will take this one.
Gajeel, you take a different dragon.

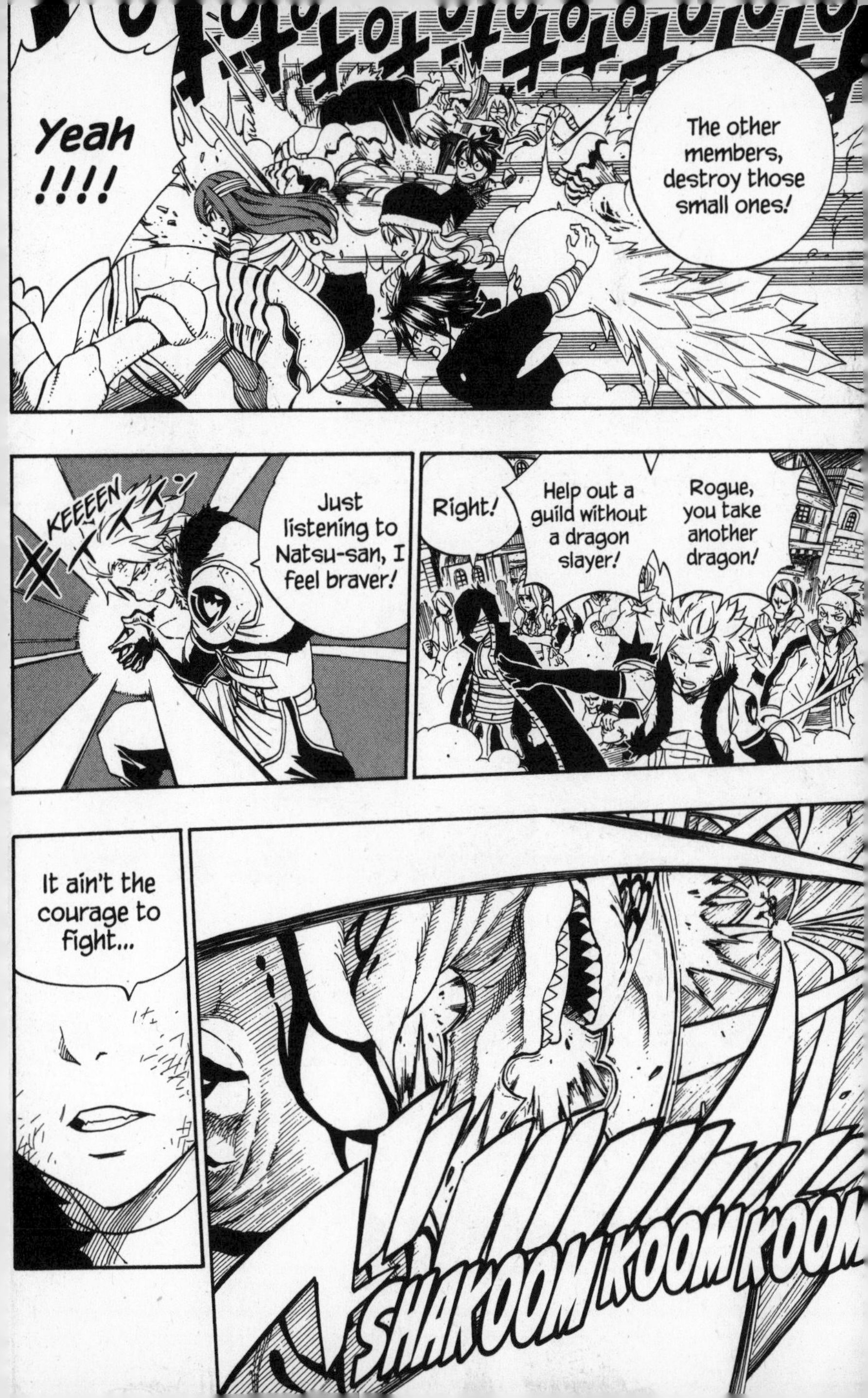
The other members, destroy those small ones!
Yeah !!!!
Rogue, you take another dragon!
Help out a guild without a dragon slayer!
Right!
Just listening to Natsu-san, I feel braver!
KEEEEN
SHAKOOM KOOM KOOM
It ain't the courage to fight...

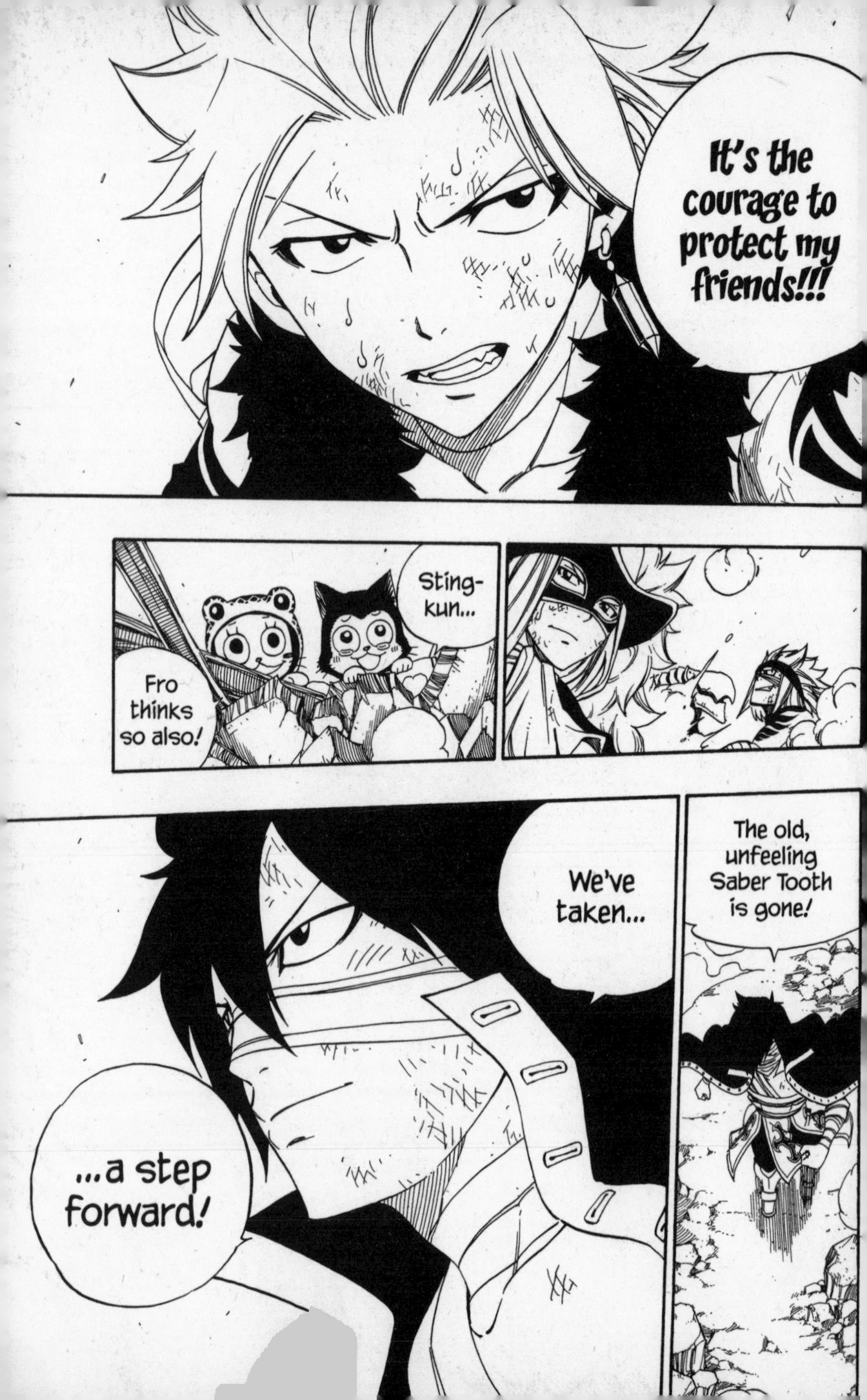
It's the courage to protect my friends!!!
Sting-kun...
Fro thinks so also!
The old, unfeeling Saber Tooth is gone!
We've taken...
...a step forward!

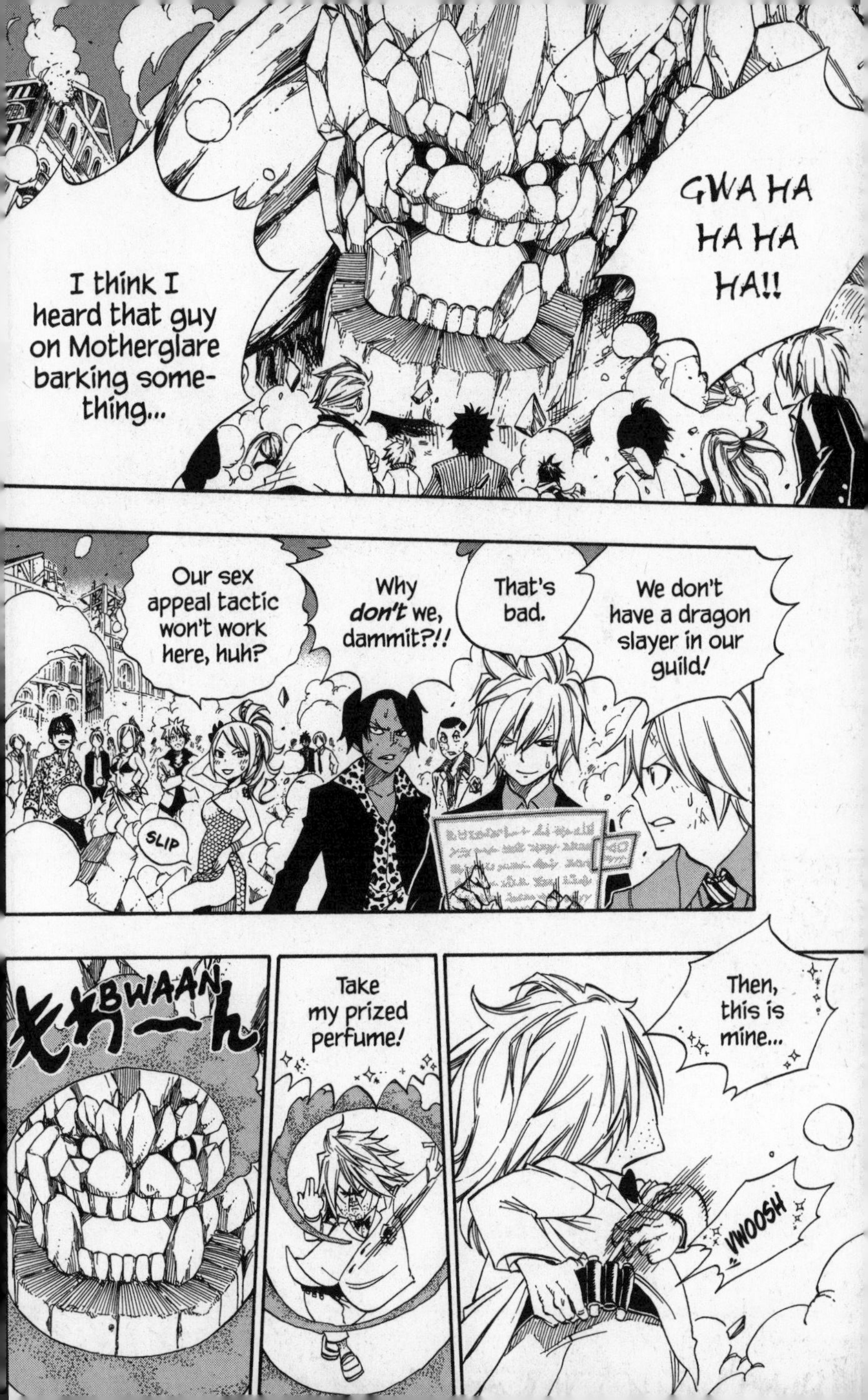
GWA HA HA HA HA!!
I think I heard that guy on Motherglare barking something...
We don't have a dragon slayer in our guild!
That's bad.
Why *don't* we, dammit?!!
Our sex appeal tactic won't work here, huh?
SLIP
Then, this is mine...
VWOOSH
Take my prized perfume!
BWAAN

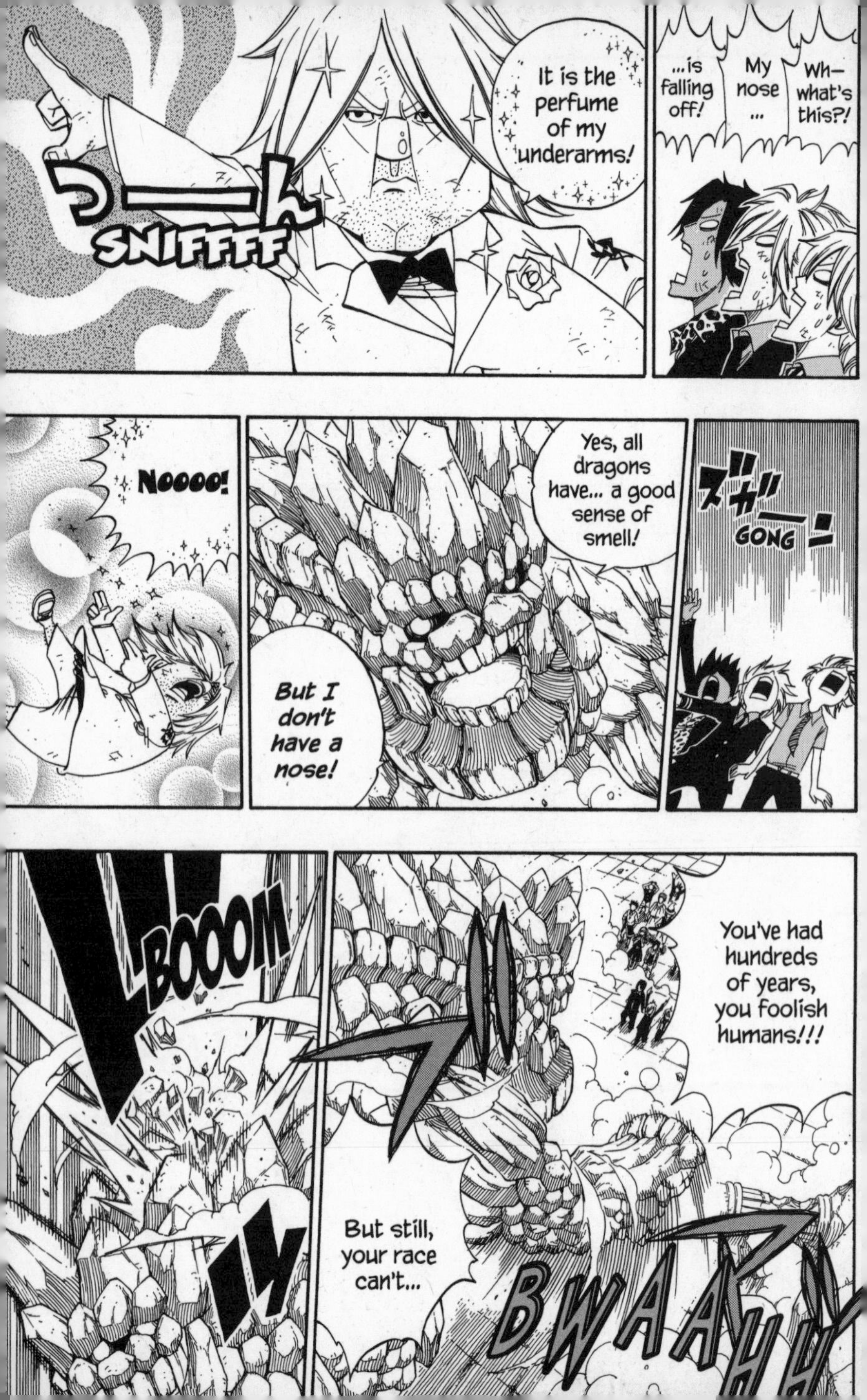
Wh— what's this?!
My nose ...
...is falling off!
It is the perfume of my underarms!
SNIFFFF
GONG
Yes, all dragons have... a good sense of smell!
But I don't have a nose!
Noooo!
You've had hundreds of years, you foolish humans!!!
But still, your race can't...
BWAAHH
BOOOM

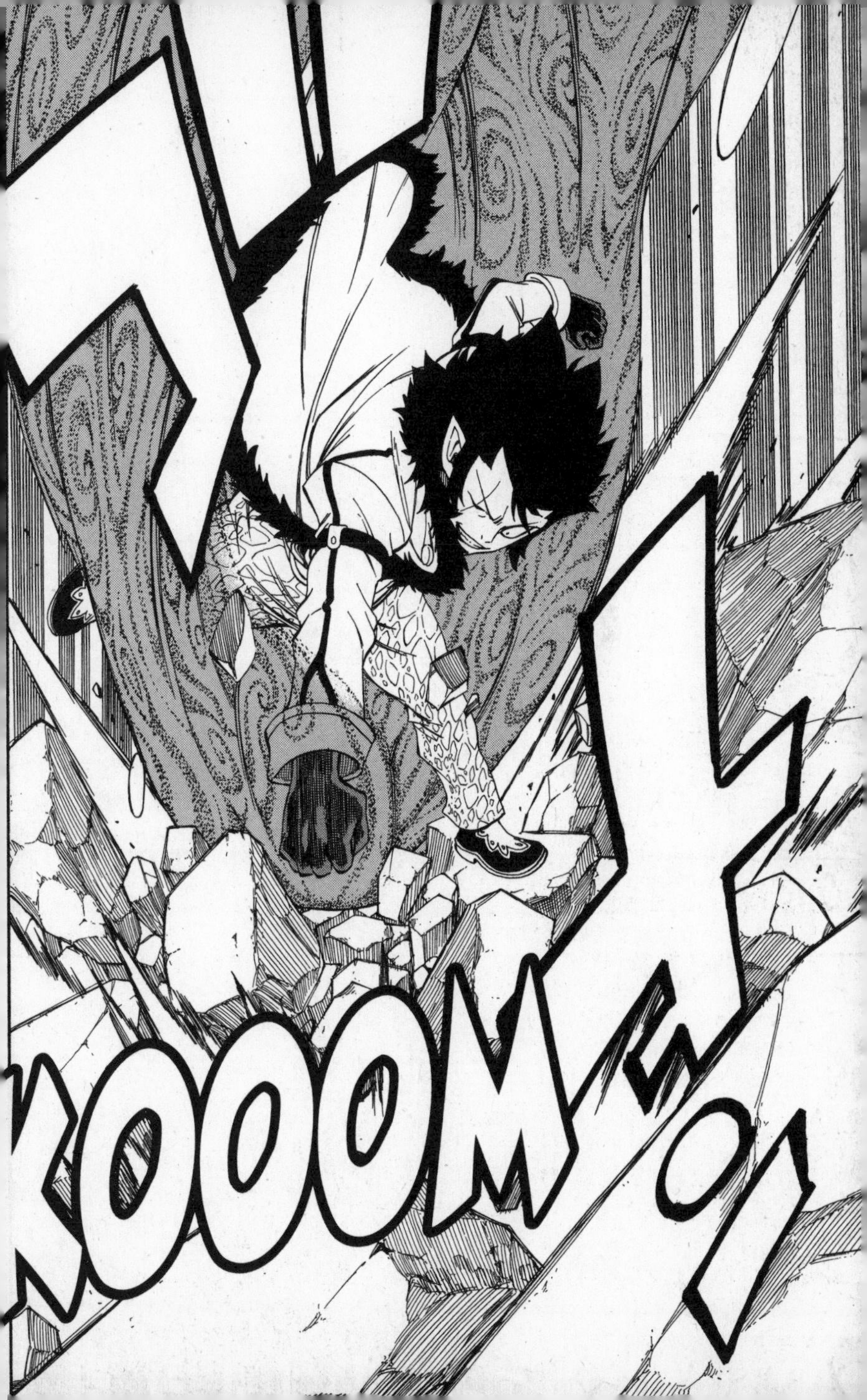
OOOM

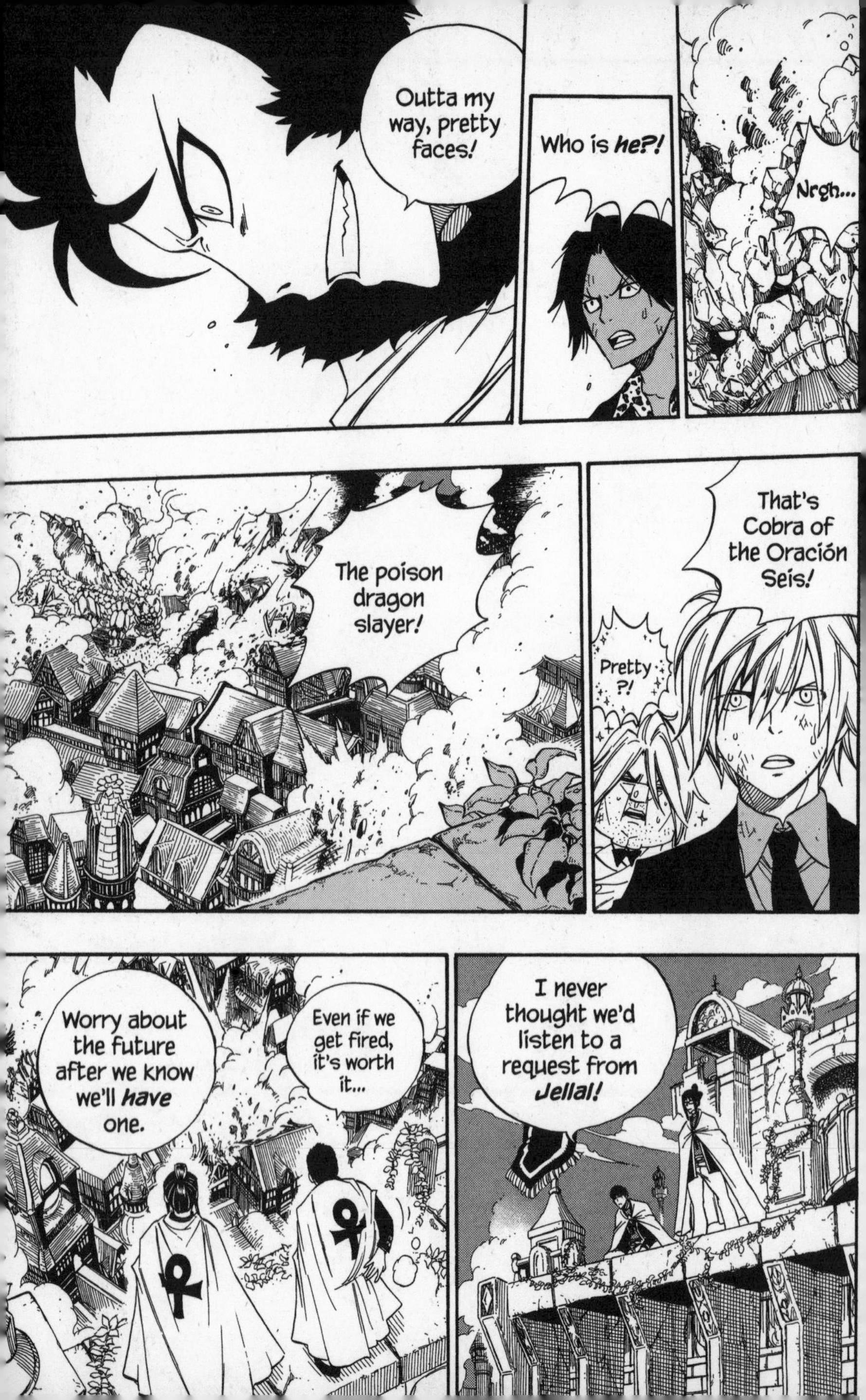
Nrgh...
Who is *he?!*
Outta my way, pretty faces!
That's Cobra of the Oración Seis!
Pretty ?!
The poison dragon slayer!
I never thought we'd listen to a request from *Jellal!*
Even if we get fired, it's worth it...
Worry about the future after we know we'll *have* one.

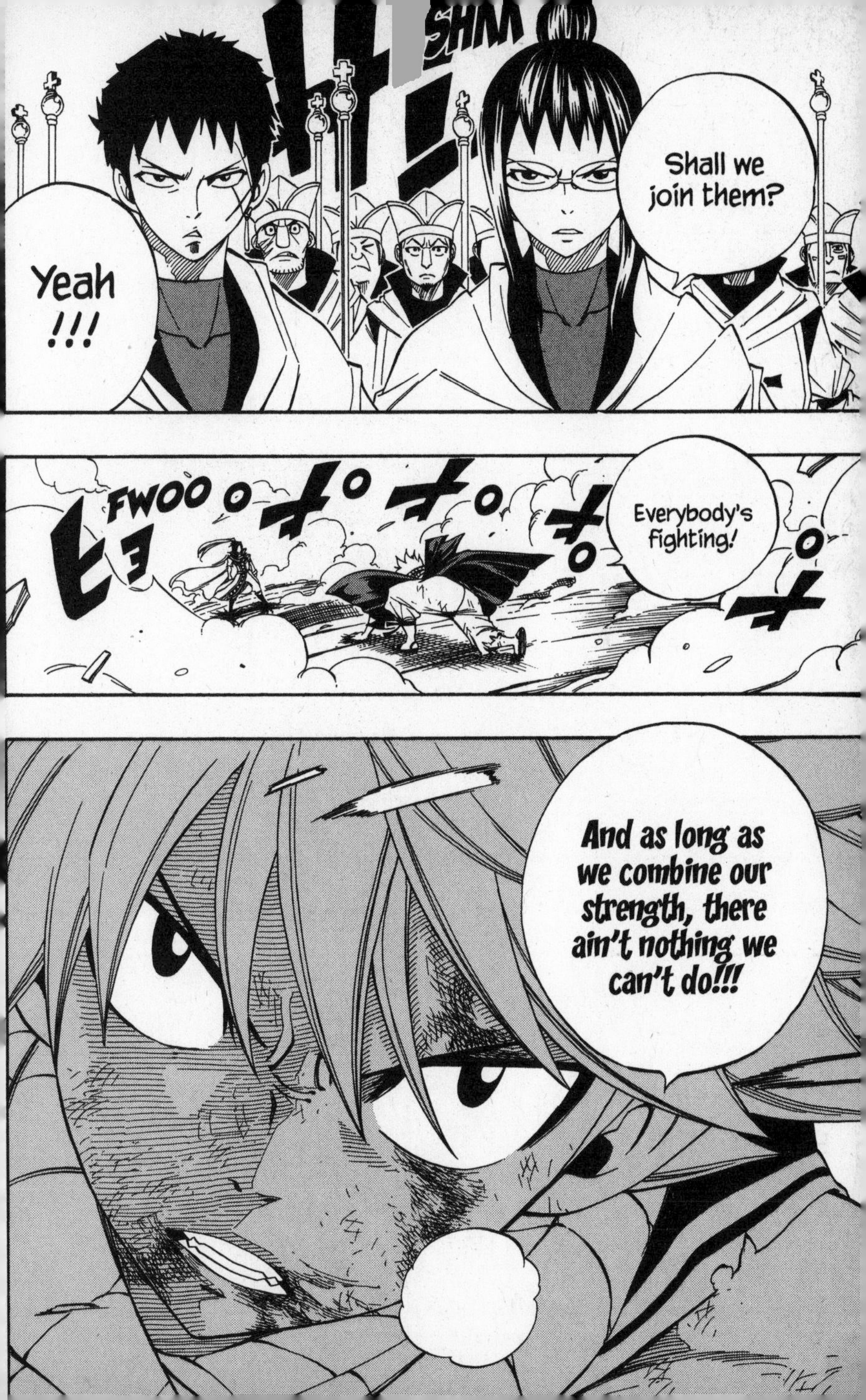
SHM
Shall we join them?
Yeah !!!
Everybody's fighting!
FWOO
ヒョ
And as long as we combine our strength, there ain't nothing we can't do!!!

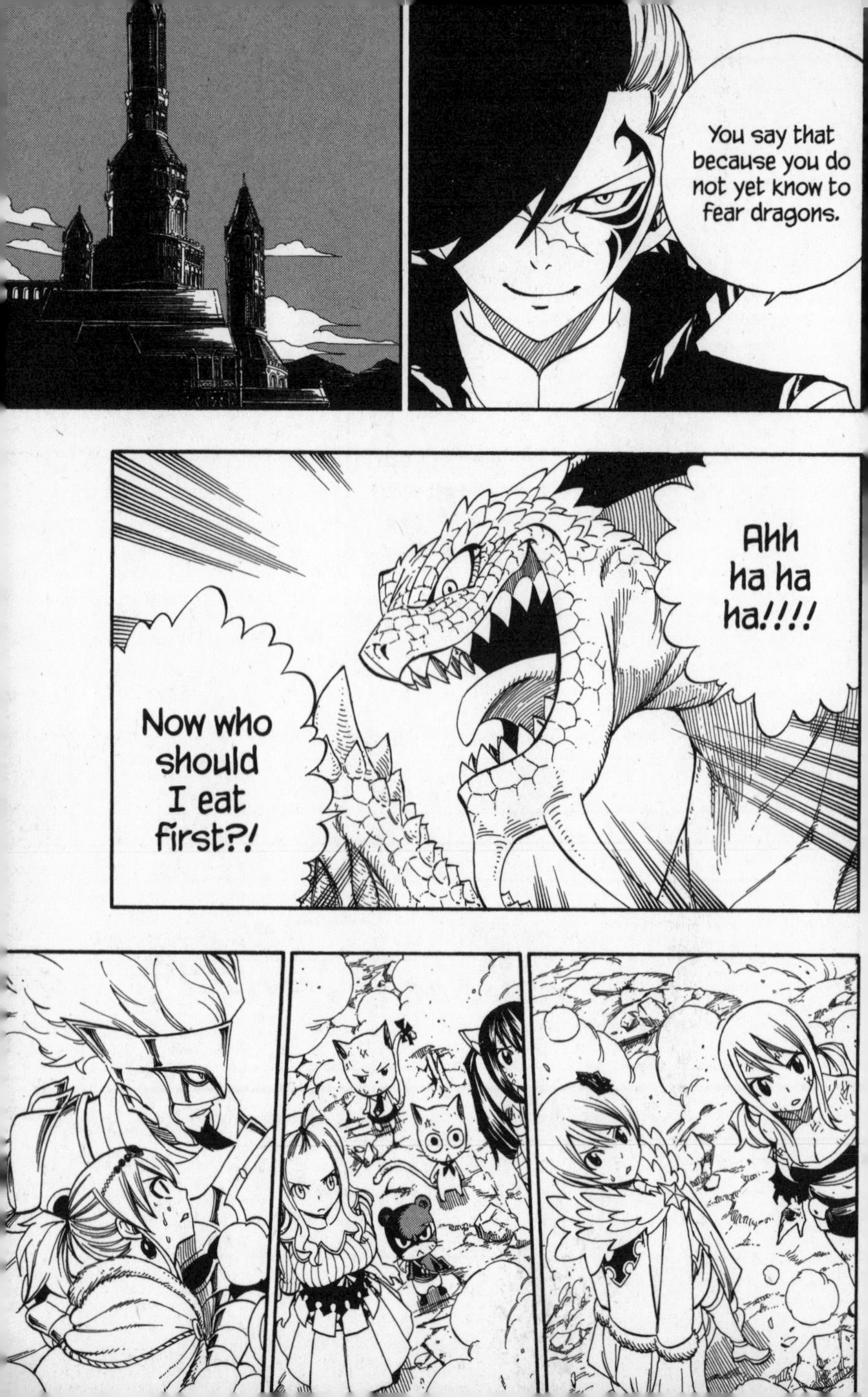
You say that because you do not yet know to fear dragons.
Ahh ha ha ha!!!!
Now who should I eat first?!

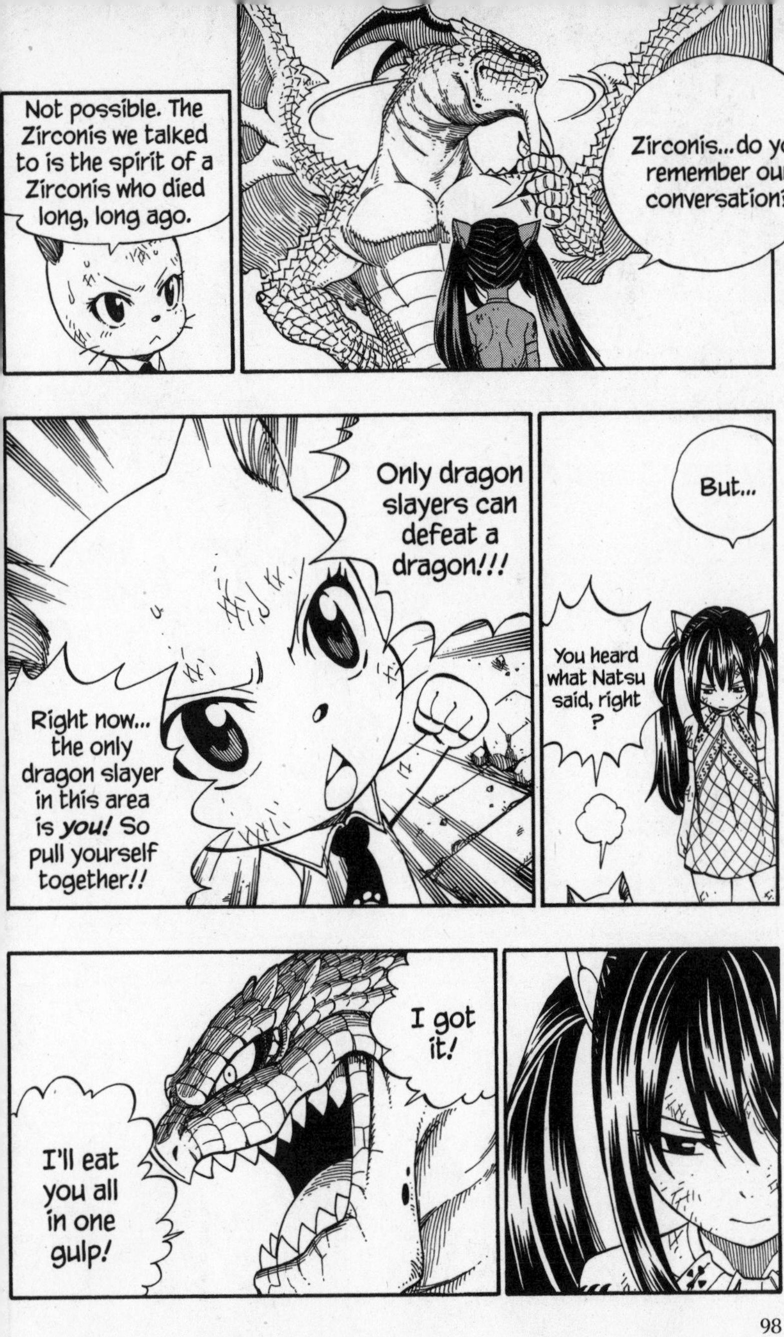

Zirconis...do you remember our conversation?
Not possible. The Zirconis we talked to is the spirit of a Zirconis who died long, long ago.
But...
You heard what Natsu said, right?
Only dragon slayers can defeat a dragon!!!
Right now... the only dragon slayer in this area is *you!* So pull yourself together!!
I got it!
I'll eat you all in one gulp!

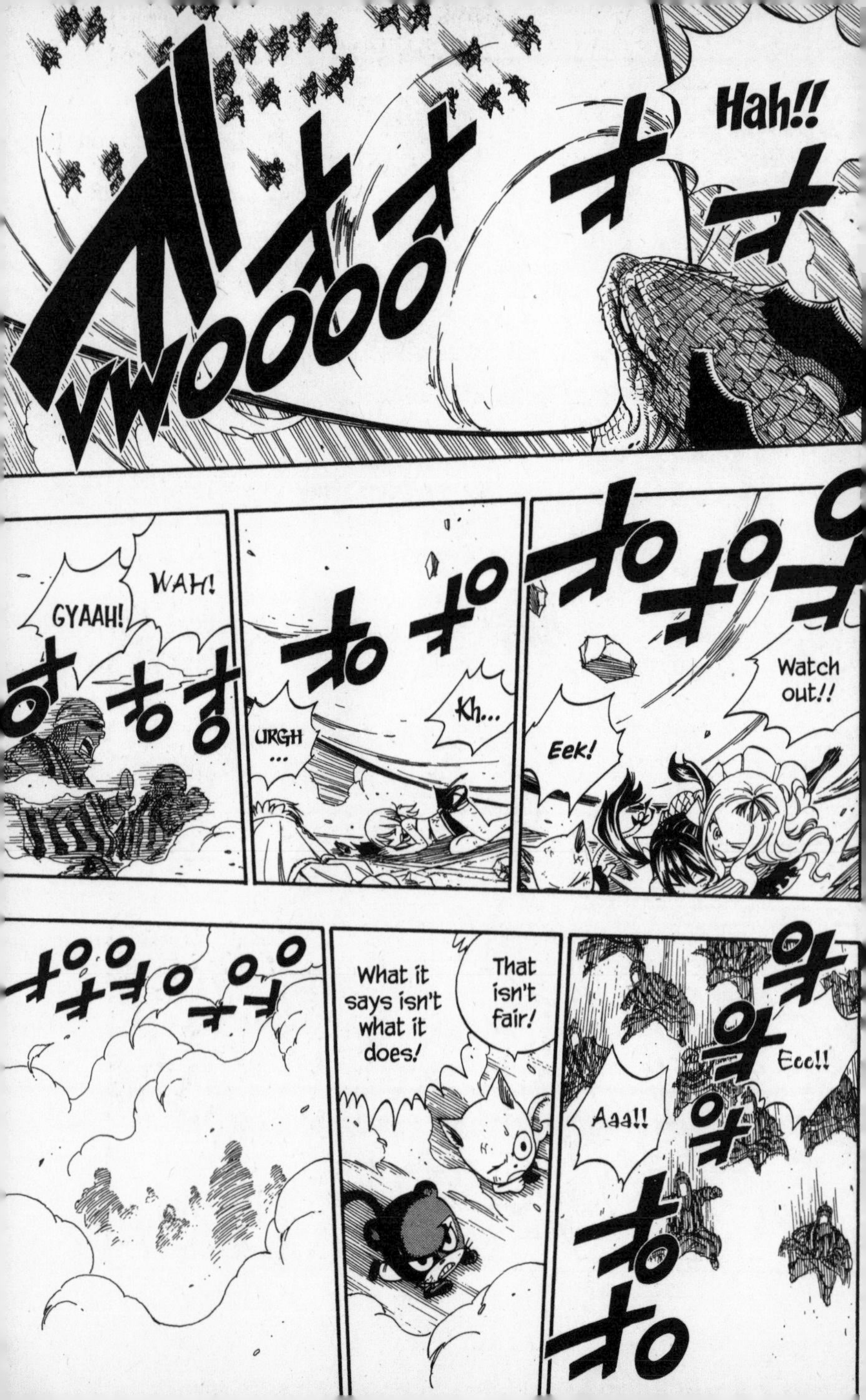

Hah!!
Watch out!!
Eek!
Kh...
URGH ...
WAH!
GYAAH!
Ecc!!
Aaa!!
That isn't fair!
What it says isn't what it does!

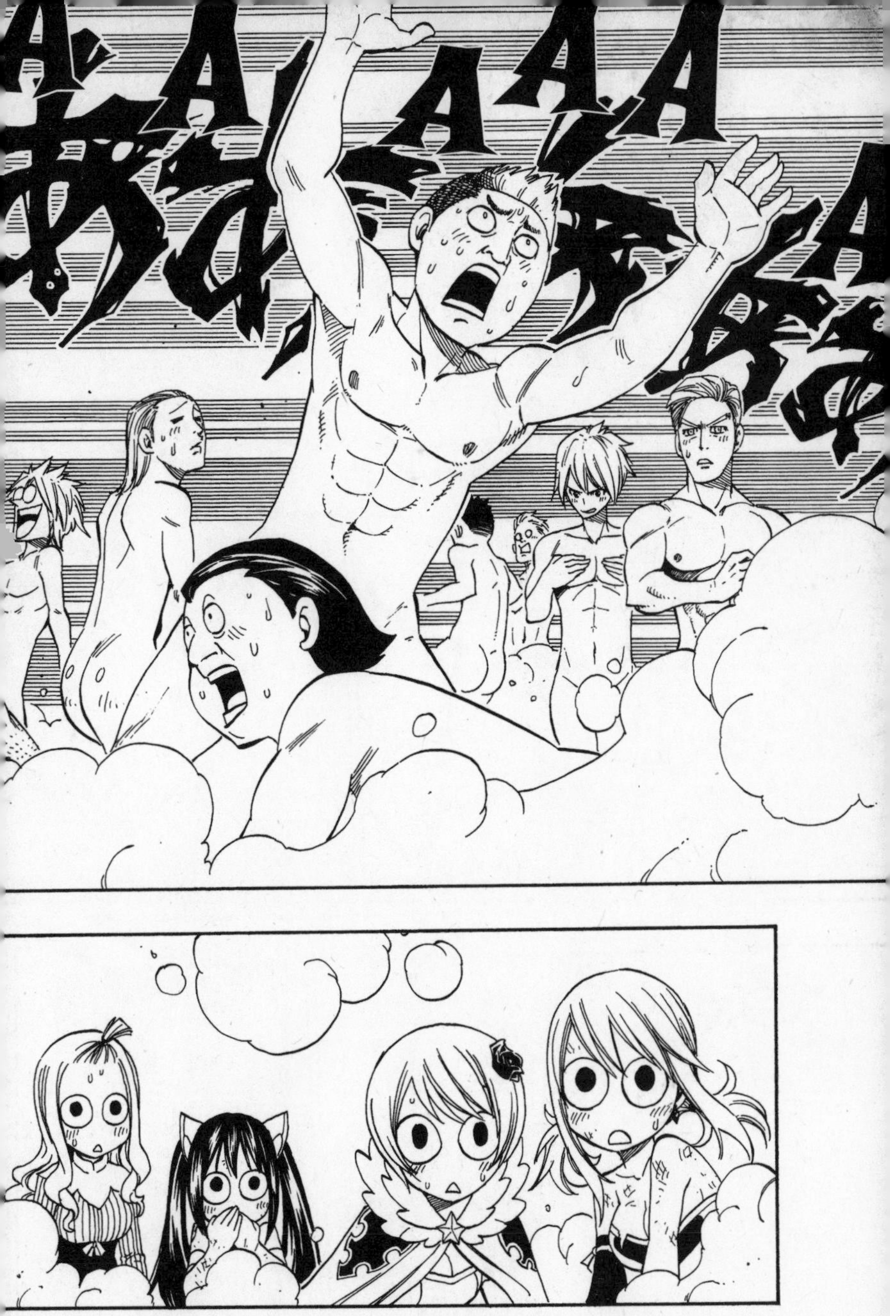
AAAAAA

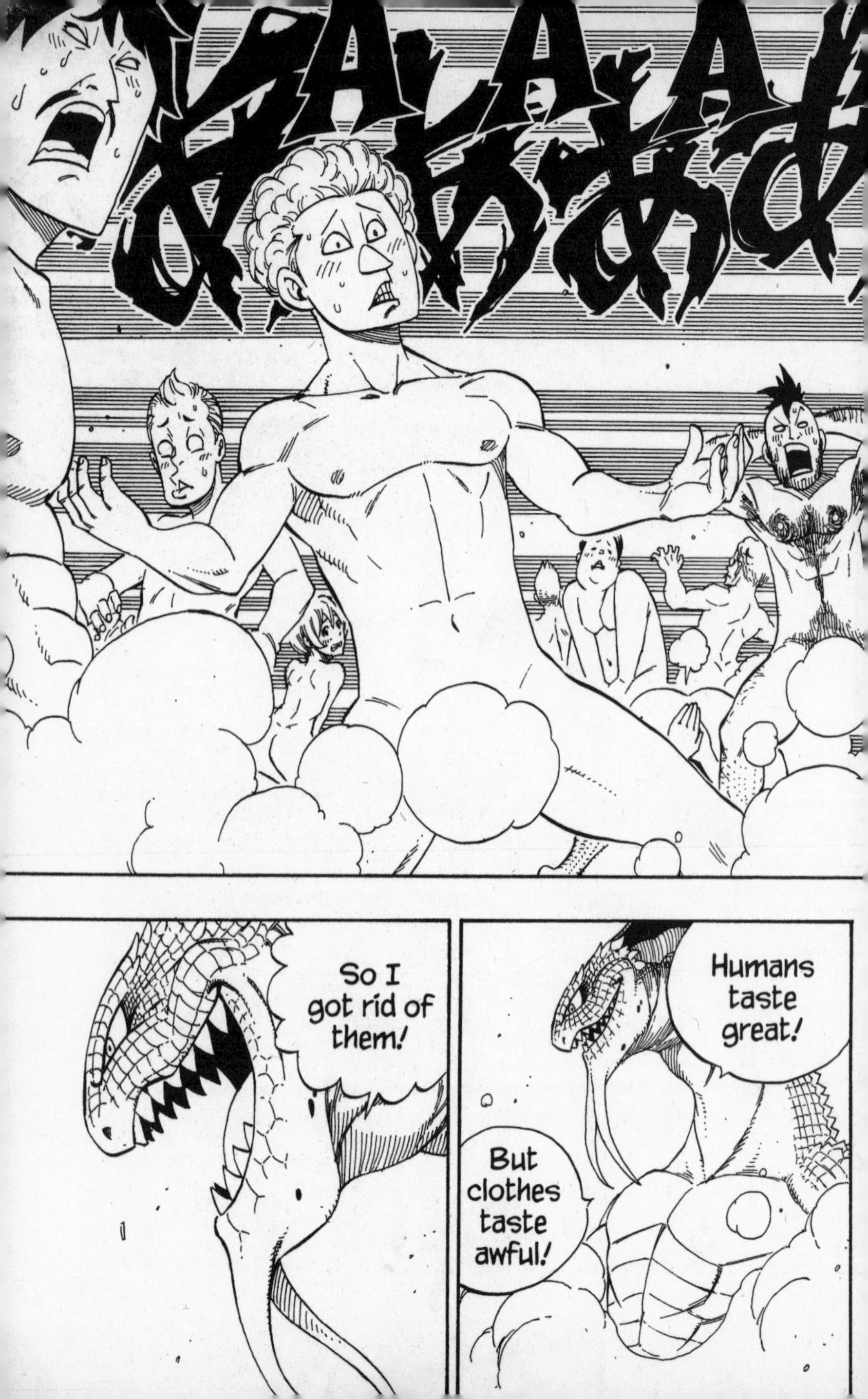
Humans taste great!
But clothes taste awful!
So I got rid of them!

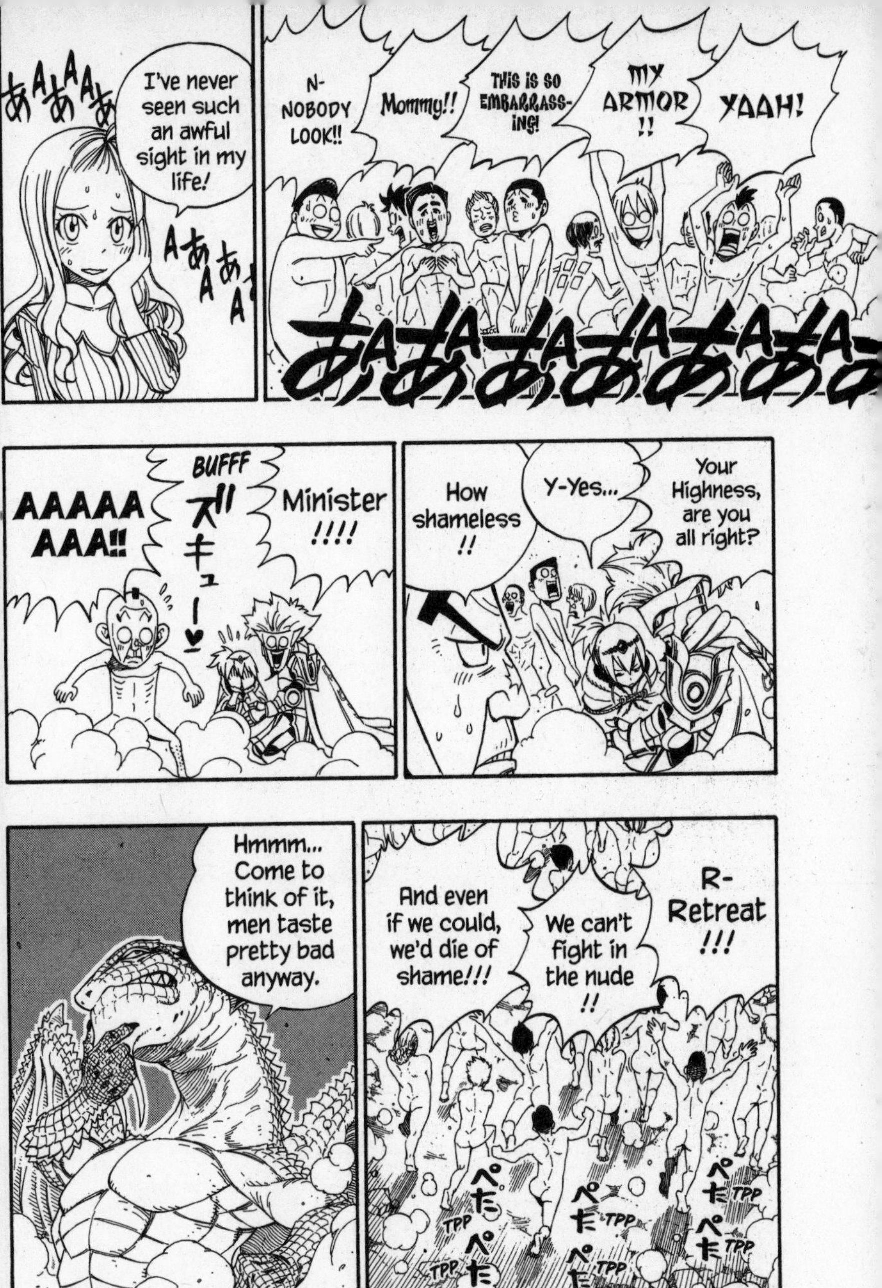
YAAH!
MY ARMOR!!
THIS IS SO EMBARRASSING!
Mommy!!
N-NOBODY LOOK!!
あAあAあAあAあAあAあ
I've never seen such an awful sight in my life!
あAあAあ
AあAあA
Your Highness, are you all right?
Y-Yes...
How shameless!!
Minister!!!!
BUFFF
ズキュー♥
AAAAAAAA!!
R-Retreat!!!
We can't fight in the nude!!
And even if we could, we'd die of shame!!!
ぺたぺた TPP TPP
ぺたぺた TPP TPP
ぺたぺた TPP TPP
Hmmm... Come to think of it, men taste pretty bad anyway.

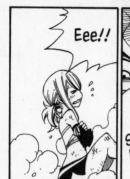

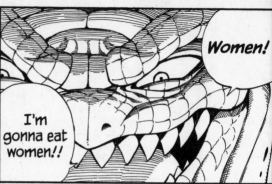

Women!
I'm gonna eat women!!
Eee!!
Was that...
...magic you used?
Yes, it was!
All dragons use magic!
PTUI!
!!

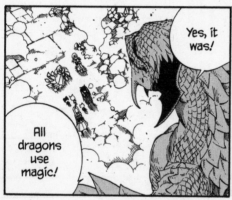

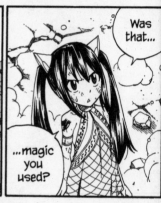

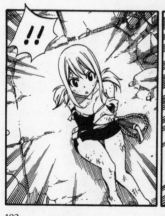

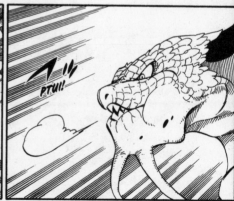

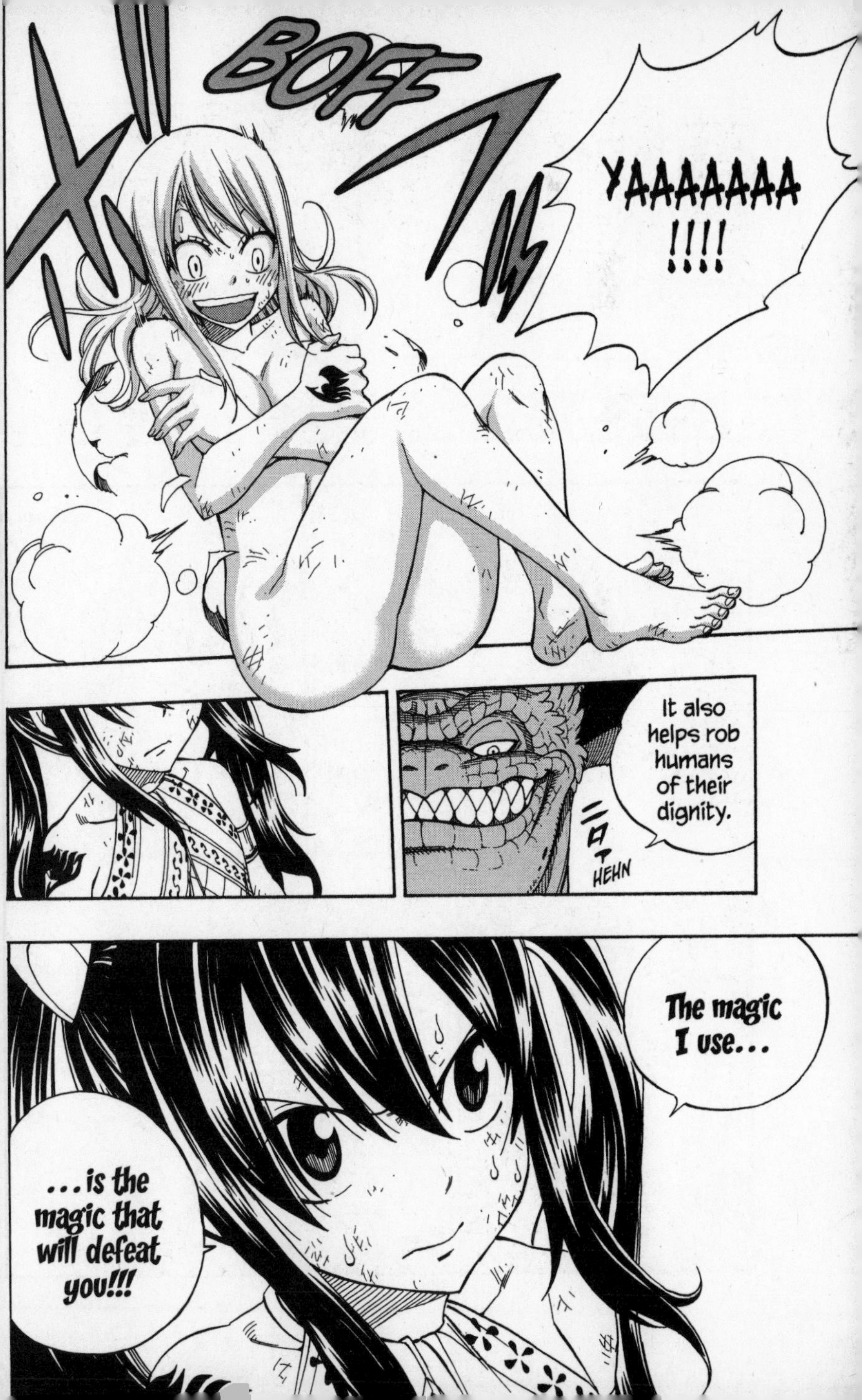
BOFF
YAAAAAAA !!!!
It also helps rob humans of their dignity.
HEHN
The magic I use...
...is the magic that will defeat you!!!

FAIRY TAIL

フェアリーテイル

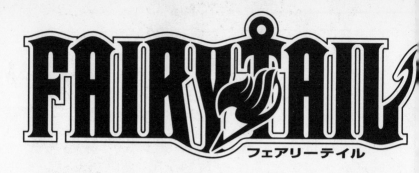

Chapter 331: Natsu's Plan

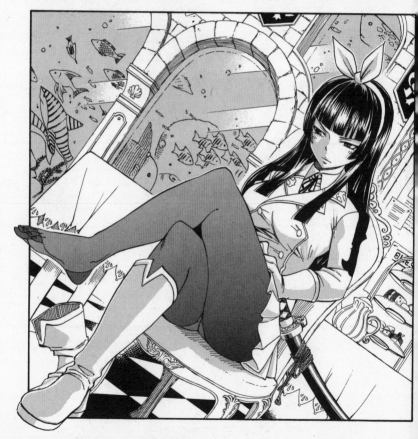

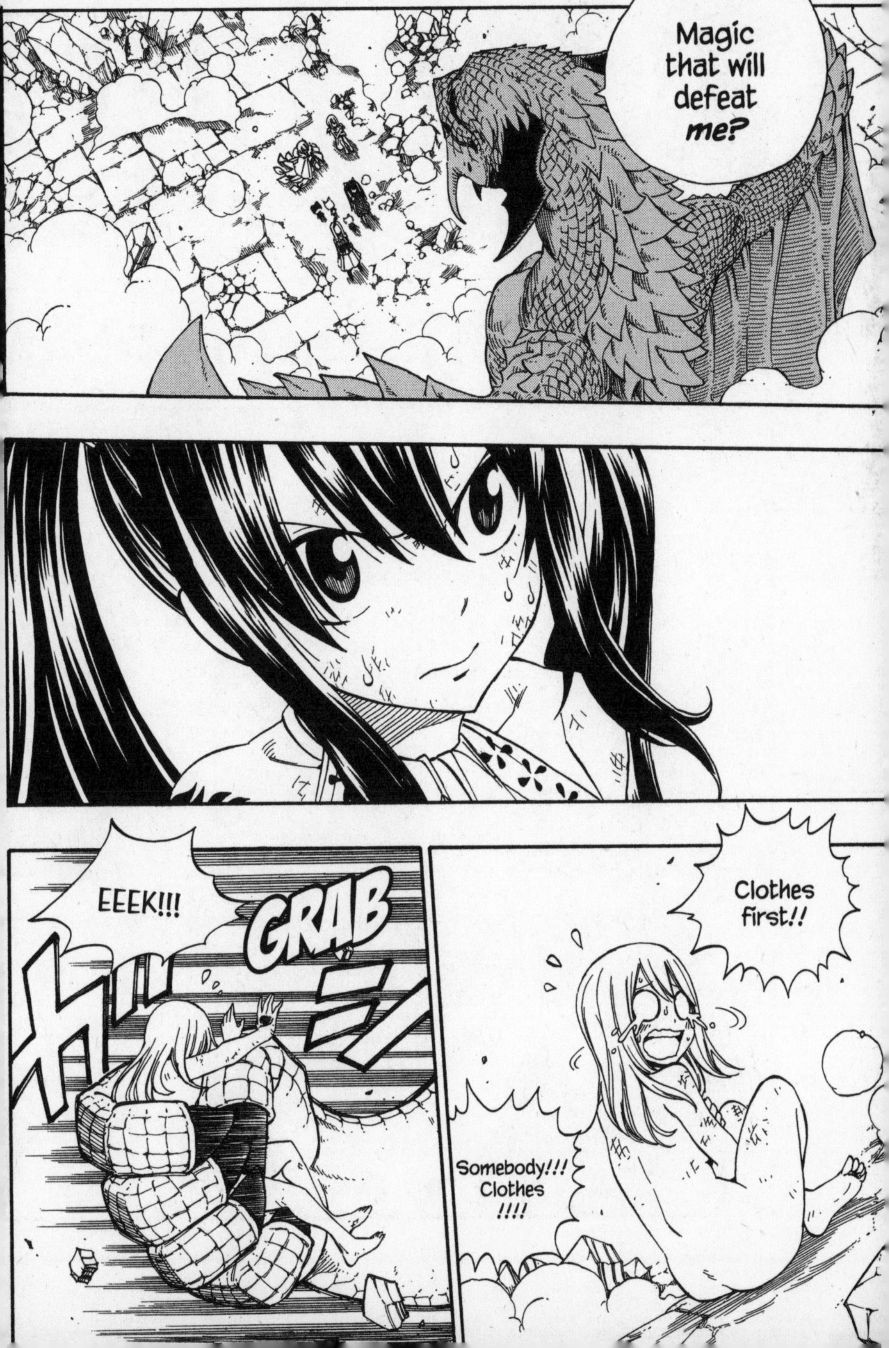
Magic that will defeat *me?*
Clothes first!!
Somebody!!! Clothes !!!!
EEEK!!!
GRAB

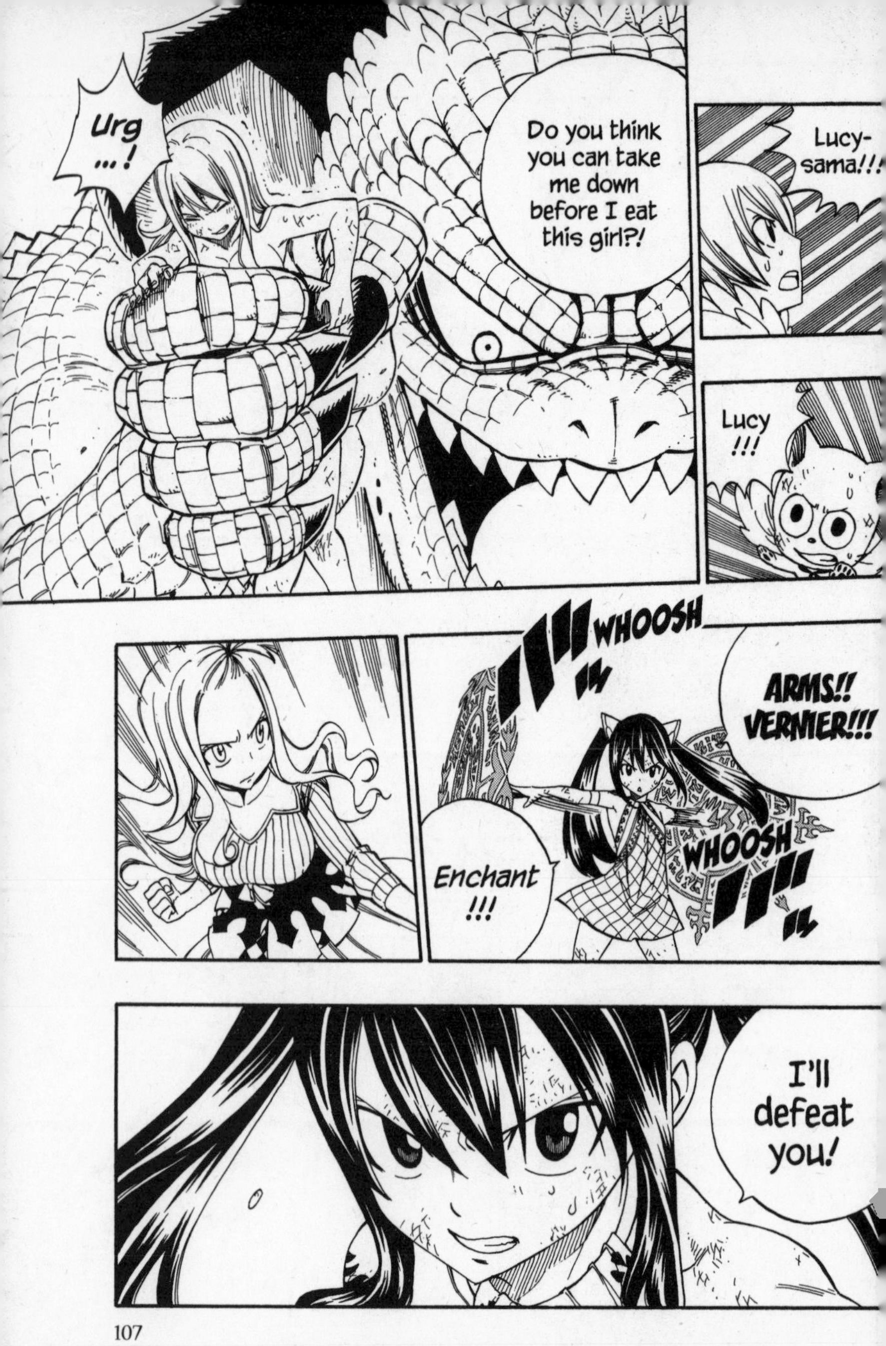
Lucy-sama!!!
Lucy !!!
Do you think you can take me down before I eat this girl?!
Urg ...!
WHOOSH
ARMS!! VERNIER!!!
Enchant !!!
WHOOSH
I'll defeat you!

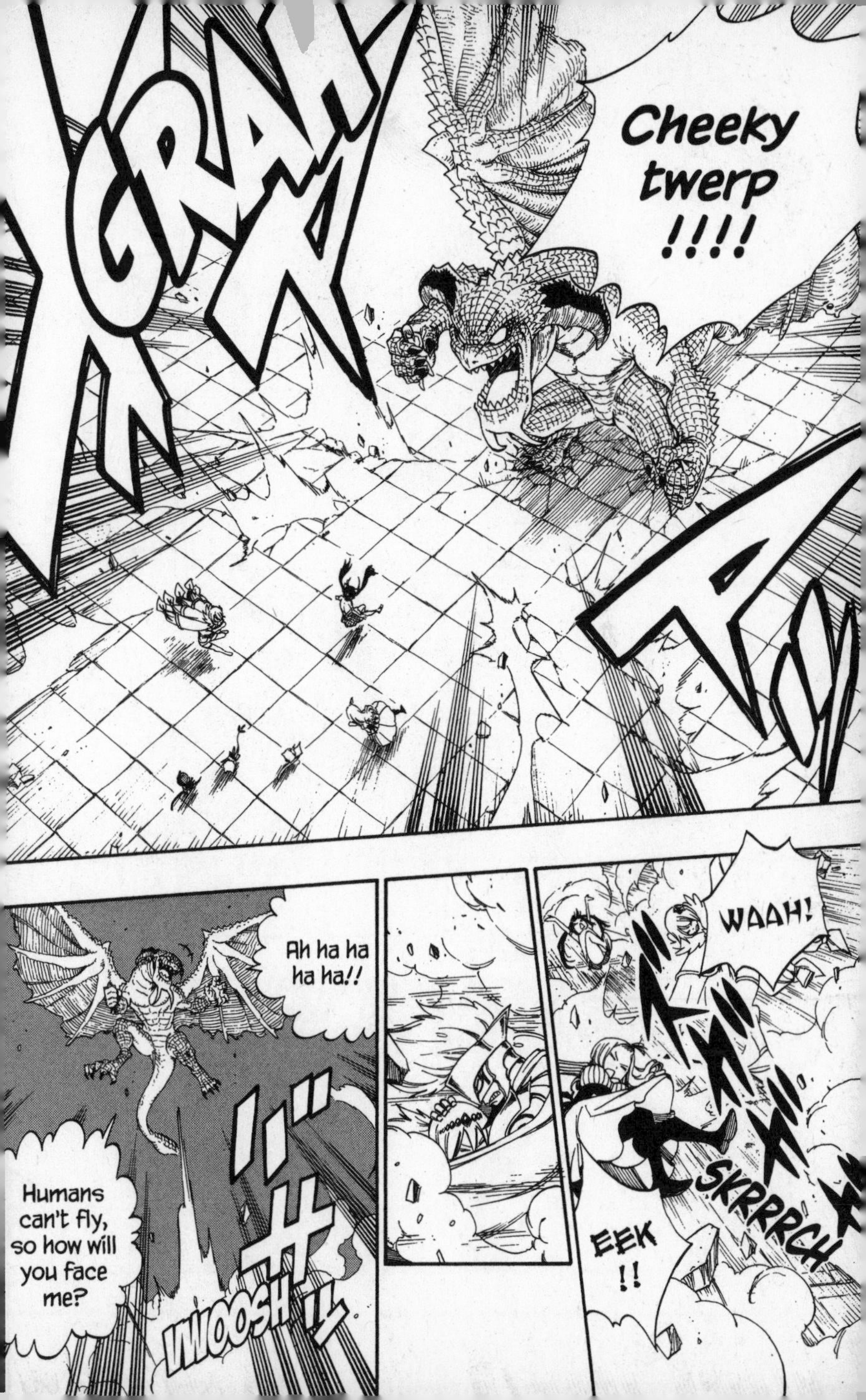
Cheeky twerp!!!!
WAAH!
SKRRRCH
EEK!!
Ah ha ha ha ha!!
Humans can't fly, so how will you face me?
WOOSH!!

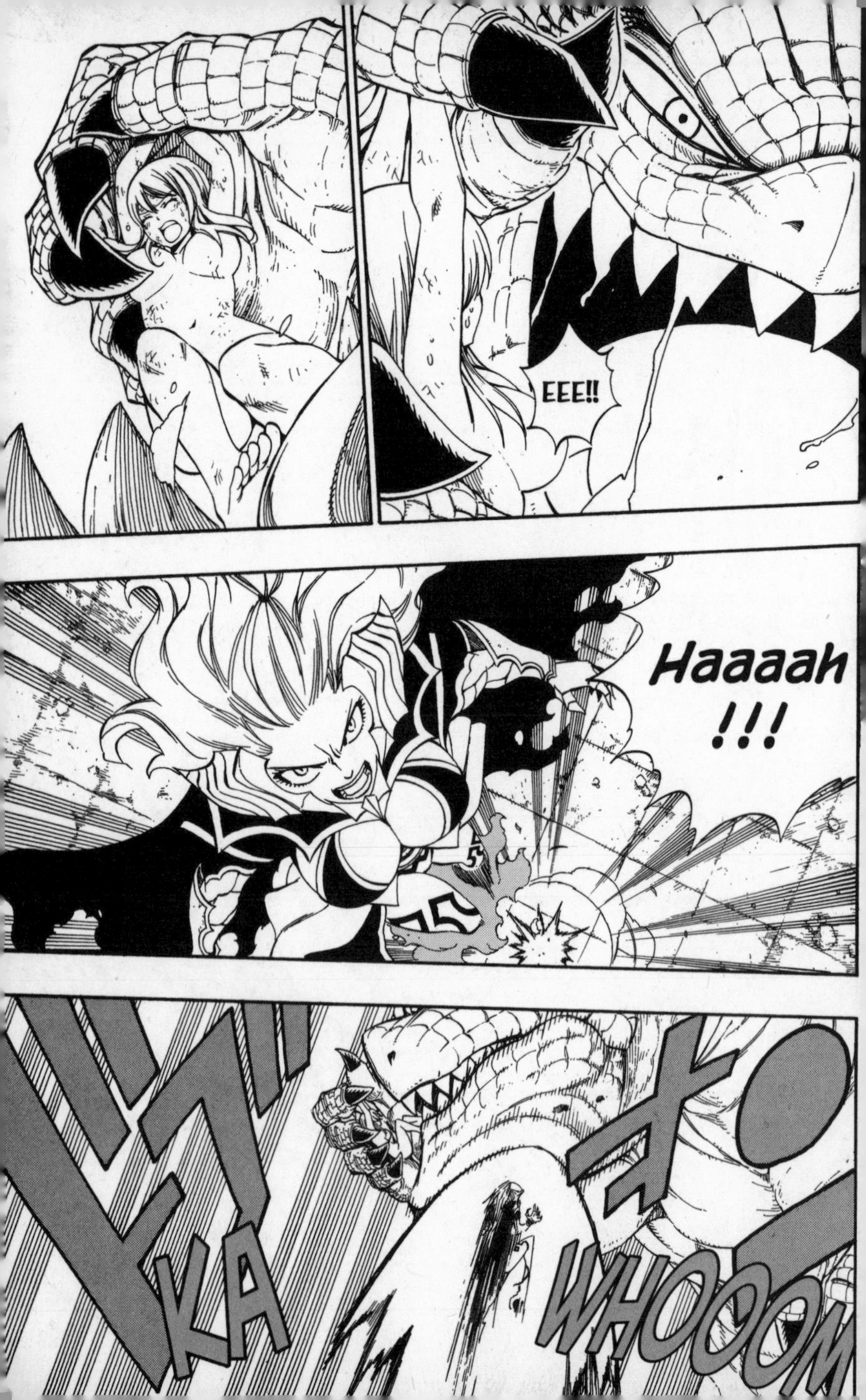
EEE!!
Haaaah !!!
KA
WHOOOM

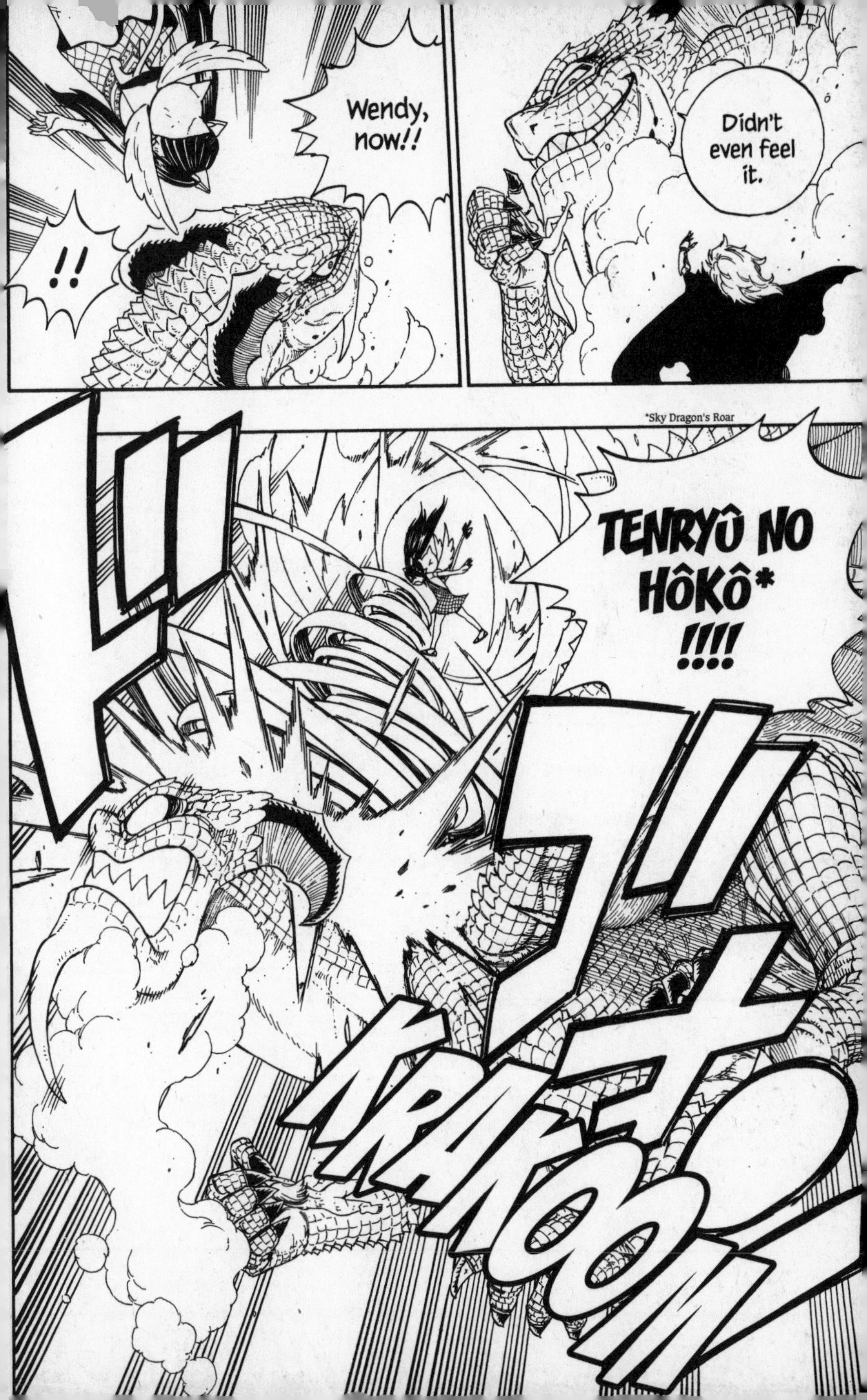
Didn't even feel it.
Wendy, now!!
!!
*Sky Dragon's Roar
TENRYÛ NO HÔKÔ* !!!!
KRAKOOM

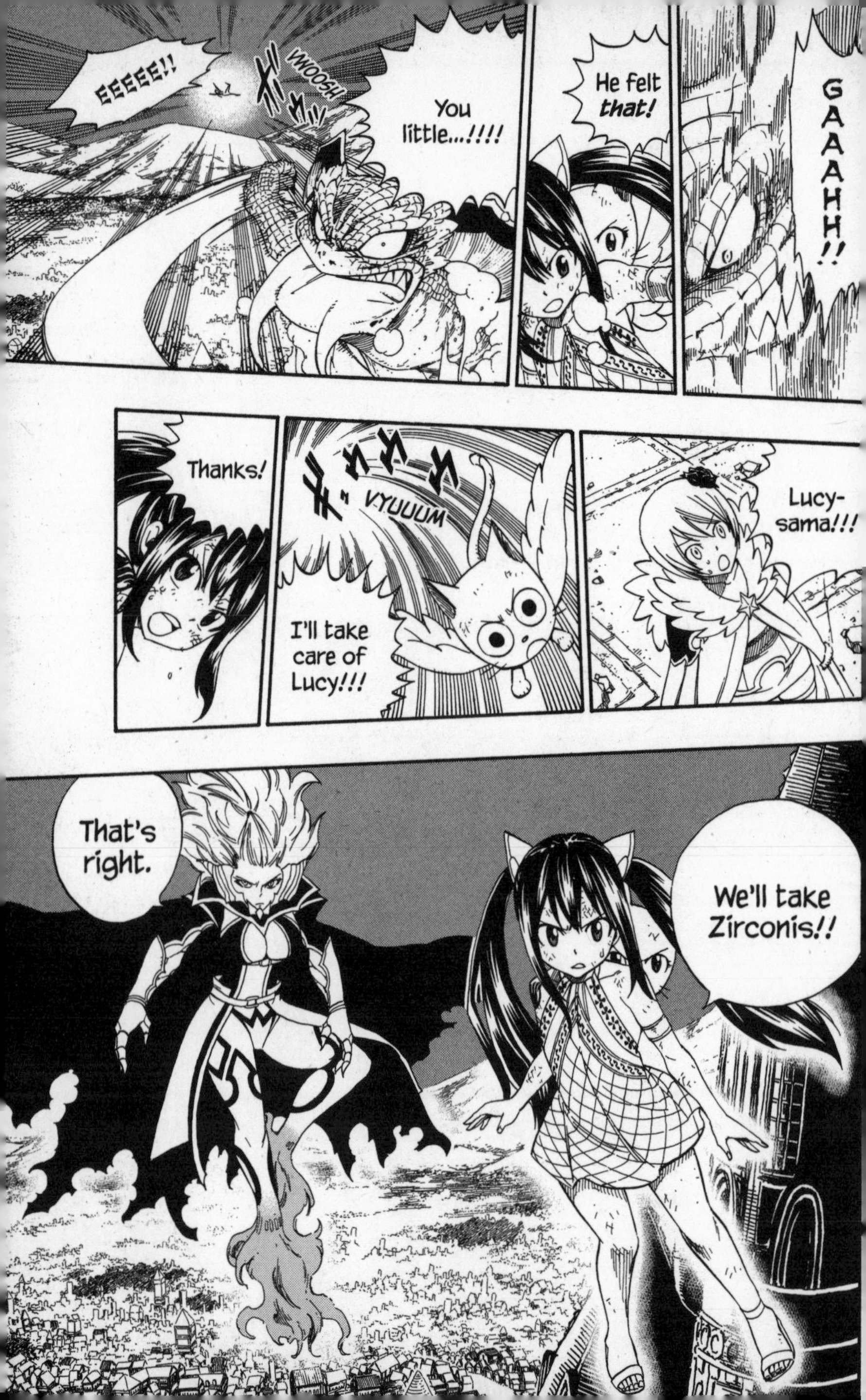
GAAAHH!!
He felt that!
You little...!!!!
WOOSH
EEEEE!!
Lucy-sama!!!
VYUUUM
I'll take care of Lucy!!!
Thanks!
We'll take Zirconis!!
That's right.

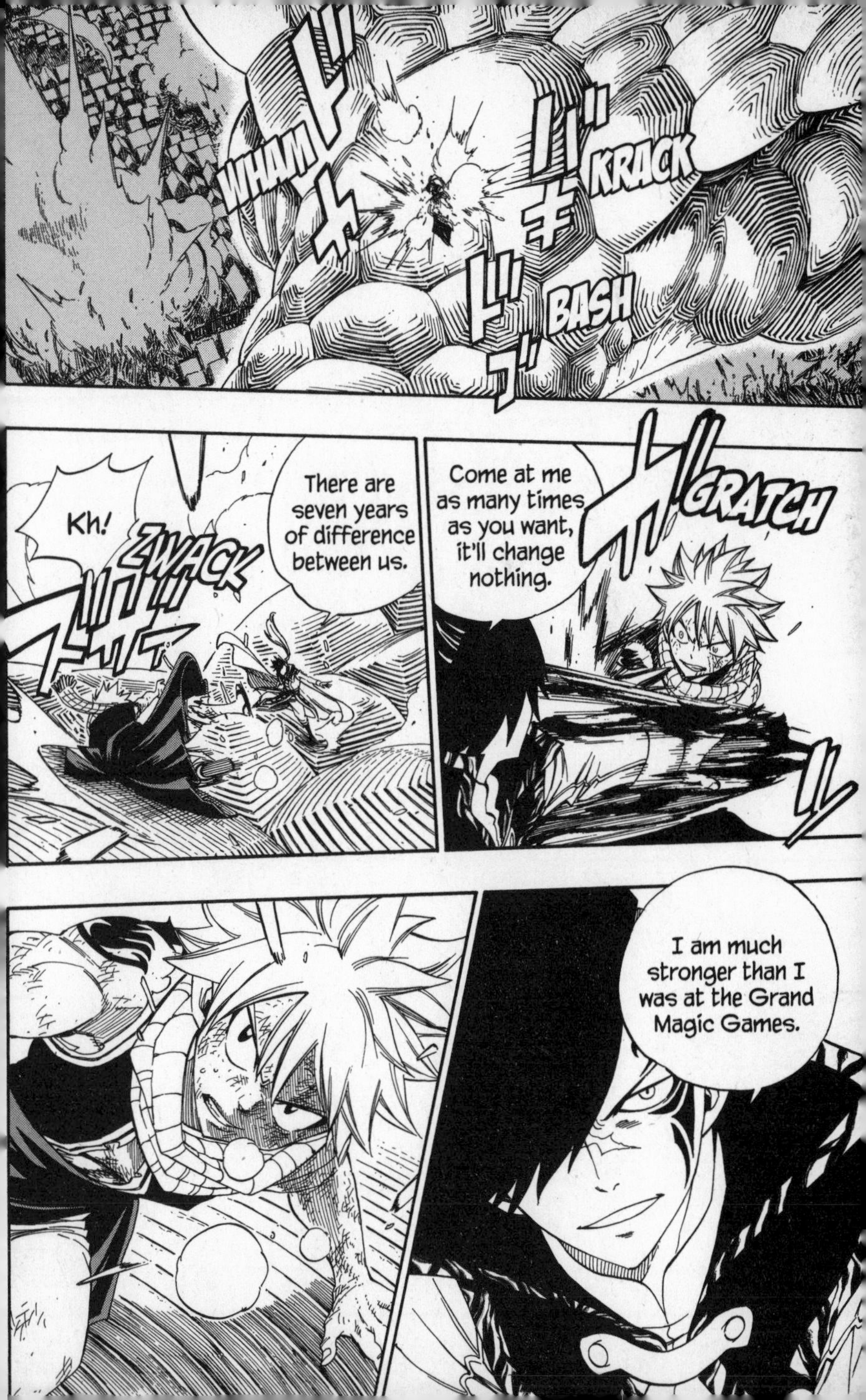
KRACK
WHAM
BASH
GRATCH
Come at me as many times as you want, it'll change nothing.
There are seven years of difference between us.
ZWACK
Kh!
I am much stronger than I was at the Grand Magic Games.

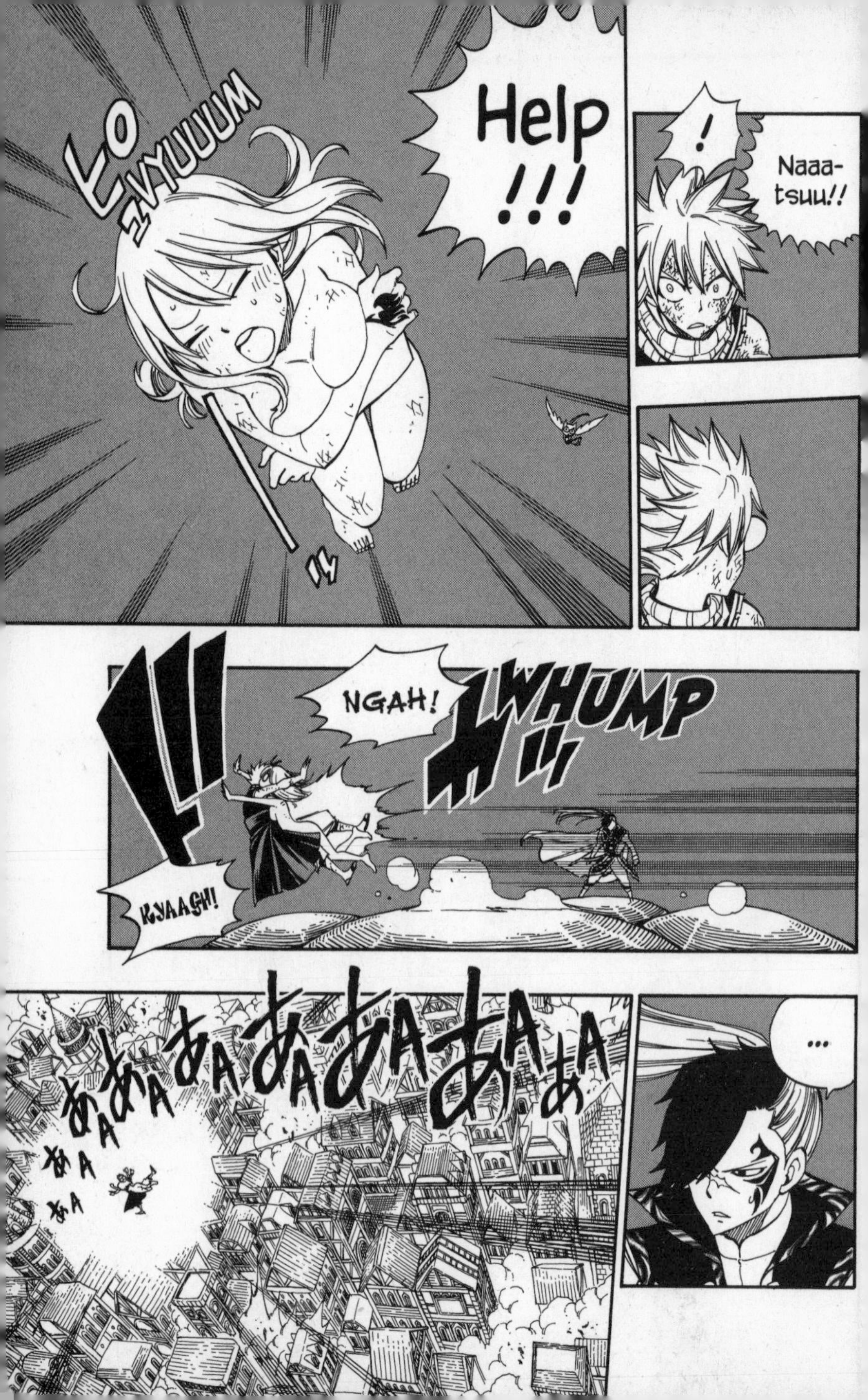

!
Naaa-tsuu!!
Help!!!
ZVYUUUM
WHUMP
NGAH!
KYAAGH!
...
あAあAあAあAあAあAあAあA

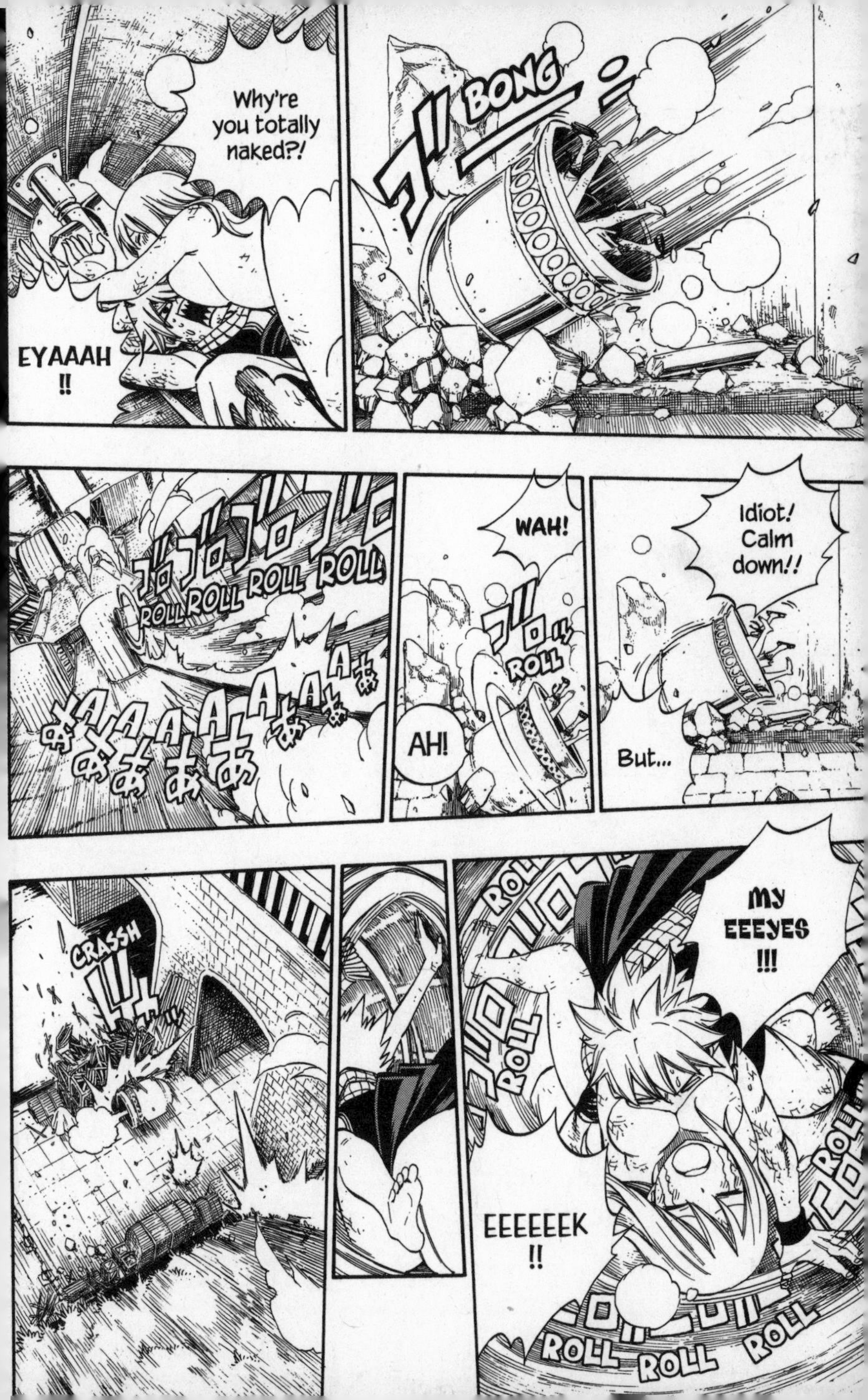
BONG
Why're you totally naked?!
EYAAAH!!
Idiot! Calm down!!
But...
WAH!
ROLL
AH!
ROLL ROLL ROLL ROLL
AAAAAAA
My EEEYES!!!
ROLL
ROLL
ROLL
EEEEEEK!!
ROLL ROLL ROLL
CRASSH!!

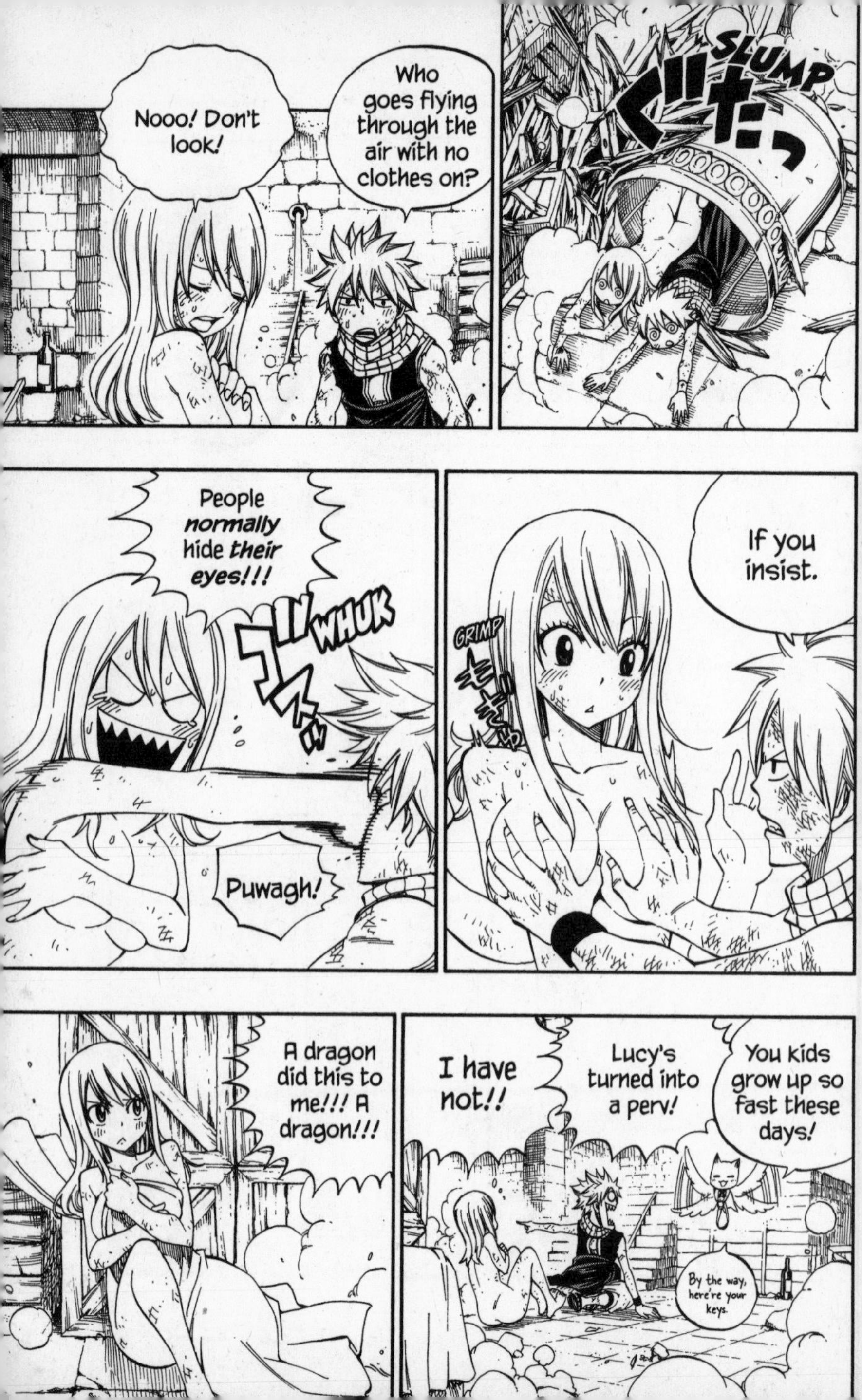
SLUMP
Who goes flying through the air with no clothes on?
Nooo! Don't look!
If you insist.
GRIMP
People *normally* hide *their* eyes!!!
WHUK
Puwagh!
You kids grow up so fast these days!
Lucy's turned into a perv!
I have not!!
By the way, here're your keys.
A dragon did this to me!!! A dragon!!!

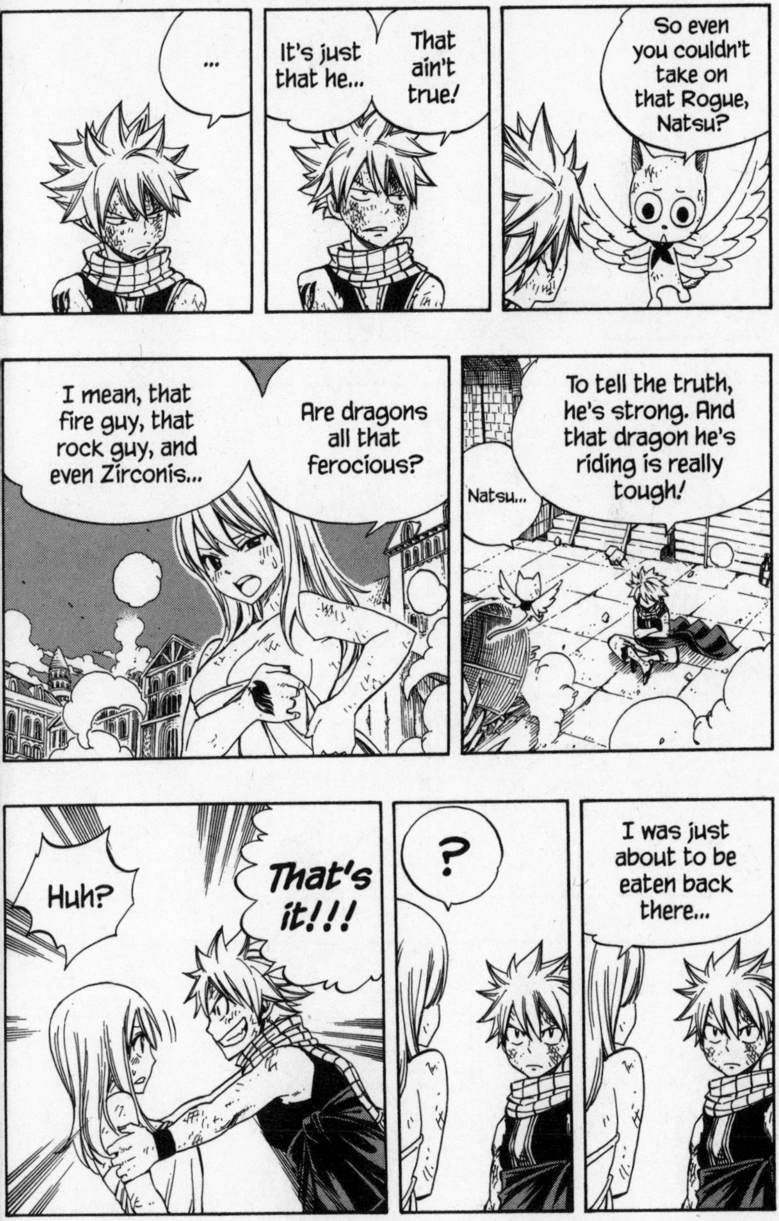
So even you couldn't take on that Rogue, Natsu?
That ain't true!
It's just that he...
...
To tell the truth, he's strong. And that dragon he's riding is really tough!
Natsu...
Are dragons all that ferocious?
I mean, that fire guy, that rock guy, and even Zirconis...
I was just about to be eaten back there...
?
That's it!!!
Huh?

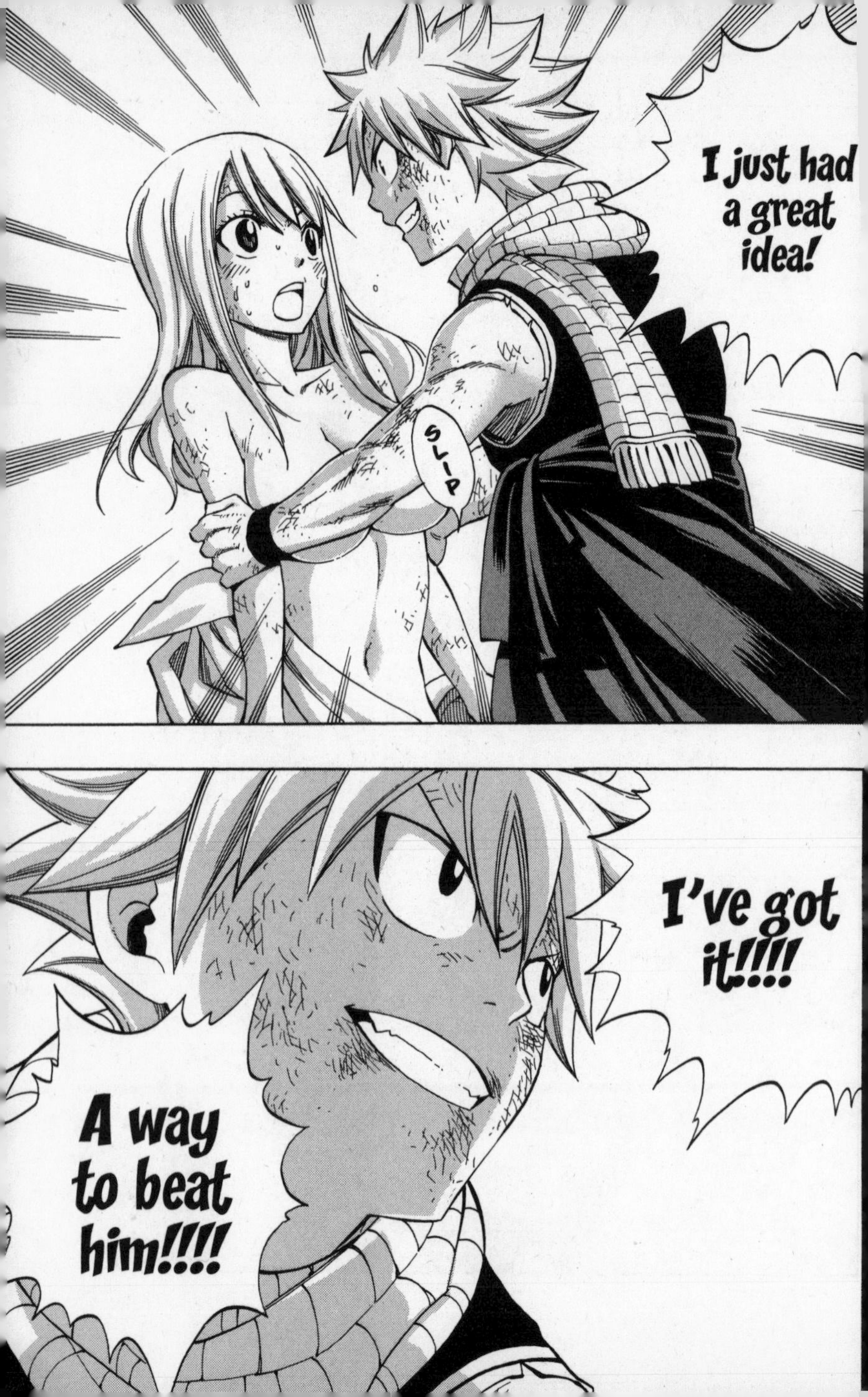
I just had a great idea!
SLIP
I've got it!!!!
A way to beat him!!!!

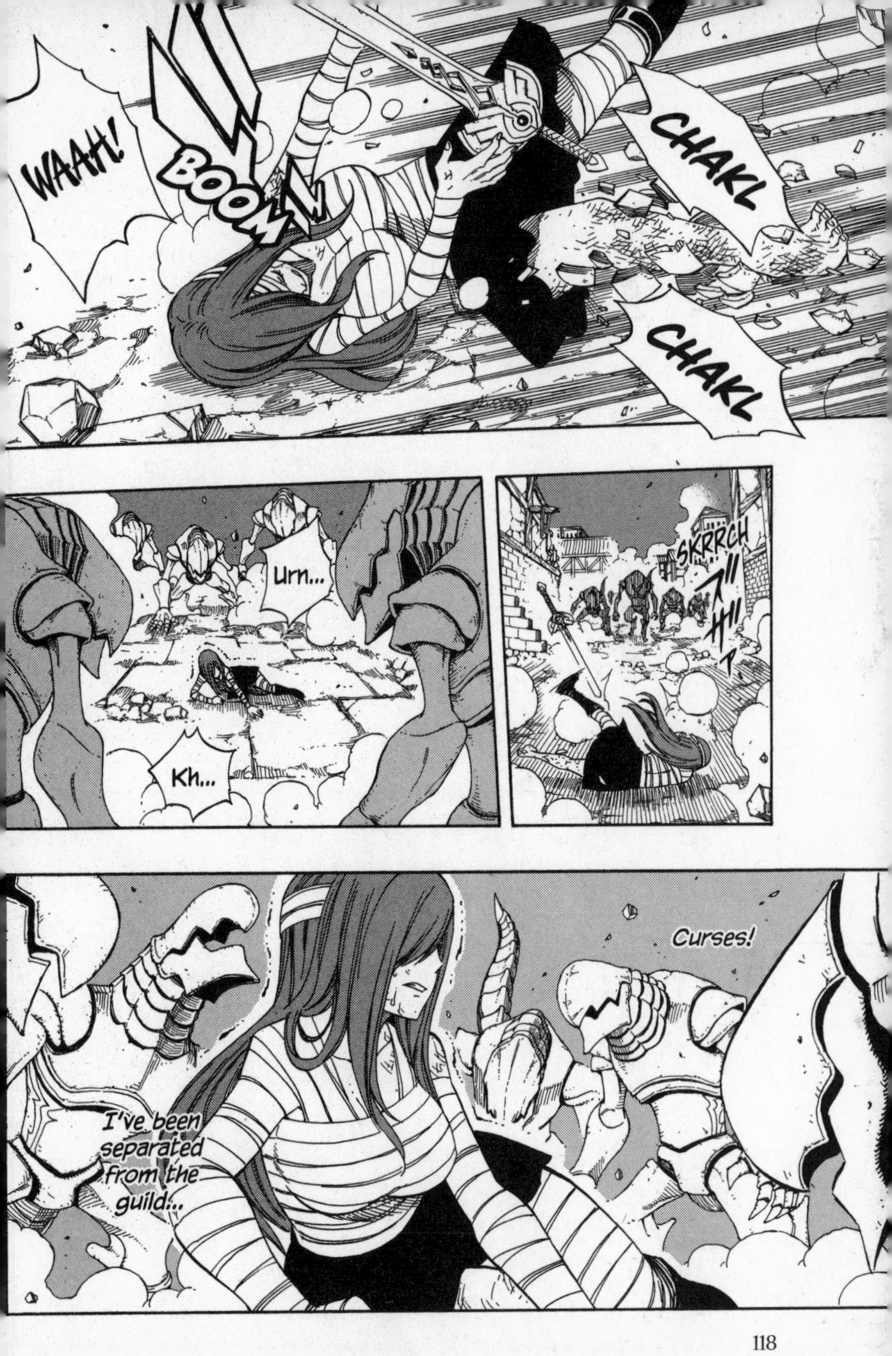
CHAKL
CHAKL
BOOM
WAAH!
SKRRCH
Urn...
Kh...
Curses!
I've been separated from the guild...

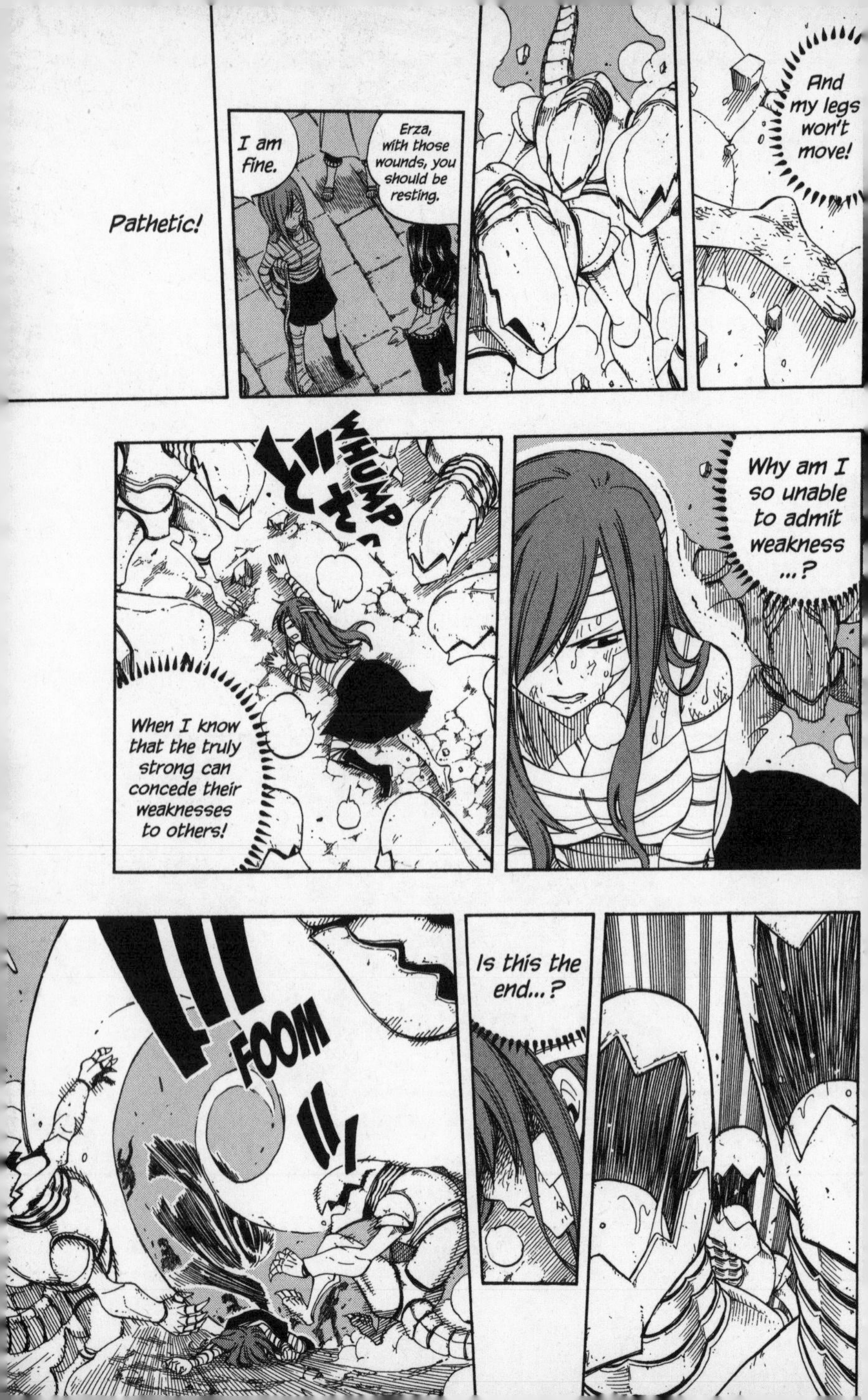
And my legs won't move!
Erza, with those wounds, you should be resting.
I am fine.
Pathetic!
Why am I so unable to admit weakness ...?
WHUMP
When I know that the truly strong can concede their weaknesses to others!
Is this the end...?
FOOM

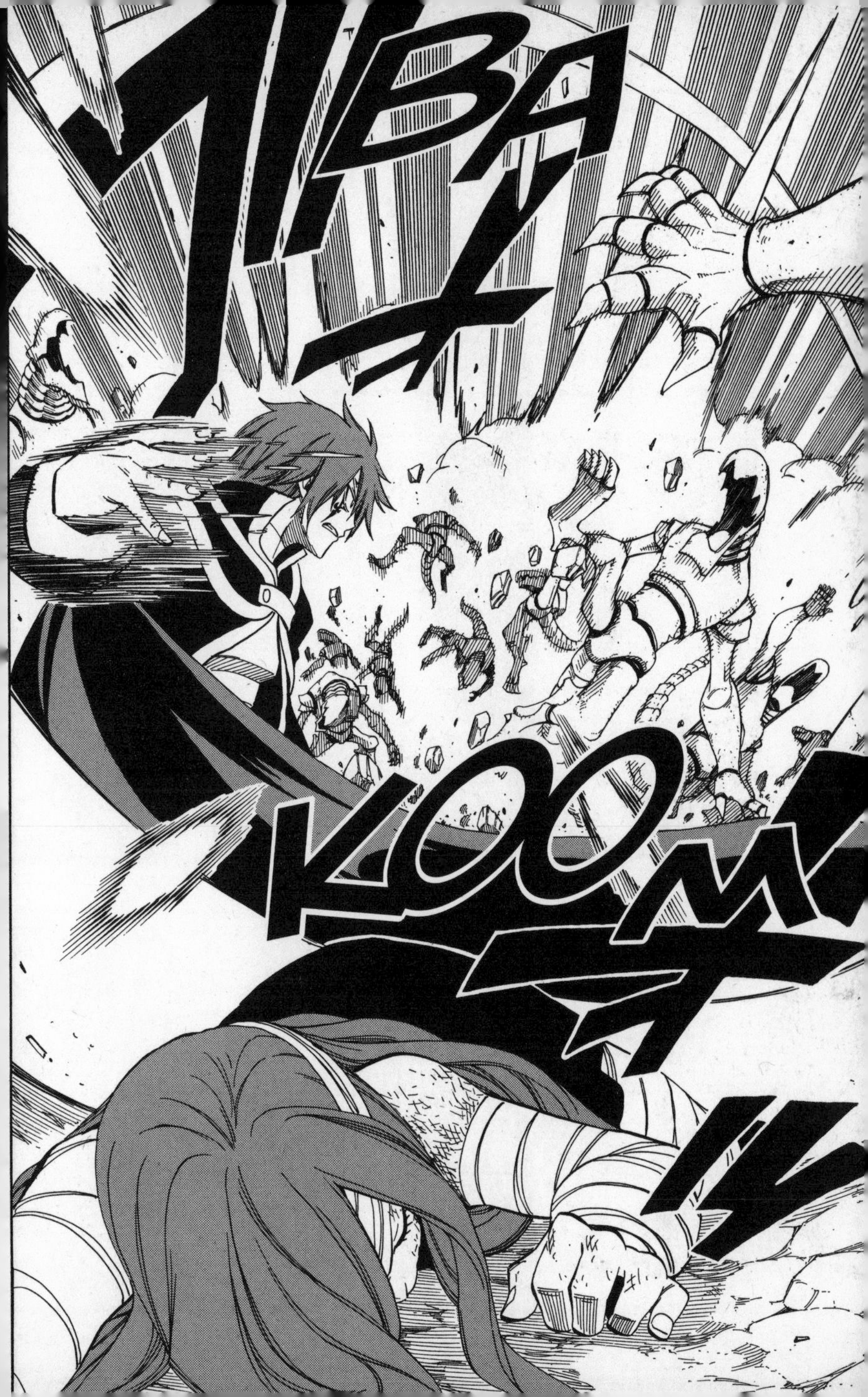

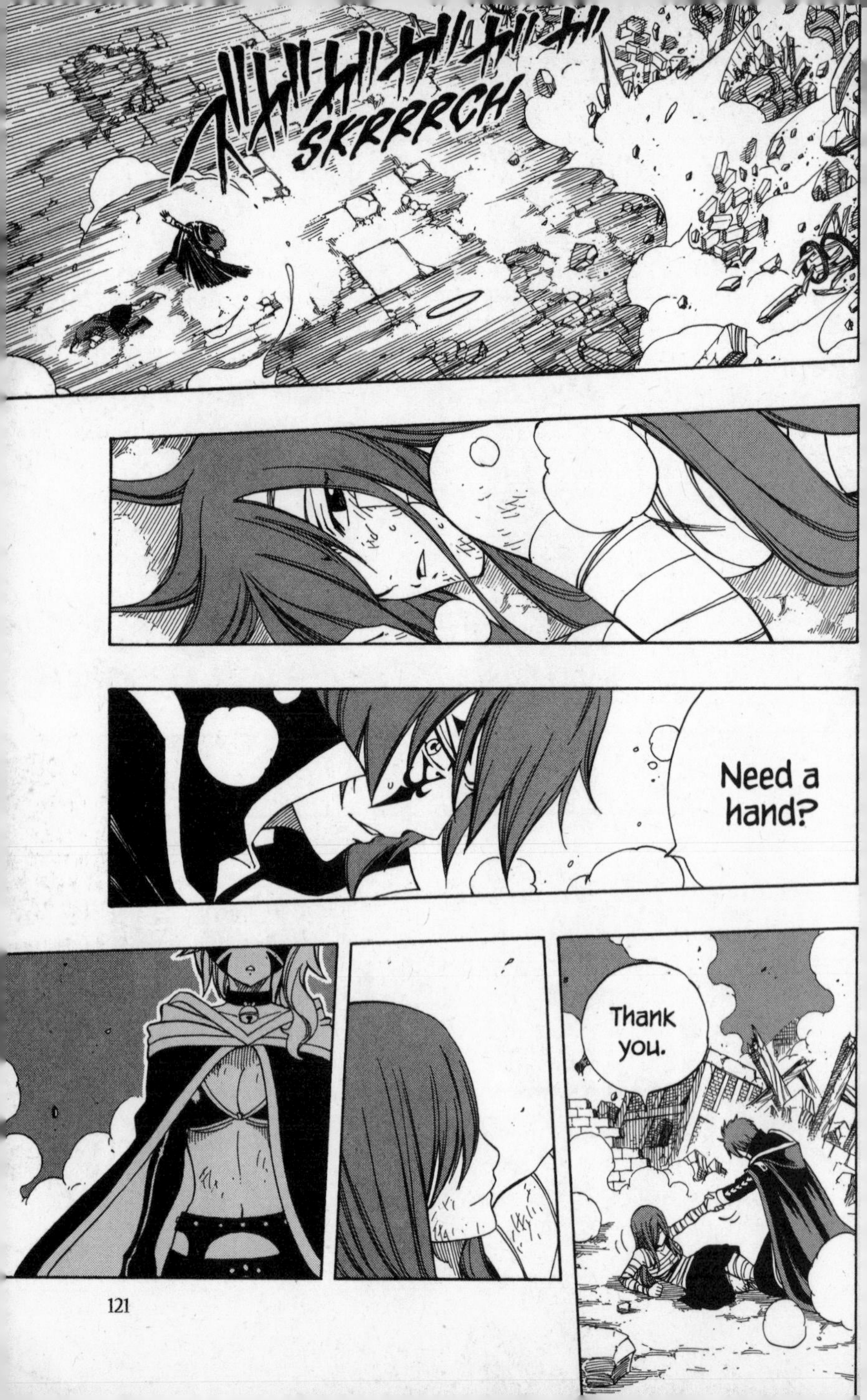
ズザザザザザザザ
SKRRRCH
Need a hand?
Thank you.

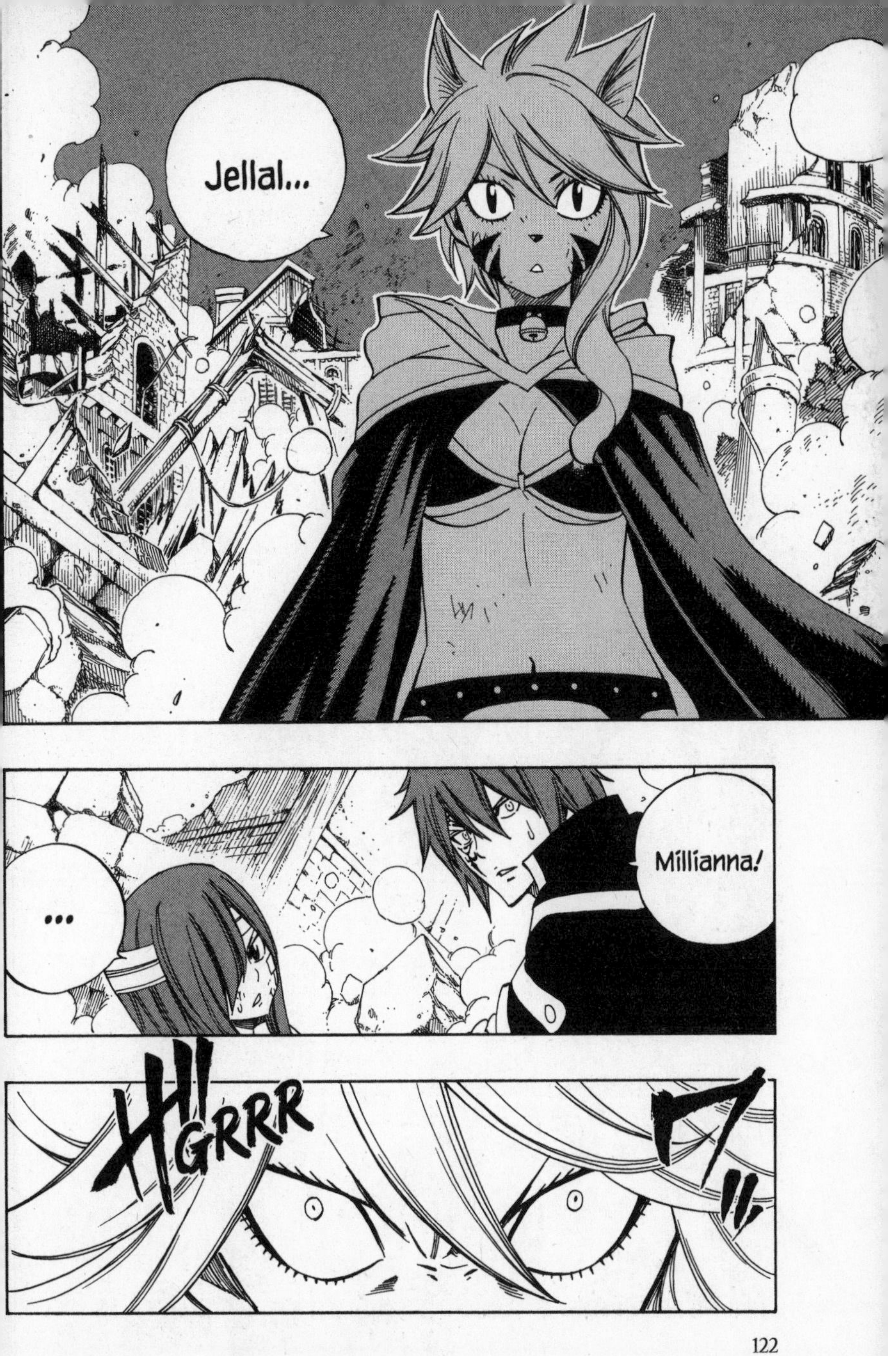
Jellal...
Millianna!
...
GRRR

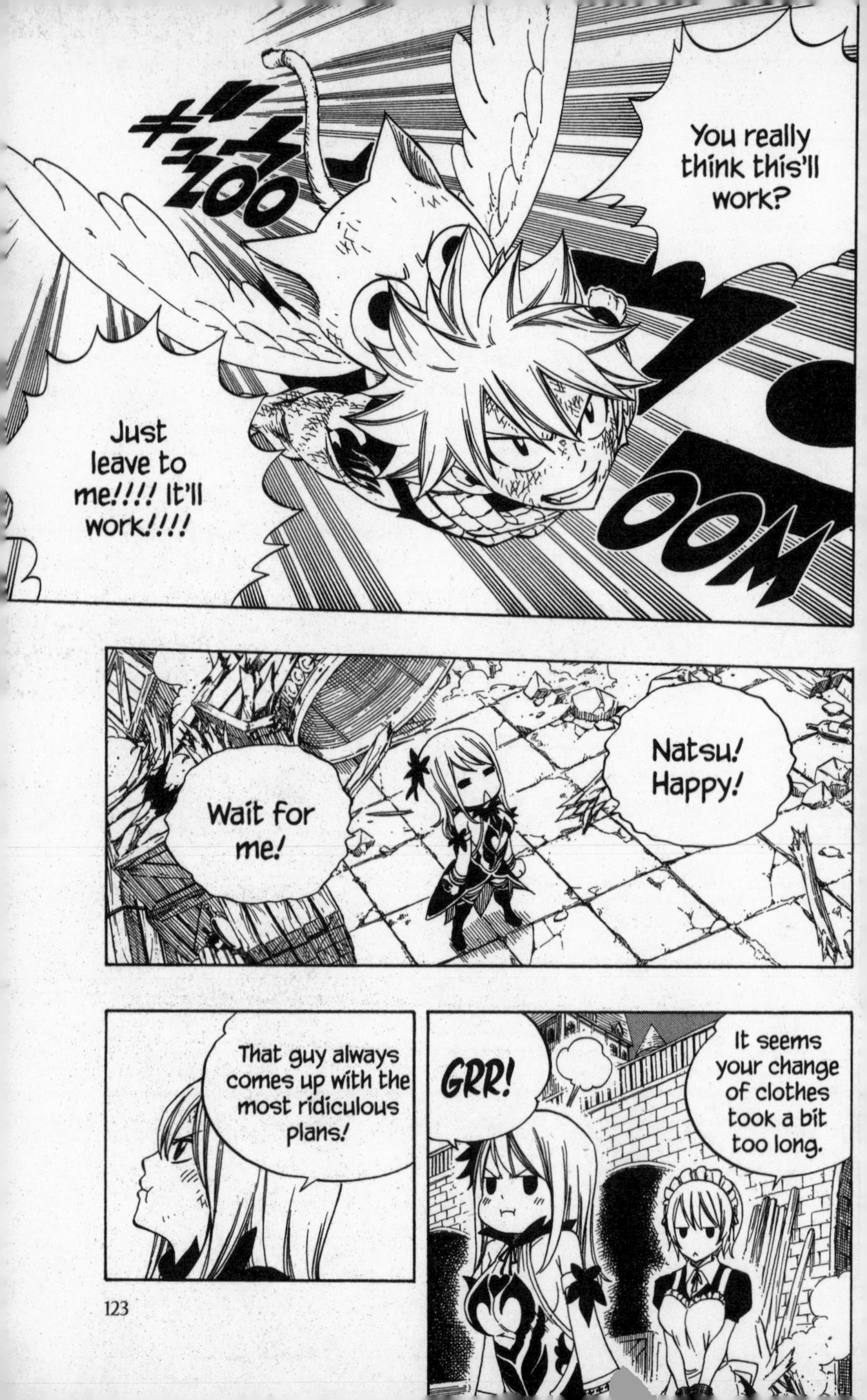
You really think this'll work?
Just leave to me!!!! It'll work!!!!
Natsu! Happy!
Wait for me!
It seems your change of clothes took a bit too long.
GRR!
That guy always comes up with the most ridiculous plans!

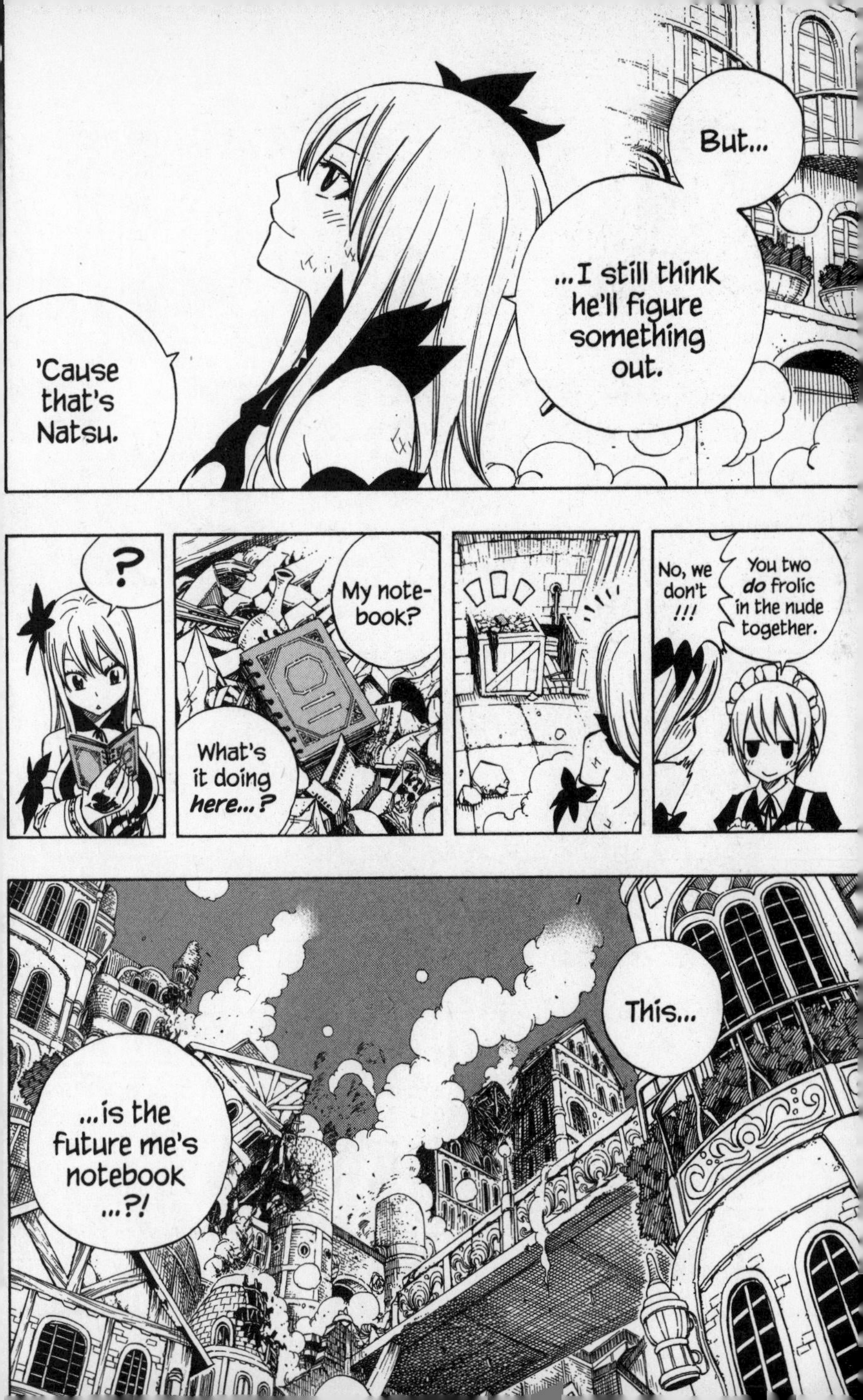
But...
...I still think he'll figure something out.
'Cause that's Natsu.
You two *do* frolic in the nude together.
No, we don't!!!
My note-book?
What's it doing *here...?*
?
This...
...is the future me's notebook ...?!

FAIRY TAIL

フェアリーテイル

Chapter 332: Firebird

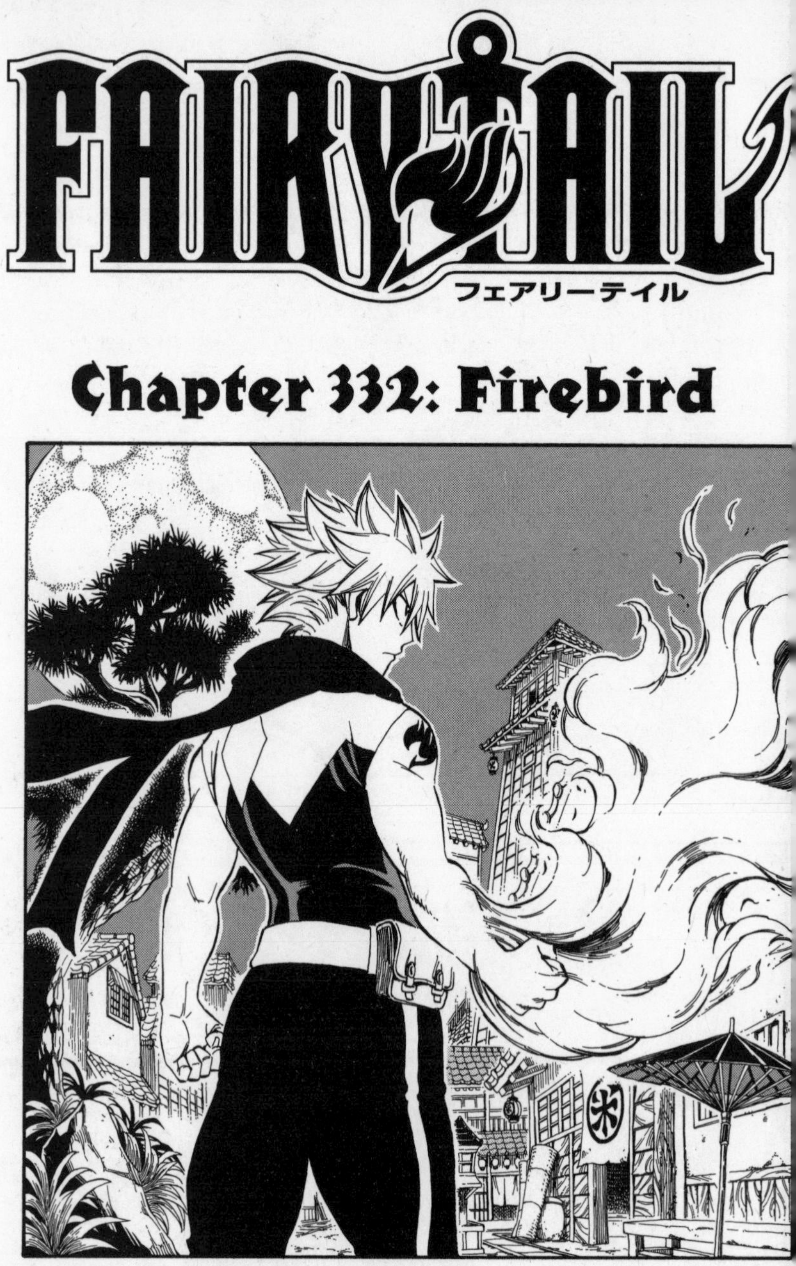

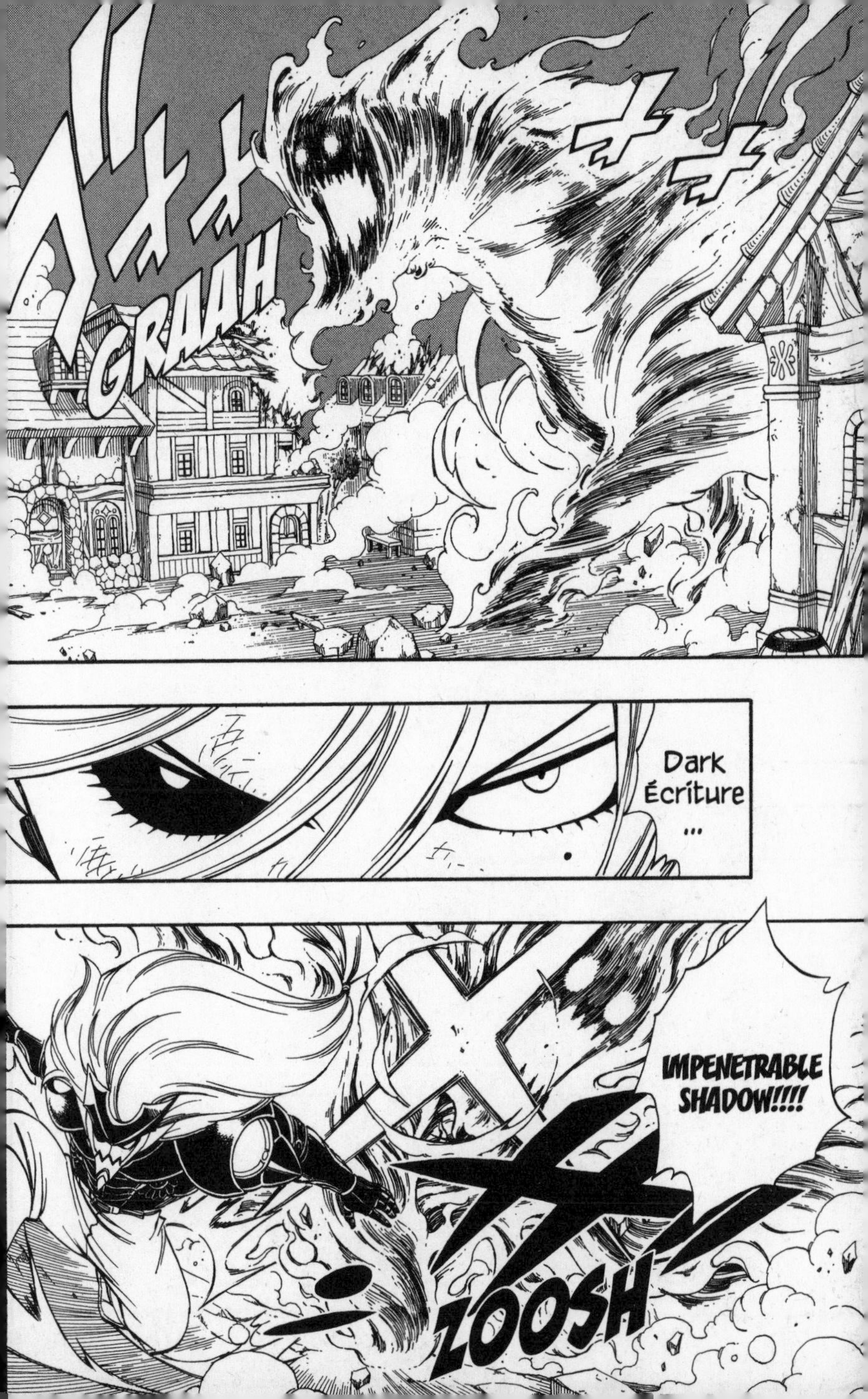
GRAAH
Dark Écriture ...
IMPENETRABLE SHADOW!!!!
ZOOSH

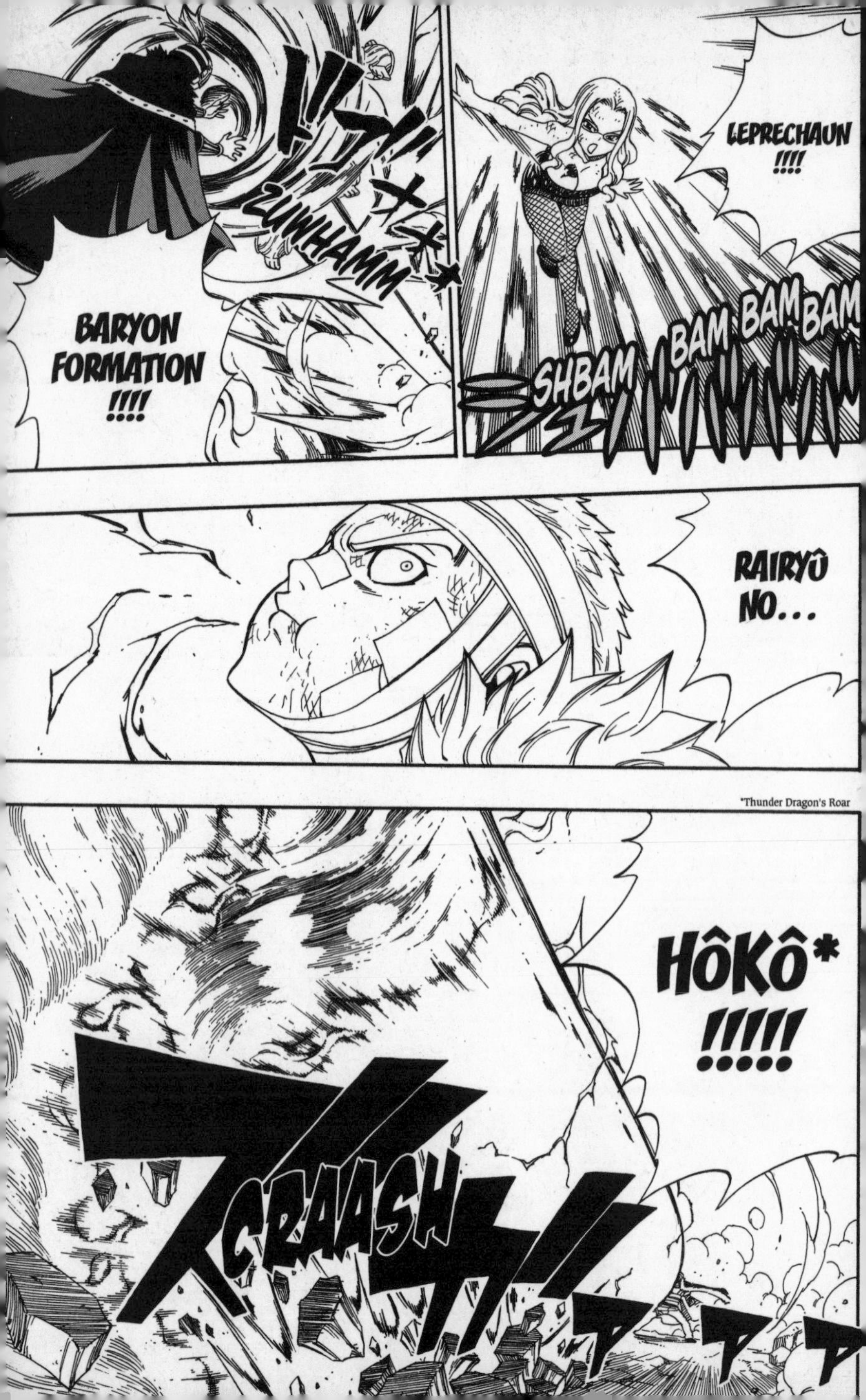
LEPRECHAUN !!!!
SHBAM BAM BAM BAM
BARYON FORMATION !!!!
ZUWHAMM
RAIRYÛ NO...
*Thunder Dragon's Roar
HÔKÔ* !!!!!
CRAASH

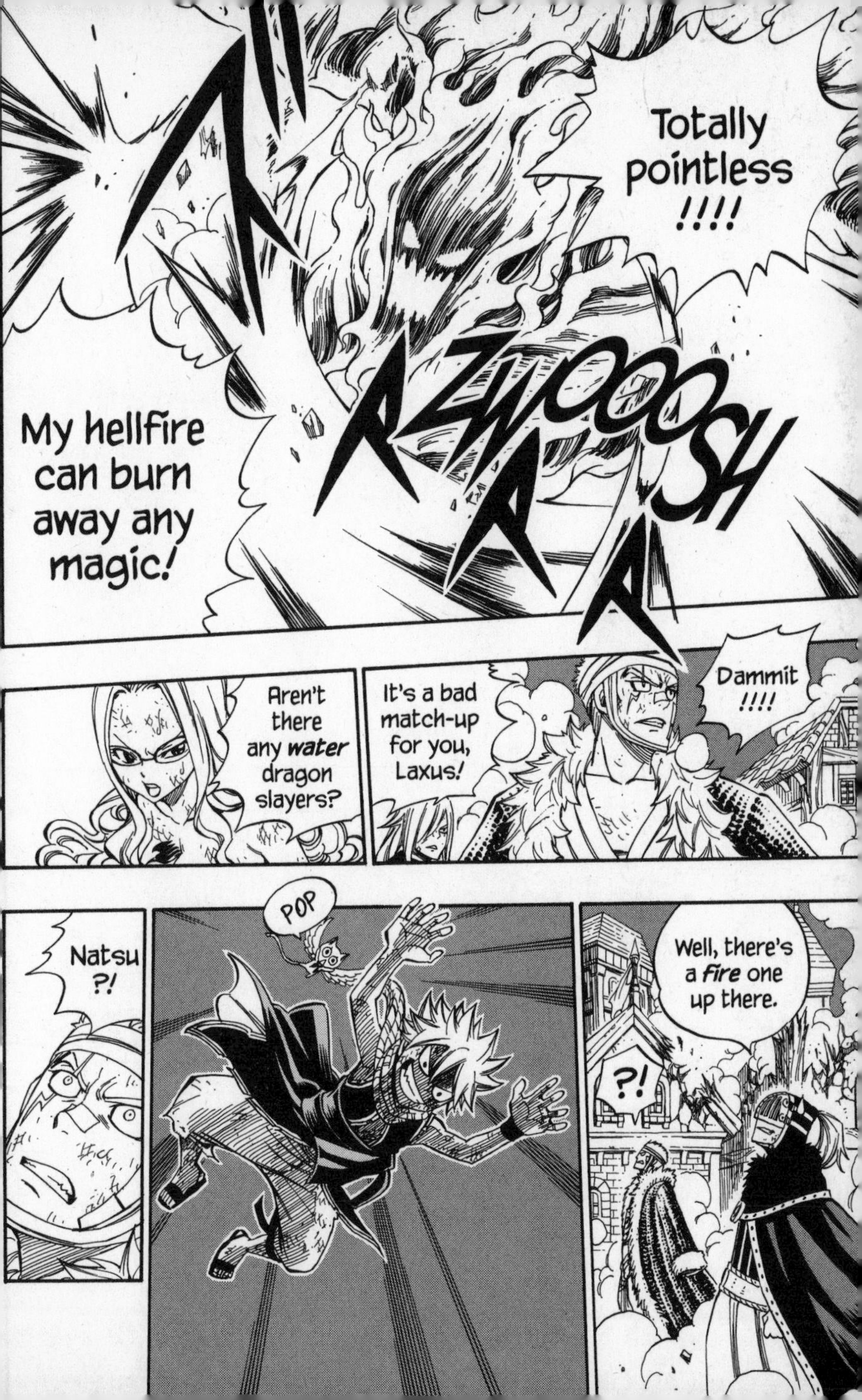
Totally pointless!!!!
A!!
AZWOOOSH
My hellfire can burn away any magic!
Dammit!!!!
It's a bad match-up for you, Laxus!
Aren't there any *water* dragon slayers?
Well, there's a *fire* one up there.
?!
POP
Natsu?!

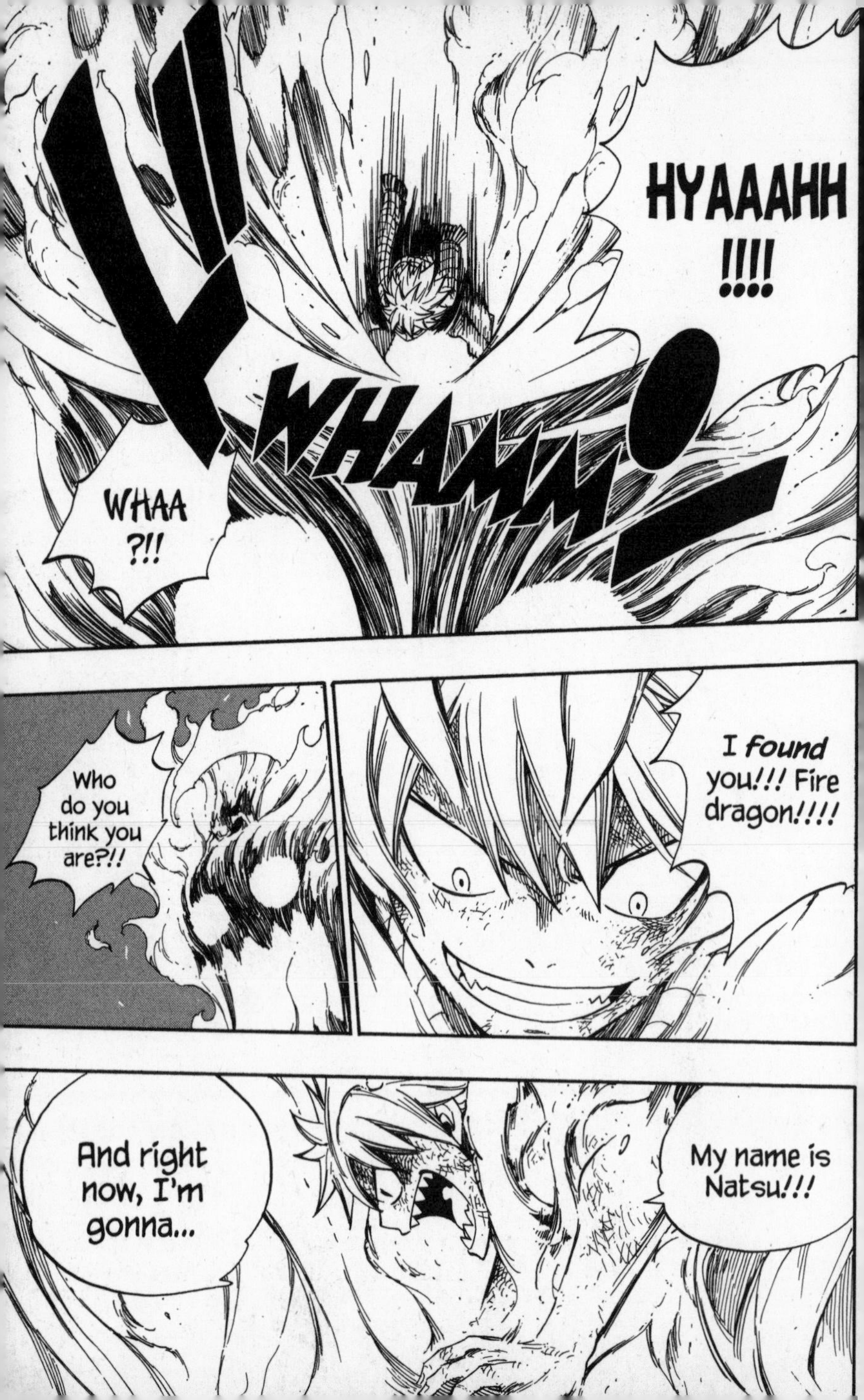
HYAAAHH!!!!
WHAMM
WHAA?!!
I *found* you!!! Fire dragon!!!!
Who do you think you are?!!
My name is Natsu!!!
And right now, I'm gonna...

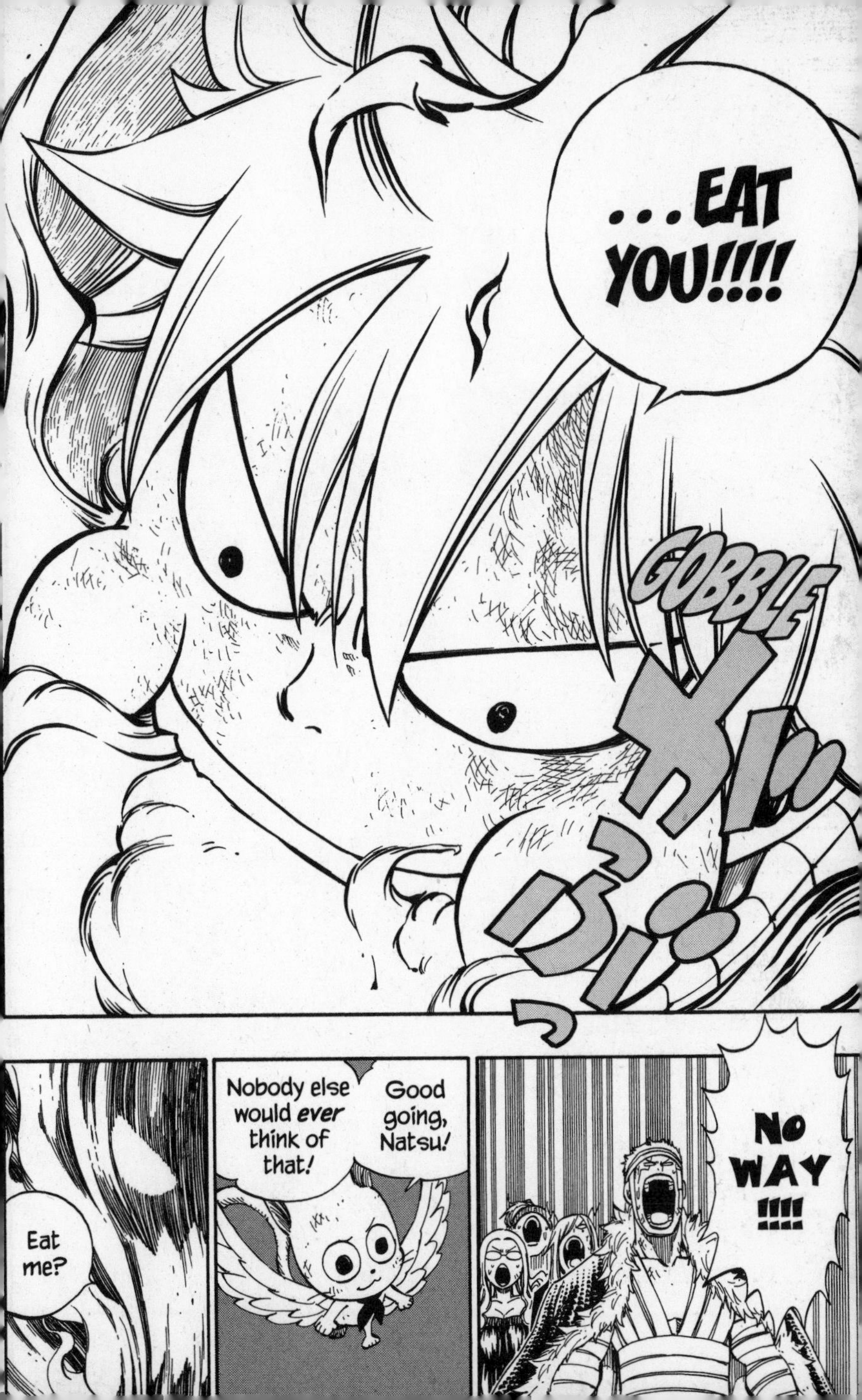
...EAT YOU!!!!
GOBBLE
NO WAY!!!!
Good going, Natsu!
Nobody else would *ever* think of that!
Eat me?

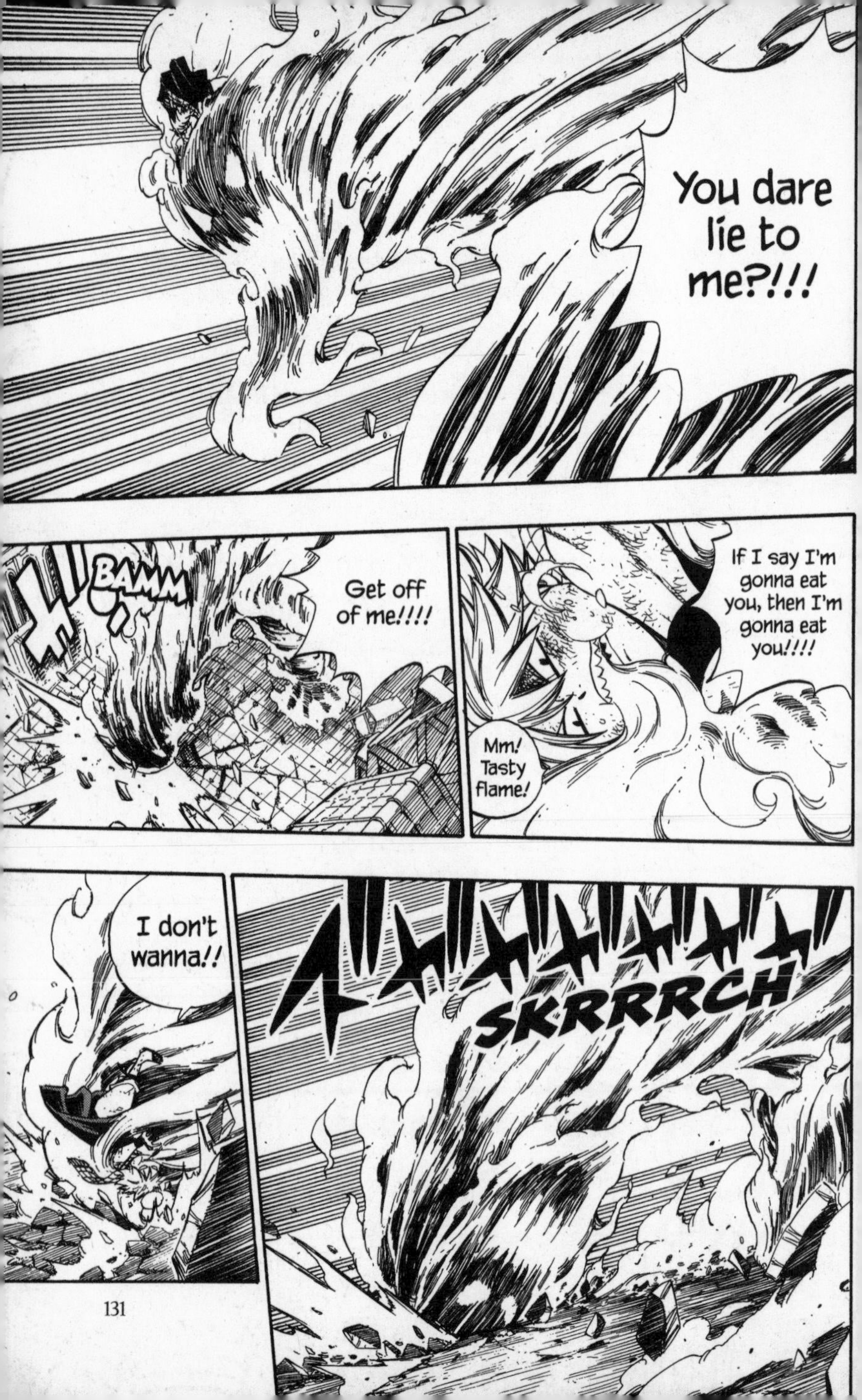
You dare lie to me?!!!
If I say I'm gonna eat you, then I'm gonna eat you!!!!
Mm! Tasty flame!
BAMM
Get off of me!!!!
SKRRRCH
I don't wanna!!

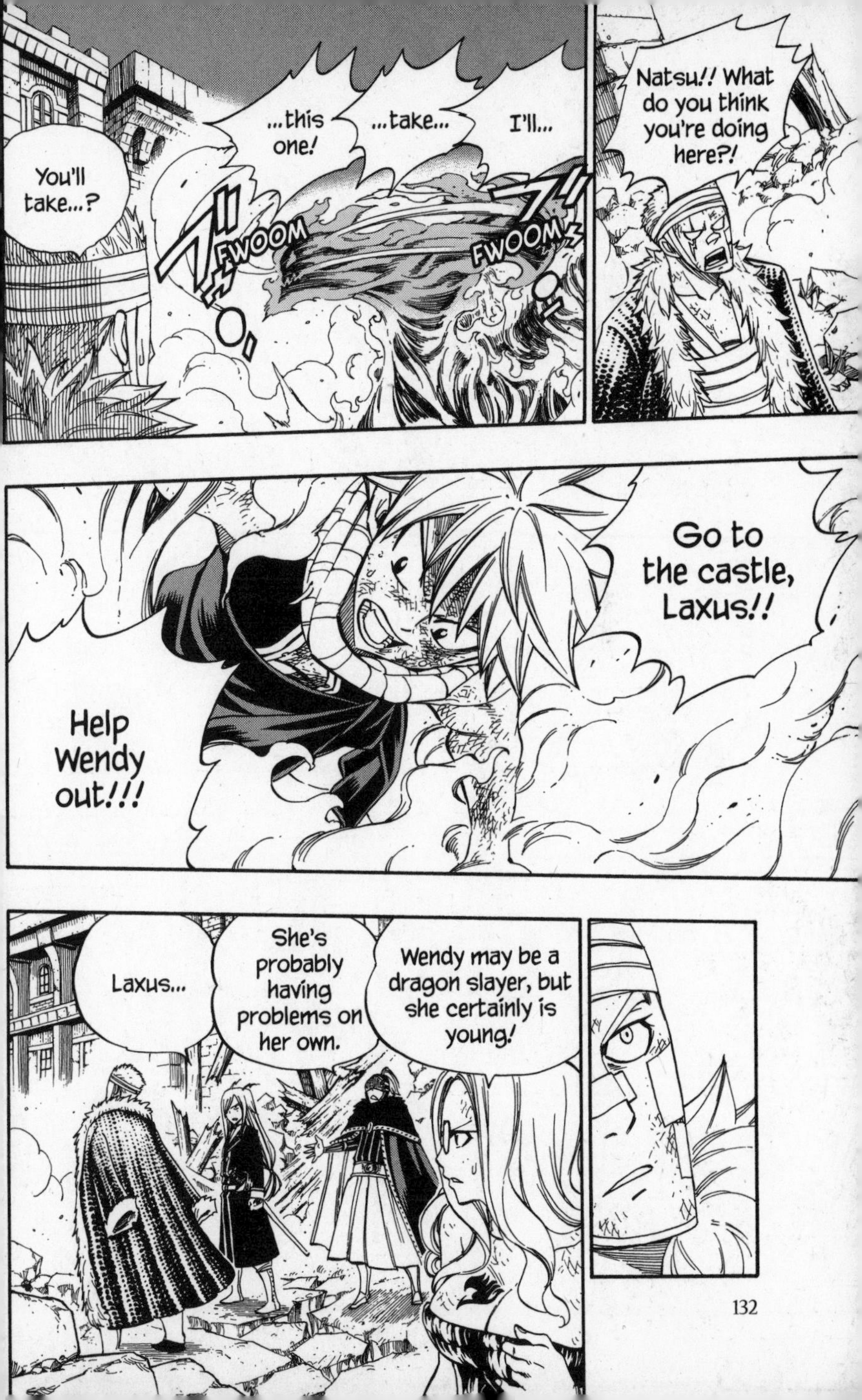
Natsu!! What do you think you're doing here?!
I'll...
...take...
...this one!
FWOOM
FWOOM
You'll take...?
Go to the castle, Laxus!!
Help Wendy out!!!
Wendy may be a dragon slayer, but she certainly is young!
She's probably having problems on her own.
Laxus...

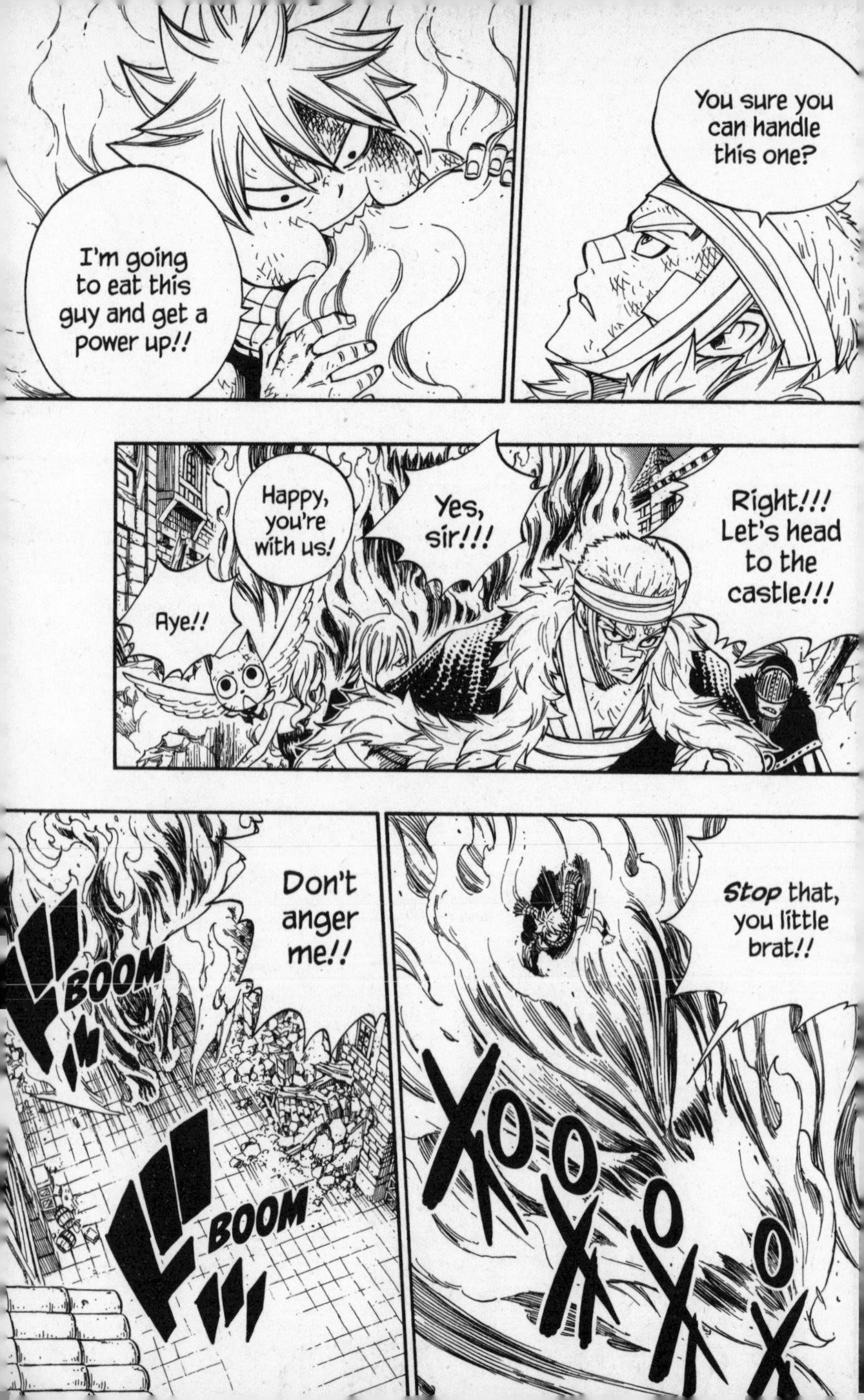
You sure you can handle this one?
I'm going to eat this guy and get a power up!!
Right!!! Let's head to the castle!!!
Yes, sir!!!
Happy, you're with us!
Aye!!
Stop that, you little brat!!
XOOOOX
Don't anger me!!
BOOM
BOOM

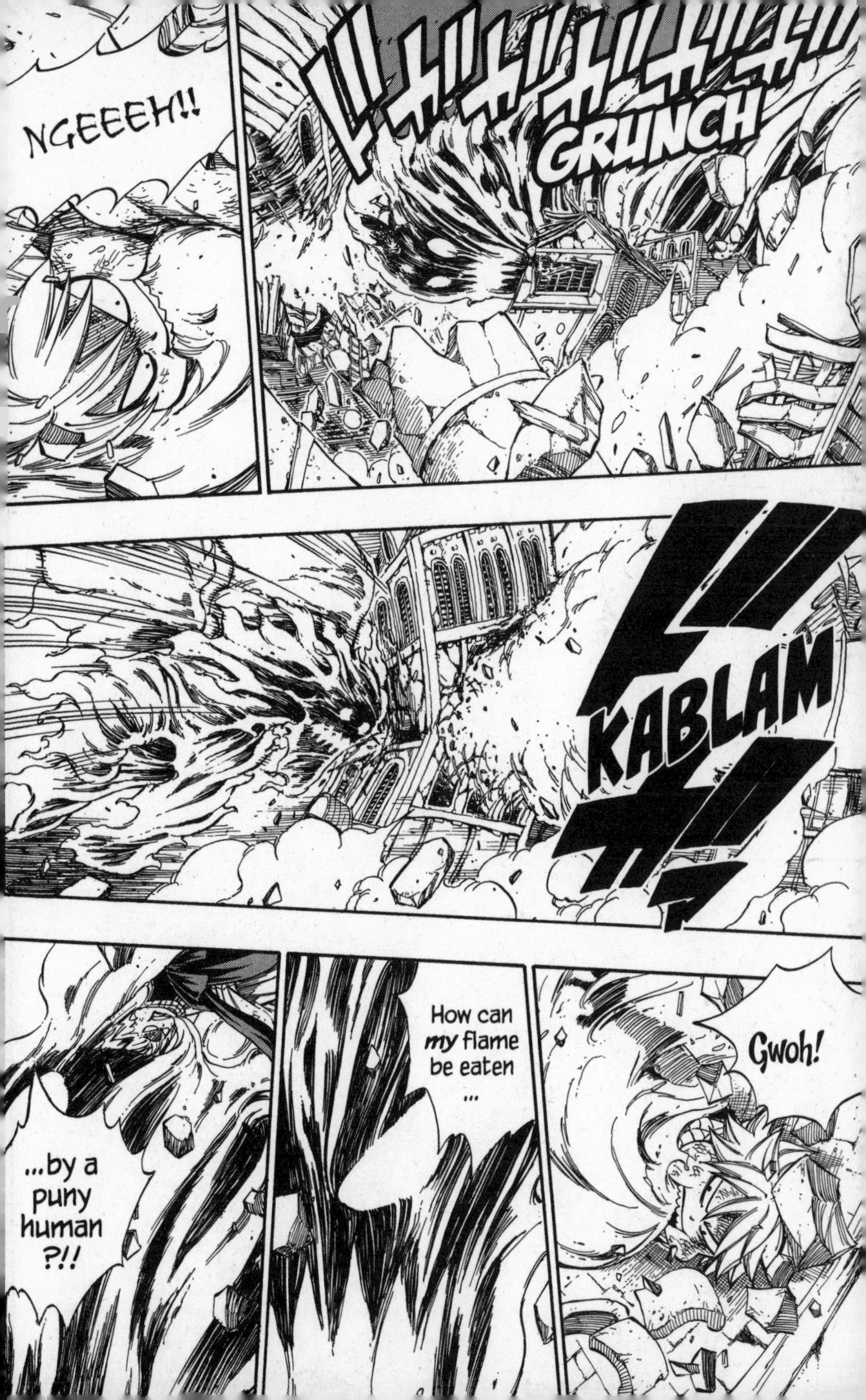
GRUNCH
NGEEEH!!
KABLAM
Gwoh!
How can *my* flame be eaten ...
...by a puny human ?!!

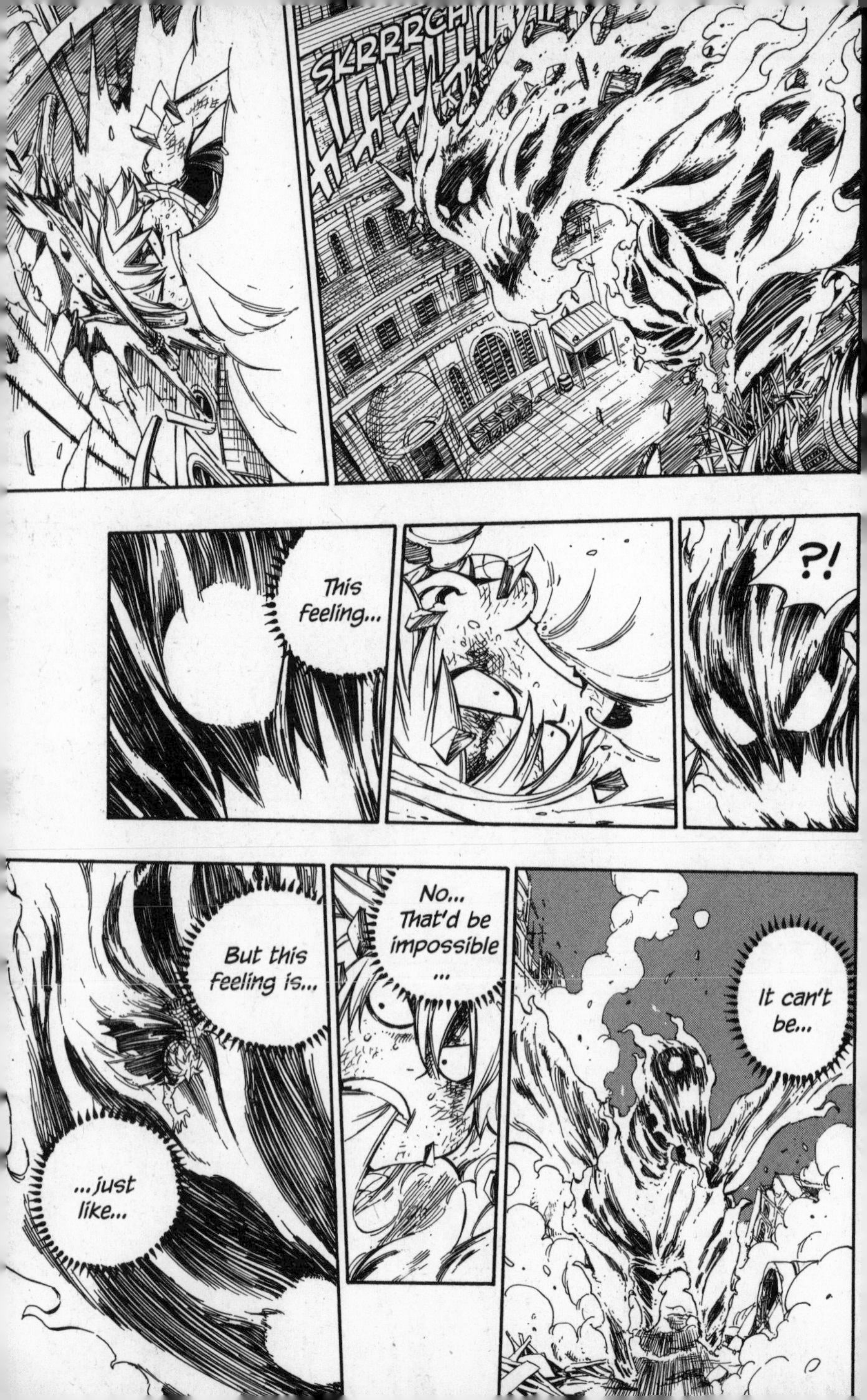
SKRRRCH
?!
This feeling...
It can't be...
No... That'd be impossible ...
But this feeling is...
...just like...

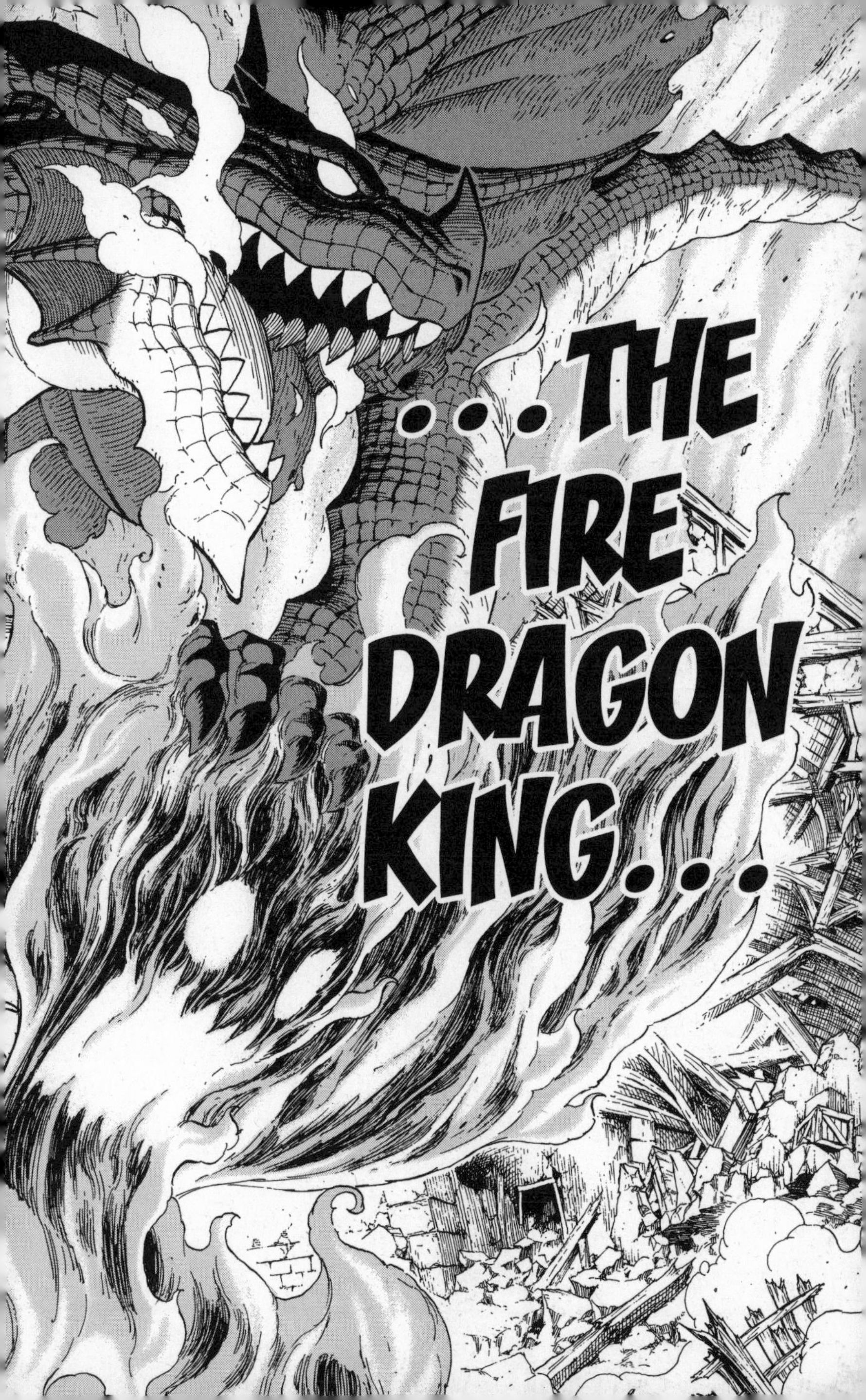
...THE FIRE DRAGON KING...

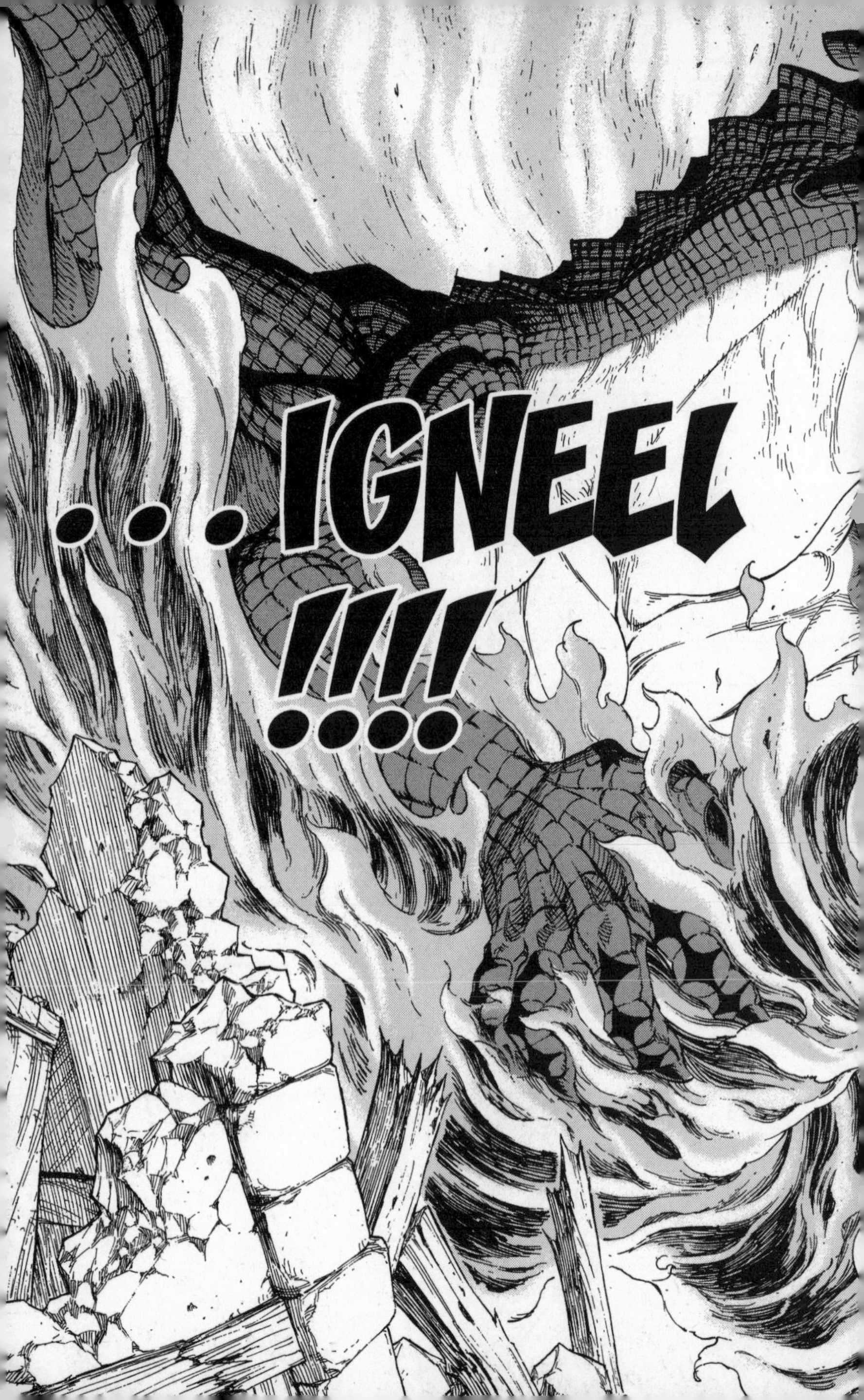

...IGNEEL
!!!
....

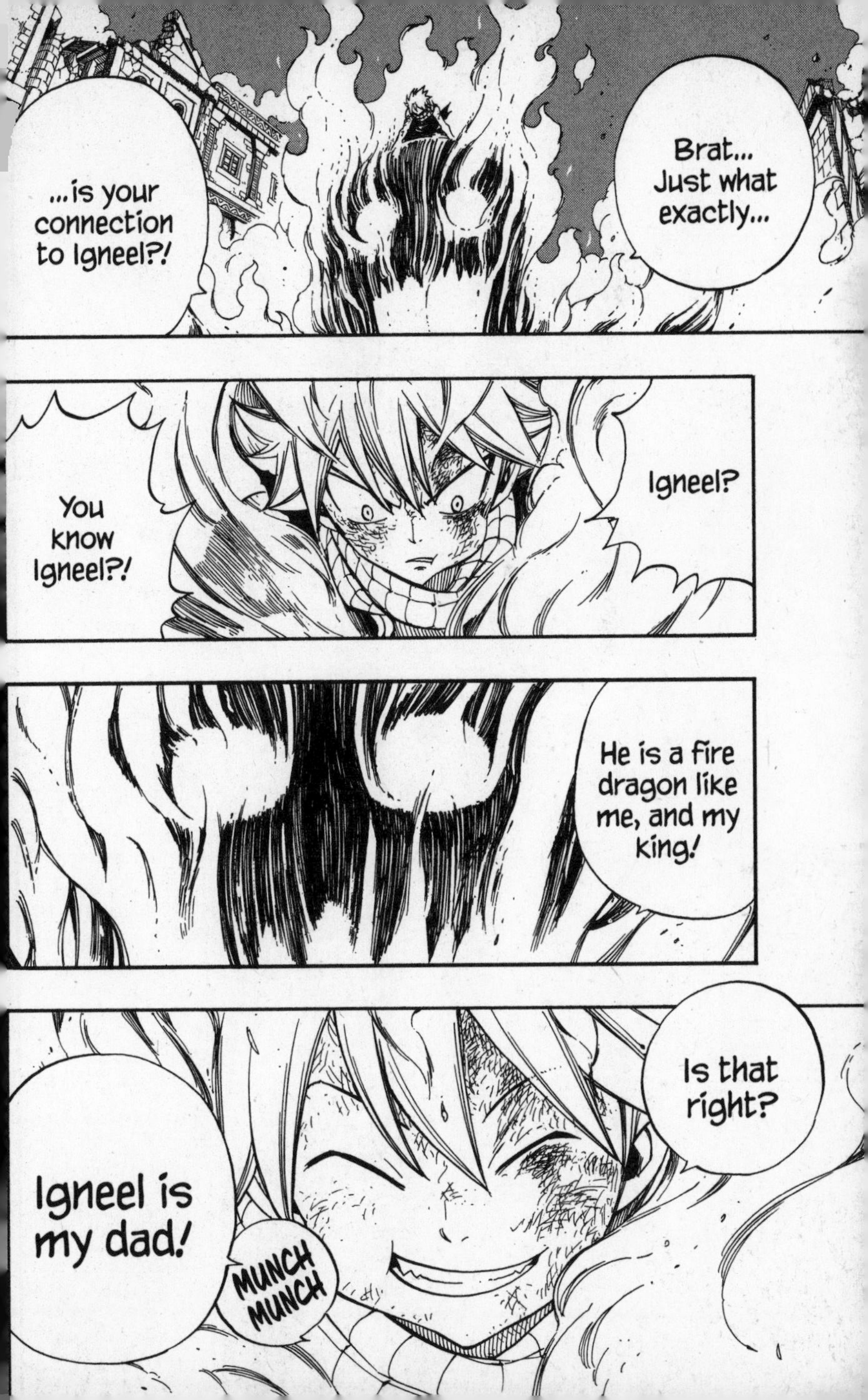
Brat... Just what exactly...
...is your connection to Igneel?!
Igneel?
You know Igneel?!
He is a fire dragon like me, and my king!
Is that right?
Igneel is my dad!
MUNCH MUNCH

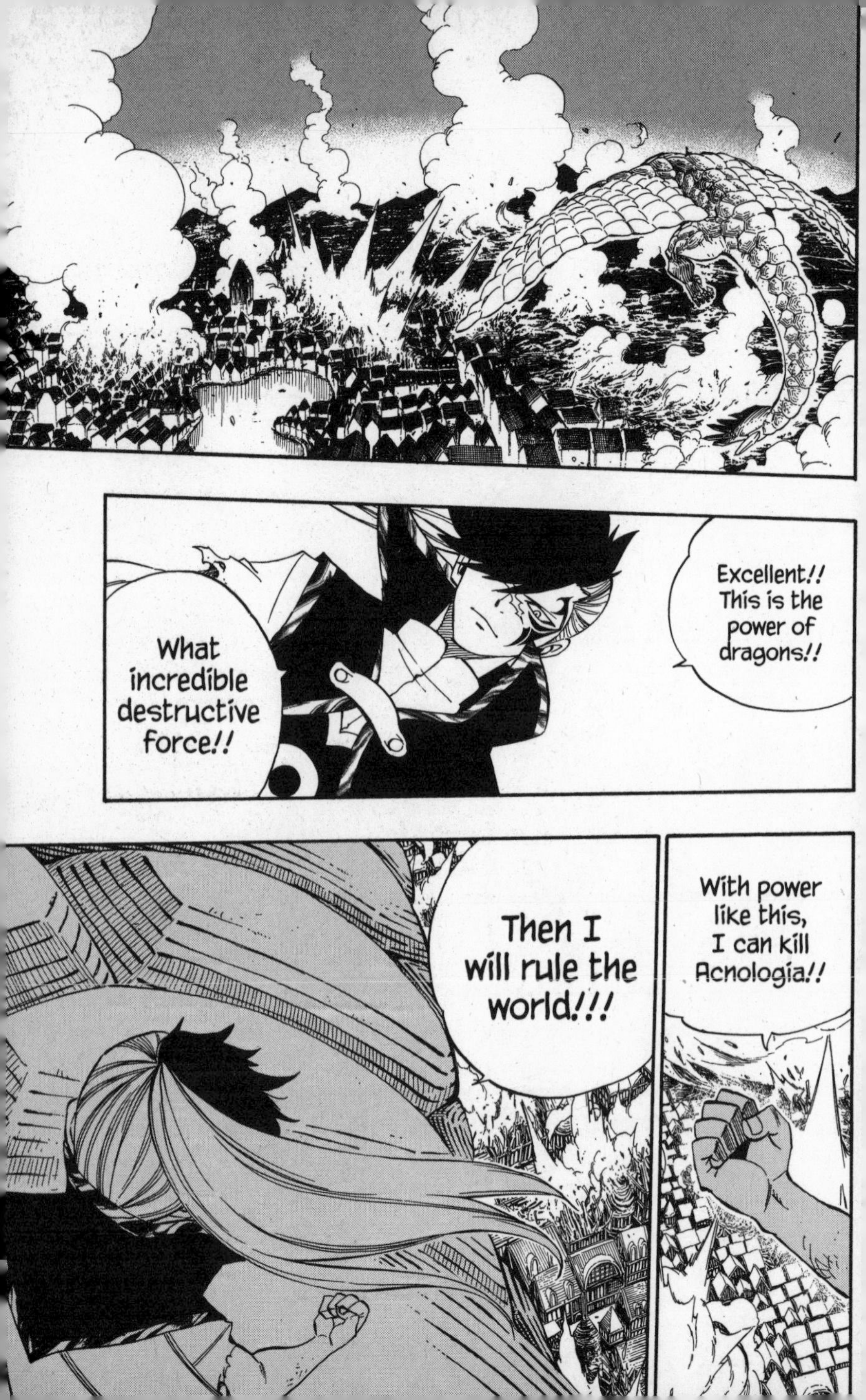
Excellent!! This is the power of dragons!!
What incredible destructive force!!
With power like this, I can kill Acnologia!!
Then I will rule the world!!!

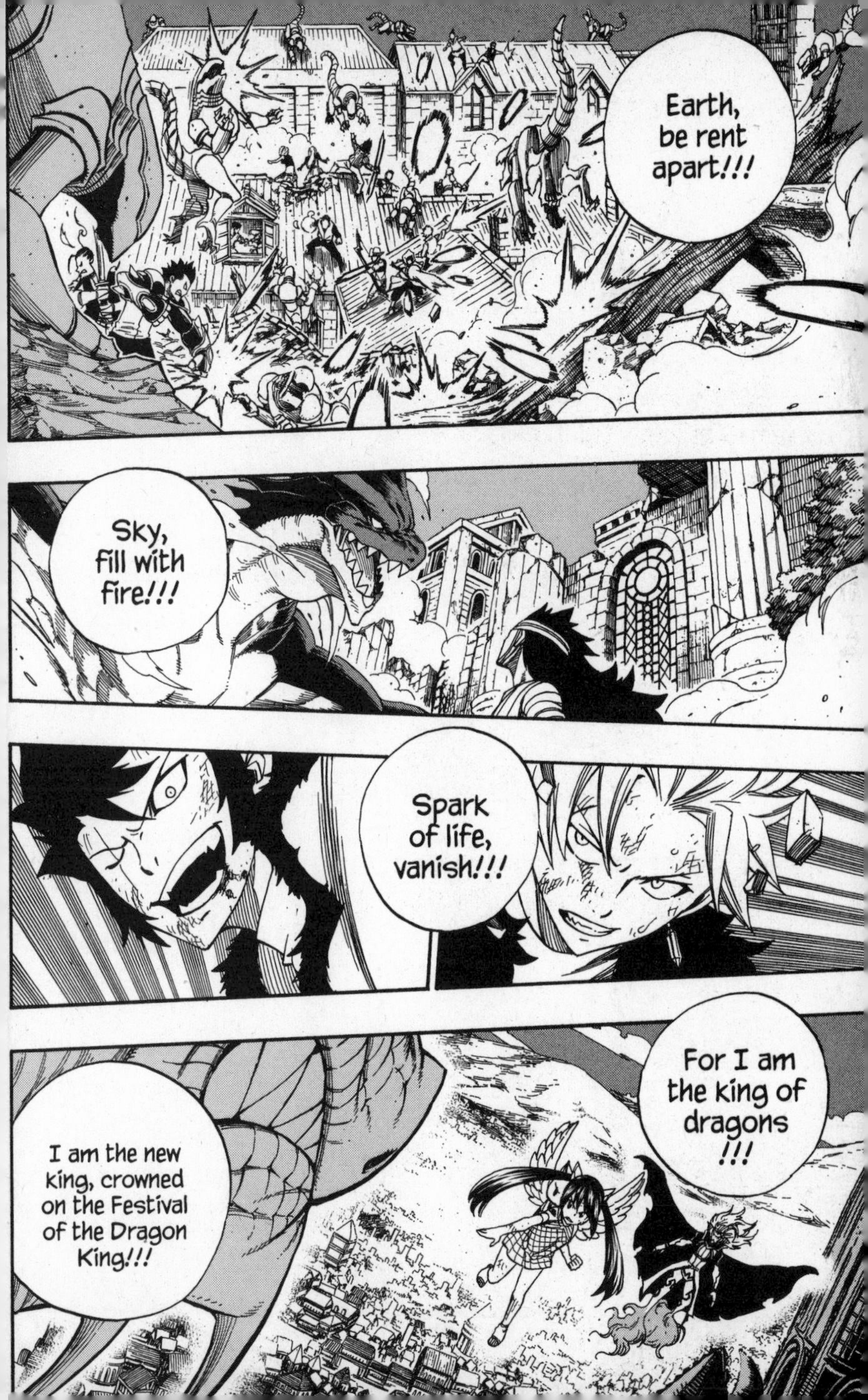
Earth, be rent apart!!!
Sky, fill with fire!!!
Spark of life, vanish!!!
For I am the king of dragons !!!
I am the new king, crowned on the Festival of the Dragon King!!!

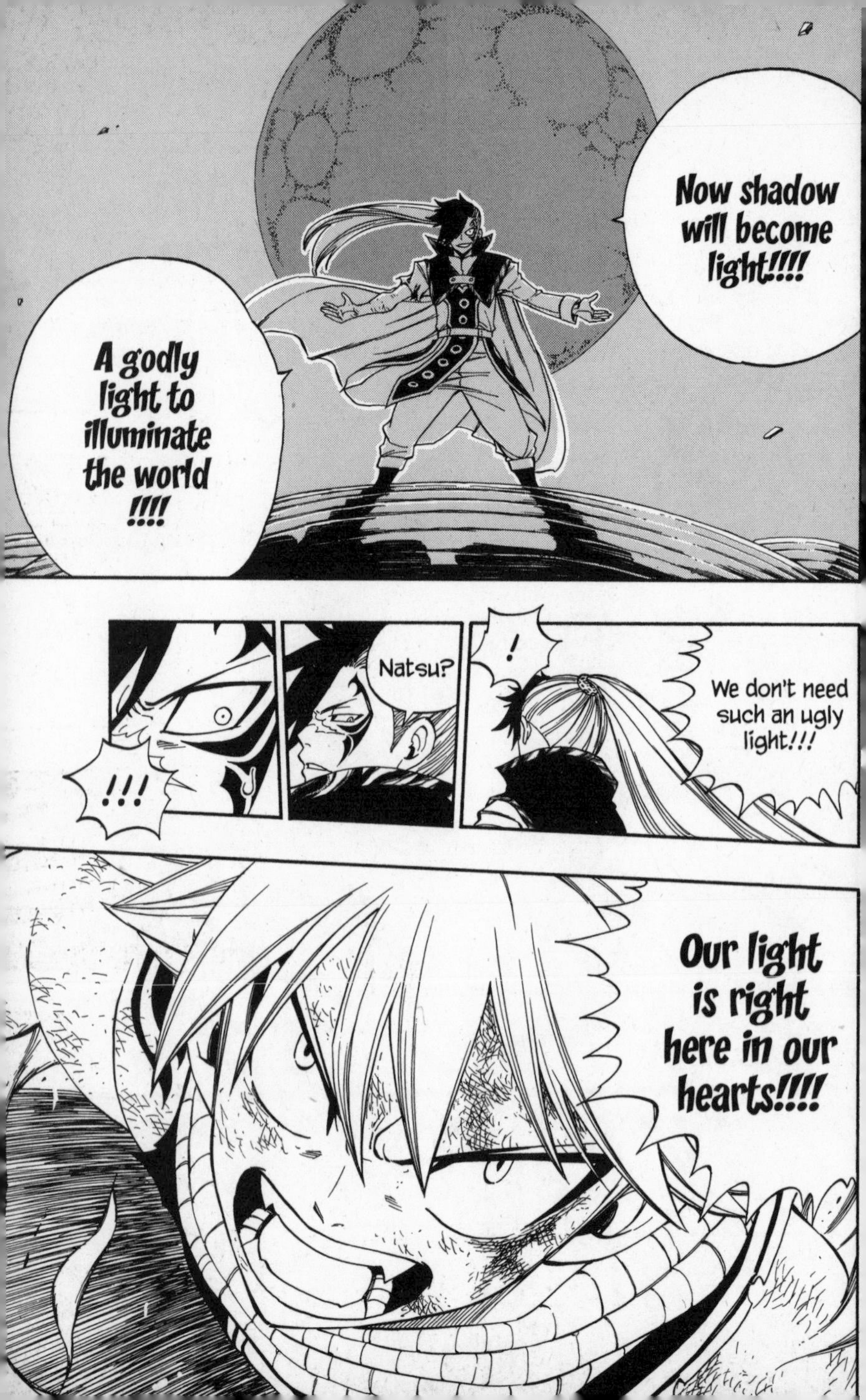
Now shadow will become light!!!!
A godly light to illuminate the world !!!!
!
We don't need such an ugly light!!!
Natsu?
!!!
Our light is right here in our hearts!!!!

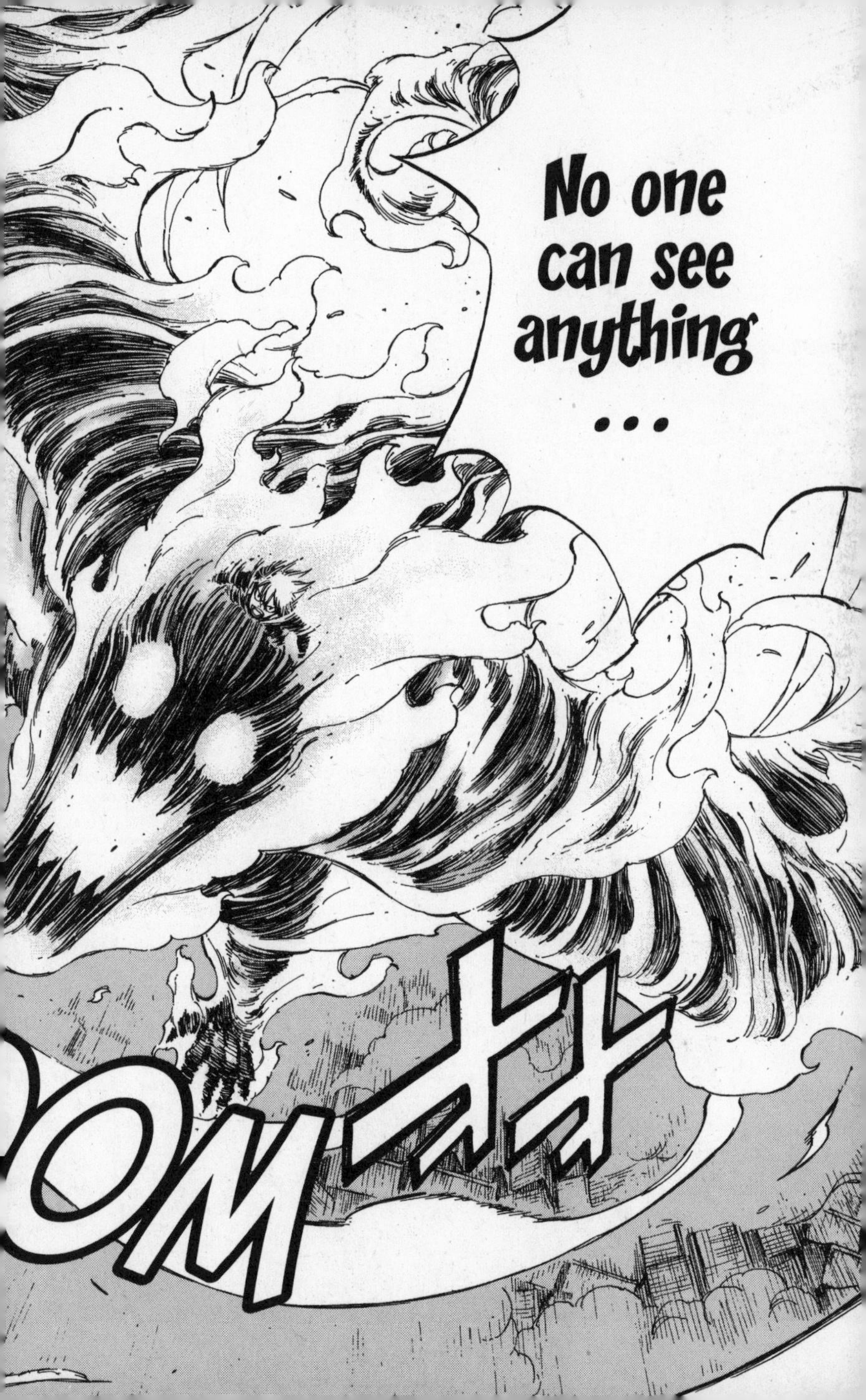
No one can see anything ...
OOM

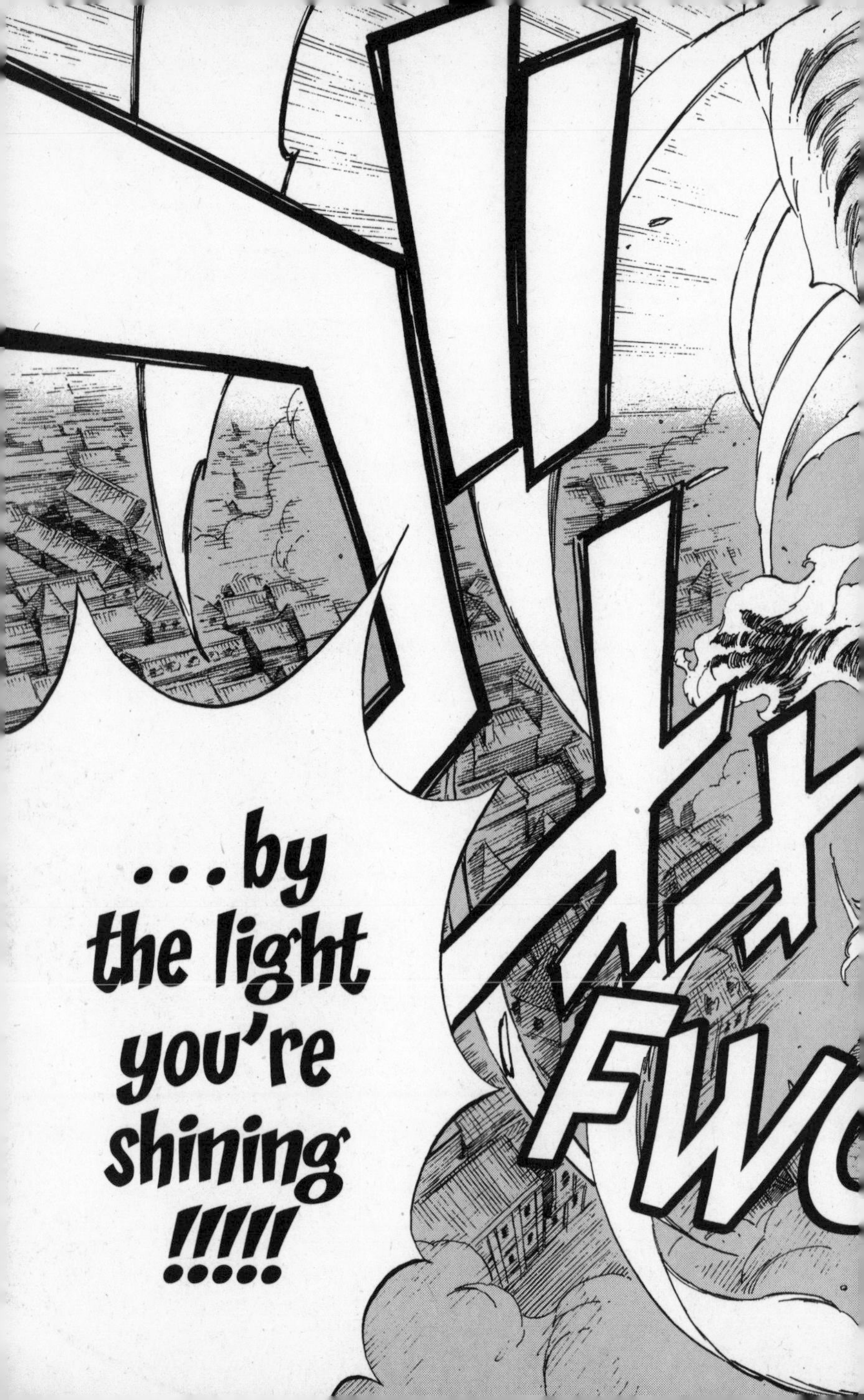
...by the light you're shining!!!!!
FWO

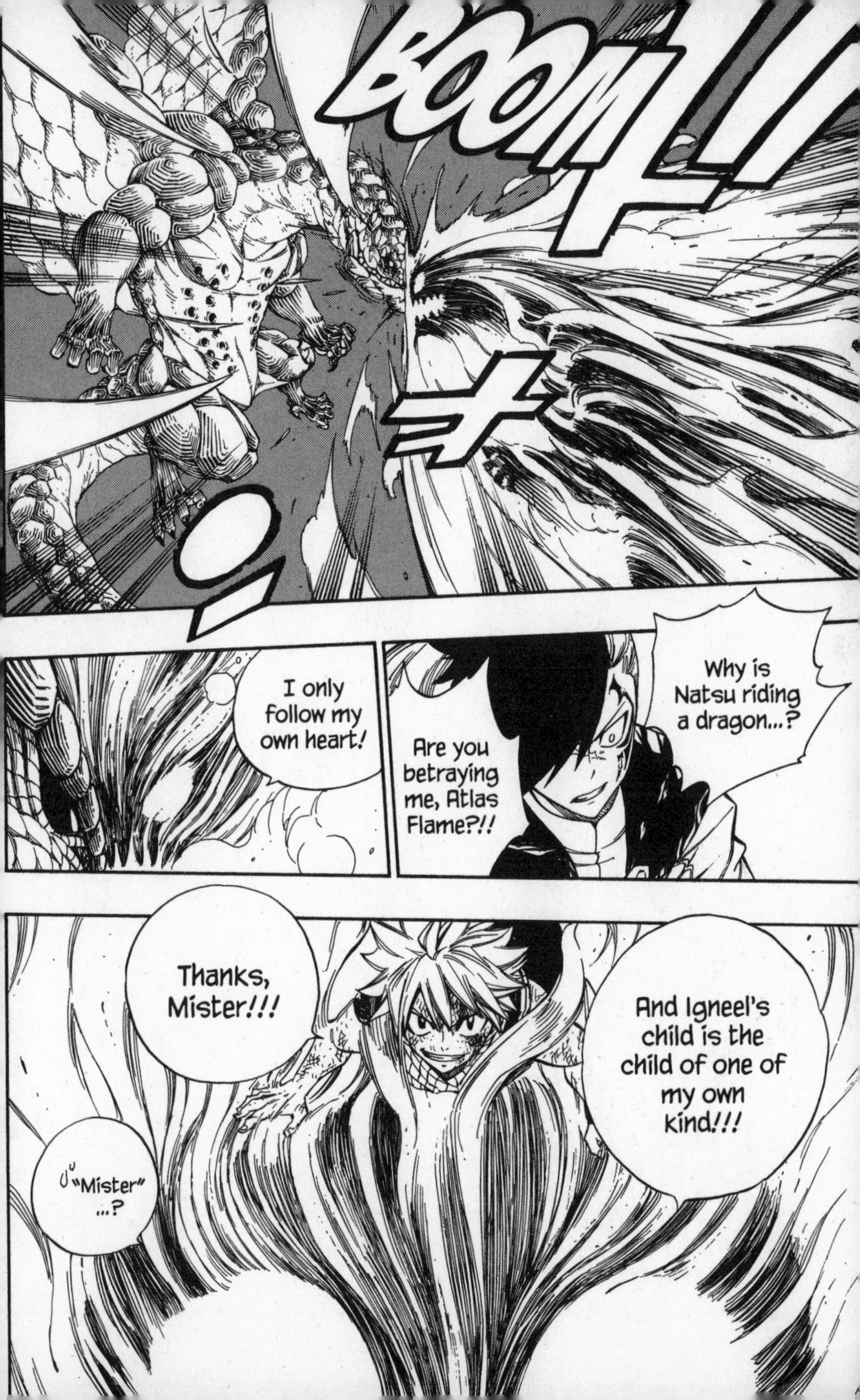
BOOM!!
Why is Natsu riding a dragon...?
Are you betraying me, Atlas Flame?!!
I only follow my own heart!
And Igneel's child is the child of one of my own kind!!!
Thanks, Mister!!!
"Mister" ...?

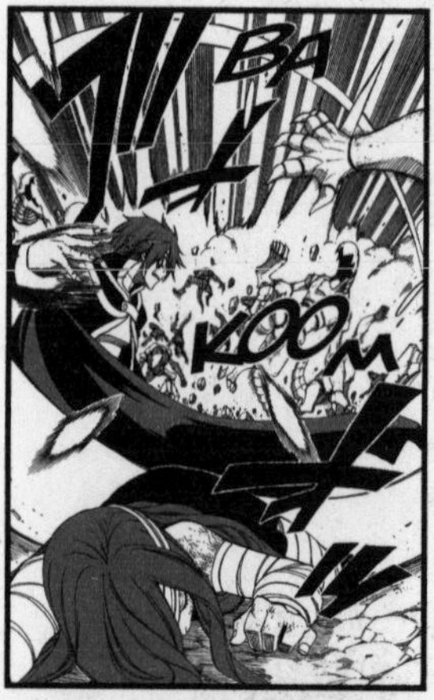
BA
KOOM

FAIRY TAIL

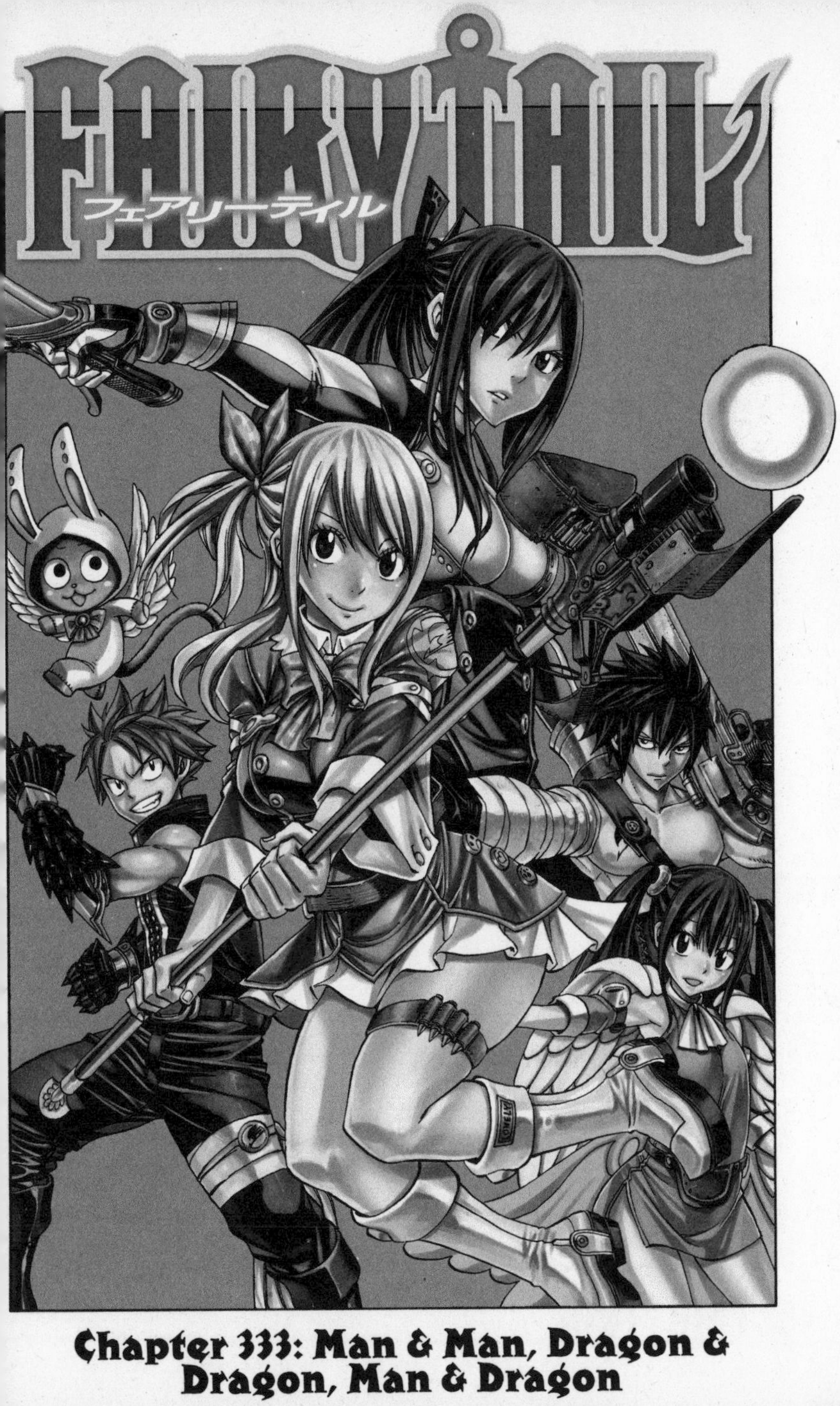
FAIRY TAIL
フェアリーテイル

Chapter 333: Man & Man, Dragon & Dragon, Man & Dragon

FAIRY TAIL Grand Magic Games Arc Timeline

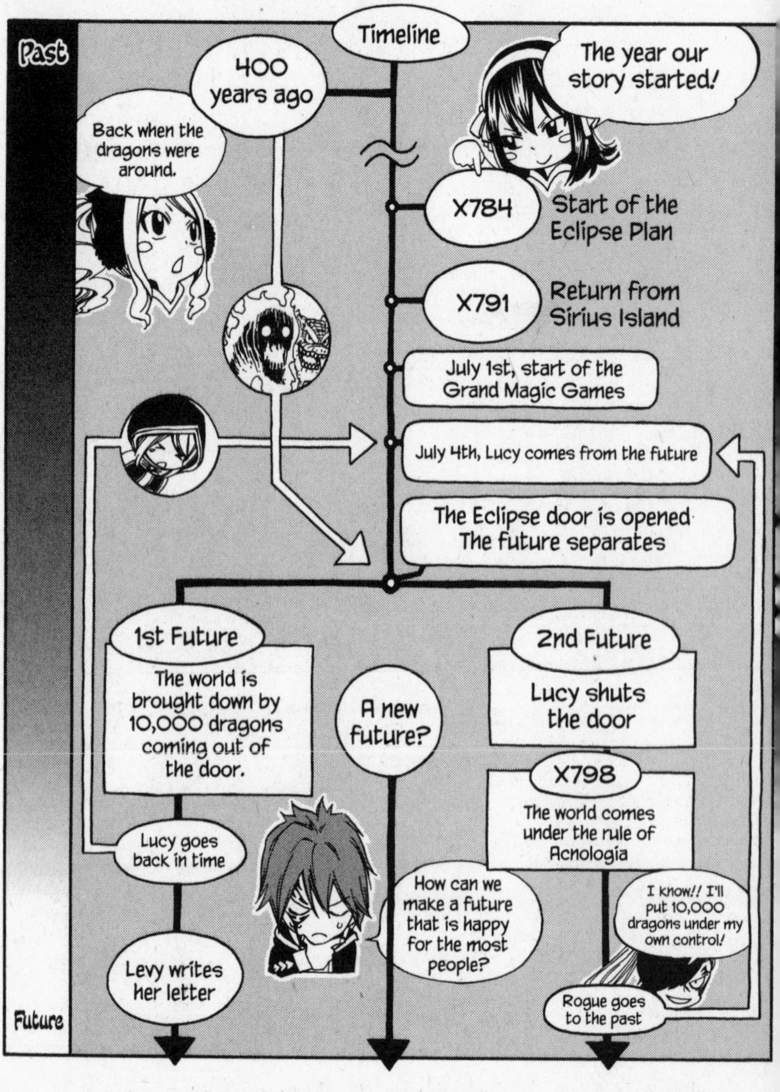
Past
Timeline
The year our story started!
400 years ago
Back when the dragons were around.
X784
Start of the Eclipse Plan
X791
Return from Sirius Island
July 1st, start of the Grand Magic Games
July 4th, Lucy comes from the future
The Eclipse door is opened
The future separates
1st Future
The world is brought down by 10,000 dragons coming out of the door.
A new future?
2nd Future
Lucy shuts the door
X798
The world comes under the rule of Acnologia
Lucy goes back in time
How can we make a future that is happy for the most people?
I know!! I'll put 10,000 dragons under my own control!
Levy writes her letter
Rogue goes to the past
Future

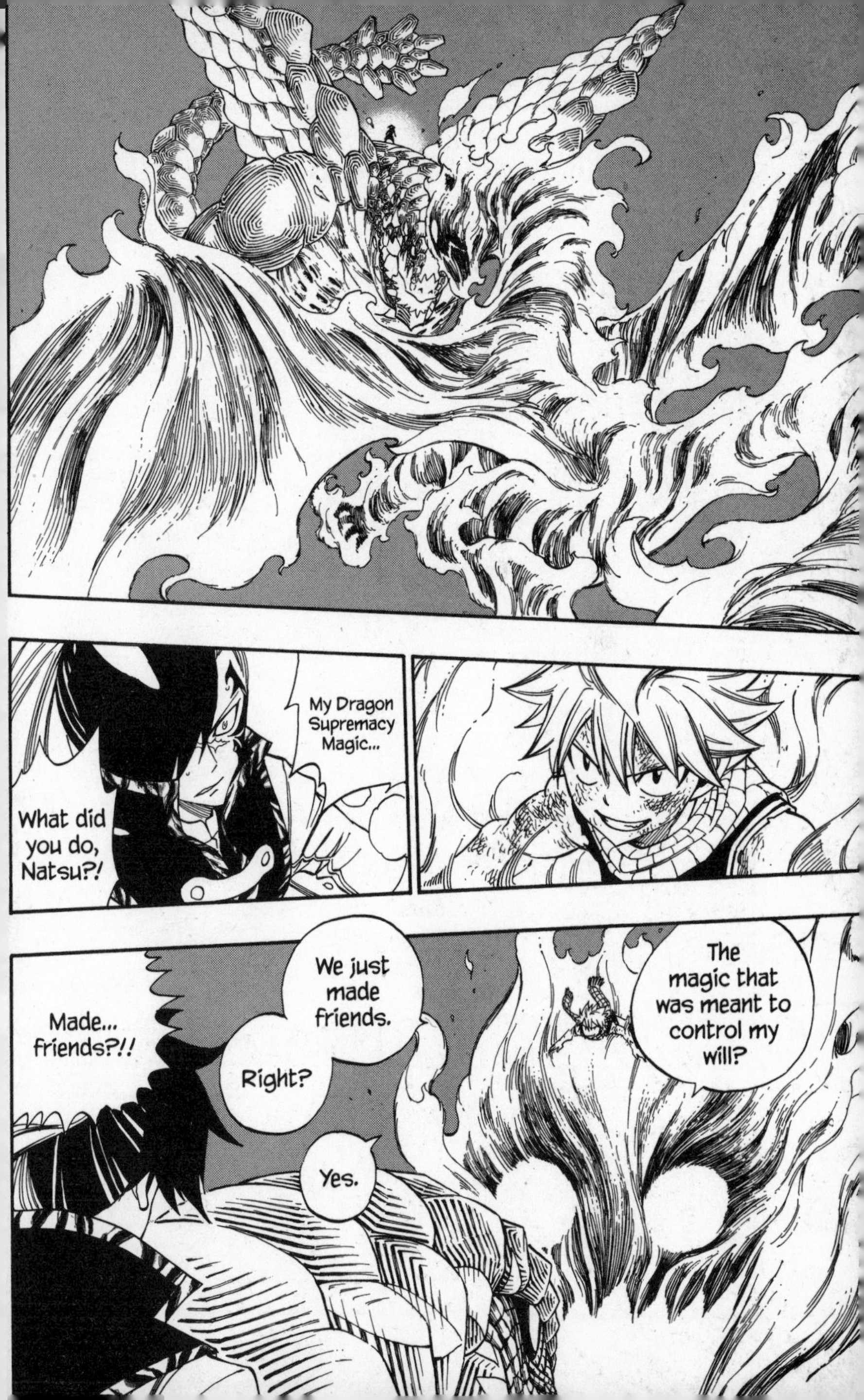
My Dragon Supremacy Magic...
What did you do, Natsu?!
The magic that was meant to control my will?
We just made friends.
Right?
Yes.
Made... friends?!!

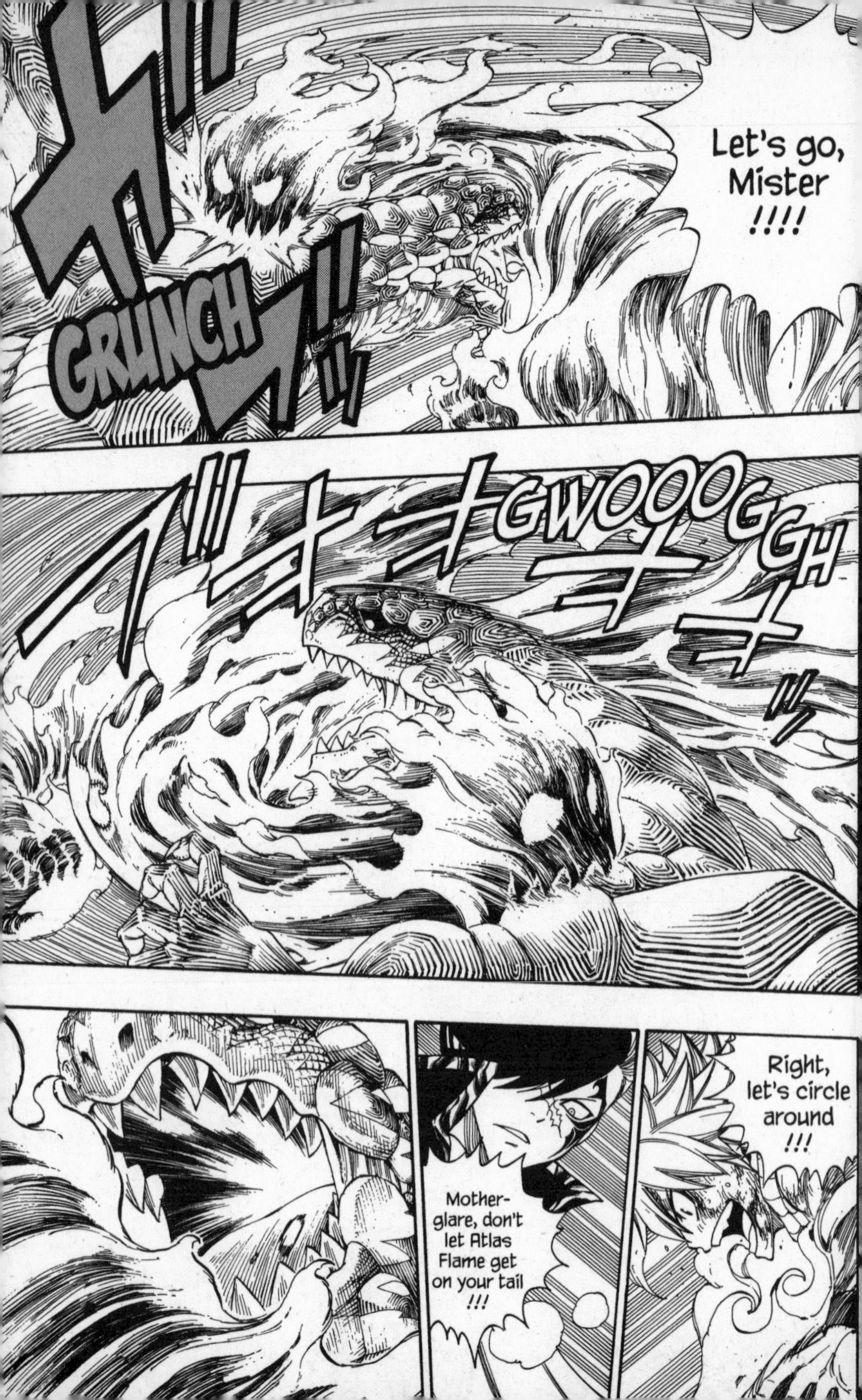
Let's go, Mister !!!!
GRUNCH
GWOOOGGH
Right, let's circle around !!!
Mother-glare, don't let Atlas Flame get on your tail !!!

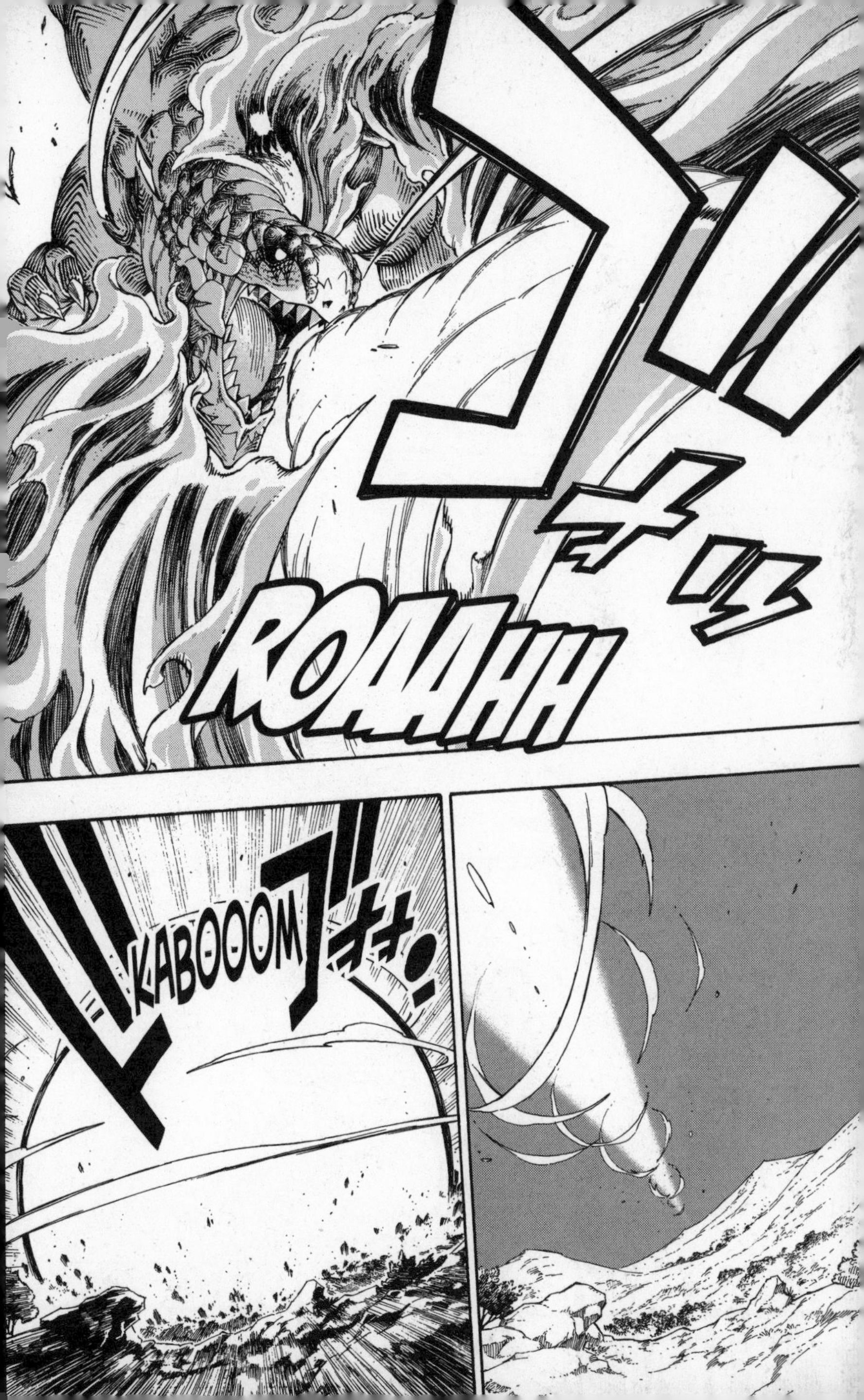
ROAAHH
KABOOOM

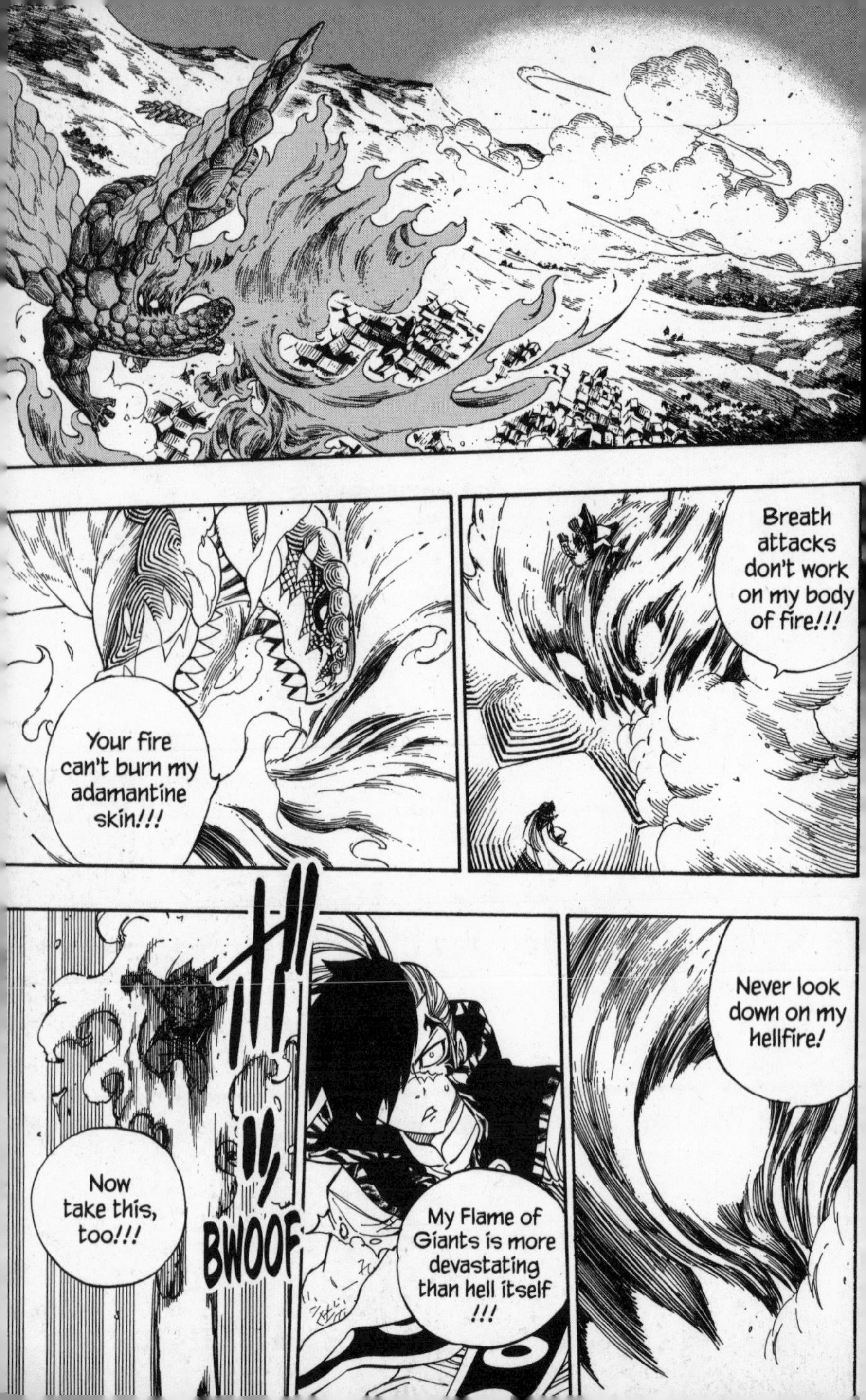
Breath attacks don't work on my body of fire!!!
Your fire can't burn my adamantine skin!!!
Never look down on my hellfire!
My Flame of Giants is more devastating than hell itself!!!
BWOOF
Now take this, too!!!

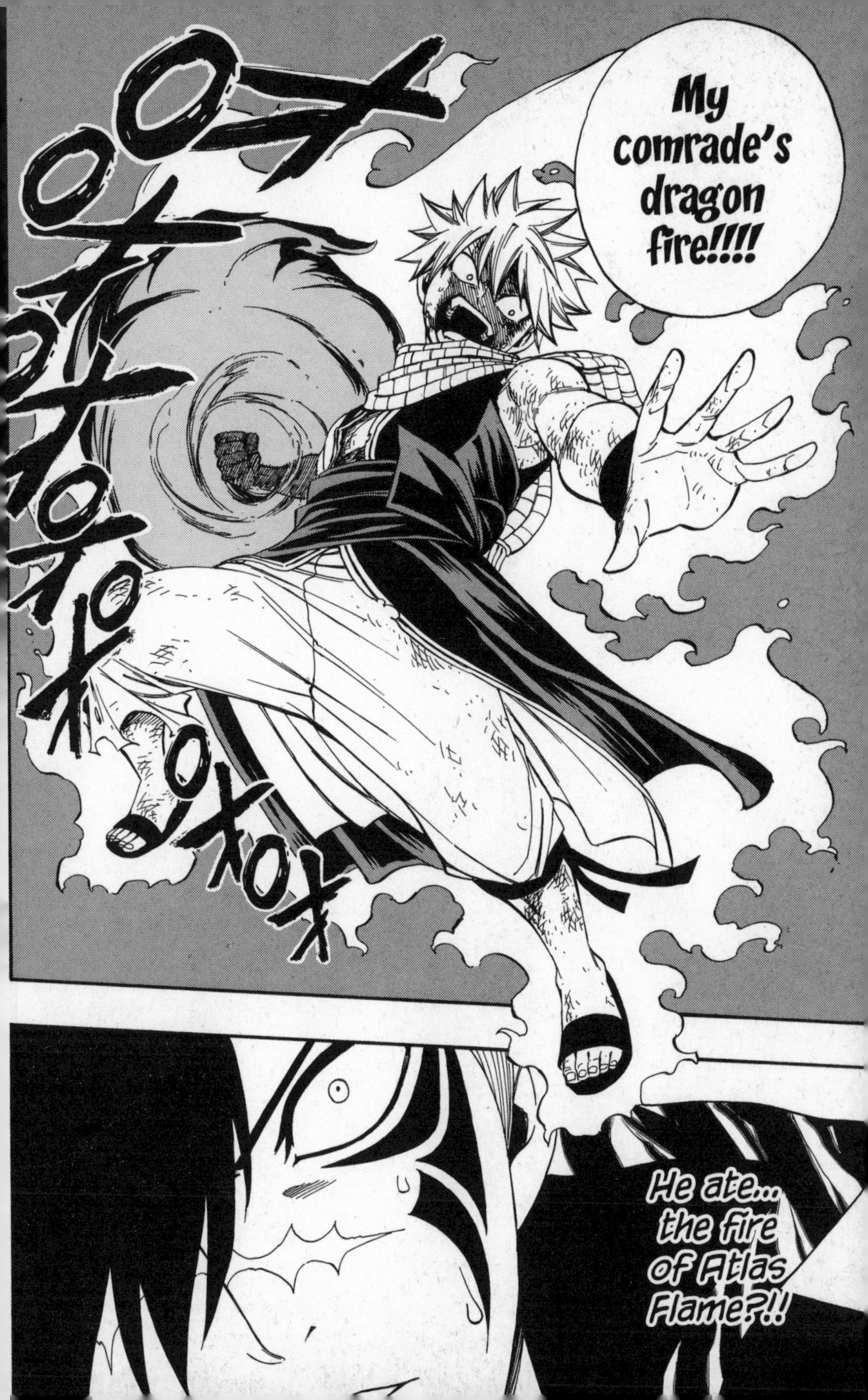
My comrade's dragon fire!!!!
He ate... the fire of Atlas Flame?!!

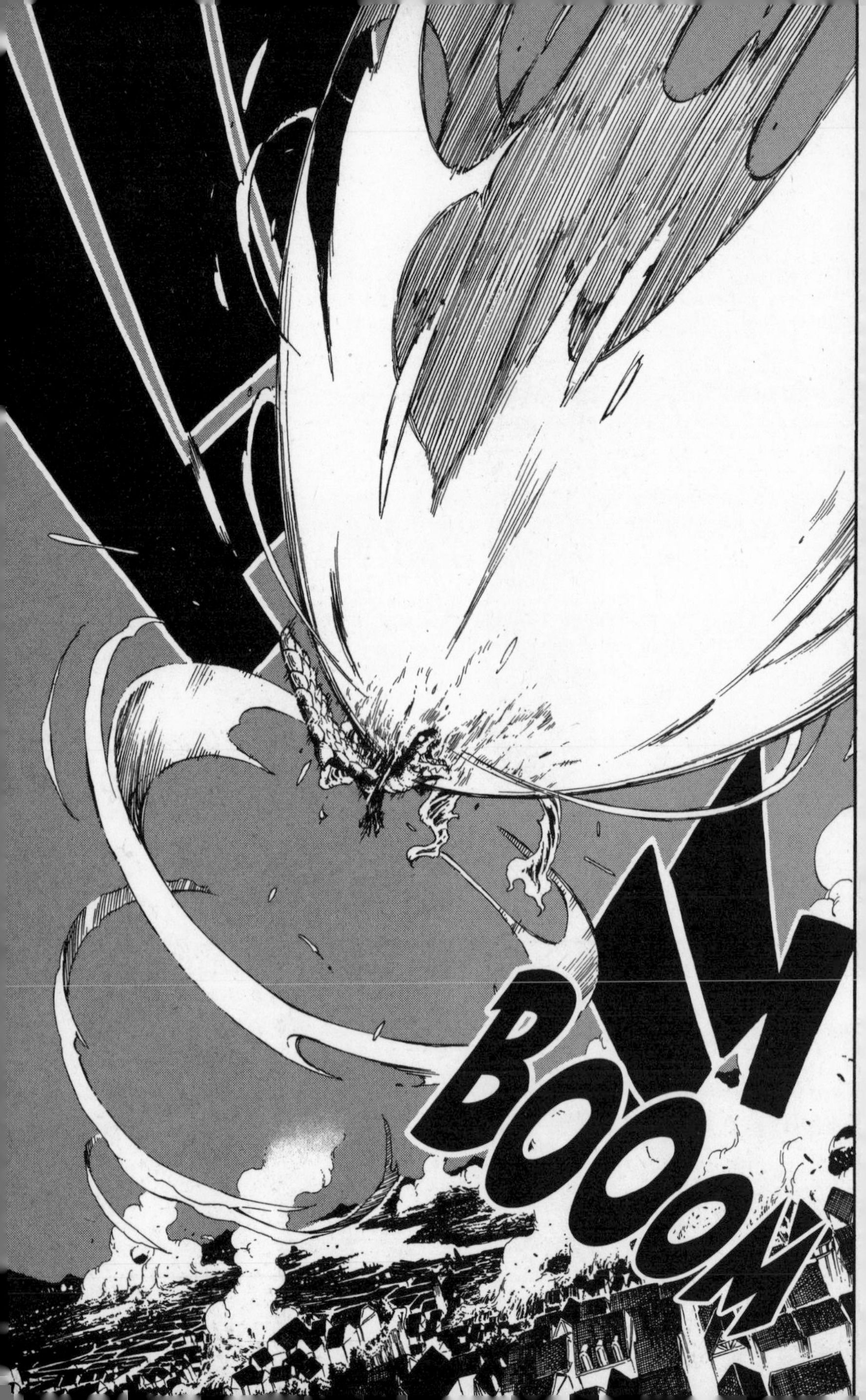
BOOOM

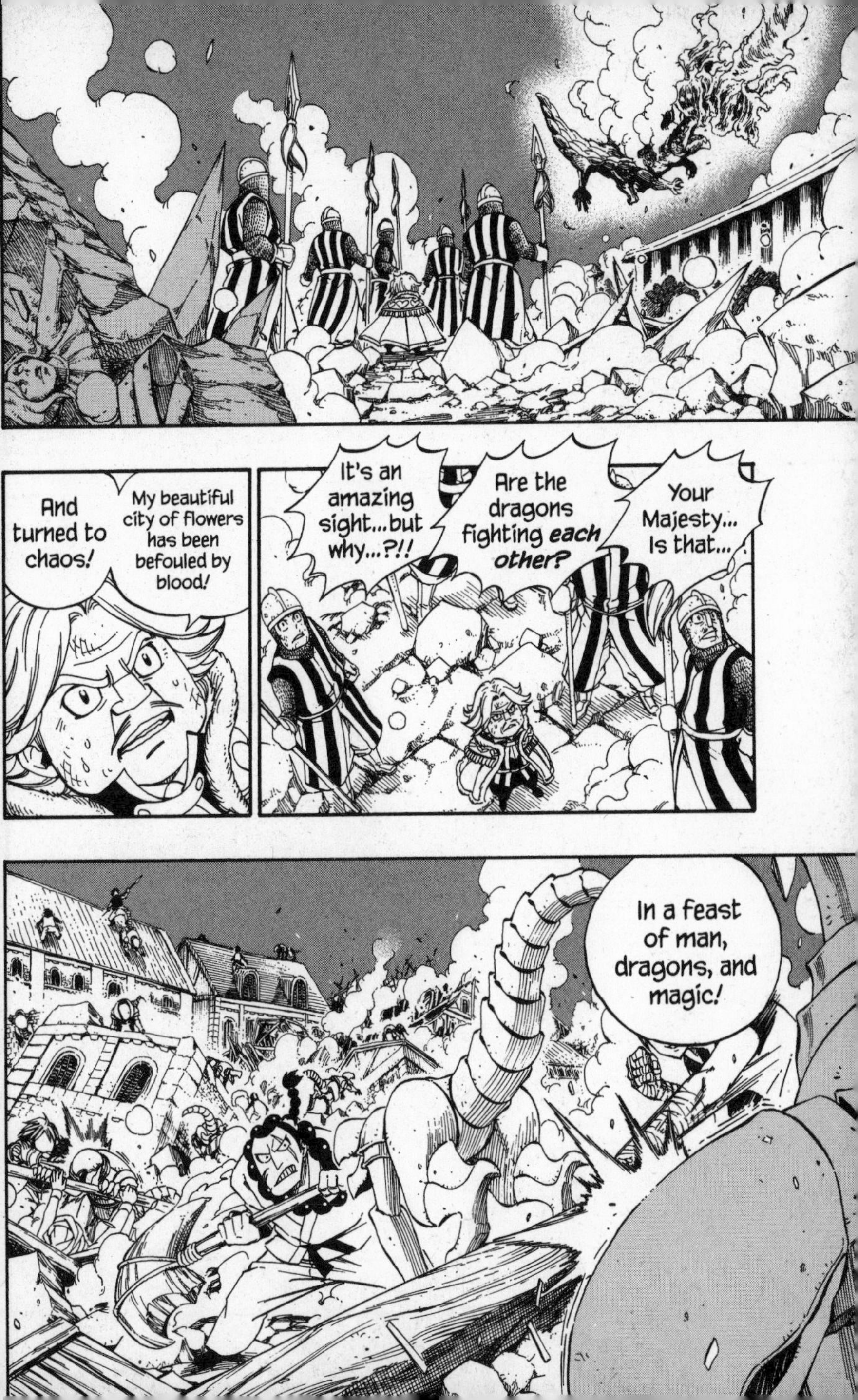
Your Majesty... Is that...
Are the dragons fighting *each other?*
It's an amazing sight...but why...?!!
My beautiful city of flowers has been befouled by blood!
And turned to chaos!
In a feast of man, dragons, and magic!

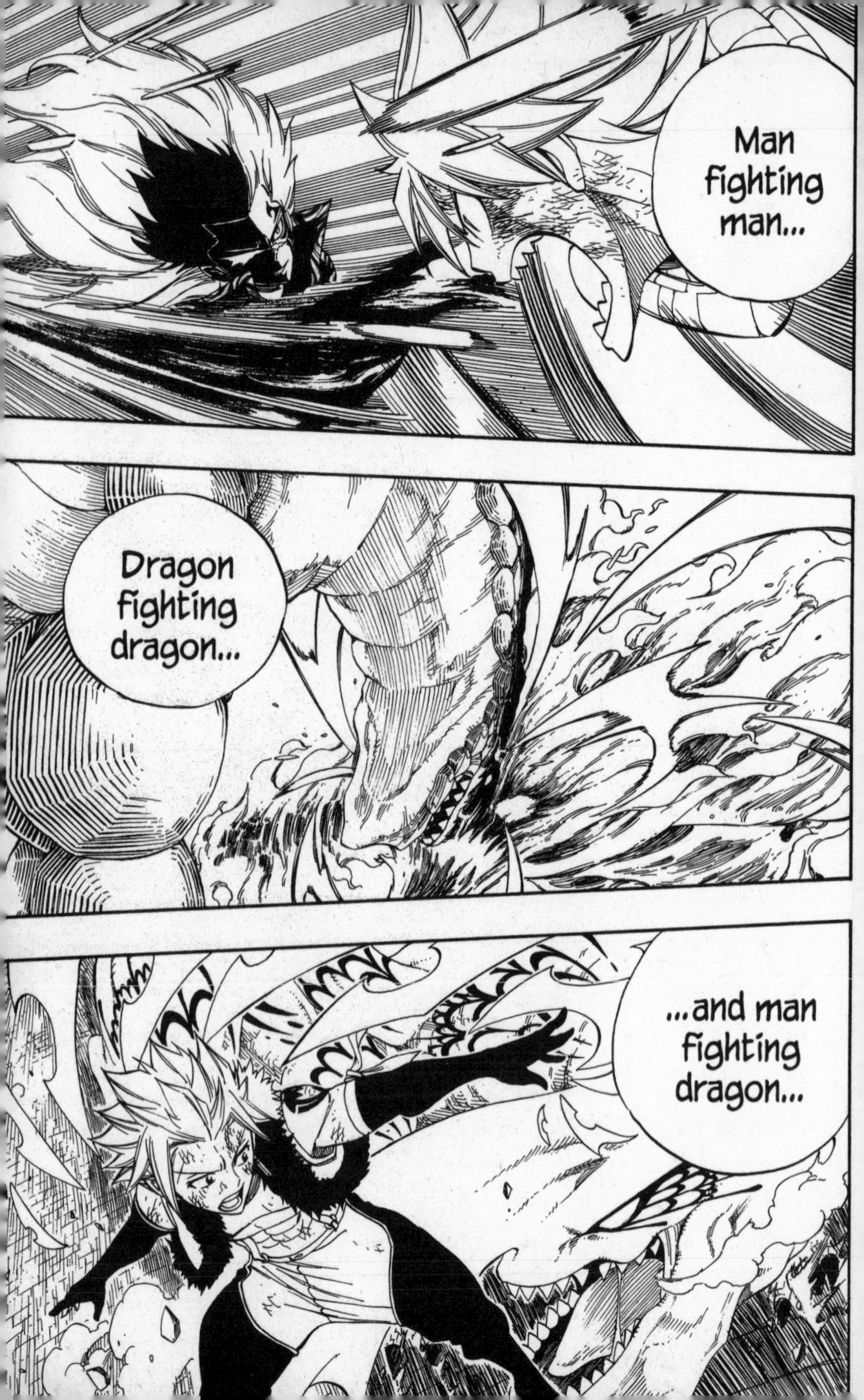
Man fighting man...
Dragon fighting dragon...
...and man fighting dragon...

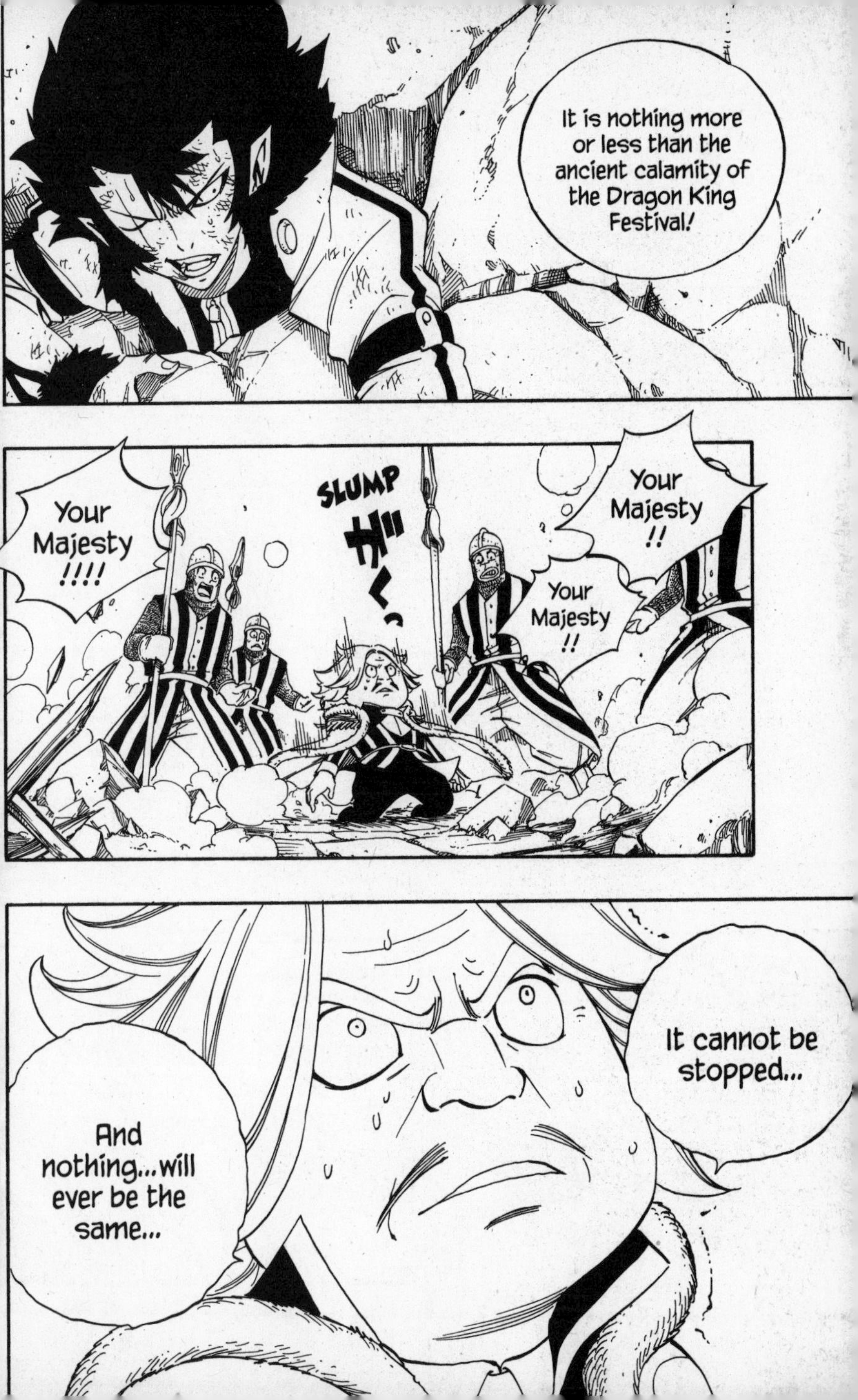

It is nothing more or less than the ancient calamity of the Dragon King Festival!
Your Majesty !!
Your Majesty !!
SLUMP
ガくっ
Your Majesty !!!!
It cannot be stopped...
And nothing...will ever be the same...

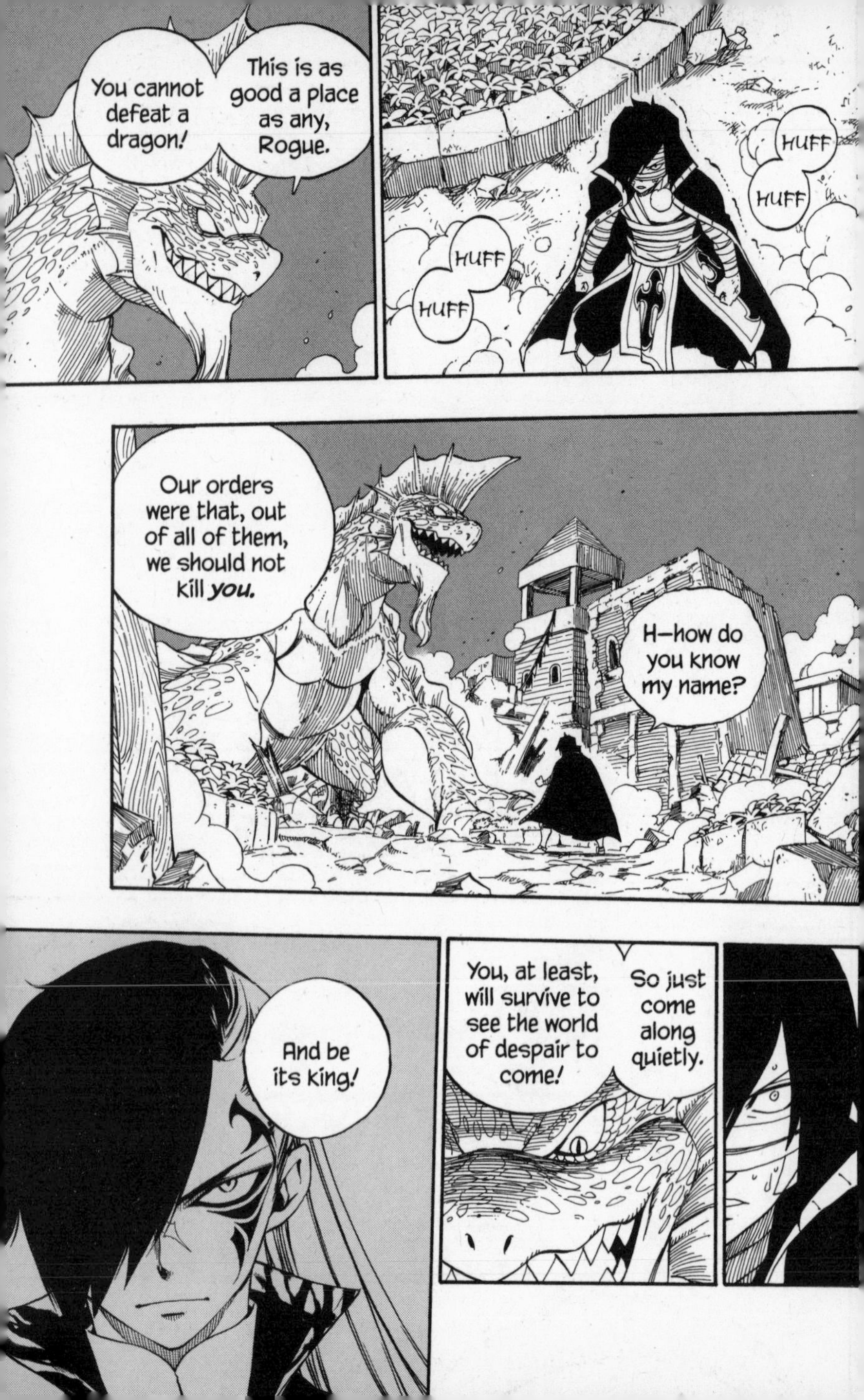
HUFF
HUFF
HUFF
HUFF
This is as good a place as any, Rogue.
You cannot defeat a dragon!
H—how do you know my name?
Our orders were that, out of all of them, we should not kill *you.*
So just come along quietly.
You, at least, will survive to see the world of despair to come!
And be its king!

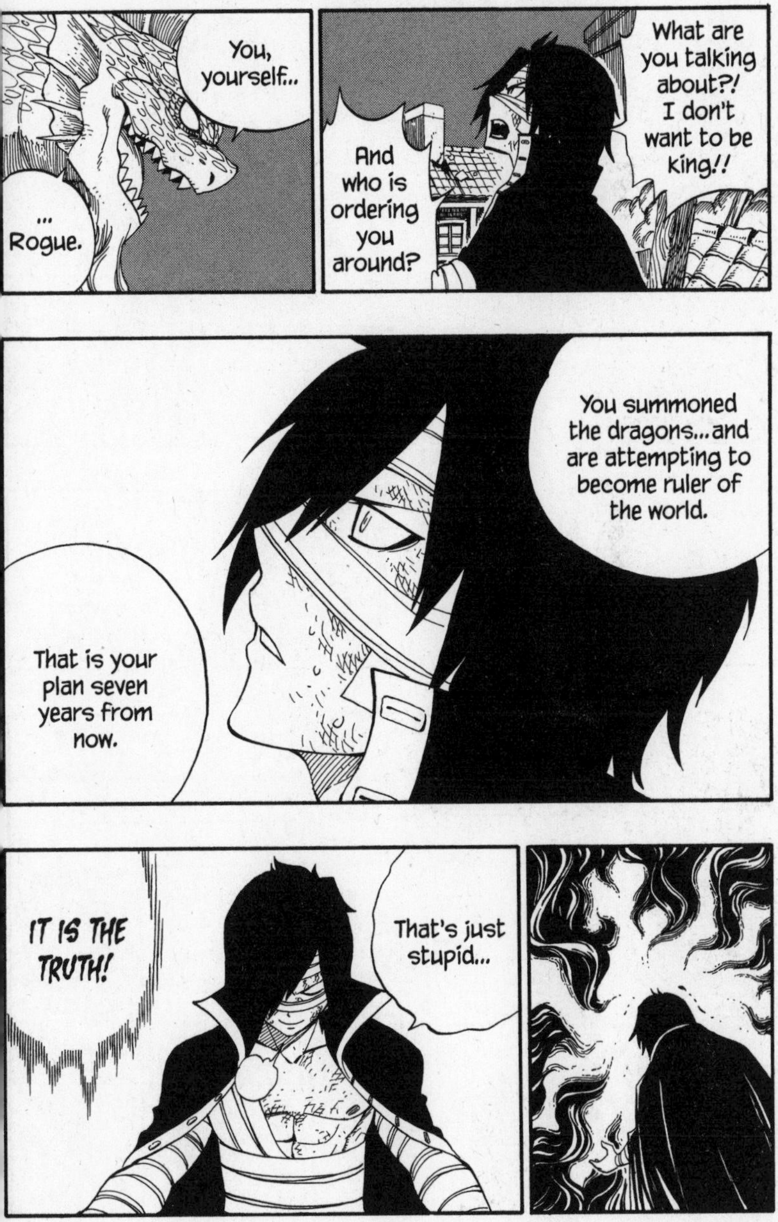
What are you talking about?! I don't want to be king!!
And who is ordering you around?
You, yourself...
... Rogue.
You summoned the dragons...and are attempting to become ruler of the world.
That is your plan seven years from now.
That's just stupid...
IT IS THE TRUTH!

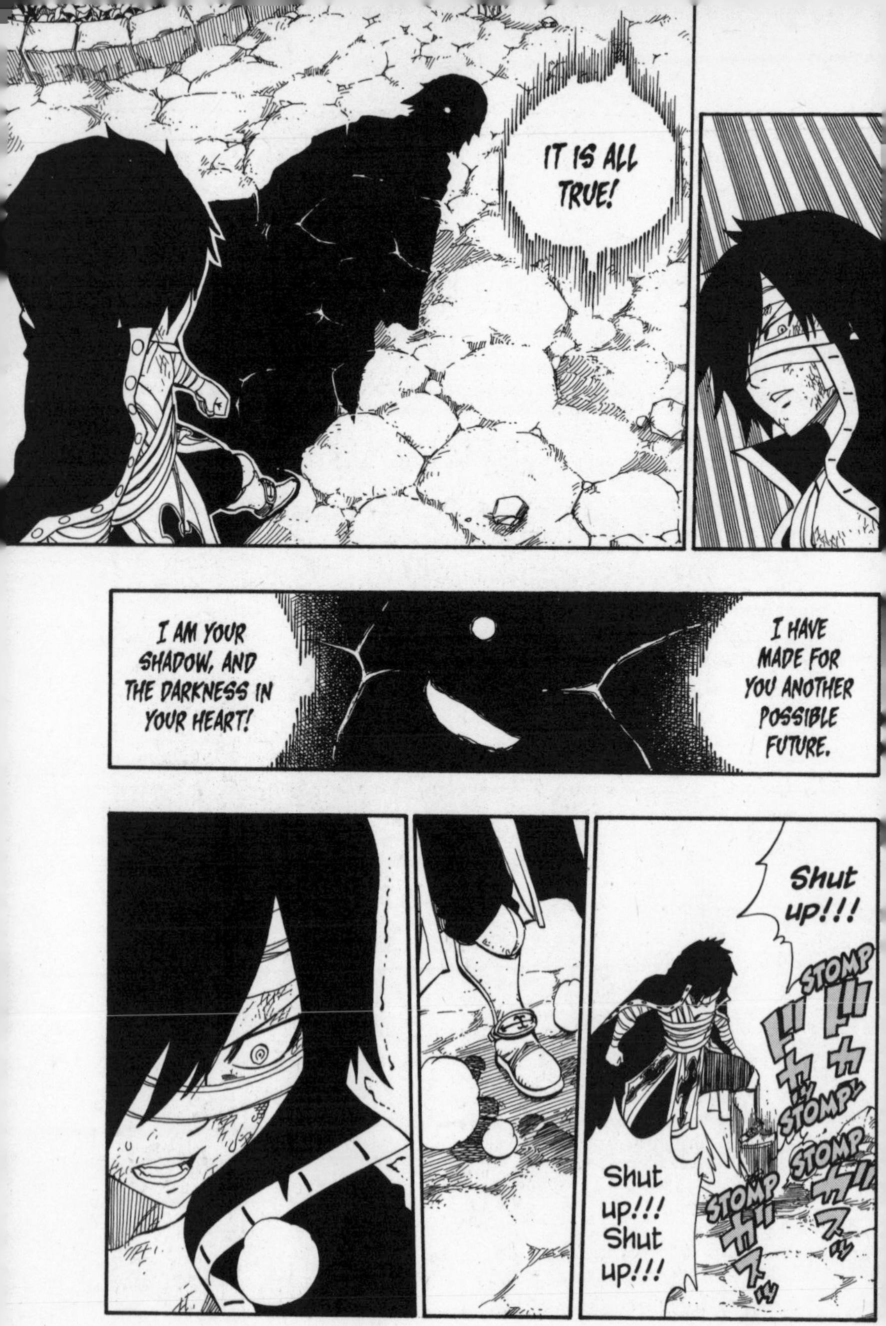
IT IS ALL TRUE!
I HAVE MADE FOR YOU ANOTHER POSSIBLE FUTURE.
I AM YOUR SHADOW, AND THE DARKNESS IN YOUR HEART!
Shut up!!!
STOMP
STOMP
STOMP
STOMP
Shut up!!! Shut up!!!

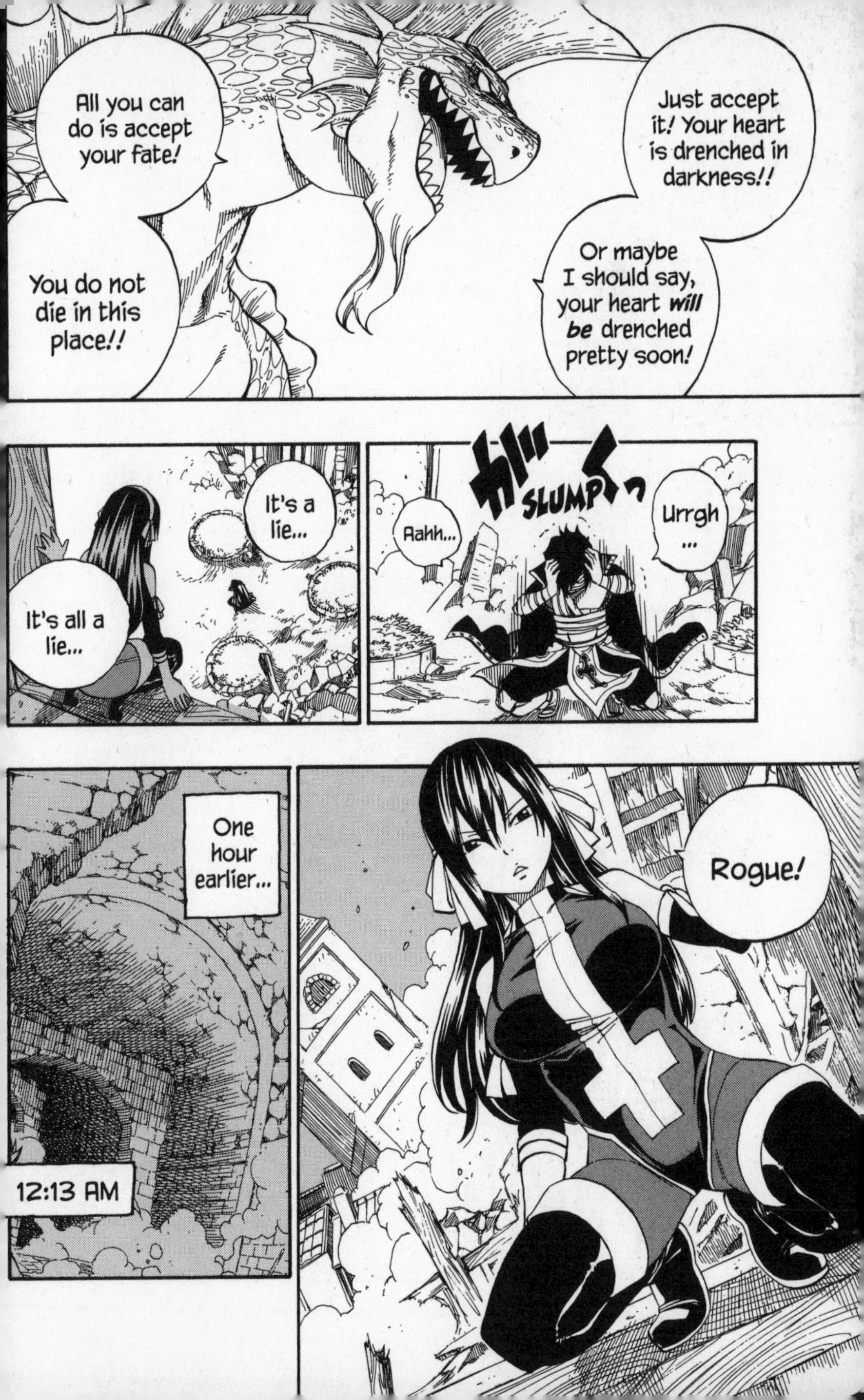
Just accept it! Your heart is drenched in darkness!!
Or maybe I should say, your heart *will be* drenched pretty soon!
All you can do is accept your fate!
You do not die in this place!!
Urrgh ...
SLUMP
Aahh...
It's a lie...
It's all a lie...
Rogue!
One hour earlier...
12:13 AM

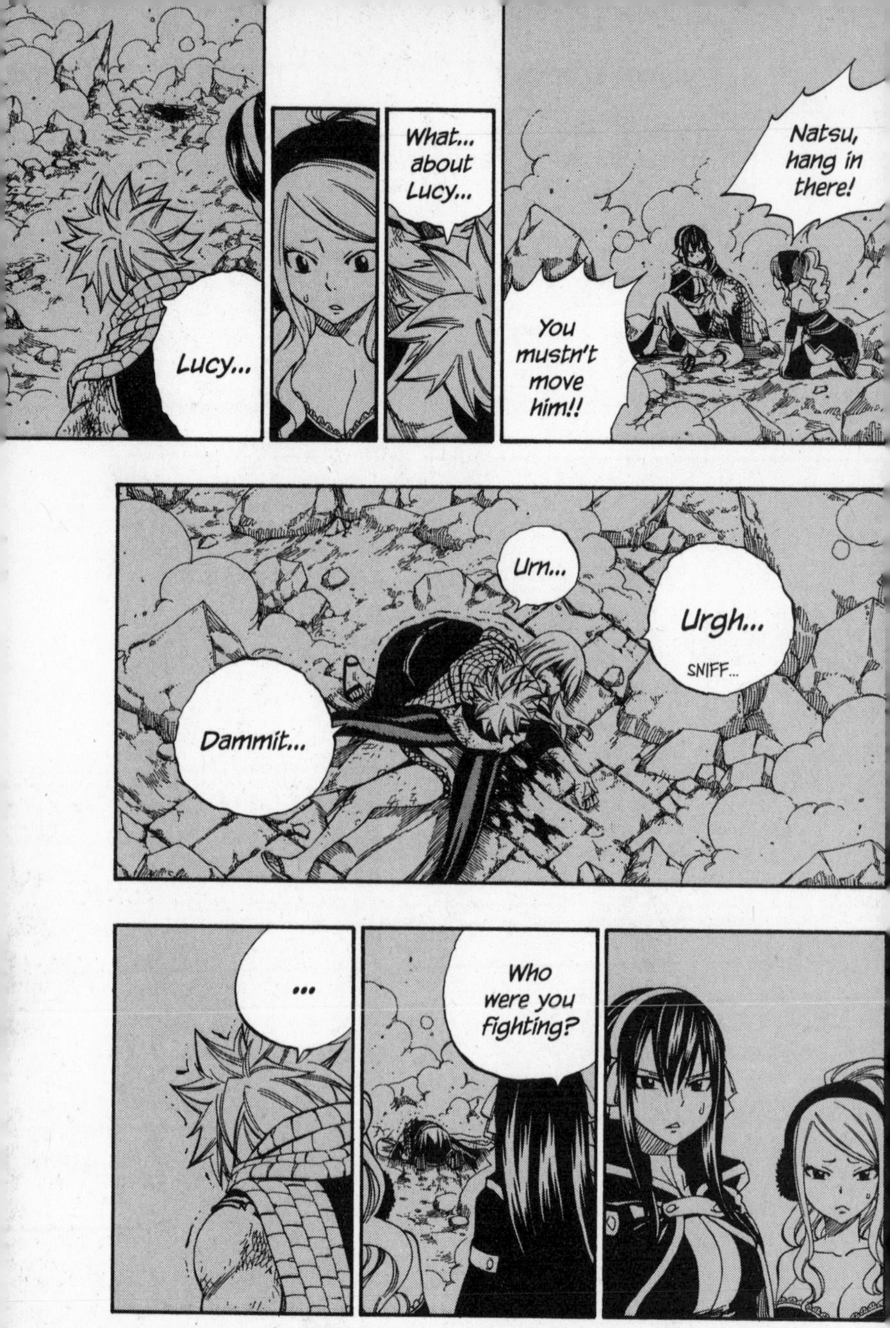
Natsu, hang in there!
You mustn't move him!!
What... about Lucy...
Lucy...
Urgh...
SNIFF...
Urn...
Dammit...
Who were you fighting?
...

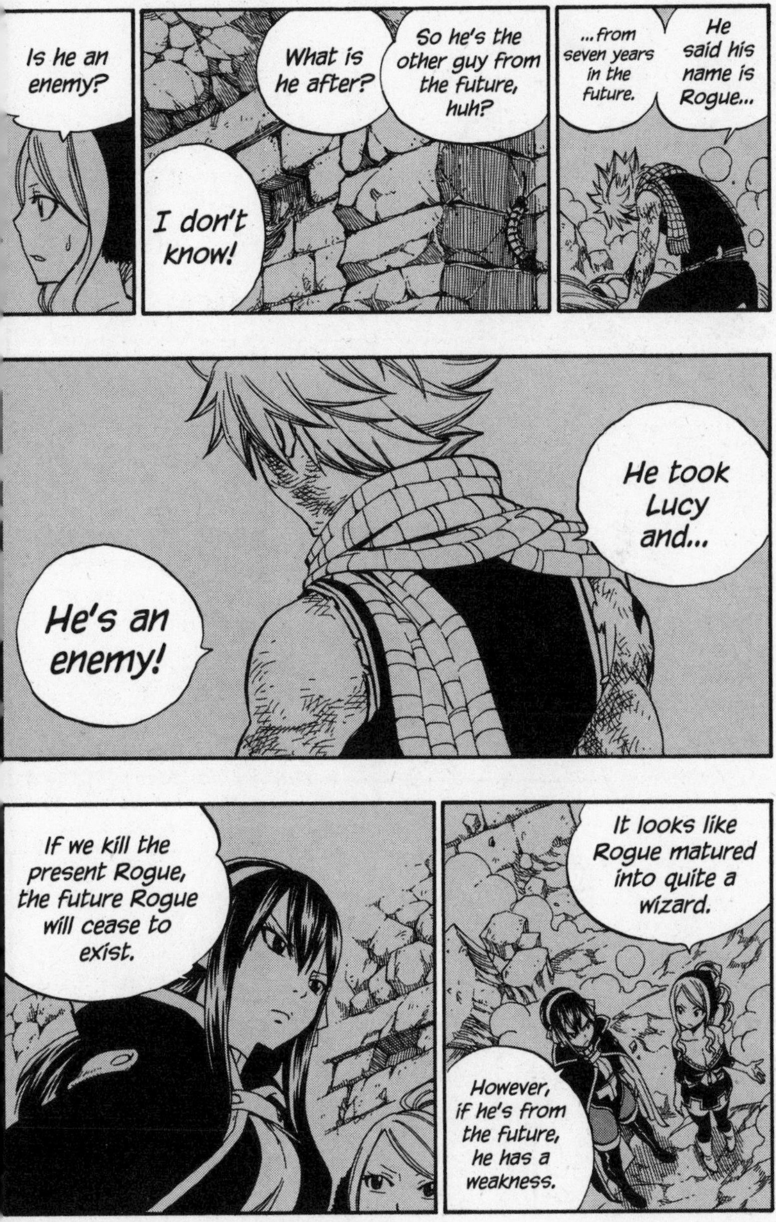
He said his name is Rogue...
...from seven years in the future.
So he's the other guy from the future, huh?
What is he after?
I don't know!
Is he an enemy?
He took Lucy and...
He's an enemy!
It looks like Rogue matured into quite a wizard.
However, if he's from the future, he has a weakness.
If we kill the present Rogue, the future Rogue will cease to exist.

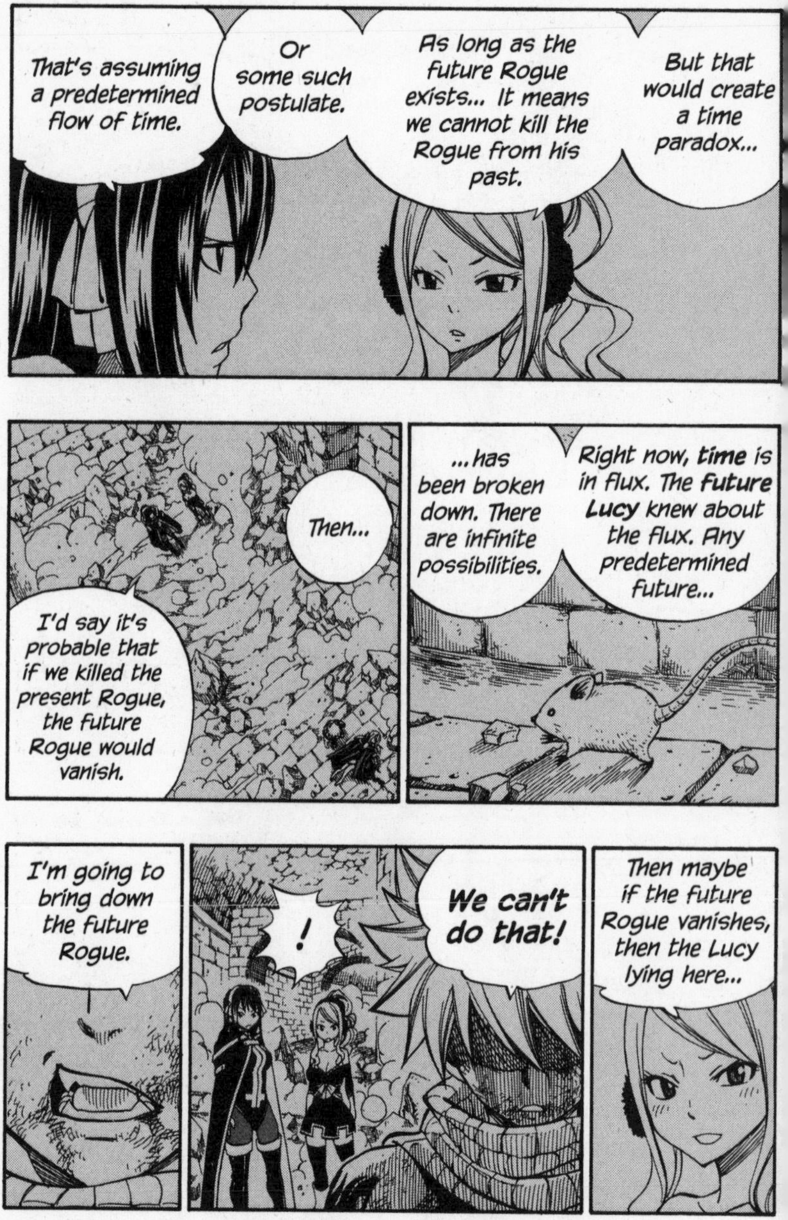
But that would create a time paradox...
As long as the future Rogue exists... It means we cannot kill the Rogue from his past.
Or some such postulate.
That's assuming a predetermined flow of time.
Right now, **time** is in flux. The **future Lucy** knew about the flux. Any predetermined future...
...has been broken down. There are infinite possibilities.
Then...
I'd say it's probable that if we killed the present Rogue, the future Rogue would vanish.
Then maybe if the future Rogue vanishes, then the Lucy lying here...
We can't do that!
!
I'm going to bring down the future Rogue.

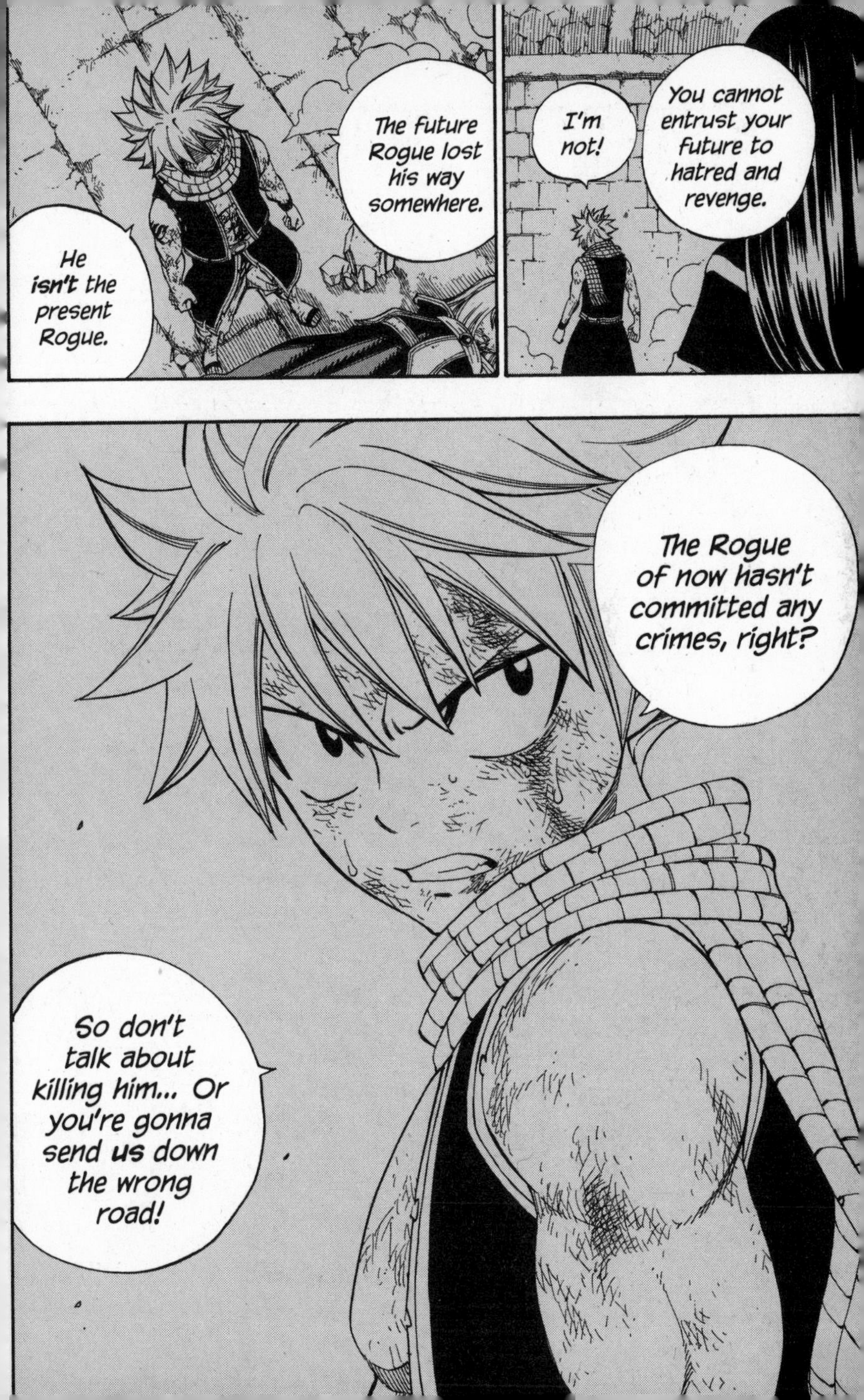
You cannot entrust your future to hatred and revenge.
I'm not!
The future Rogue lost his way somewhere.
He **isn't** the present Rogue.
The Rogue of now hasn't committed any crimes, right?
So don't talk about killing him... Or you're gonna send **us** down the wrong road!

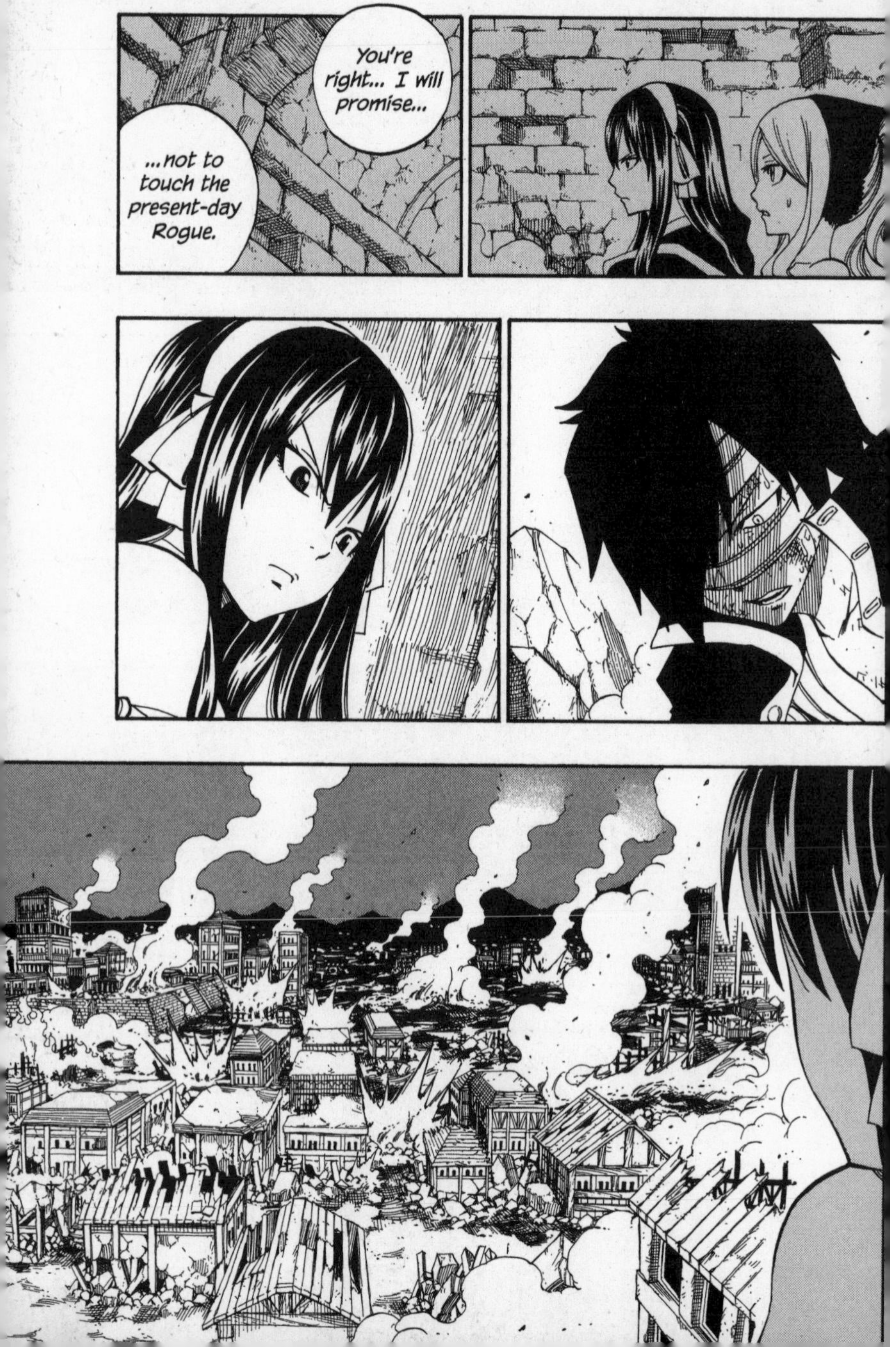
You're right... I will promise...
...not to touch the present-day Rogue.

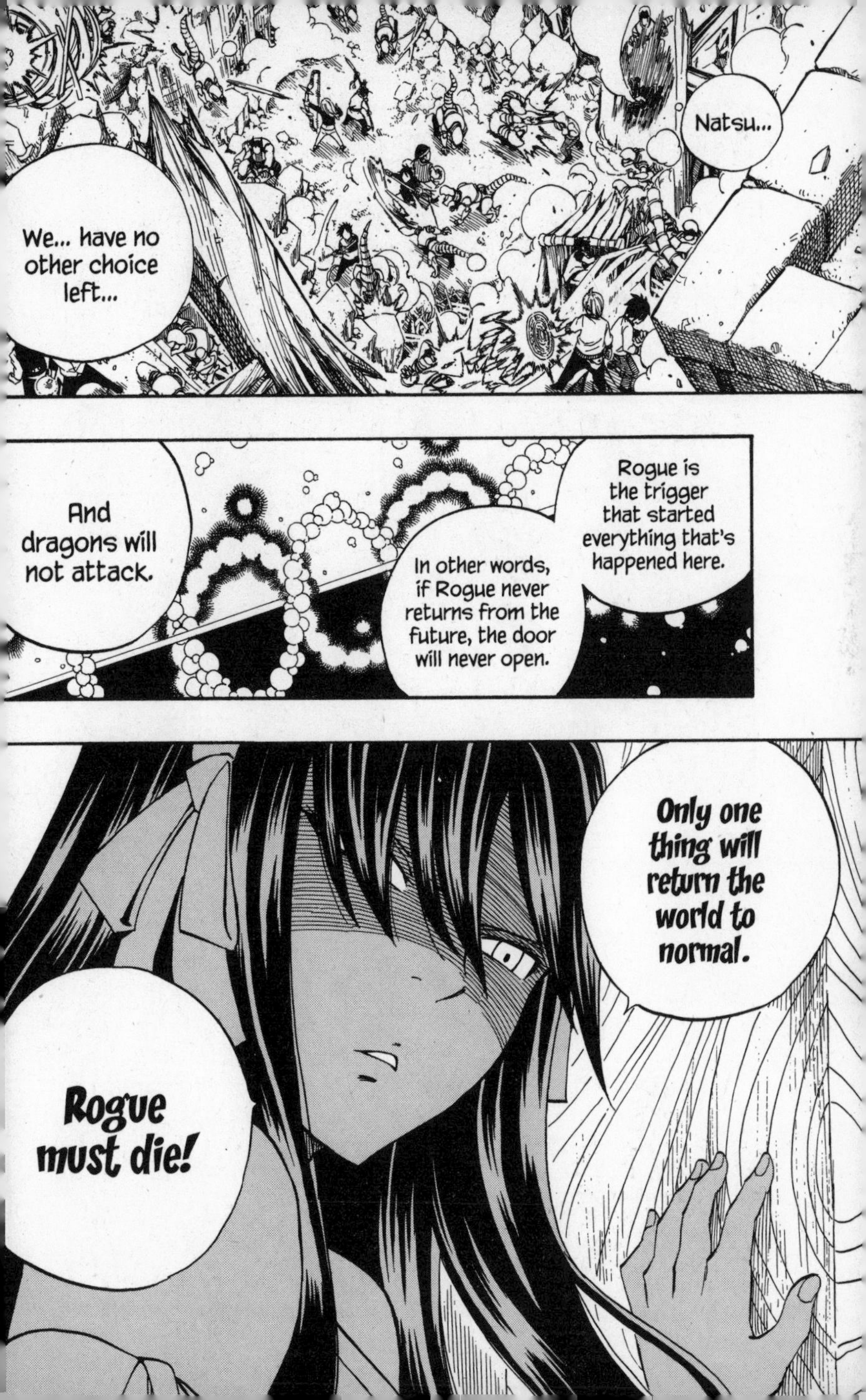
Natsu...
We... have no other choice left...
Rogue is the trigger that started everything that's happened here.
In other words, if Rogue never returns from the future, the door will never open.
And dragons will not attack.
Only one thing will return the world to normal.
Rogue must die!

FAIRY TAIL

フェアリーテイル

Chapter 334: Sin and Sacrifice

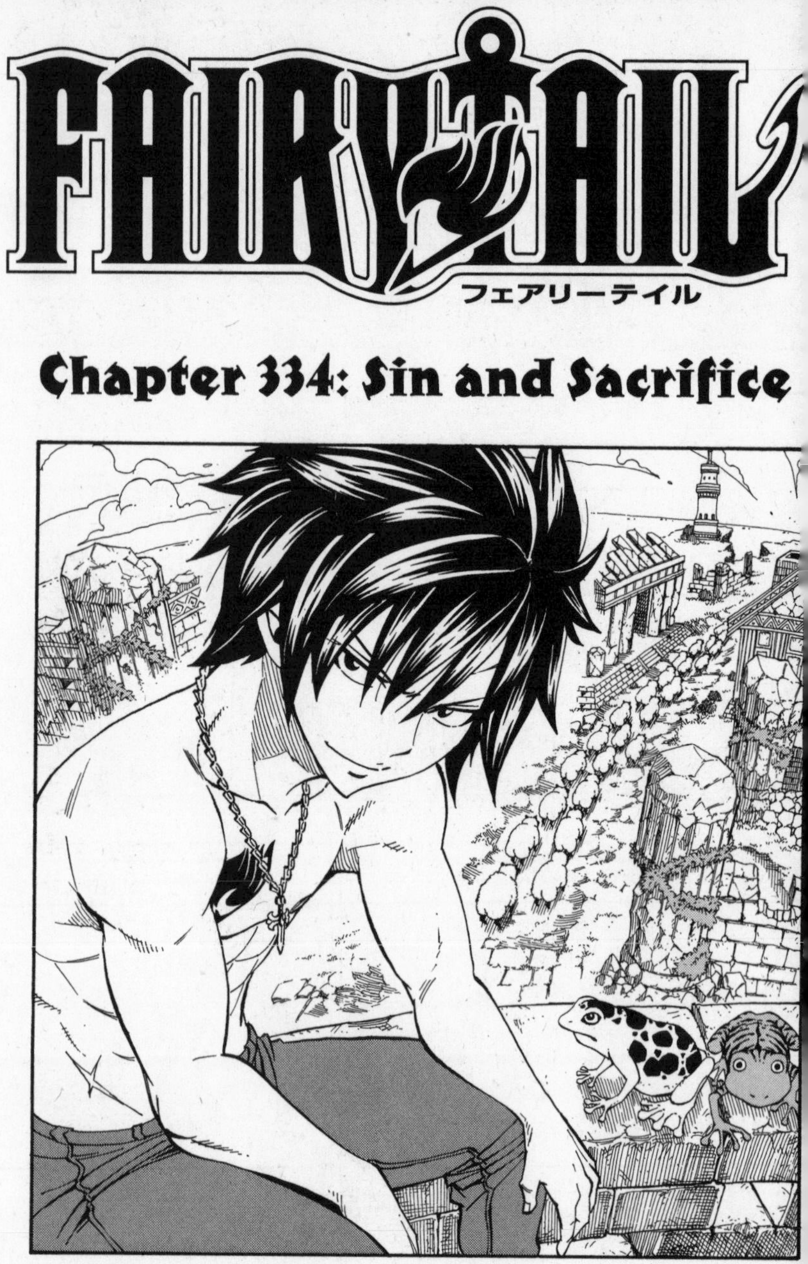

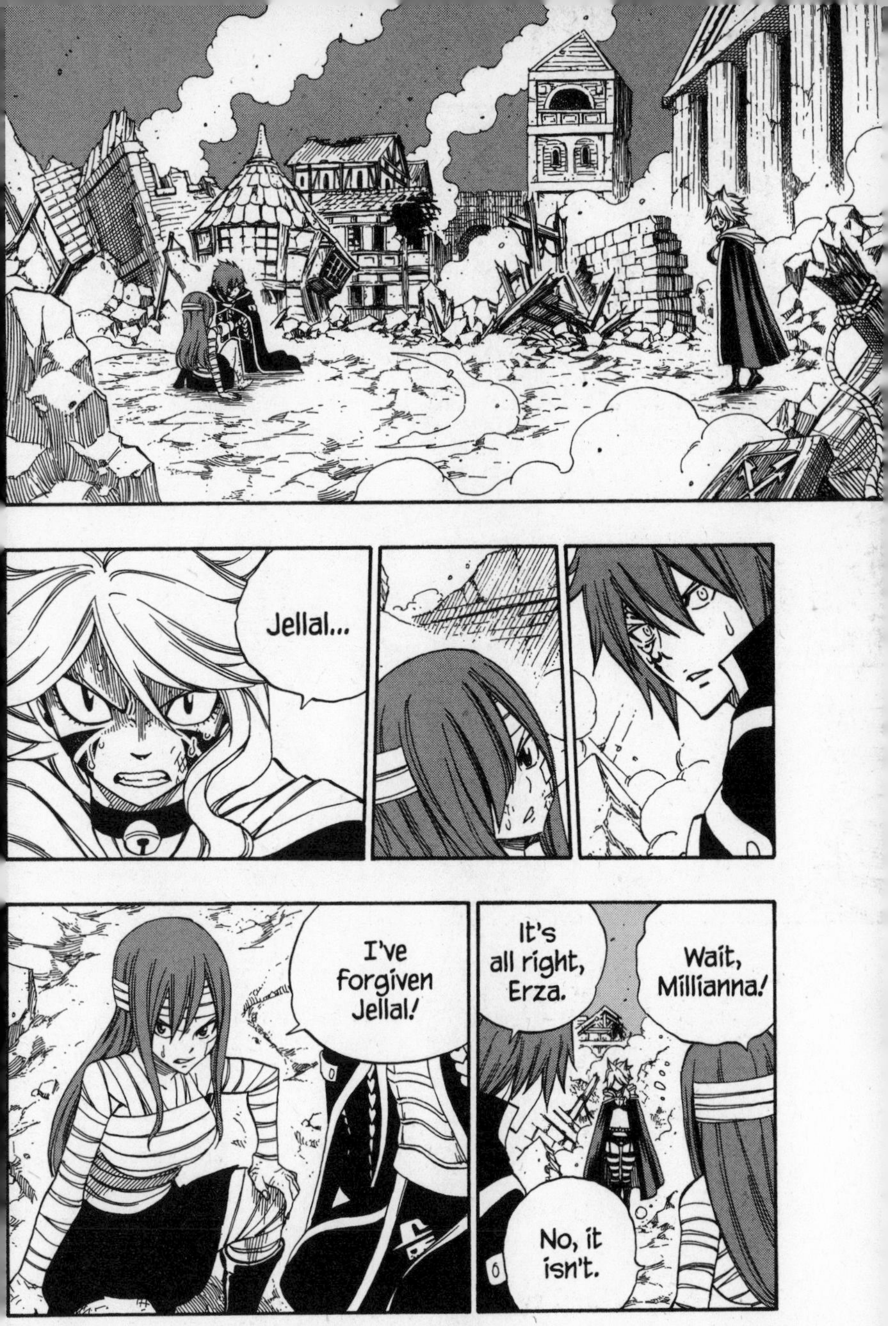
Jellal...
Wait, Millianna!
It's all right, Erza.
No, it isn't.
I've forgiven Jellal!

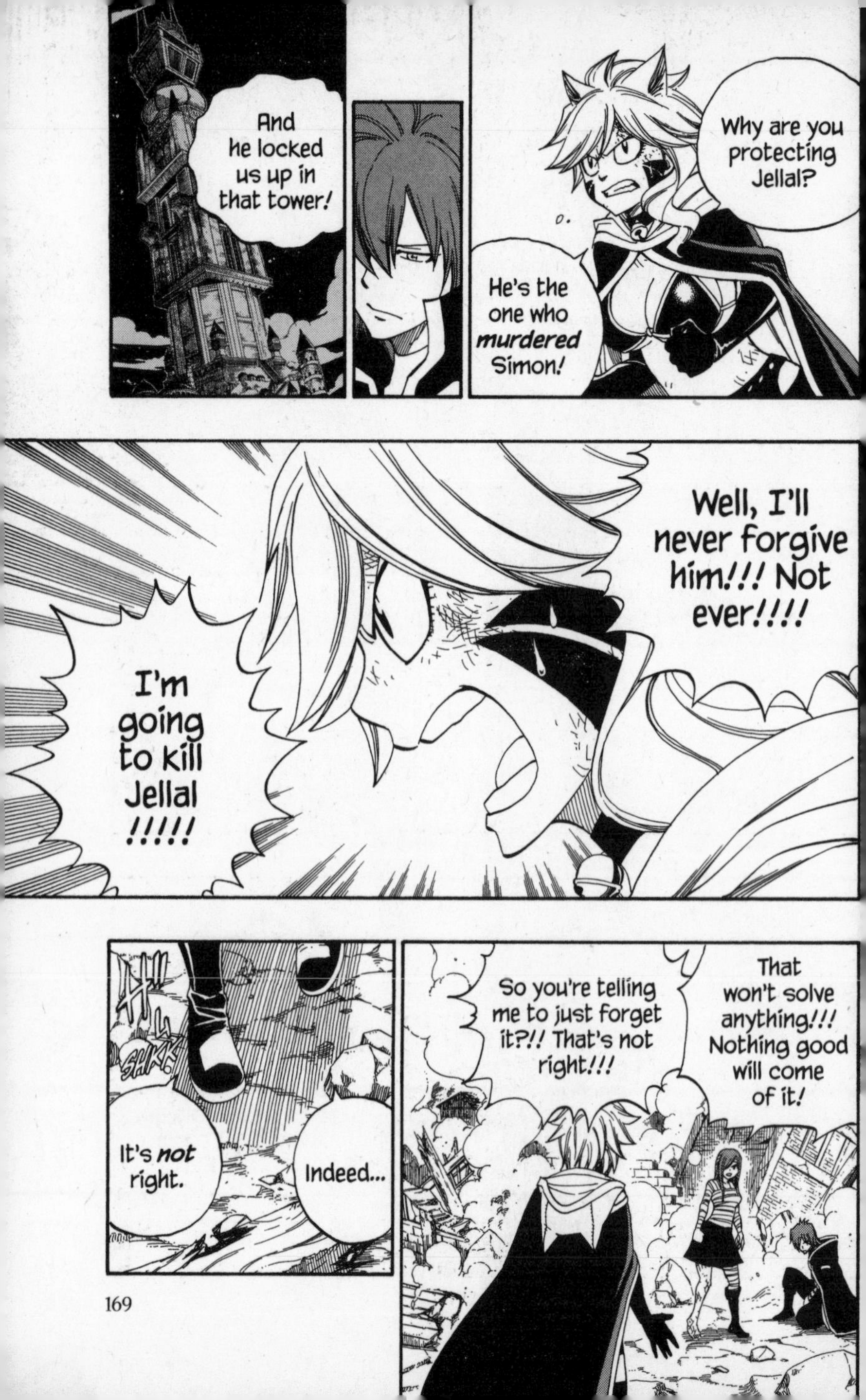

Why are you protecting Jellal?
He's the one who *murdered* Simon!
And he locked us up in that tower!
Well, I'll never forgive him!!! Not ever!!!!
I'm going to kill Jellal !!!!!
That won't solve anything!!! Nothing good will come of it!
So you're telling me to just forget it?!! That's not right!!!
SHKK
Indeed...
It's *not* right.

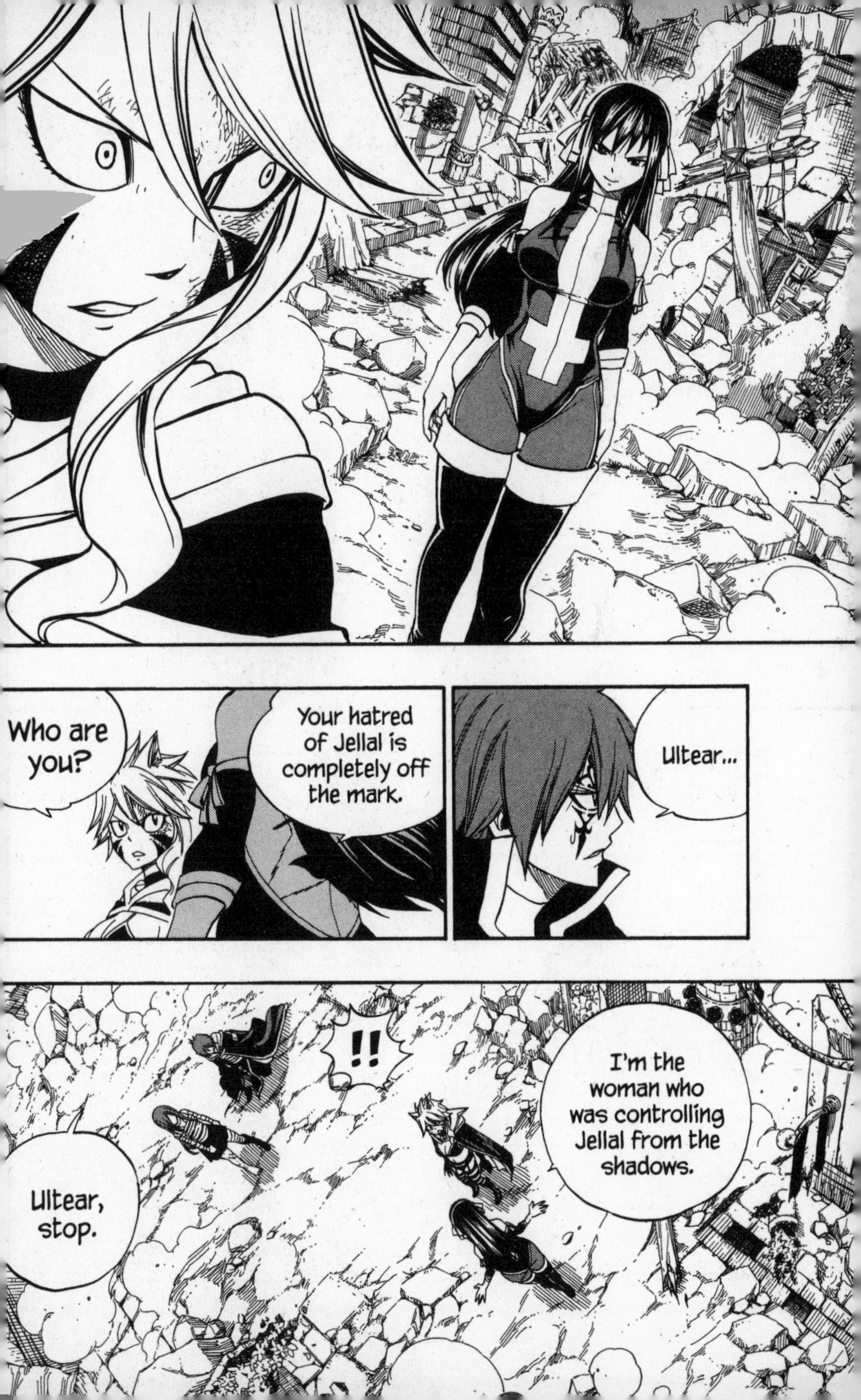
Ultear...
Your hatred of Jellal is completely off the mark.
Who are you?
I'm the woman who was controlling Jellal from the shadows.
!!
Ultear, stop.

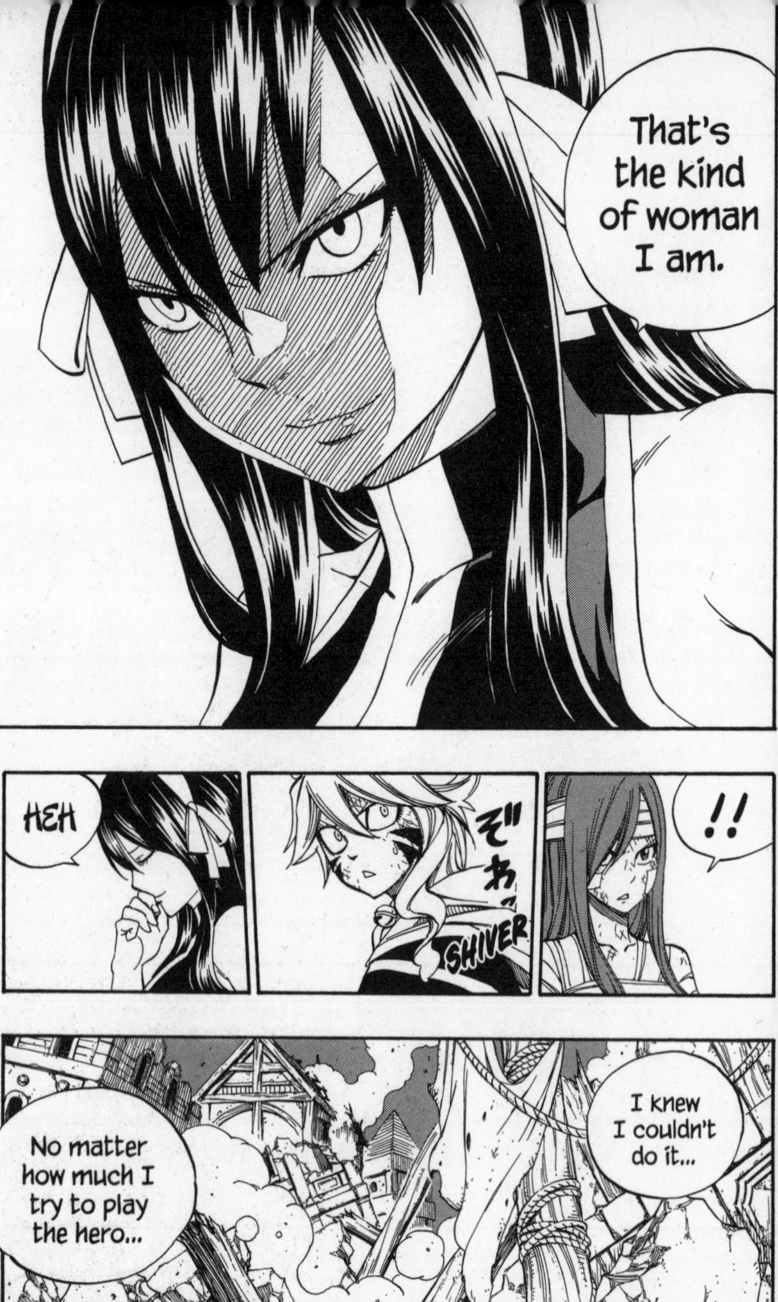
That's the kind of woman I am.
!!
ぞわっ
SHIVER
HEH
I knew I couldn't do it...
No matter how much I try to play the hero...

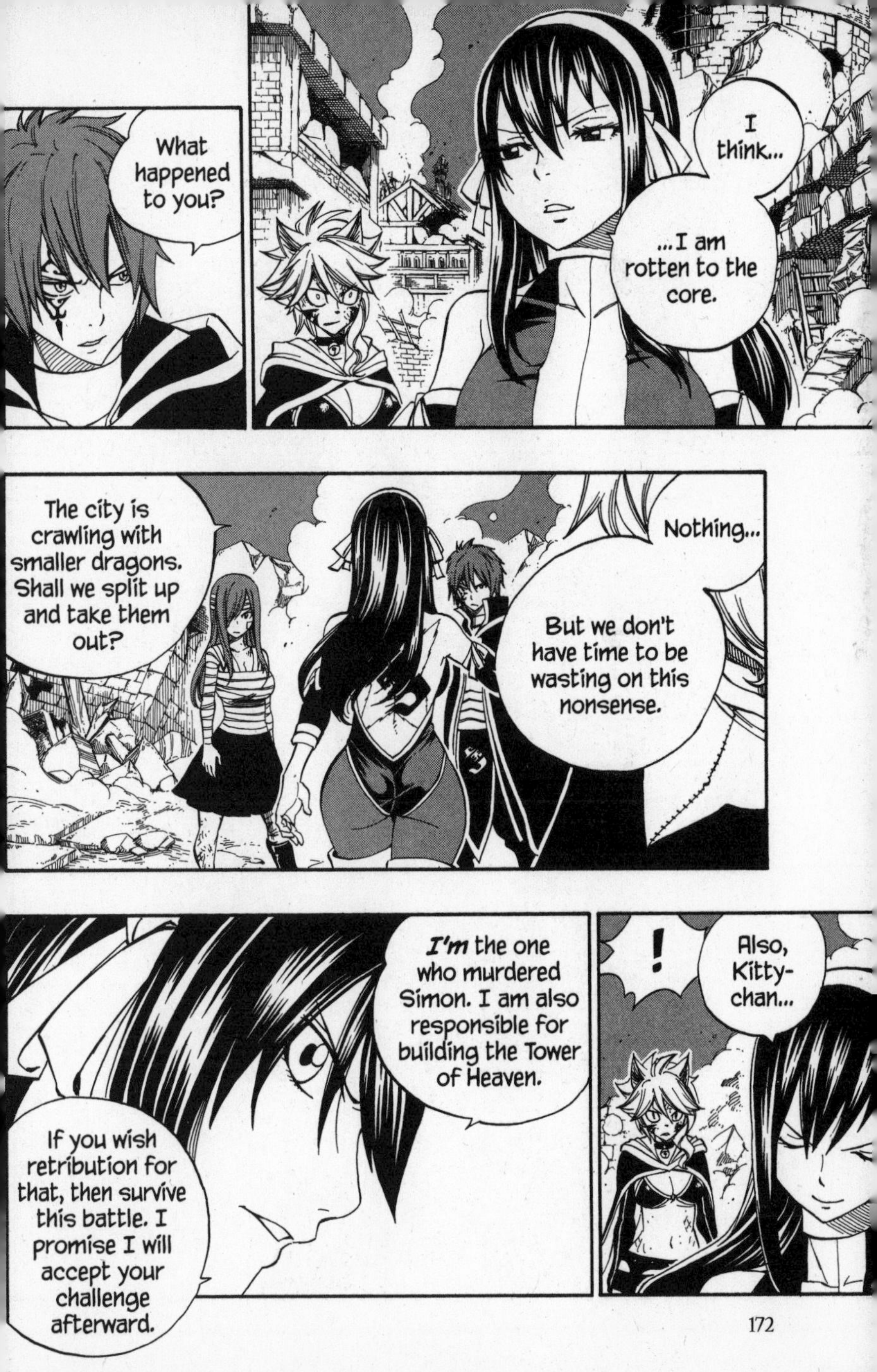
I think...
...I am rotten to the core.
What happened to you?
Nothing...
But we don't have time to be wasting on this nonsense.
The city is crawling with smaller dragons. Shall we split up and take them out?
!
Also, Kitty-chan...
I'm the one who murdered Simon. I am also responsible for building the Tower of Heaven.
If you wish retribution for that, then survive this battle. I promise I will accept your challenge afterward.

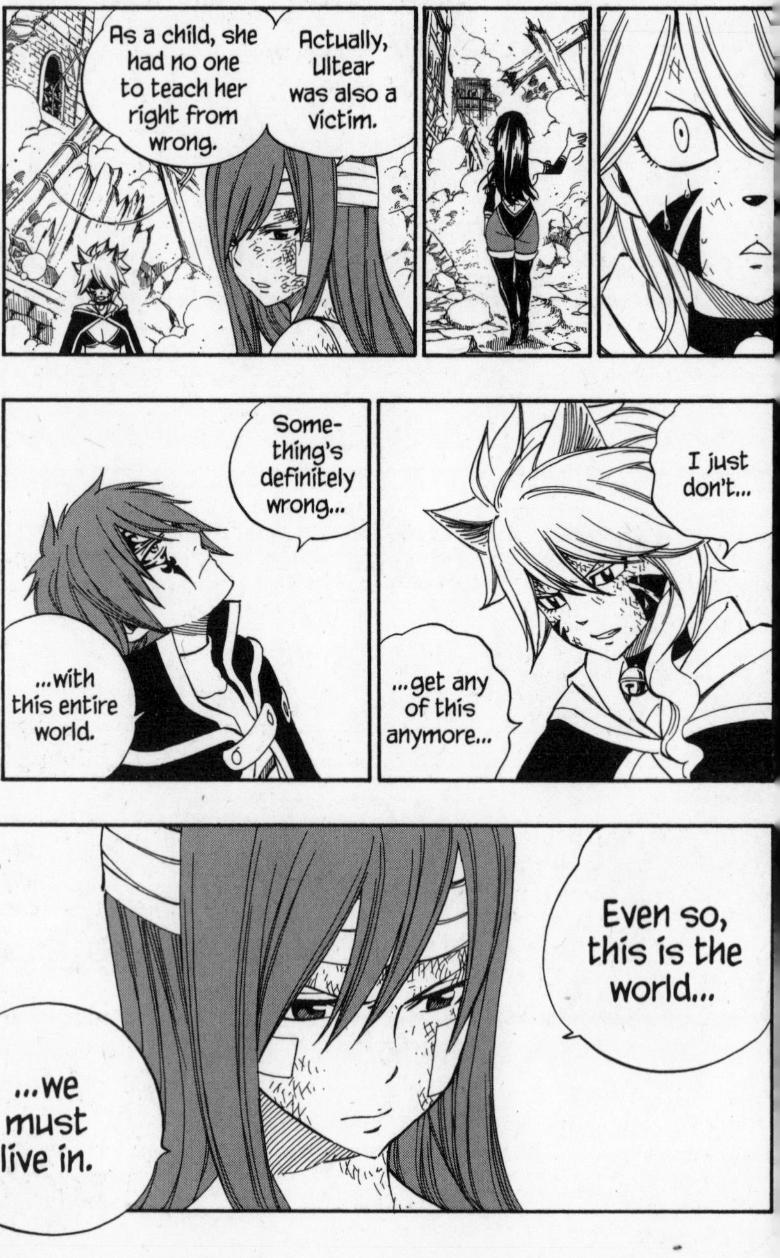
Actually, Ultear was also a victim.
As a child, she had no one to teach her right from wrong.
I just don't...
...get any of this anymore...
Some-thing's definitely wrong...
...with this entire world.
Even so, this is the world...
...we must live in.

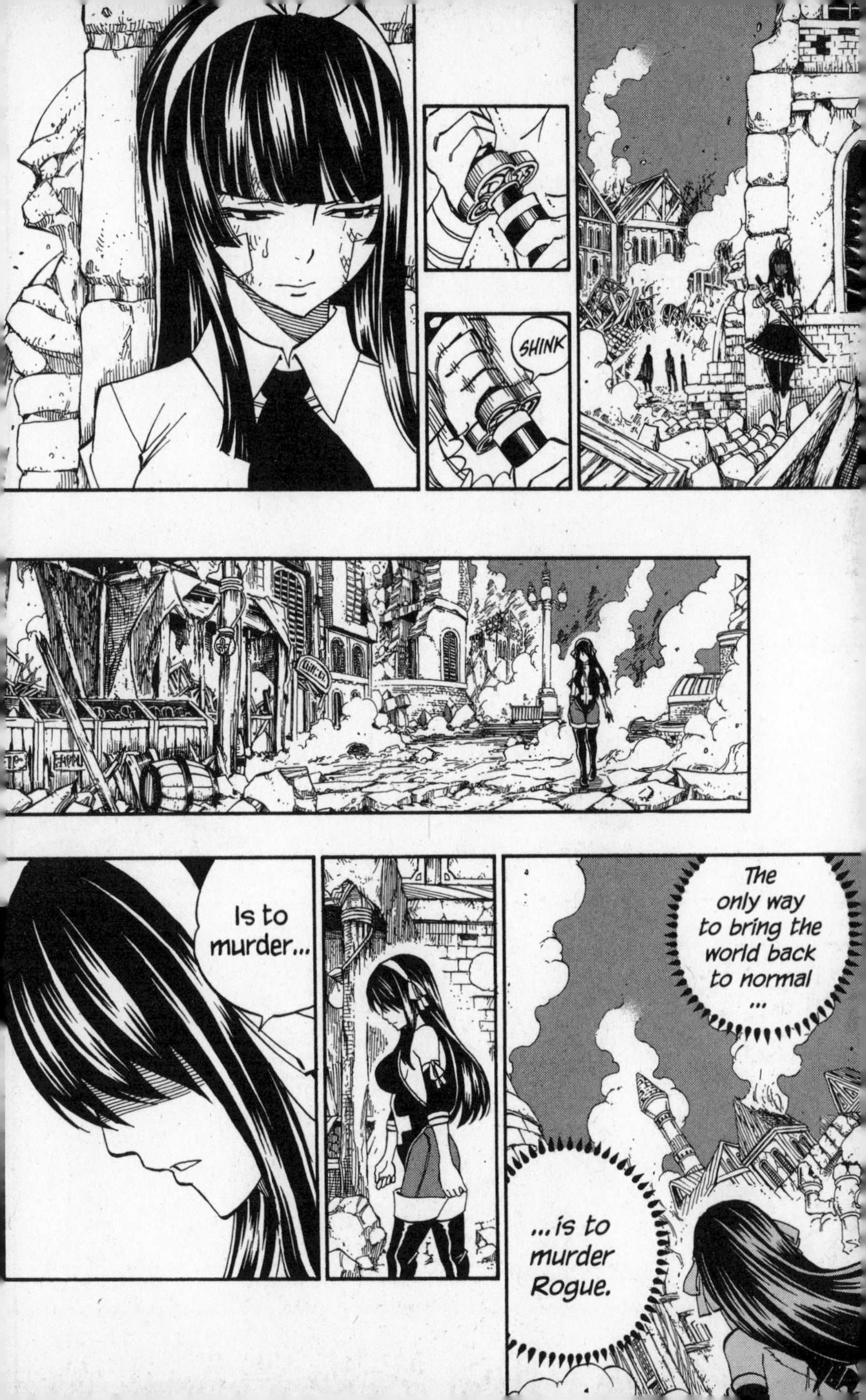
SHINK
The only way to bring the world back to normal ...
...is to murder Rogue.
Is to murder...

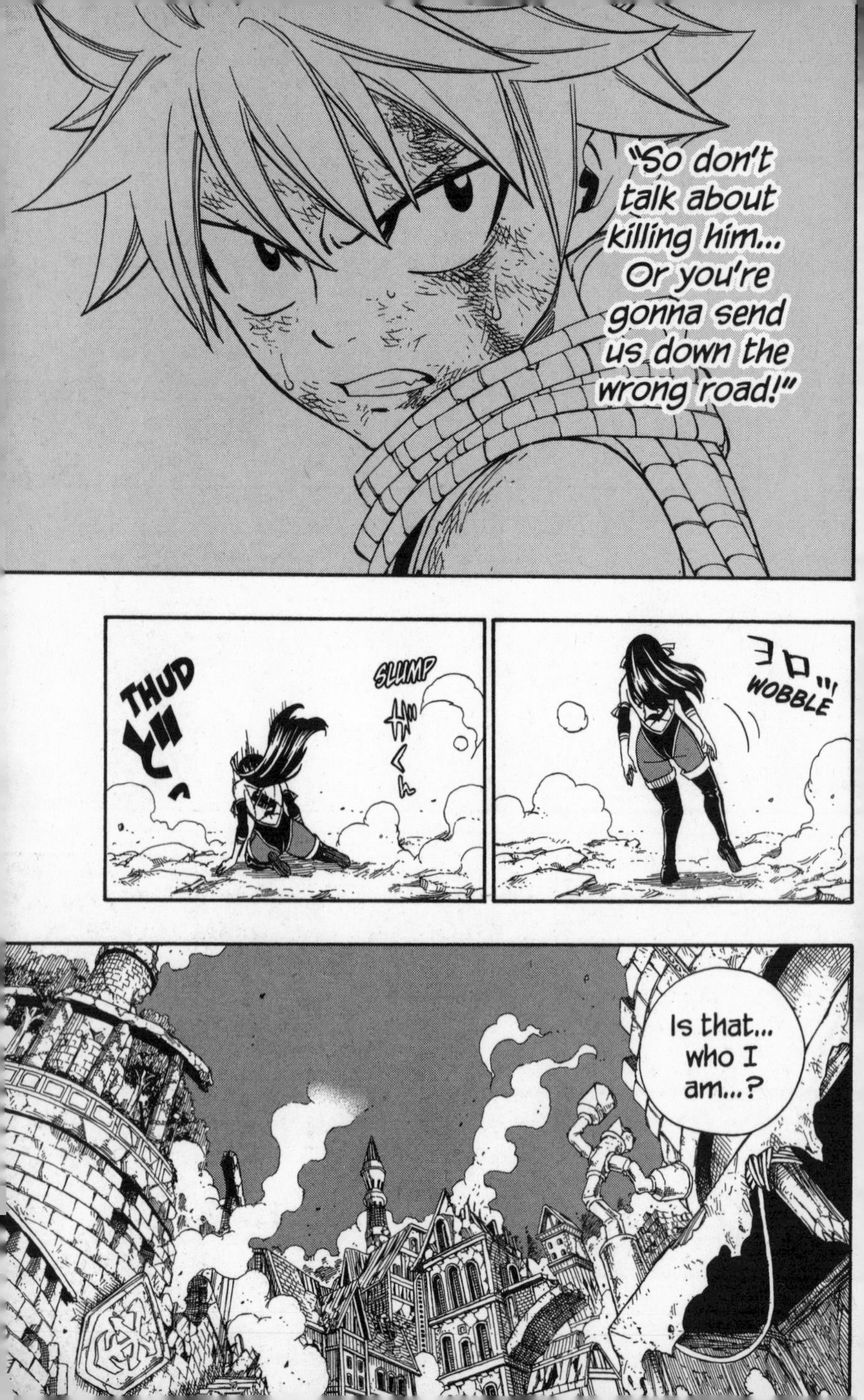
"So don't talk about killing him... Or you're gonna send us down the wrong road!"
ヨロ
WOBBLE
SLUMP
THUD
Is that... who I am...?

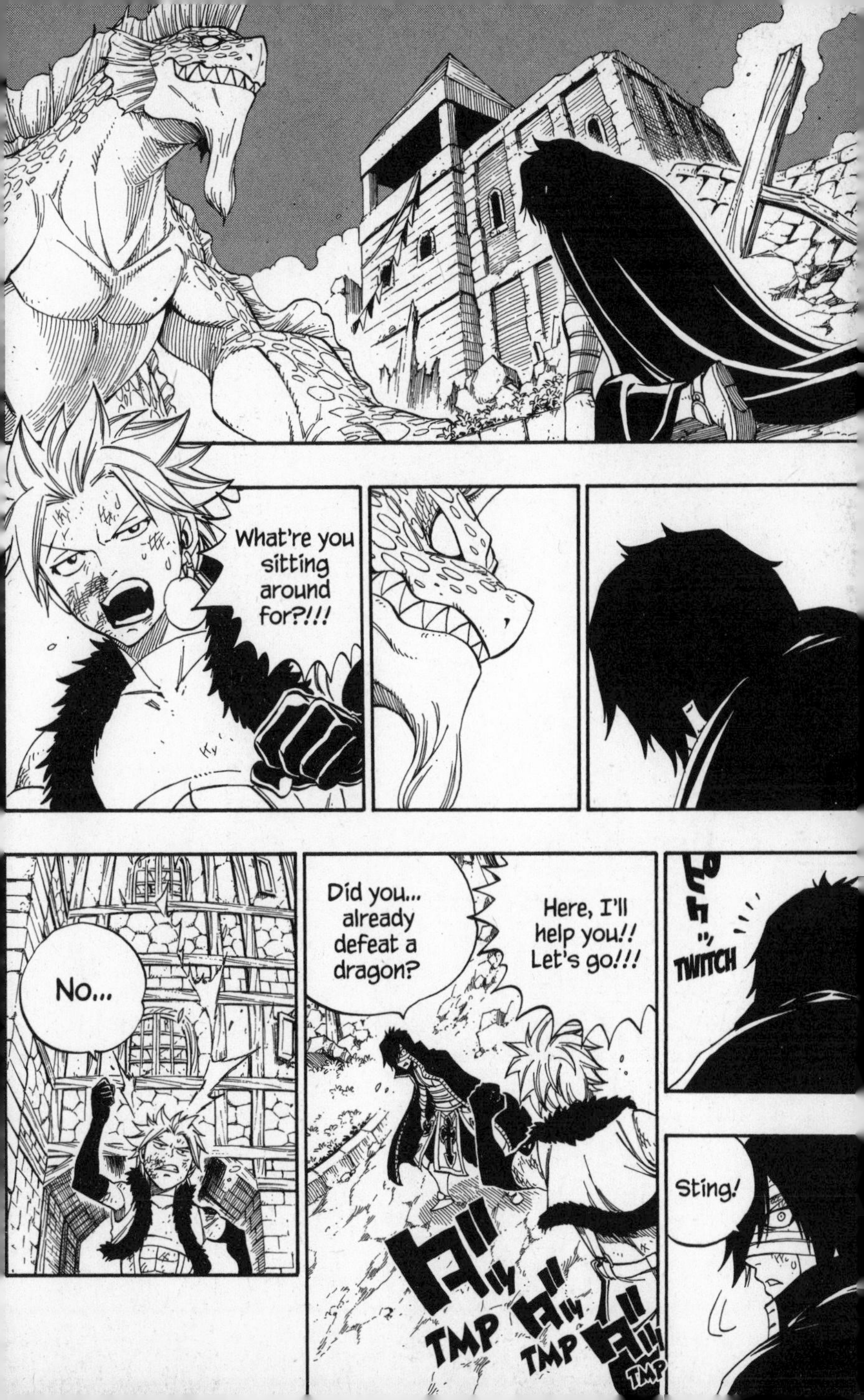
What're you sitting around for?!!!
TWITCH
Sting!
Here, I'll help you!! Let's go!!!
Did you... already defeat a dragon?
TMP
TMP
TMP
No...

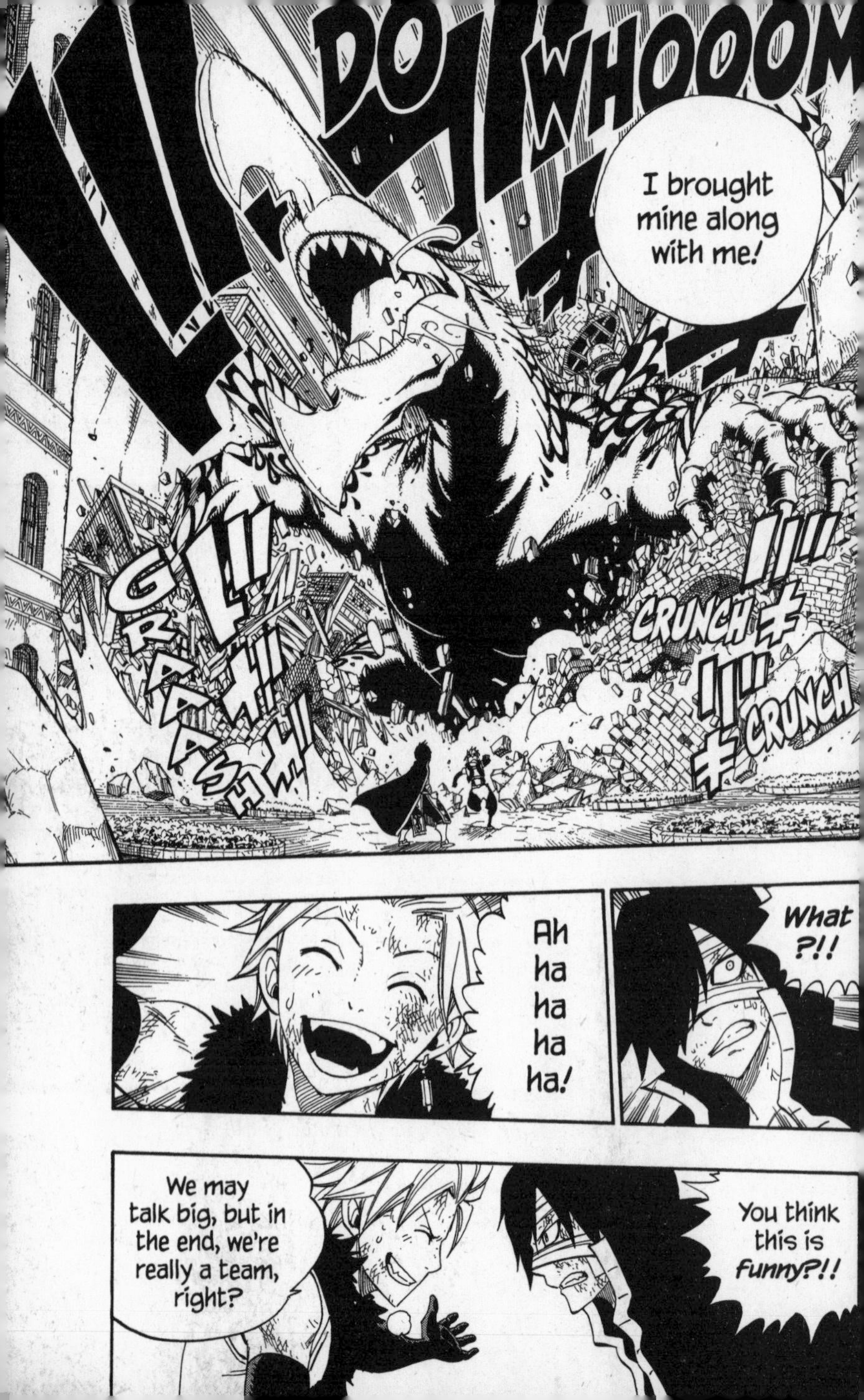
DO WHOOOM
I brought mine along with me!
CRUNCH
CRUNCH
GRAAASH!!
What?!!
Ah ha ha ha ha!
You think this is funny?!!
We may talk big, but in the end, we're really a team, right?

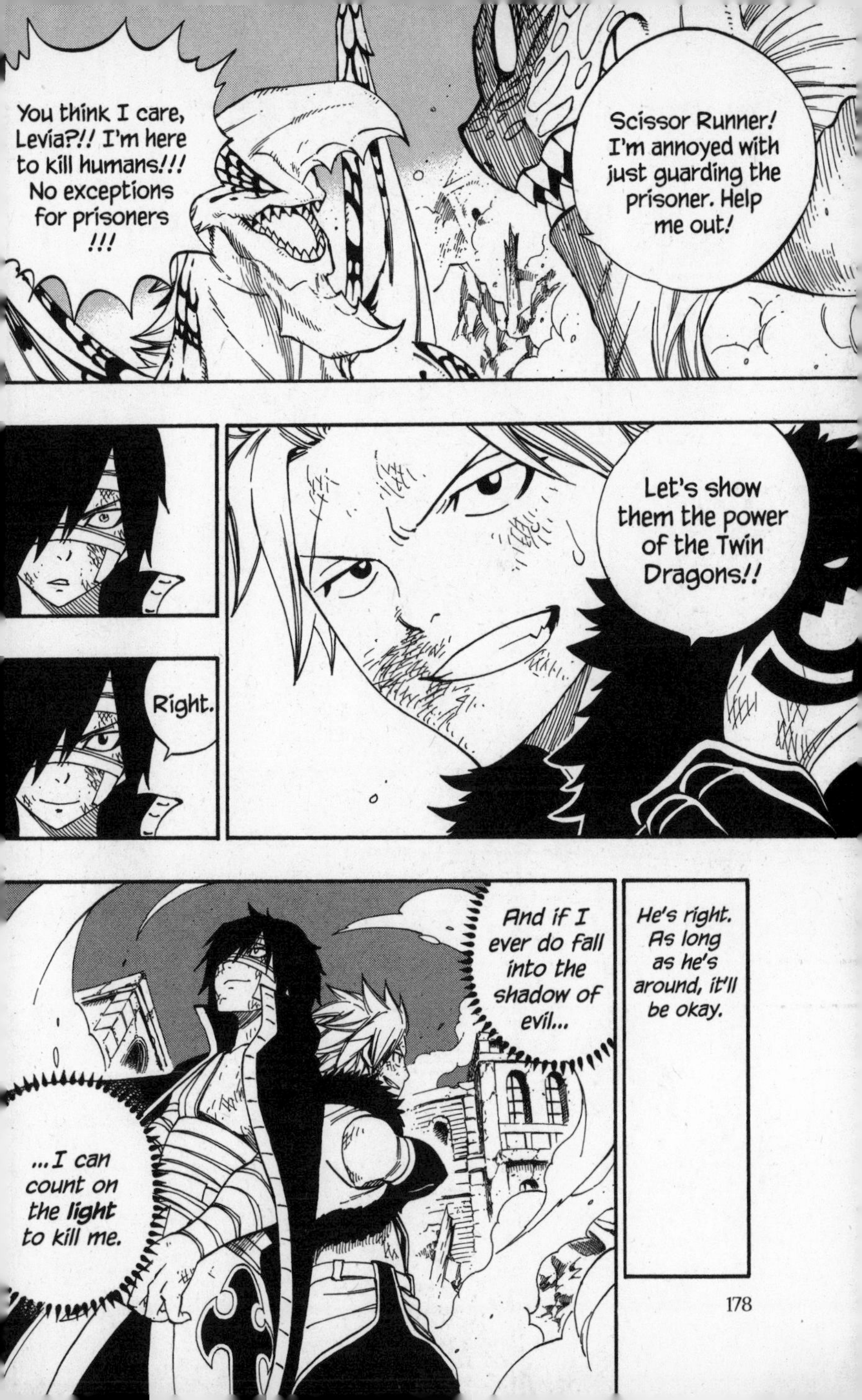
Scissor Runner! I'm annoyed with just guarding the prisoner. Help me out!
You think I care, Levia?!! I'm here to kill humans!!! No exceptions for prisoners!!!
Let's show them the power of the Twin Dragons!!
Right.
He's right. As long as he's around, it'll be okay.
And if I ever do fall into the shadow of evil...
...I can count on the **light** to kill me.

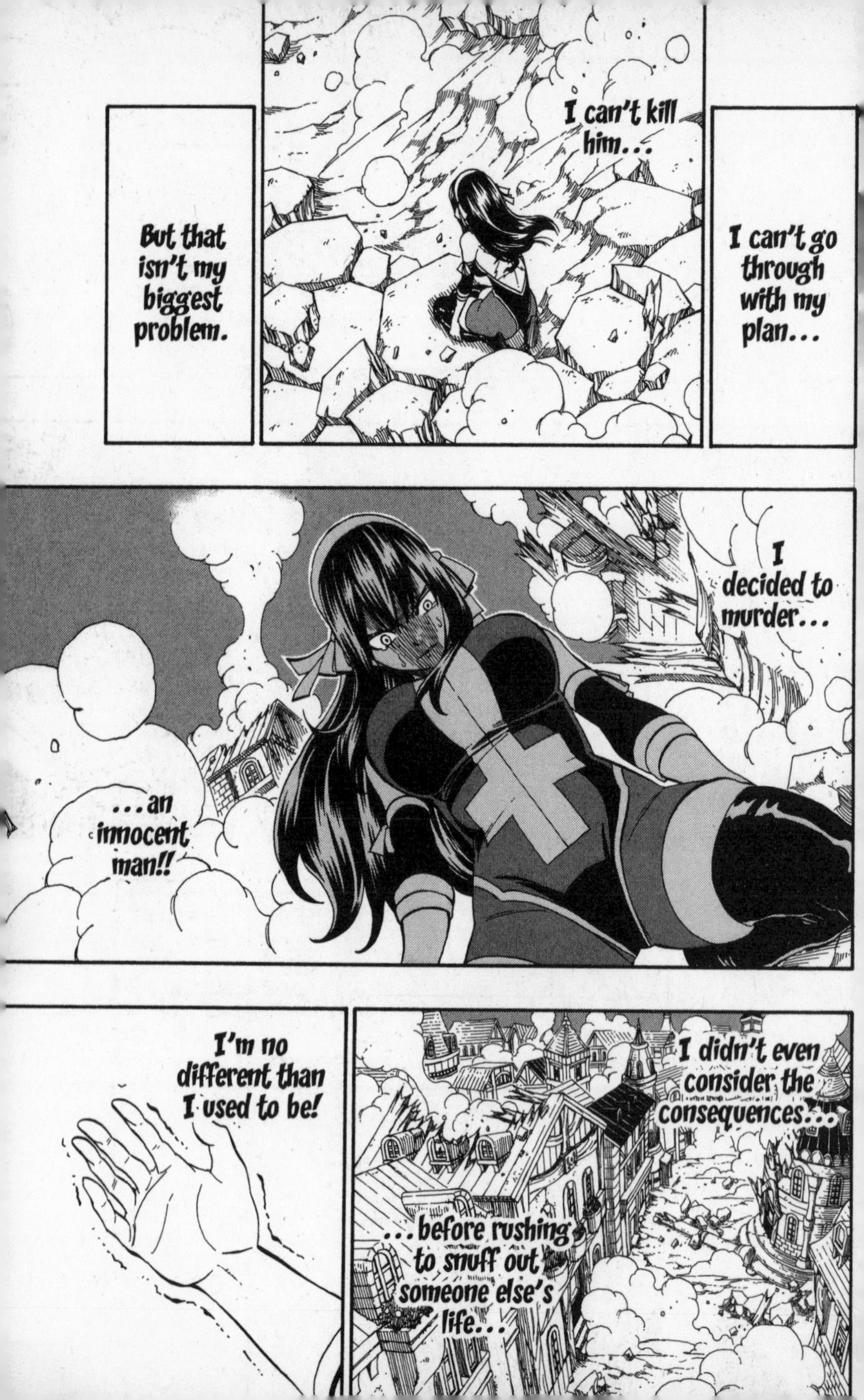
I can't go through with my plan...
I can't kill him...
But that isn't my biggest problem.
I decided to murder...
...an innocent man!!
I didn't even consider the consequences...
...before rushing to snuff out someone else's life...
I'm no different than I used to be!

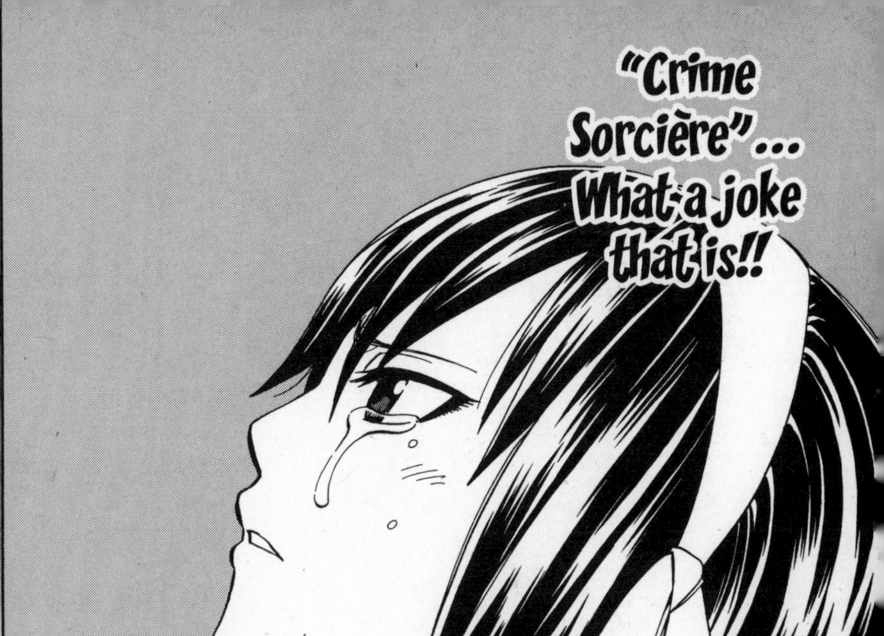
"Crime Sorcière"... What a joke that is!!
I'll never be able to wash my sins away!

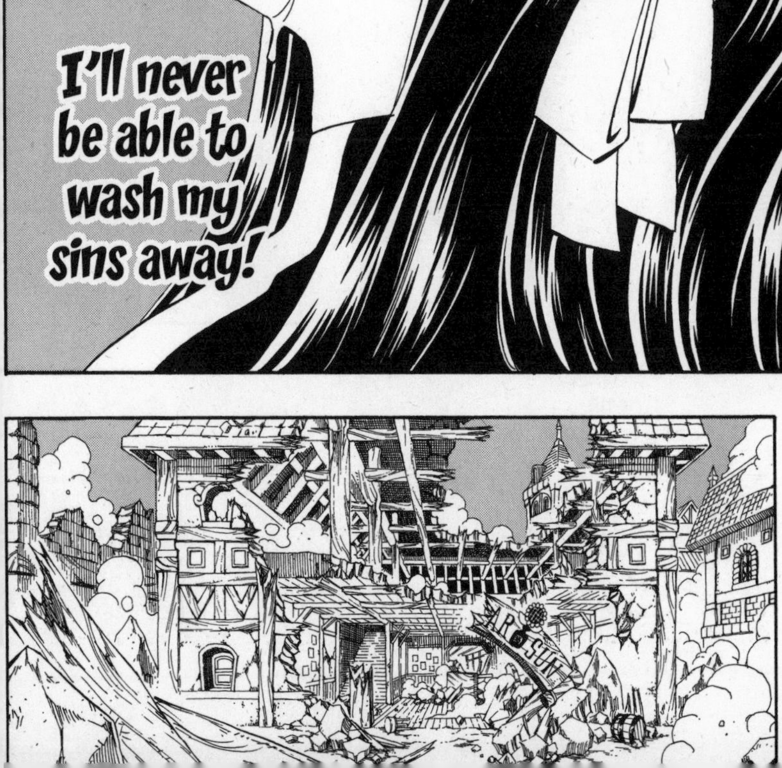

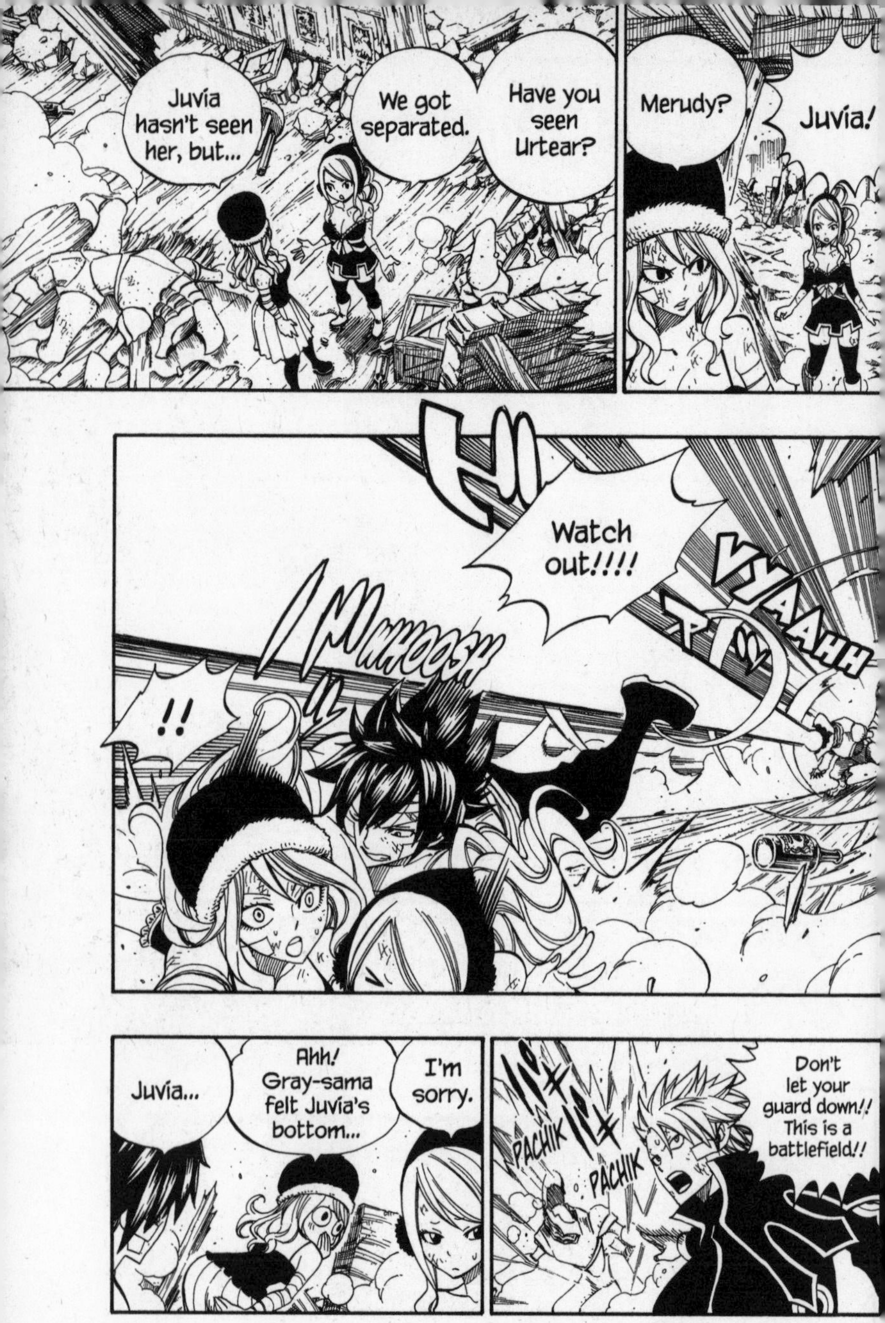

Juvia!
Merudy?
Have you seen Urtear?
We got separated.
Juvia hasn't seen her, but...
Watch out!!!!
VYAAHH
WHOOSH
!!
Don't let your guard down!! This is a battlefield!!
PACHIK
PACHIK
I'm sorry.
Ahh! Gray-sama felt Juvia's bottom...
Juvia...

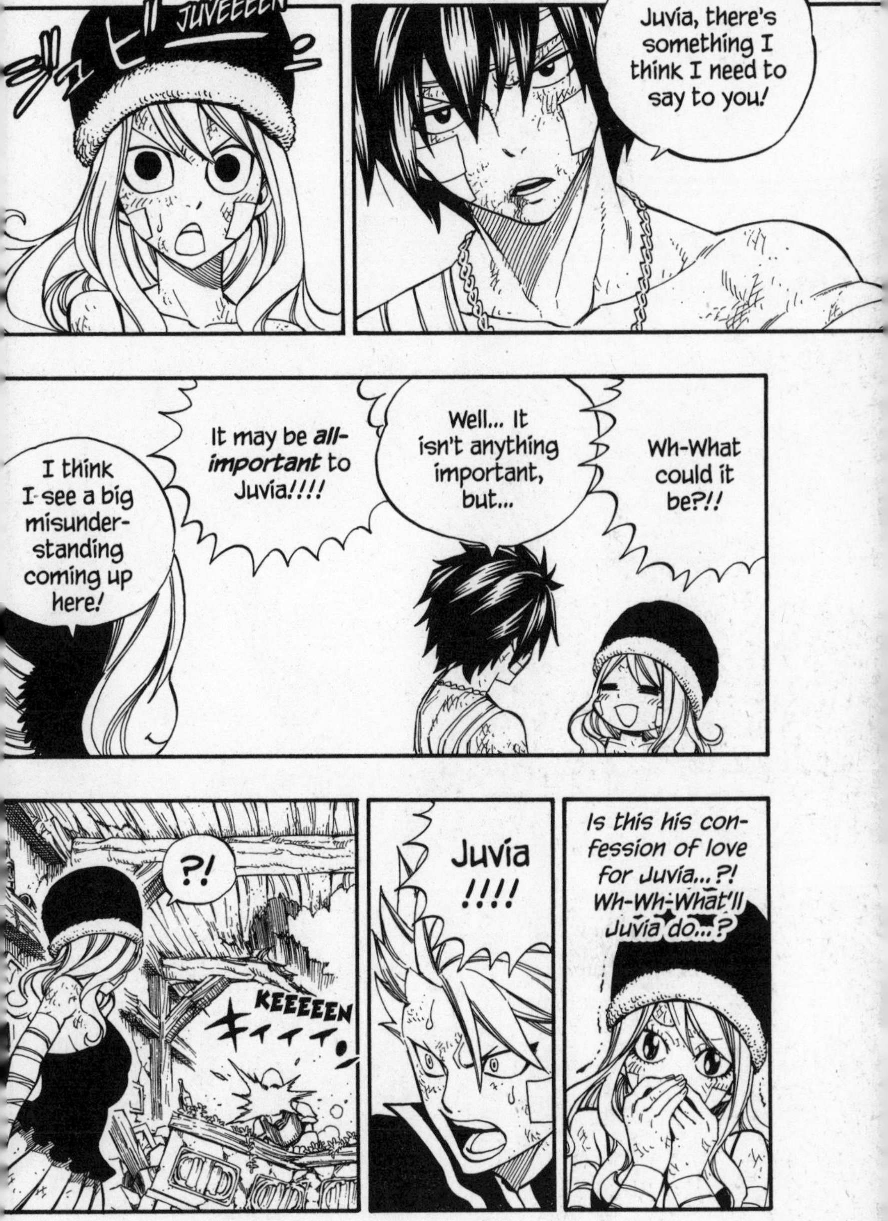
Juvia, there's something I think I need to say to you!
JUVEEEEN
Wh-What could it be?!!
Well... It isn't anything important, but...
It may be *all-important* to Juvia!!!!
I think I see a big misunderstanding coming up here!
Is this his confession of love for Juvia...?! Wh-Wh-What'll Juvia do...?
Juvia !!!!
?!
KEEEEEN

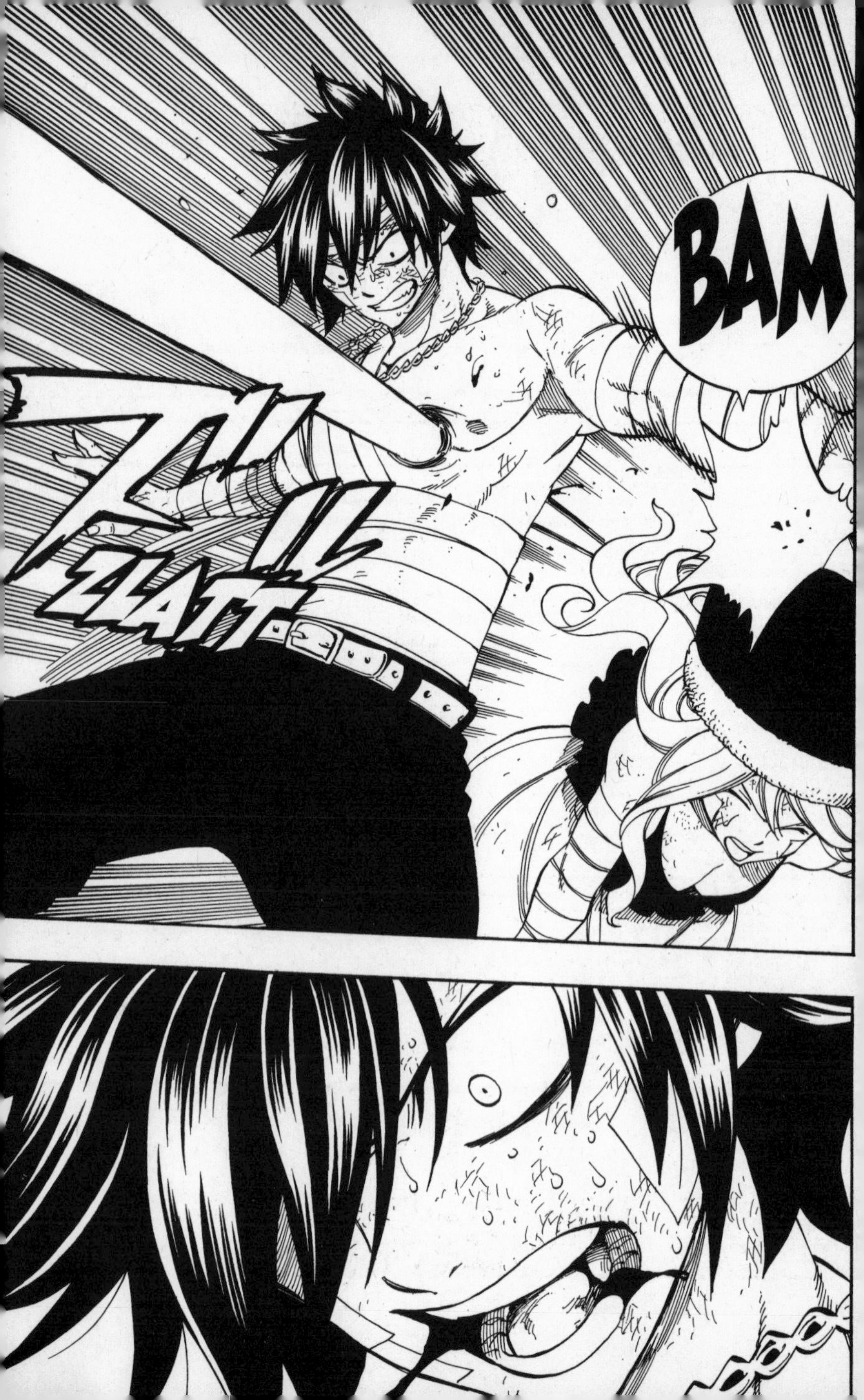
BAM
ZLATT

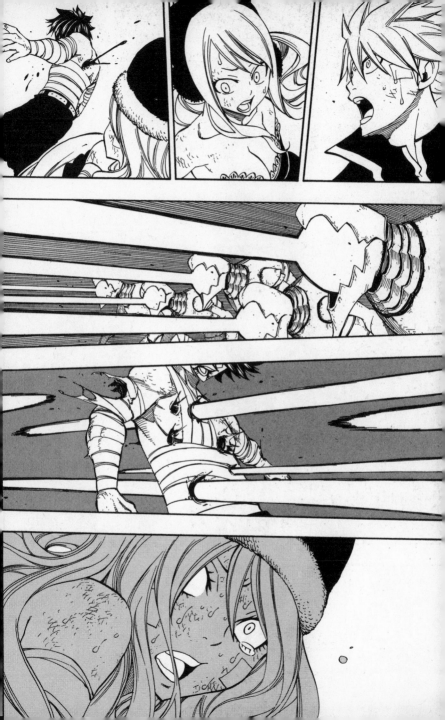

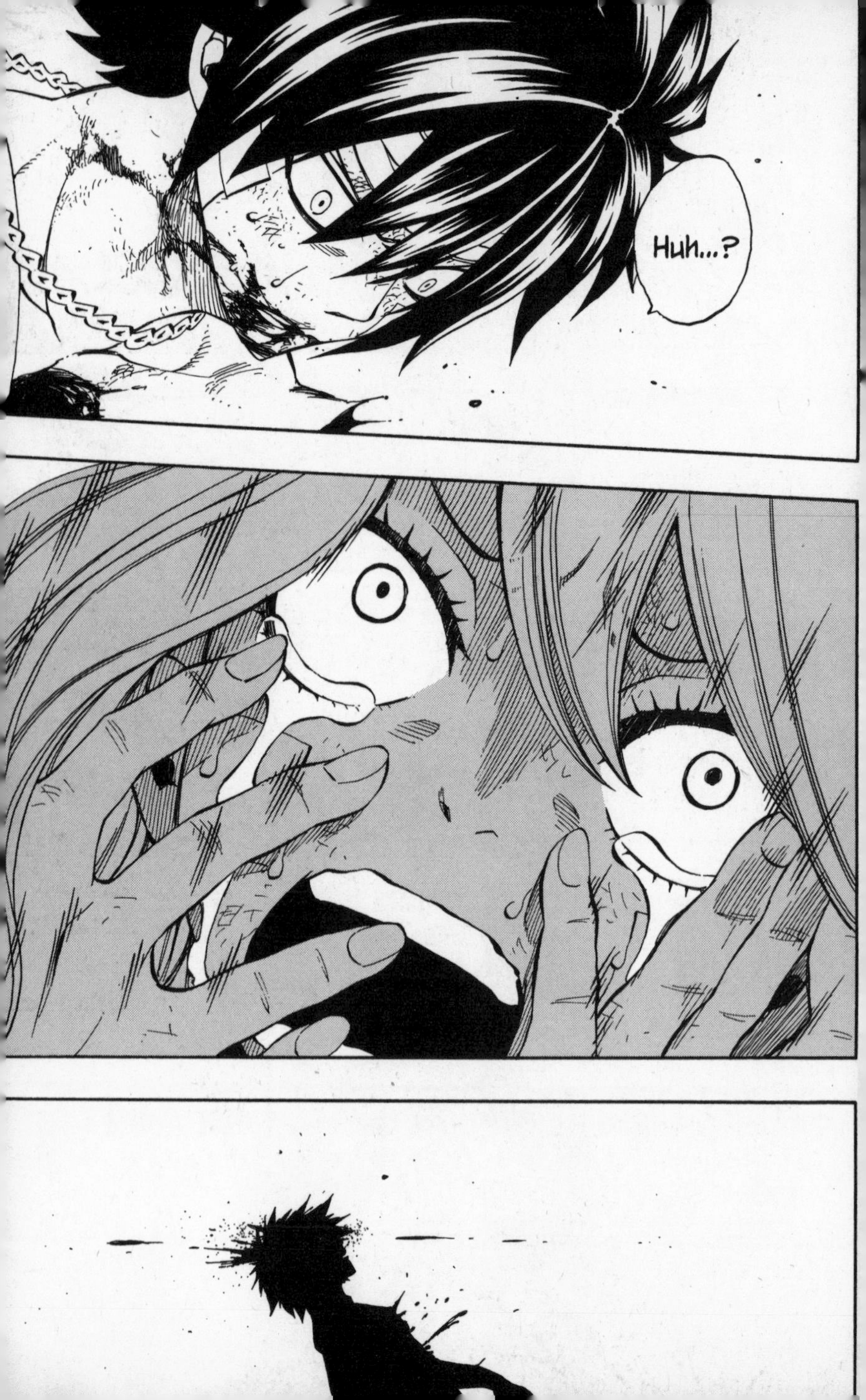
Huh...?

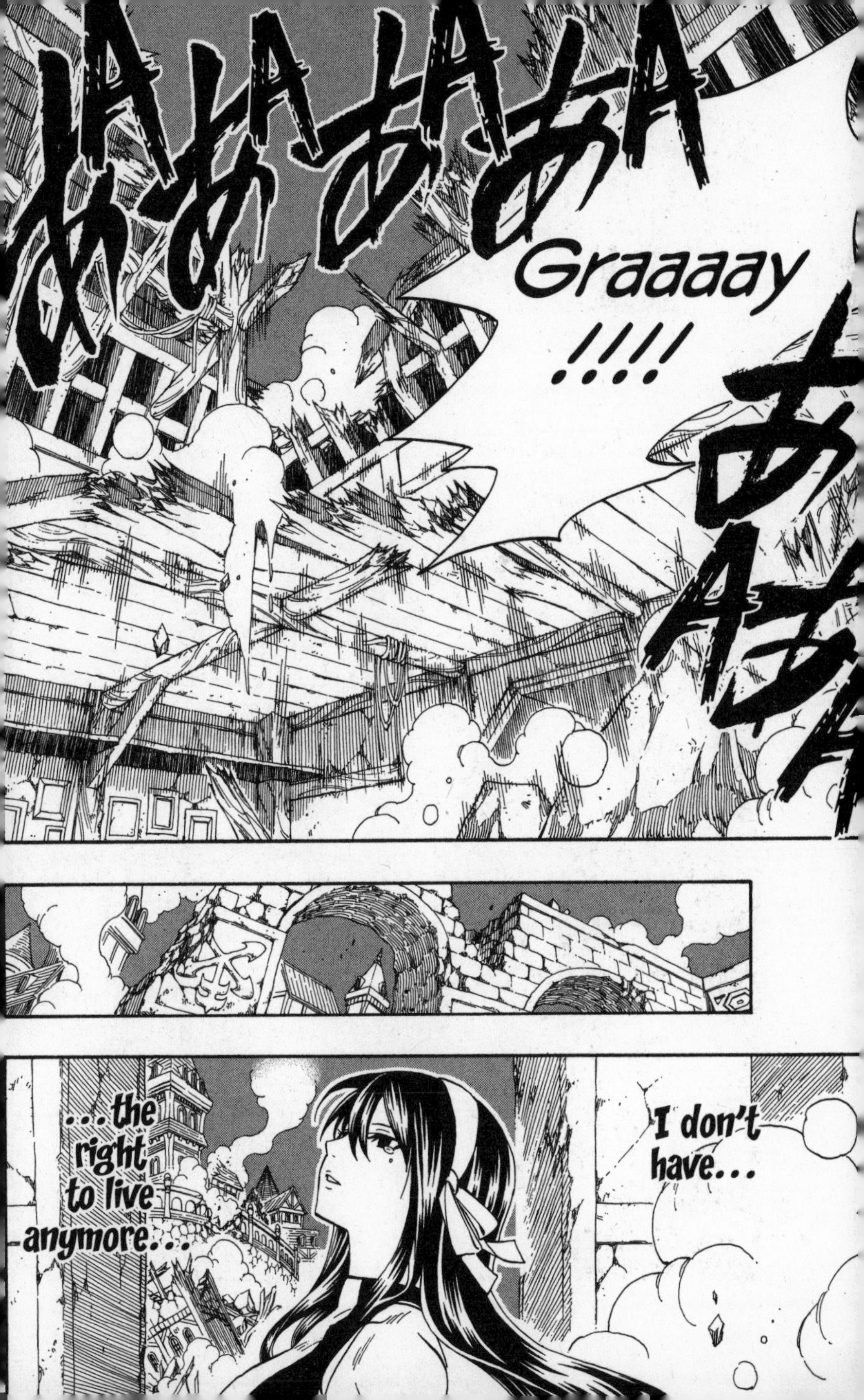
Graaaay !!!!
I don't have...
...the right to live anymore...

FAIRY TAIL

フェアリーテイル

Chapter 335: Time of Life

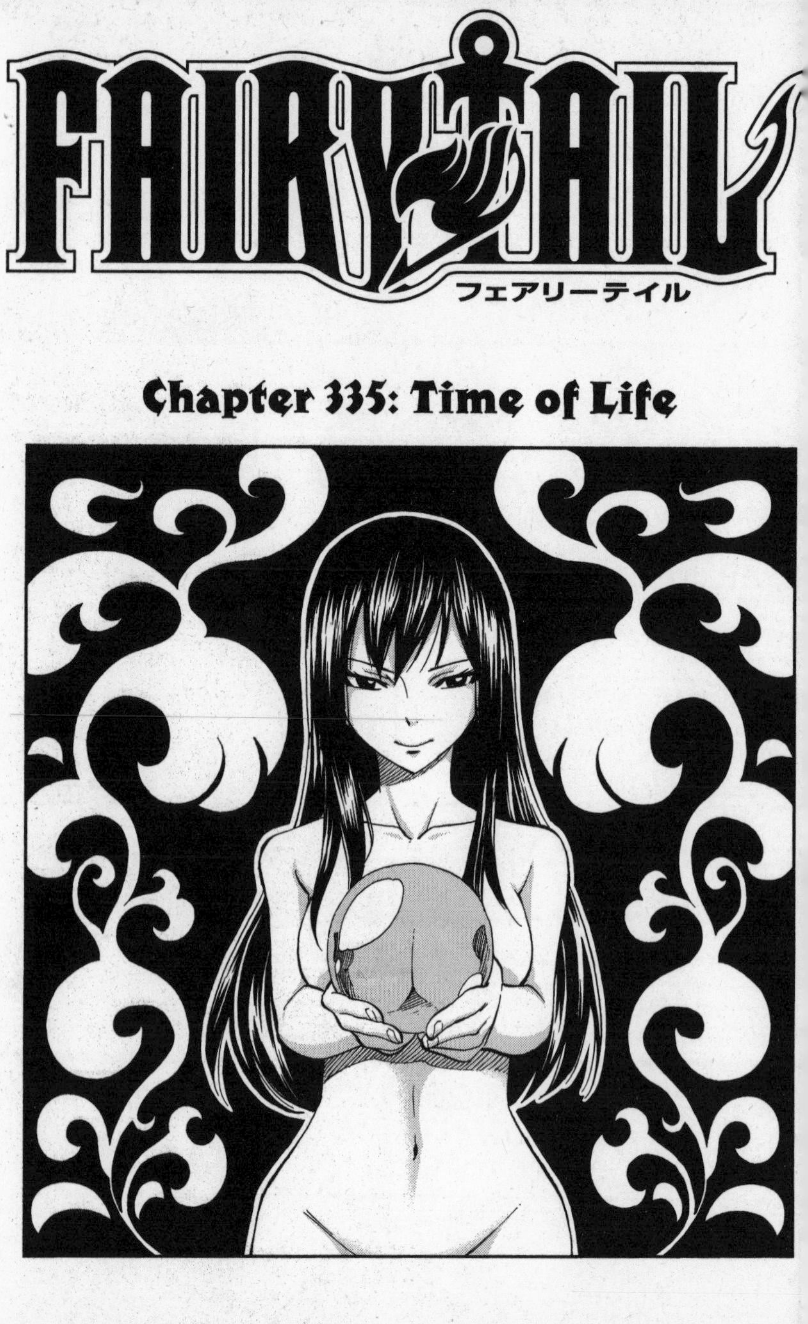

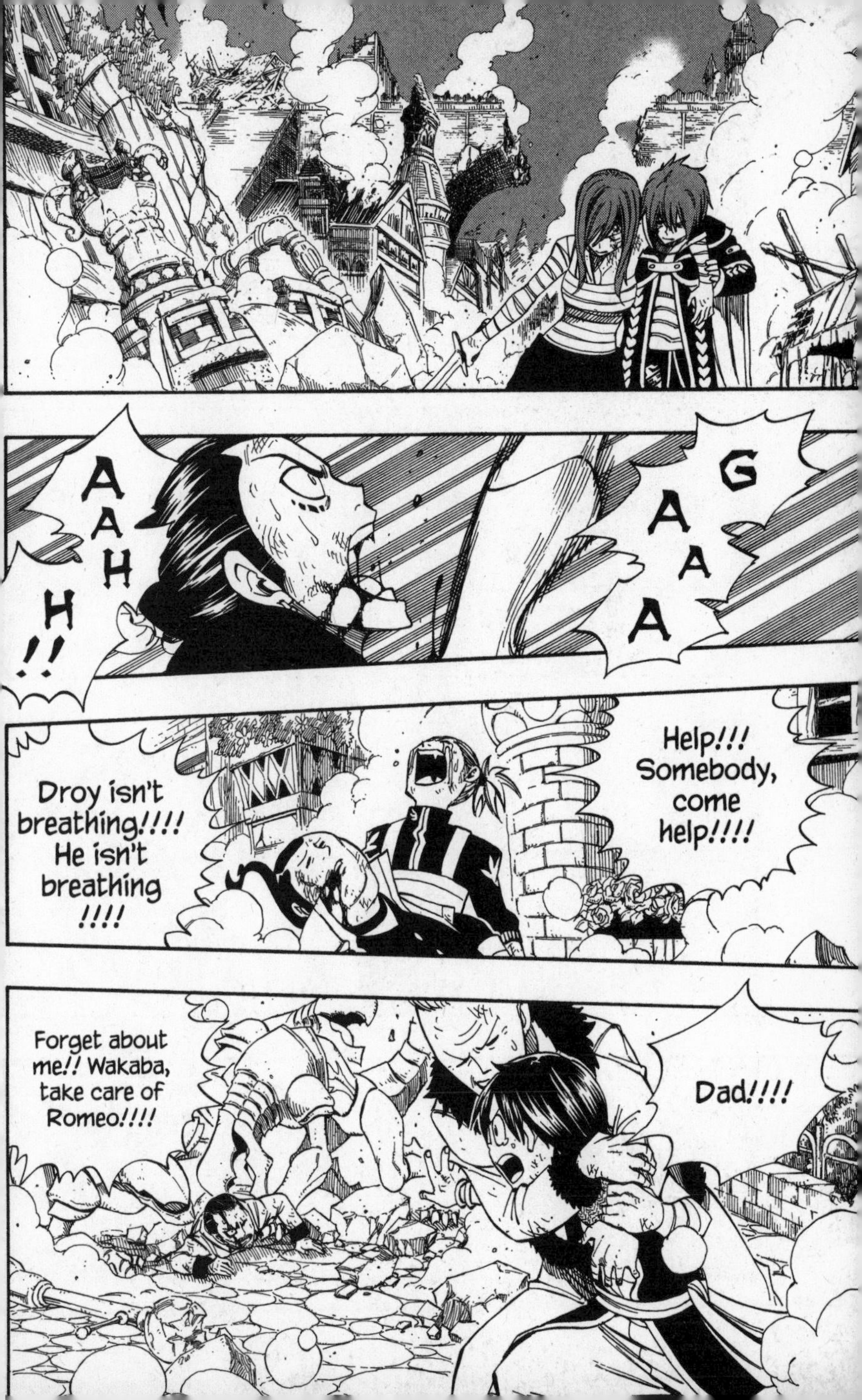
GAAAA
AAHH!!
Help!!! Somebody, come help!!!!
Droy isn't breathing!!!! He isn't breathing !!!!
Dad!!!!
Forget about me!! Wakaba, take care of Romeo!!!!

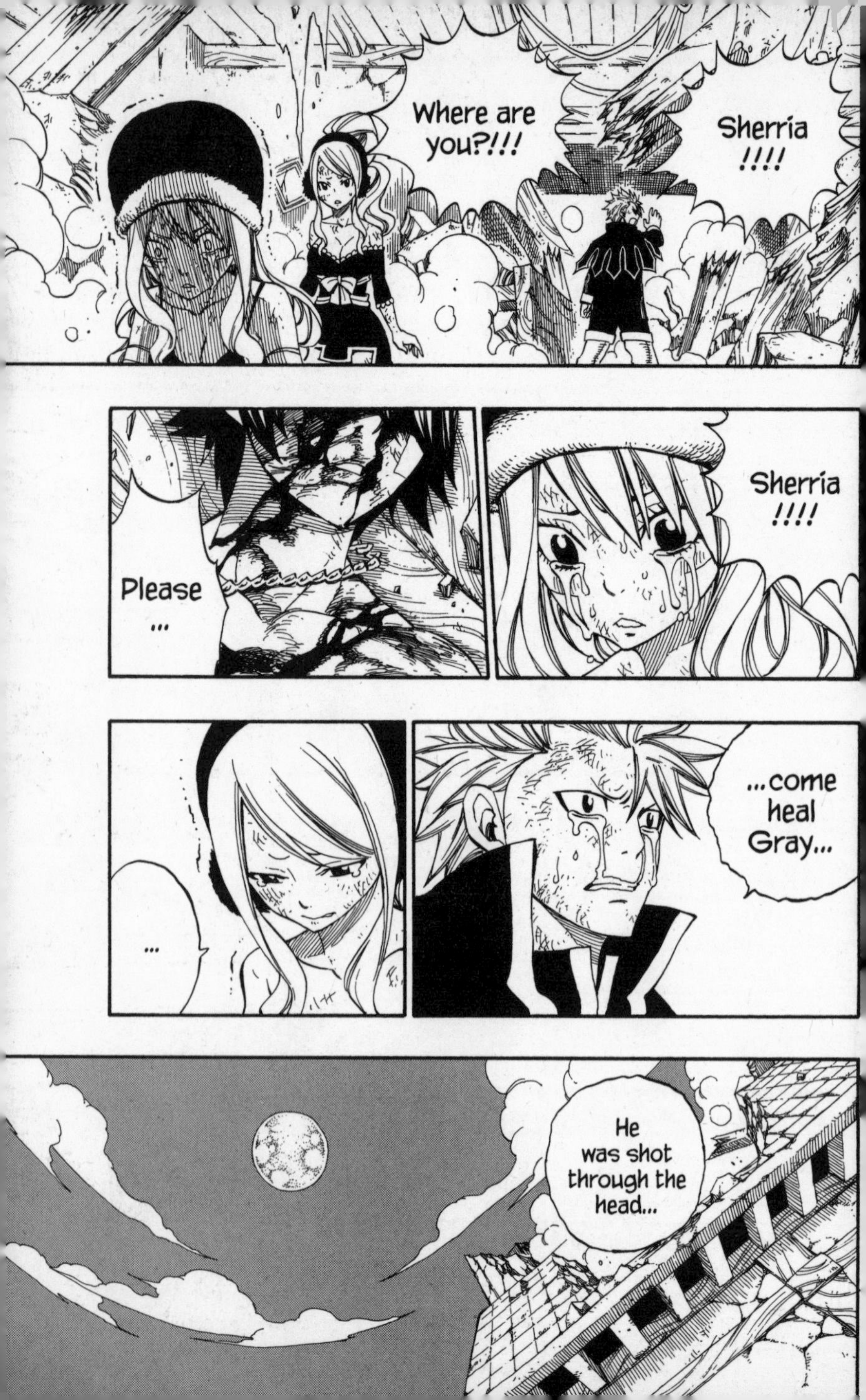
Sherria !!!!
Where are you?!!!
Sherria !!!!
Please ...
...come heal Gray...
...
He was shot through the head...

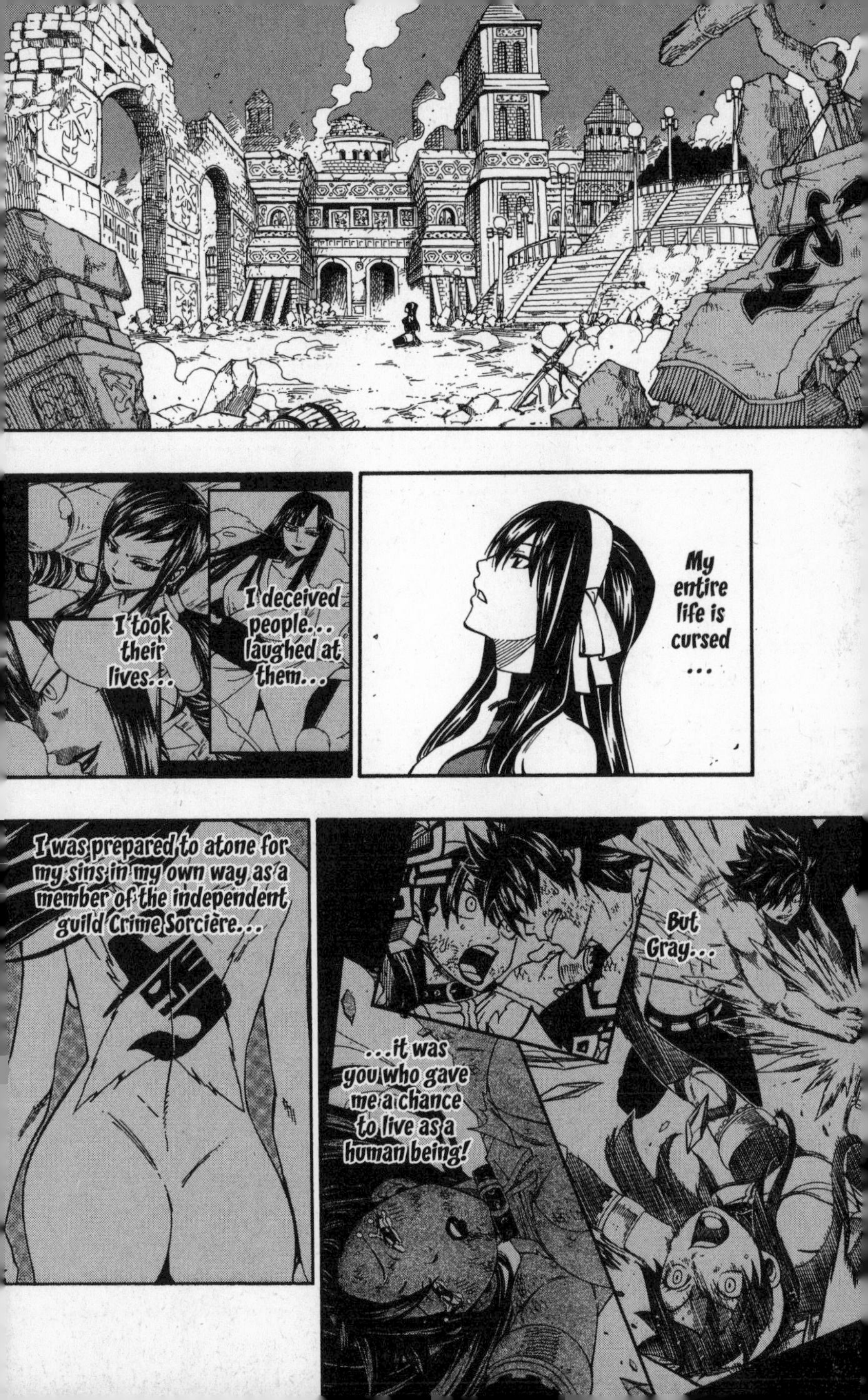
My entire life is cursed...
I deceived people... laughed at them...
I took their lives...
But Gray...
...it was you who gave me a chance to live as a human being!
I was prepared to atone for my sins in my own way as a member of the independent guild Crime Sorcière...

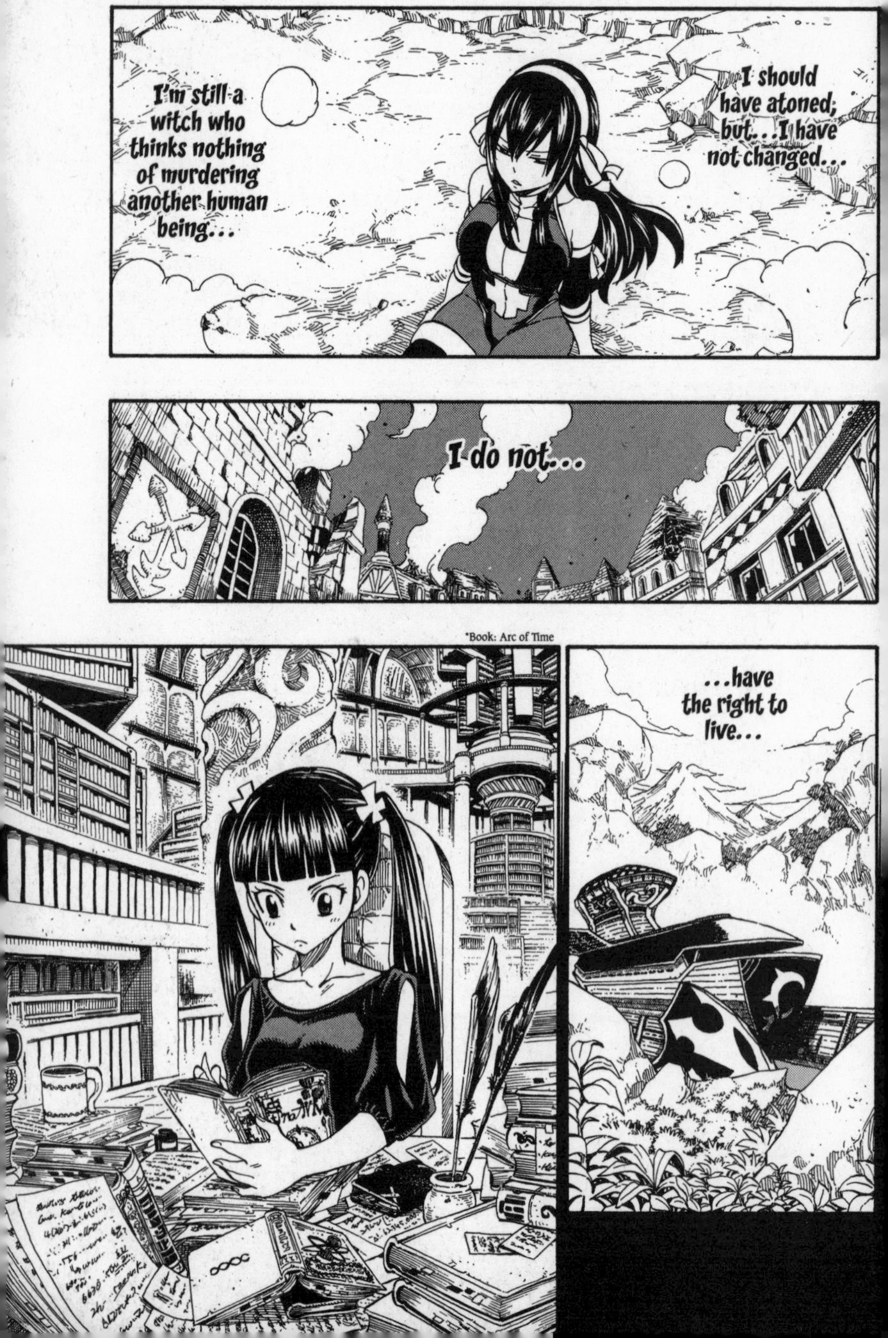
I should have atoned; but...I have not changed...
I'm still a witch who thinks nothing of murdering another human being...
I do not...
...have the right to live...

*Book: Arc of Time

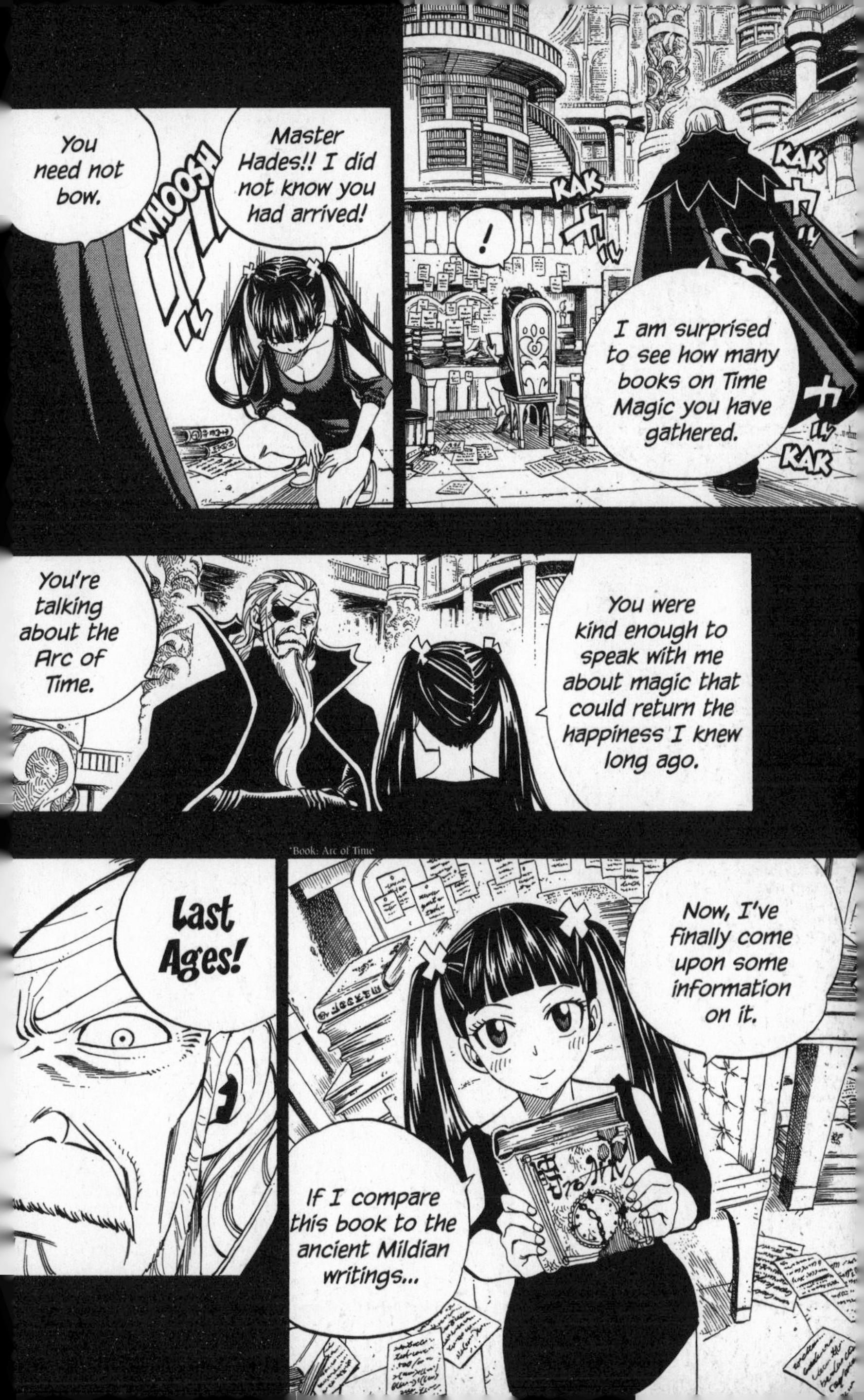
KAK
KAK
!
I am surprised to see how many books on Time Magic you have gathered.
KAK
Master Hades!! I did not know you had arrived!
WHOOSH
You need not bow.
You were kind enough to speak with me about magic that could return the happiness I knew long ago.
You're talking about the Arc of Time.
*Book: Arc of Time
Now, I've finally come upon some information on it.
If I compare this book to the ancient Mildian writings...
Last Ages!

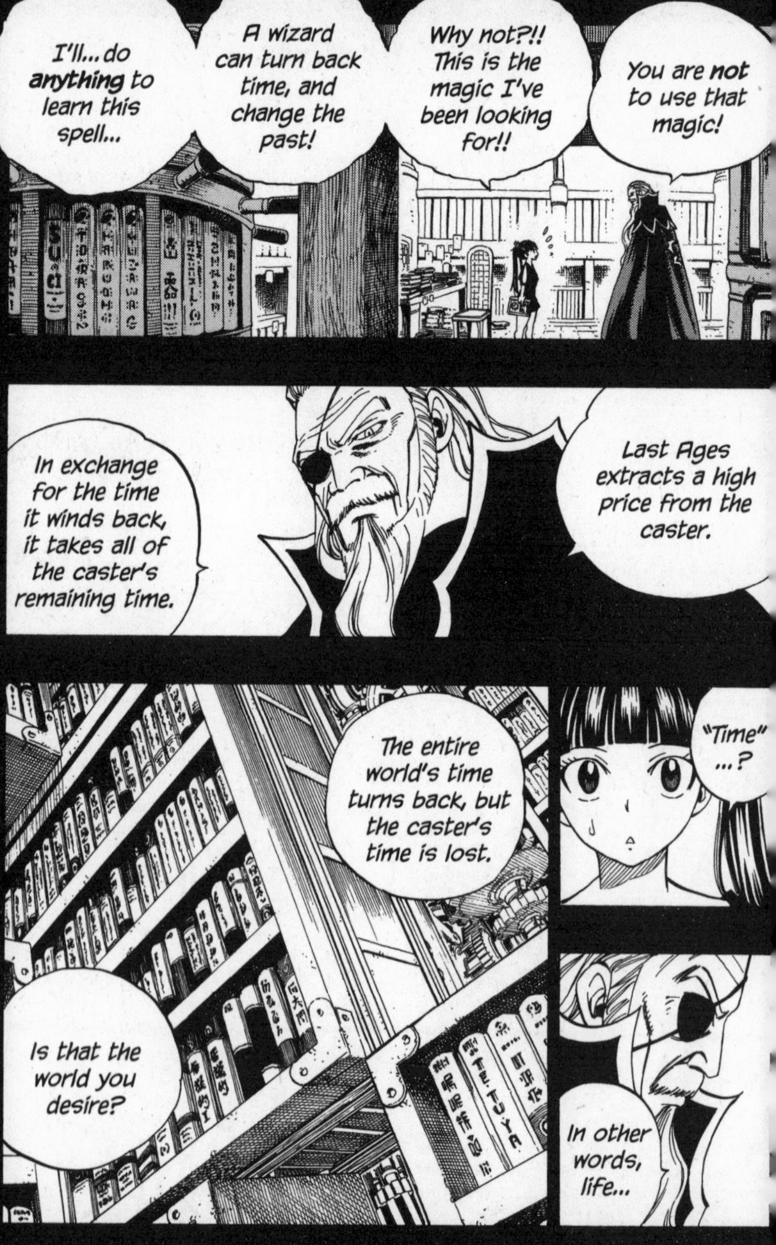
You are **not** to use that magic!
Why not?!! This is the magic I've been looking for!!
A wizard can turn back time, and change the past!
I'll...do **anything** to learn this spell...
Last Ages extracts a high price from the caster.
In exchange for the time it winds back, it takes all of the caster's remaining time.
"Time" ...?
In other words, life...
The entire world's time turns back, but the caster's time is lost.
Is that the world you desire?

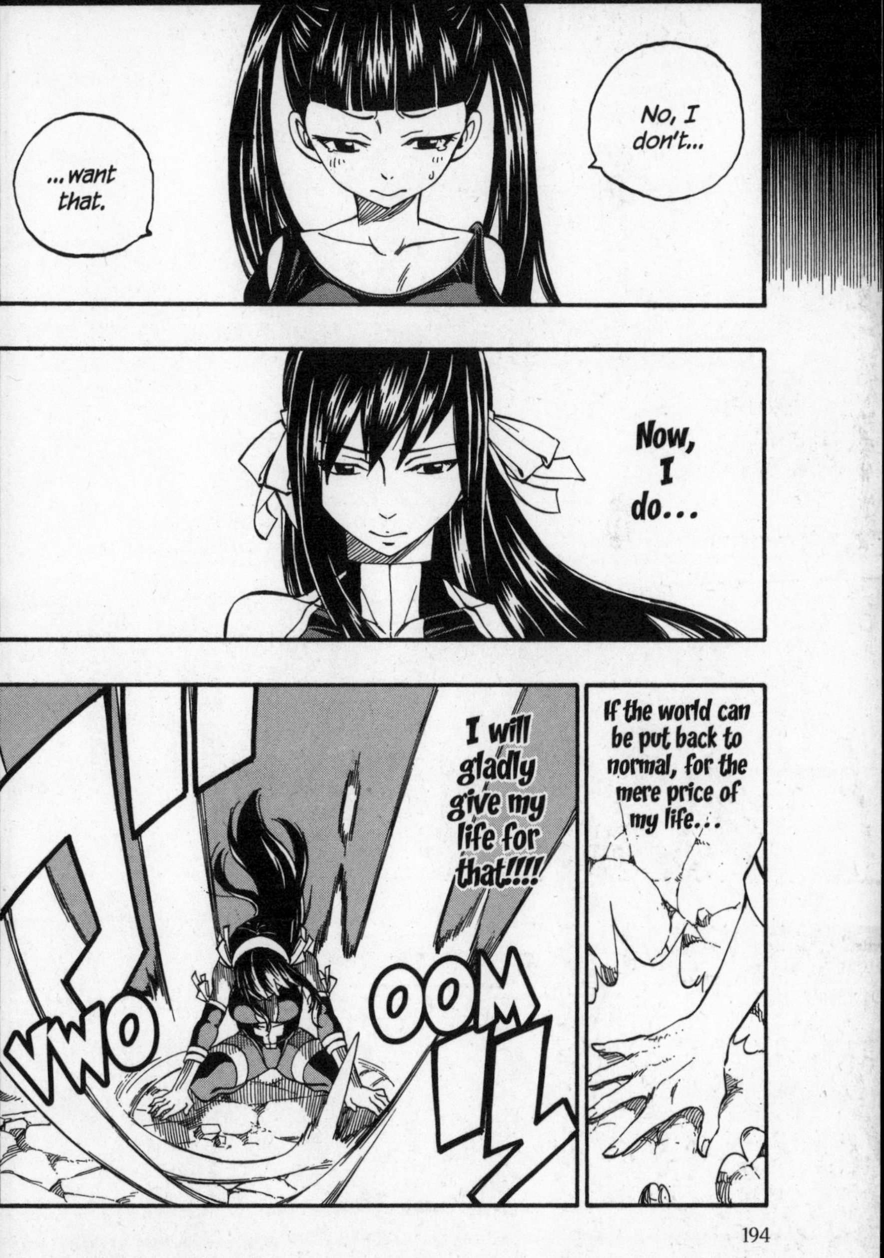
No, I don't...
...want that.
Now, I do...
If the world can be put back to normal, for the mere price of my life...
I will gladly give my life for that!!!!
VWO OOM

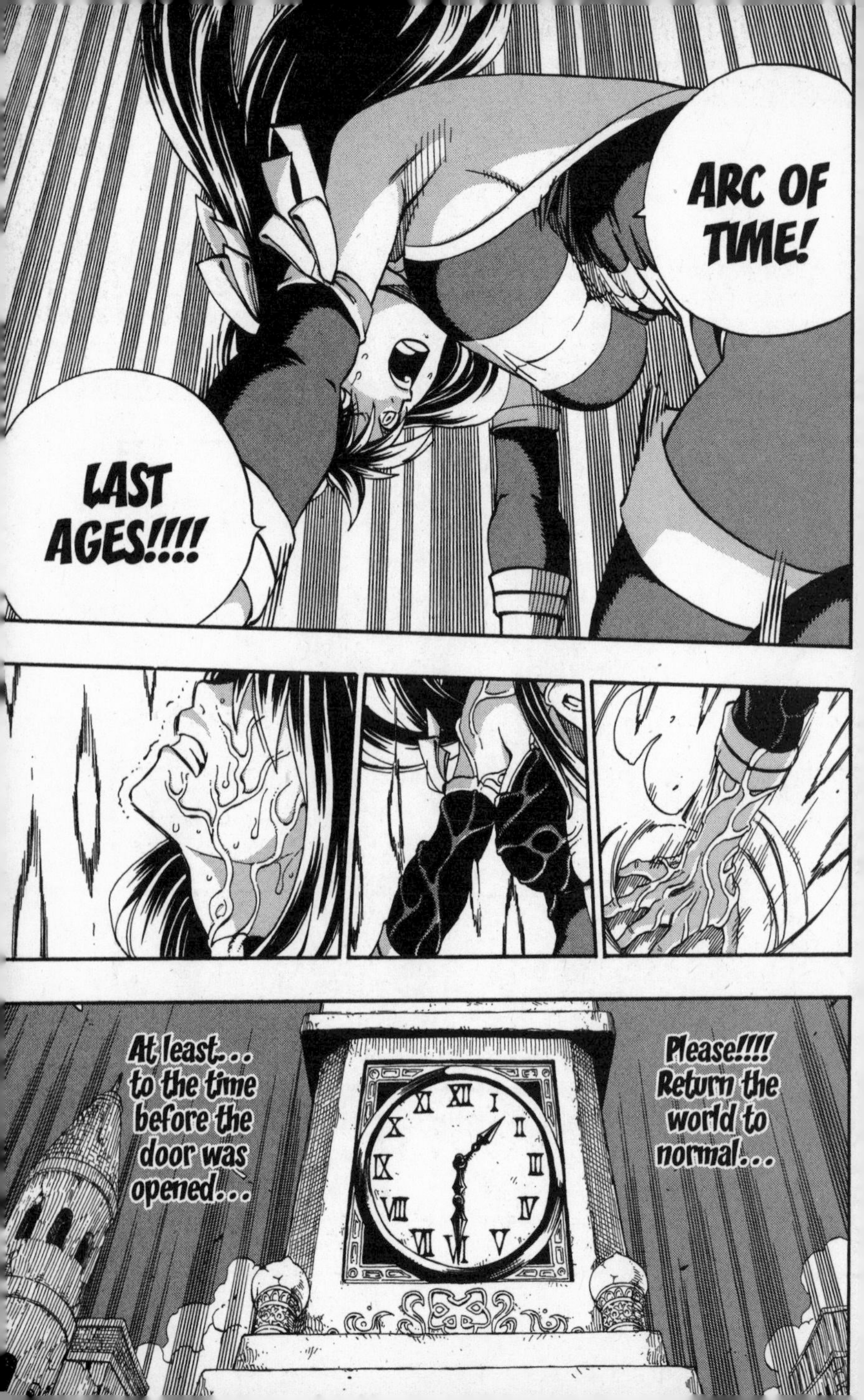
ARC OF TIME!
LAST AGES!!!!
Please!!!! Return the world to normal...
At least... to the time before the door was opened...

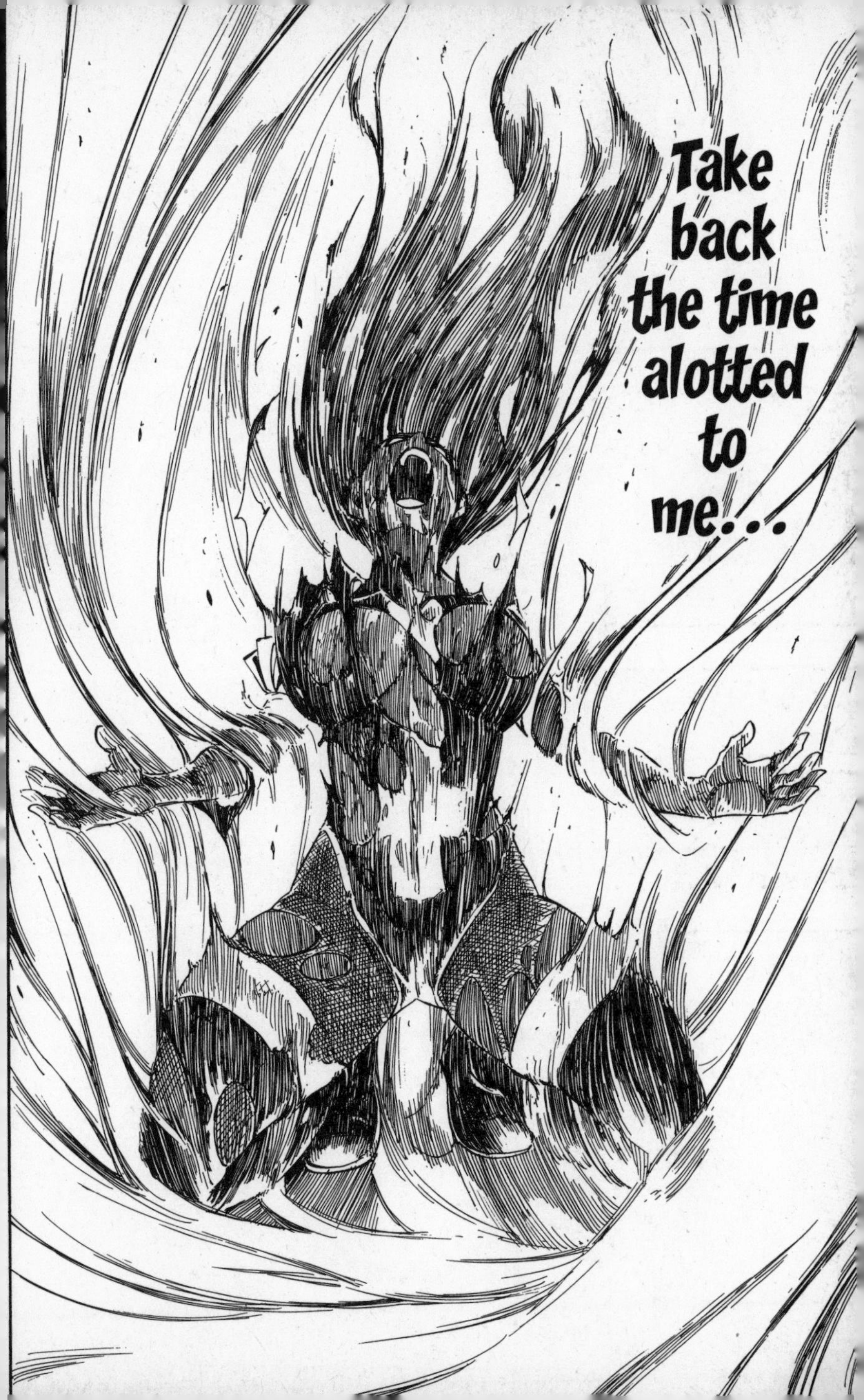
Take back the time alotted to me...

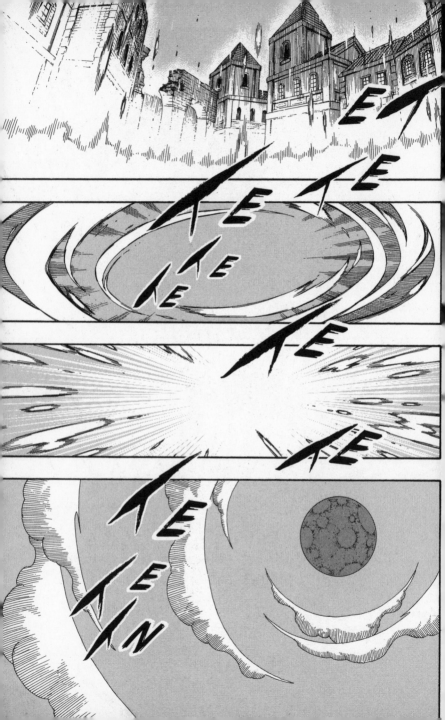

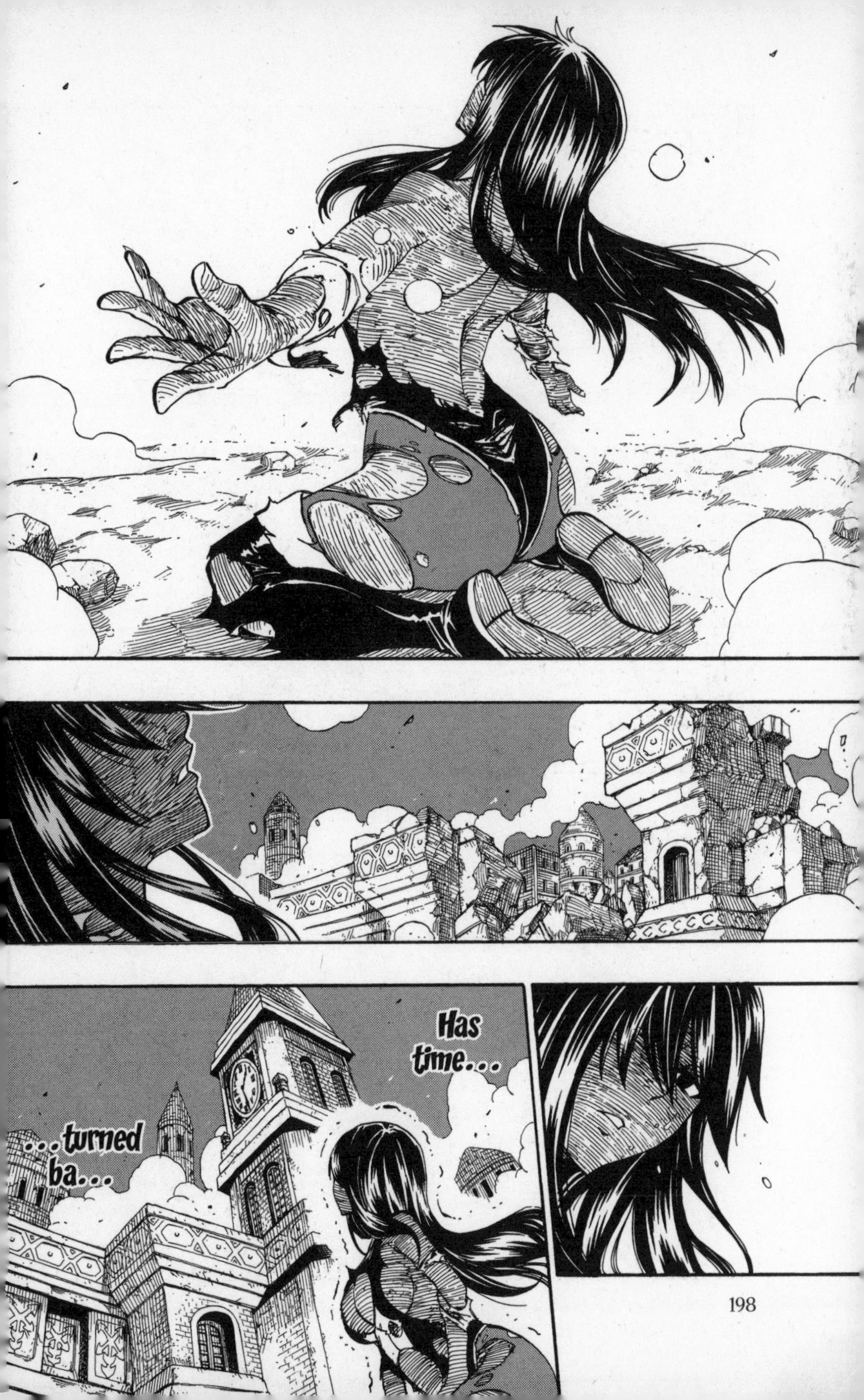
Has time...
...turned ba...

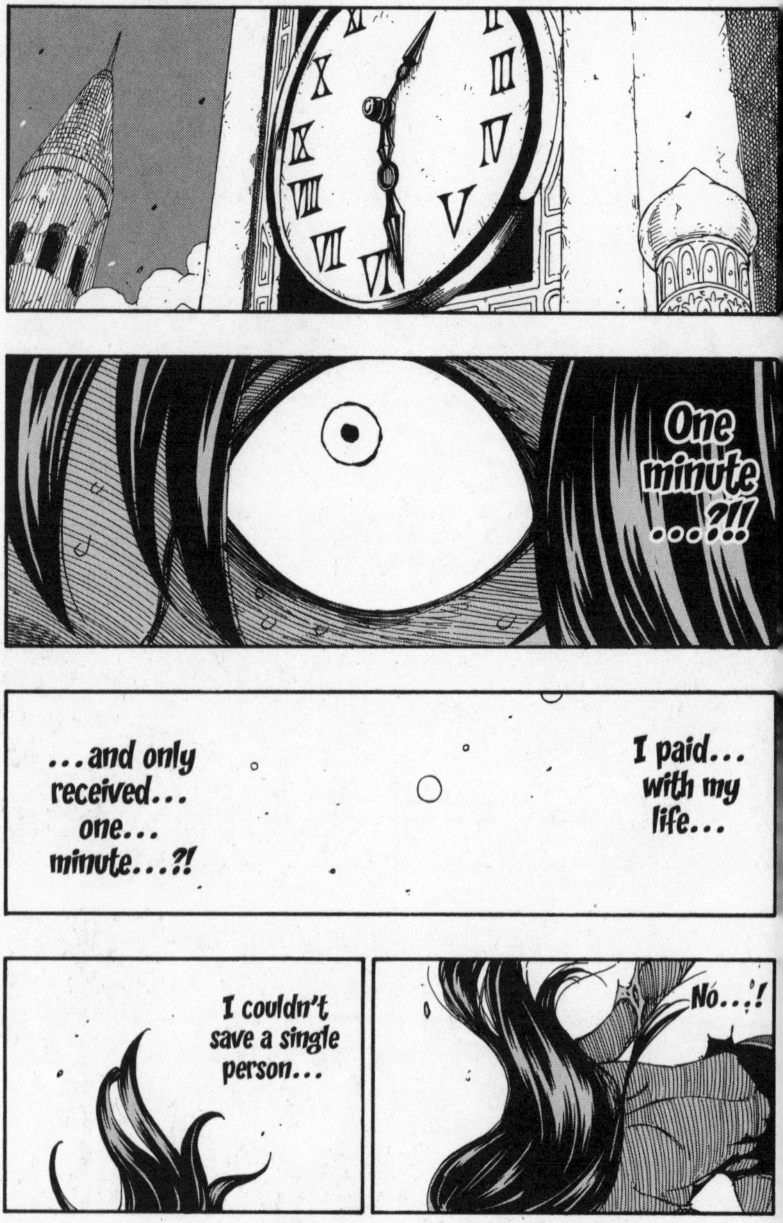
One minute...?!!
I paid... with my life...
...and only received... one... minute...?!
No...!
I couldn't save a single person...

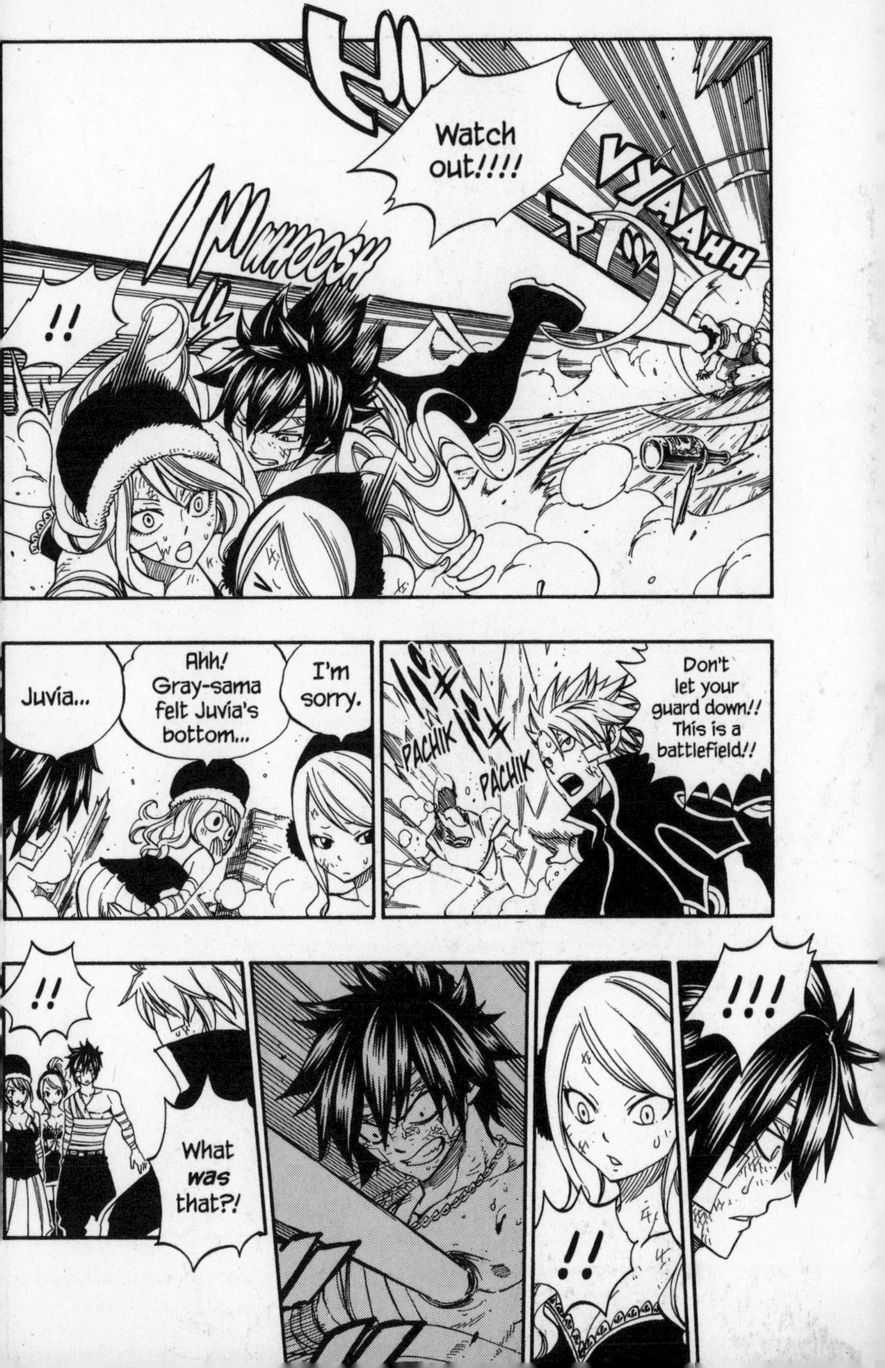

Watch out!!!!
VYAAHH
WHOOSH
!!
Don't let your guard down!! This is a battlefield!!
PACHIK
PACHIK
I'm sorry.
Ahh! Gray-sama felt Juvia's bottom...
Juvia...
!!!
!!
What was that?!
!!

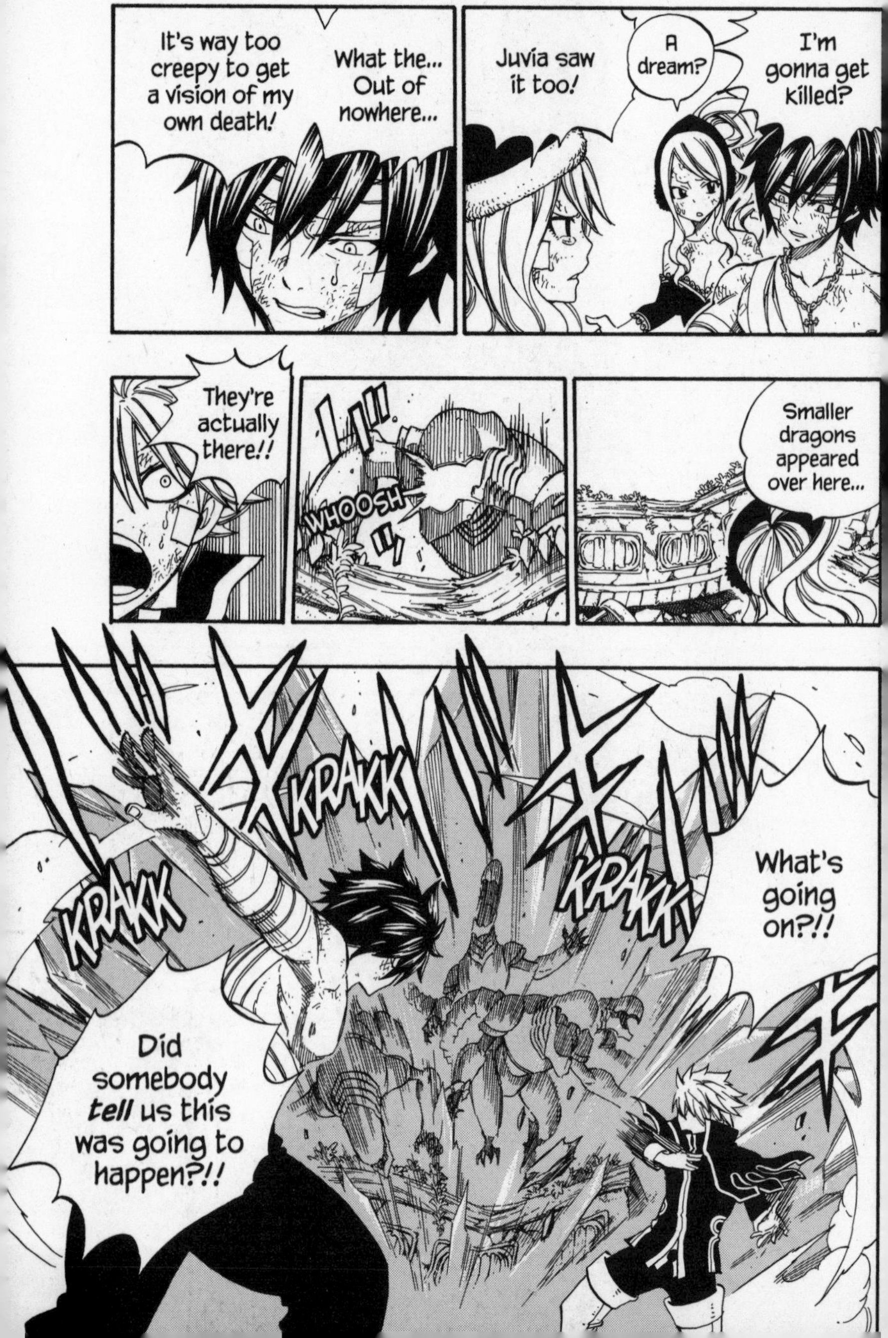

I'm gonna get killed?
A dream?
Juvia saw it too!
What the... Out of nowhere...
It's way too creepy to get a vision of my own death!
Smaller dragons appeared over here...
WHOOSH
They're actually there!!
What's going on?!!
KRAKK
KRAKK
KRAKK
Did somebody *tell* us this was going to happen?!!

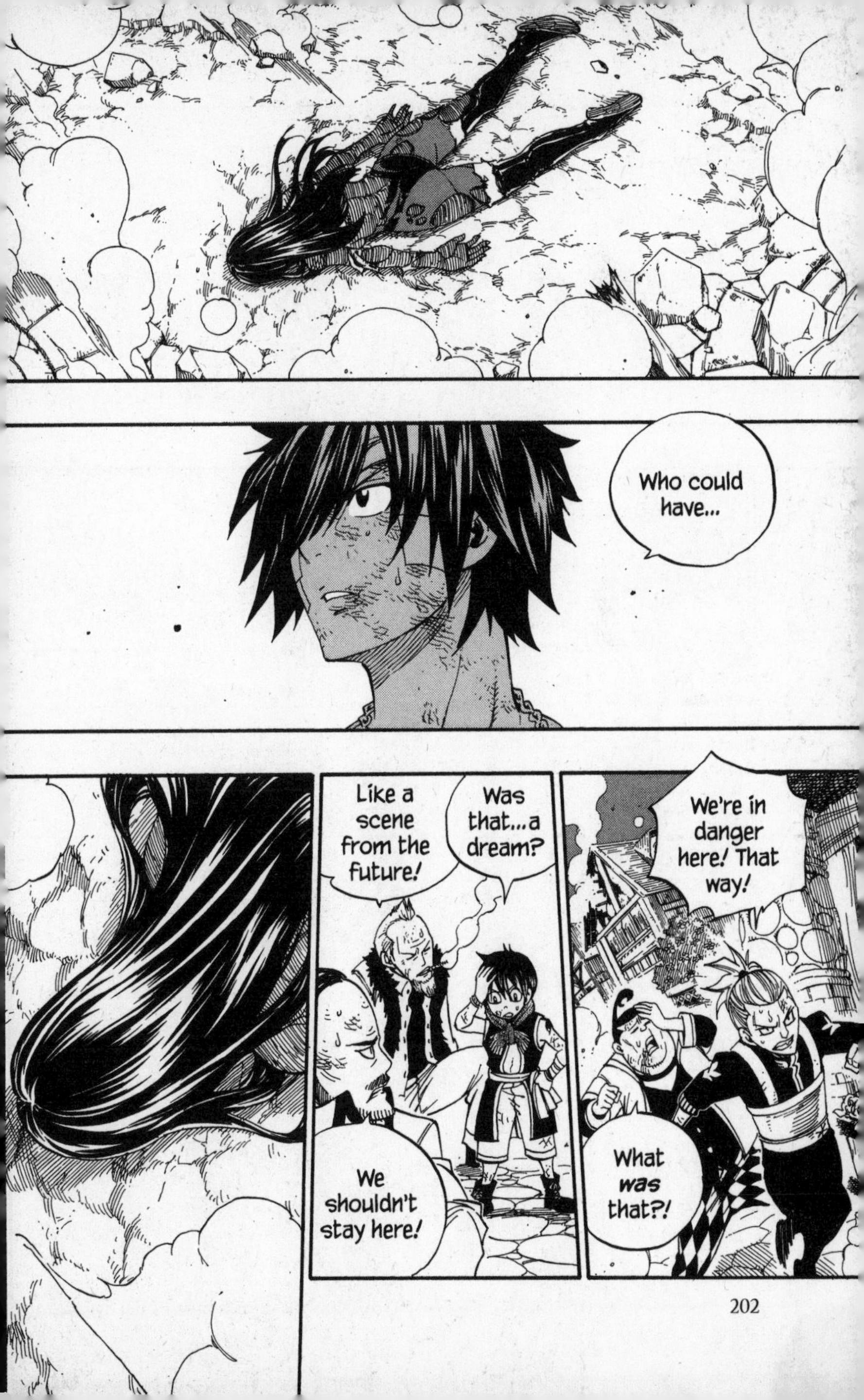
Who could have...
We're in danger here! That way!
What *was* that?!
Was that...a dream?
Like a scene from the future!
We shouldn't stay here!

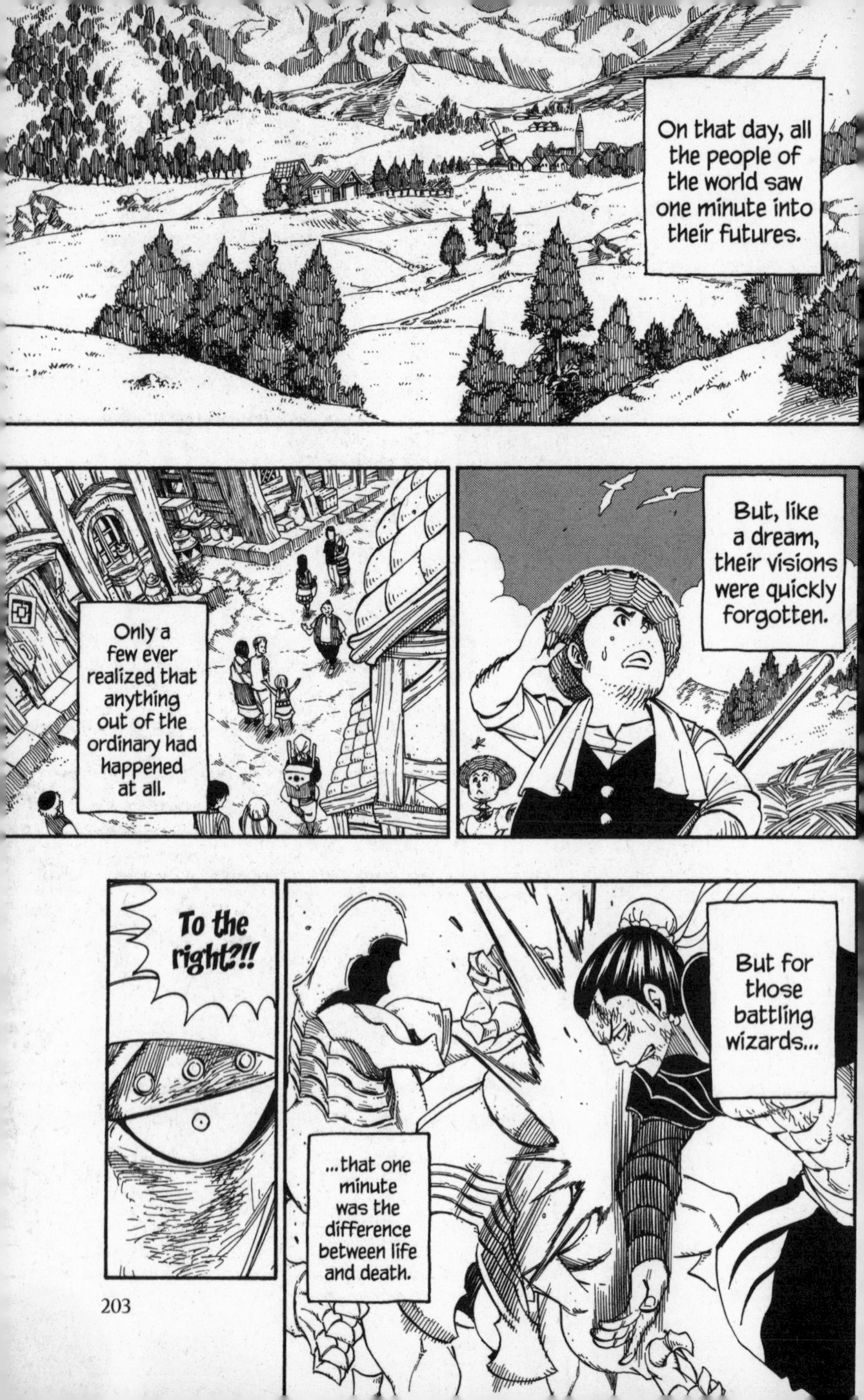
On that day, all the people of the world saw one minute into their futures.
But, like a dream, their visions were quickly forgotten.
Only a few ever realized that anything out of the ordinary had happened at all.
But for those battling wizards...
...that one minute was the difference between life and death.
To the right?!!

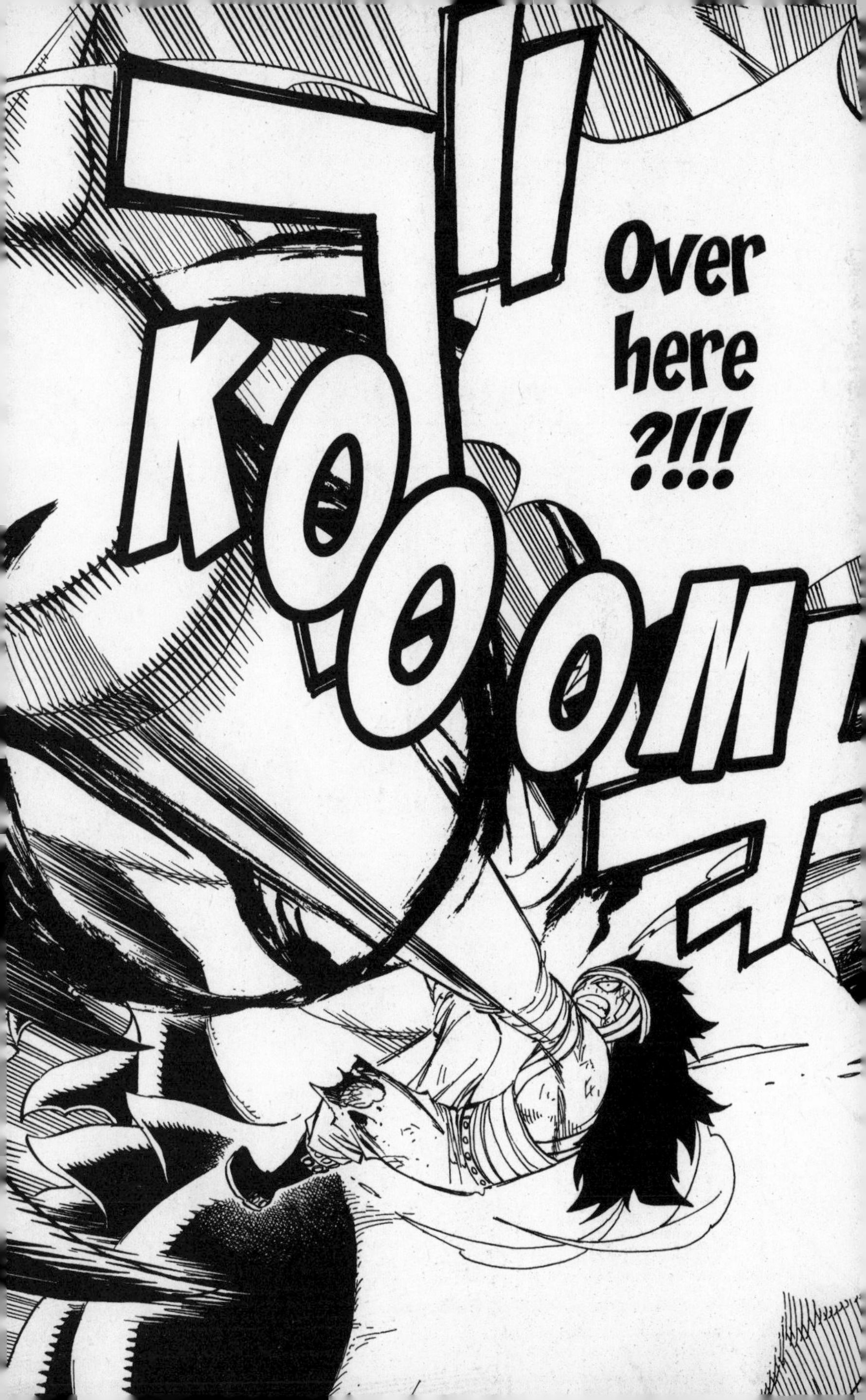
KOOOM!!
Over here?!!!

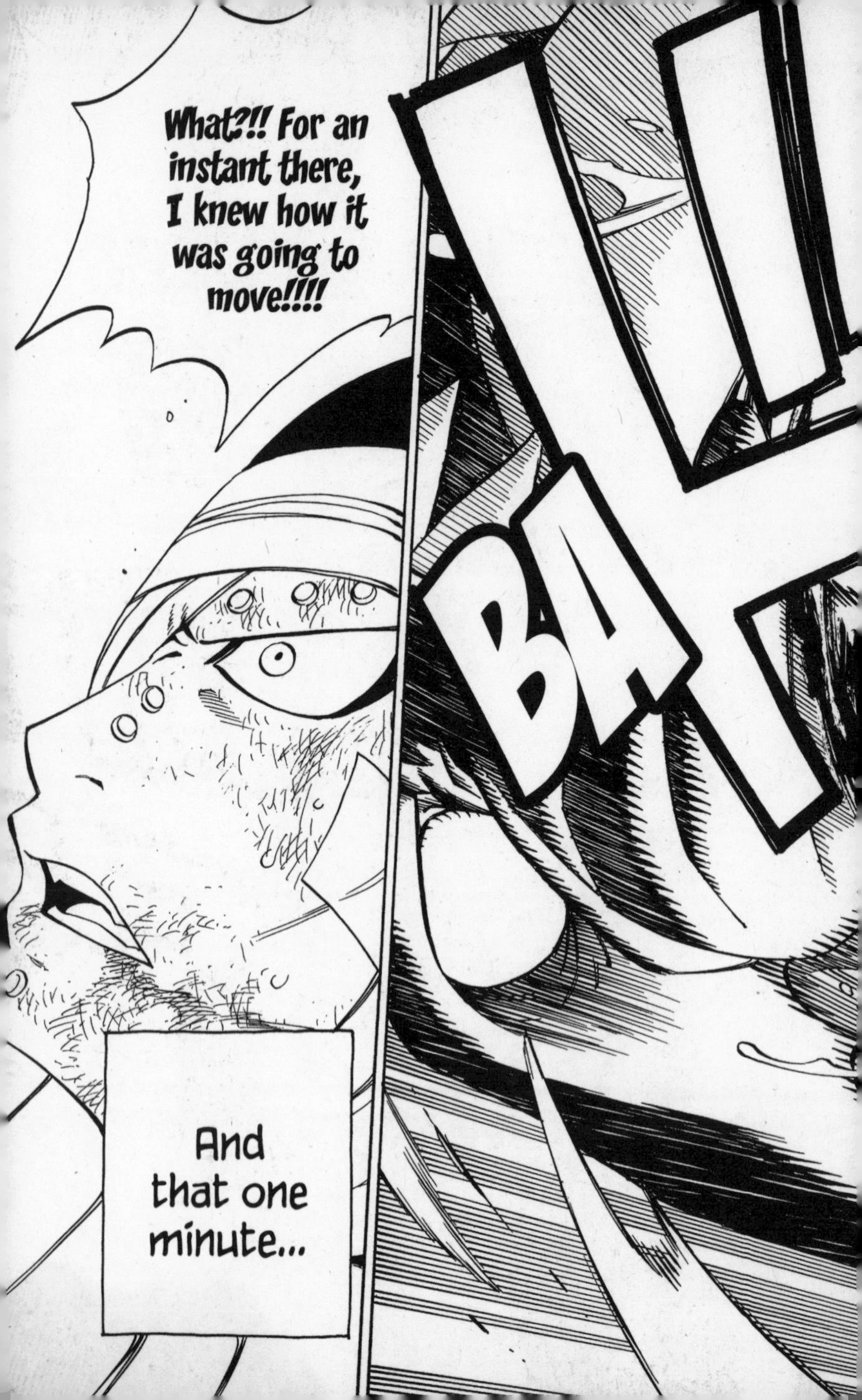
BA
What?!! For an instant there, I knew how it was going to move!!!!
And that one minute...

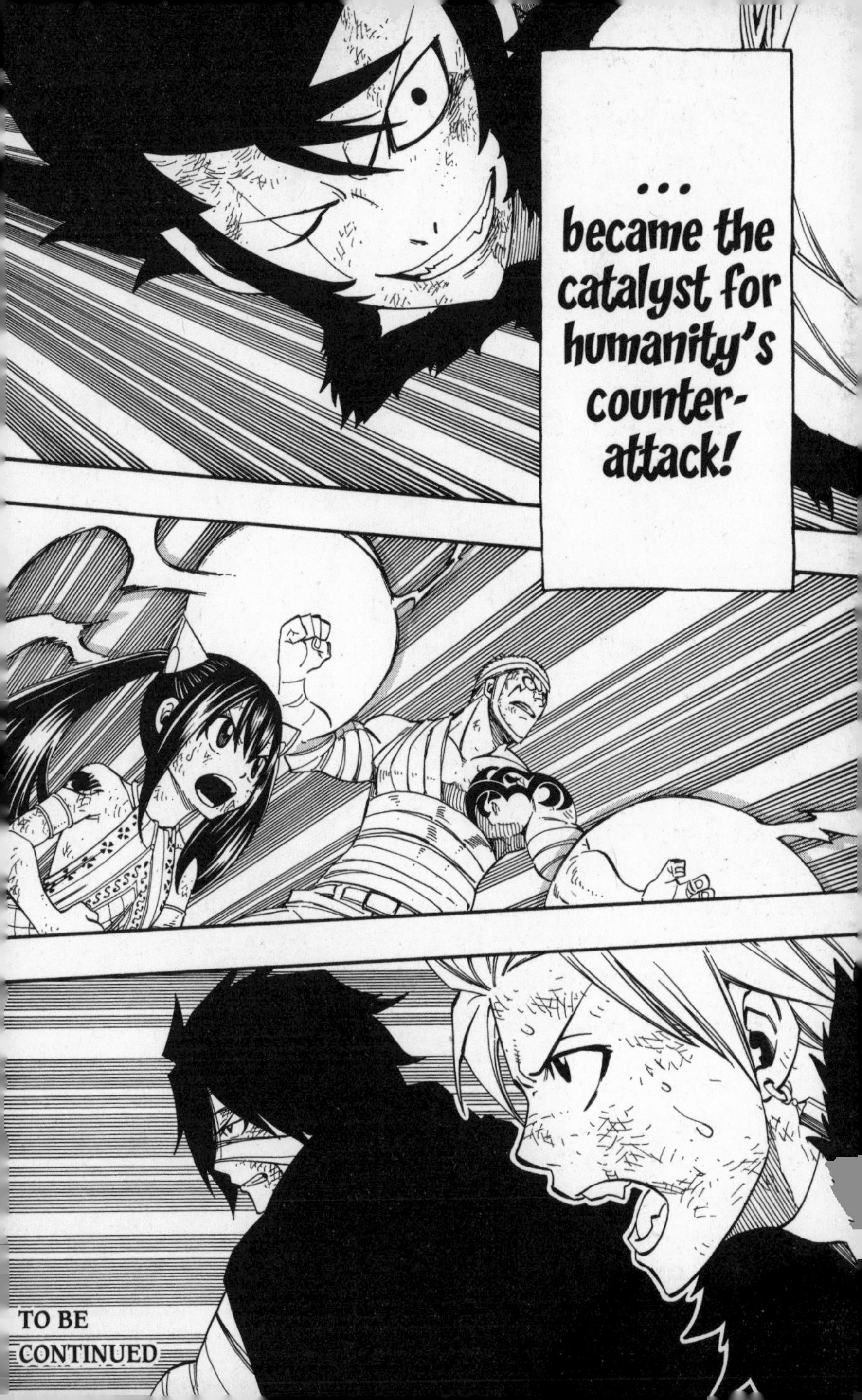
...became the catalyst for humanity's counter-attack!
TO BE CONTINUED

あとがき
Afterword

Well, it looks like the main story has turned out to be a really big thing, and in the next volume, the Grand Magic Games arc finally comes to a close. Wow, this one was long! I have a shorter episode planned for the next one. But even saying that, the next episode foreshadows a long story afterward. I still can't say much about it, but the next long arc will have more plot twists than you've seen before, and the entire story of Fairy Tail will change in a very big way.

We're getting close to **that one thing that was in the original setup that has always been a mystery!**

Now, the Japanese "Special Edition" version of this graphic novel includes the anime DVD of the Fairy Tail and Rave Master collaboration manga! I tried to write it so that even if you've never caught a glimpse of my earlier work, Rave Master, you can still enjoy it. It took quite a bit of figuring out. Sure, if you know it, you'll have even more fun with it, but if you've never encountered it, it'll make me really happy if you think, "Hey, that Haru guy is pretty cool," or, "The girl Elie sure is cute!"

I get embarrassed by my old work, so I hardly ever read my old books I put out a long time ago, but there have been so many comments saying, "I still love Rave," or, "The first time I bought your manga was when you did Rave," that it really boosts my spirits! So maybe I'll just come out and say, "If there is anybody out there who hasn't read it, maybe you can take this chance to check it out…"

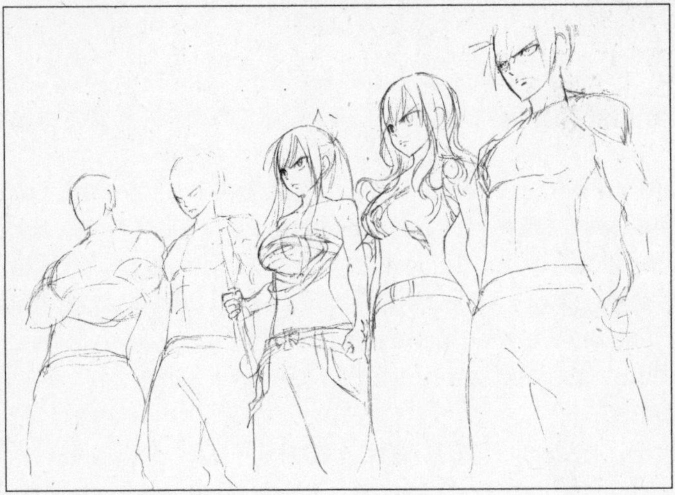

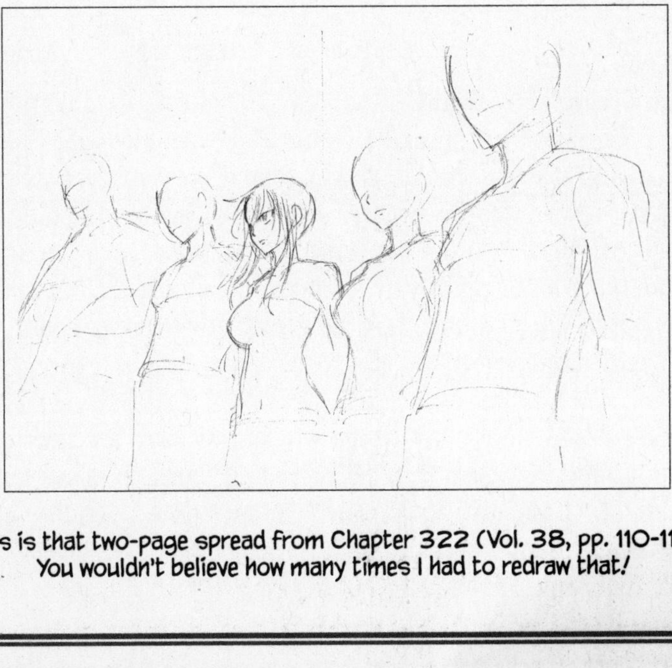

This is that two-page spread from Chapter 322 (Vol. 38, pp. 110-111).
You wouldn't believe how many times I had to redraw that!

FAIRY TAIL

フェアリーテイル

39

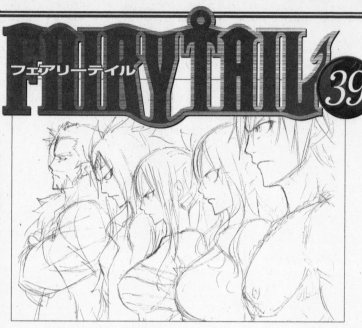

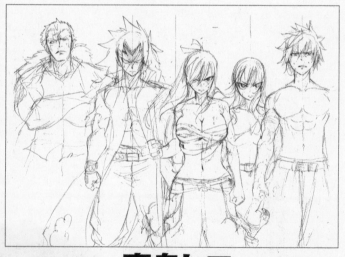

HIRO 真島ヒロ MASHIMA

FROM HIRO MASHIMA

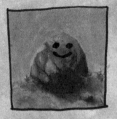

This time, there are very few bonus pages, but in exchange, the main story goes on longer than normal. I've written this many times before, but sometimes there is nothing an author can do when it comes to how many main-story pages and how many bonus pages are in a book. Things seem a little complicated, and even after all this time, I don't think I could explain it.

If any of you become manga artists in the future, and if you put out a graphic novel, I'm sure you'll be pretty surprised too. You'll say, "Yeah, I don't get it either."

Original Jacket Design: Hisao Ogawa

Preview of *Fairy Tail*, volume 40

We're pleased to present you with a preview from Fairy Tail, volume 40, coming soon to print and digital platforms. Please check our Web site (www.kodanshacomics.com) to see when this volume will be available.

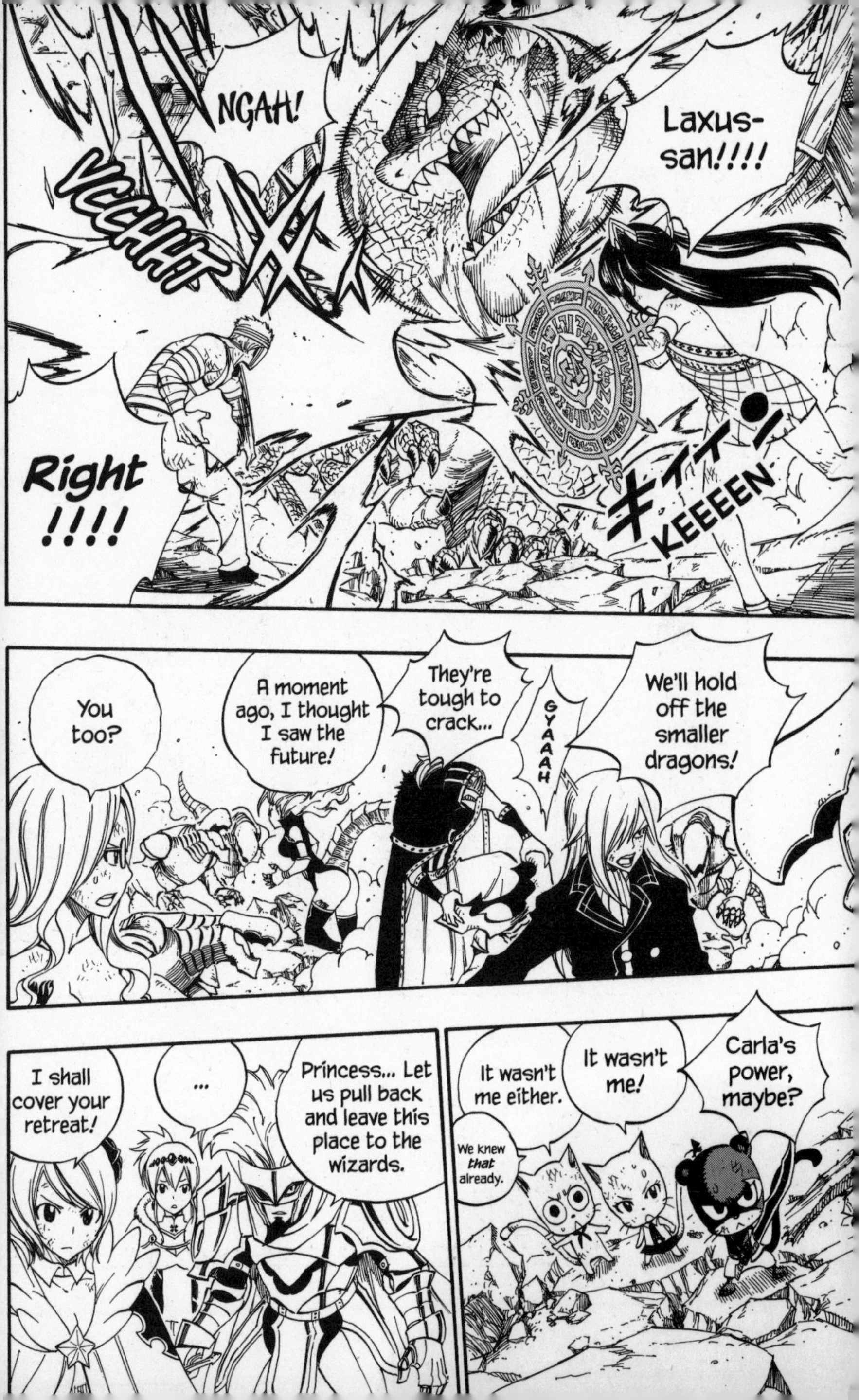

Laxus-san!!!!
KEEEEN
NGAH!
VCCHHT
Right !!!!
We'll hold off the smaller dragons!
GYAAAAH
They're tough to crack...
A moment ago, I thought I saw the future!
You too?
Carla's power, maybe?
It wasn't me!
It wasn't me either.
We knew *that* already.
Princess... Let us pull back and leave this place to the wizards.
...
I shall cover your retreat!

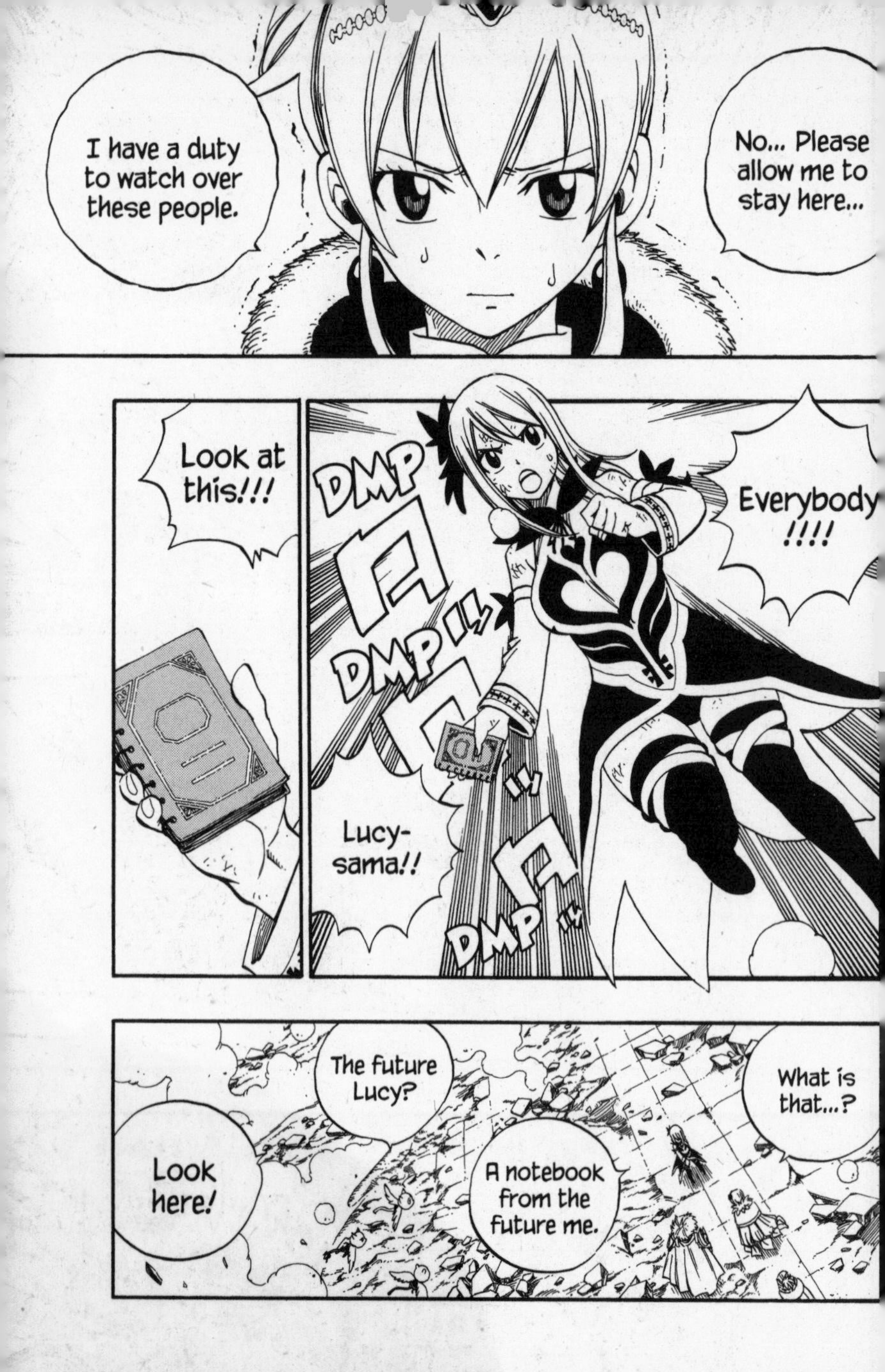
No... Please allow me to stay here...
I have a duty to watch over these people.
Everybody!!!!
DMP
DMP!!
DMP!!
Lucy-sama!!
Look at this!!!
What is that...?
The future Lucy?
A notebook from the future me.
Look here!

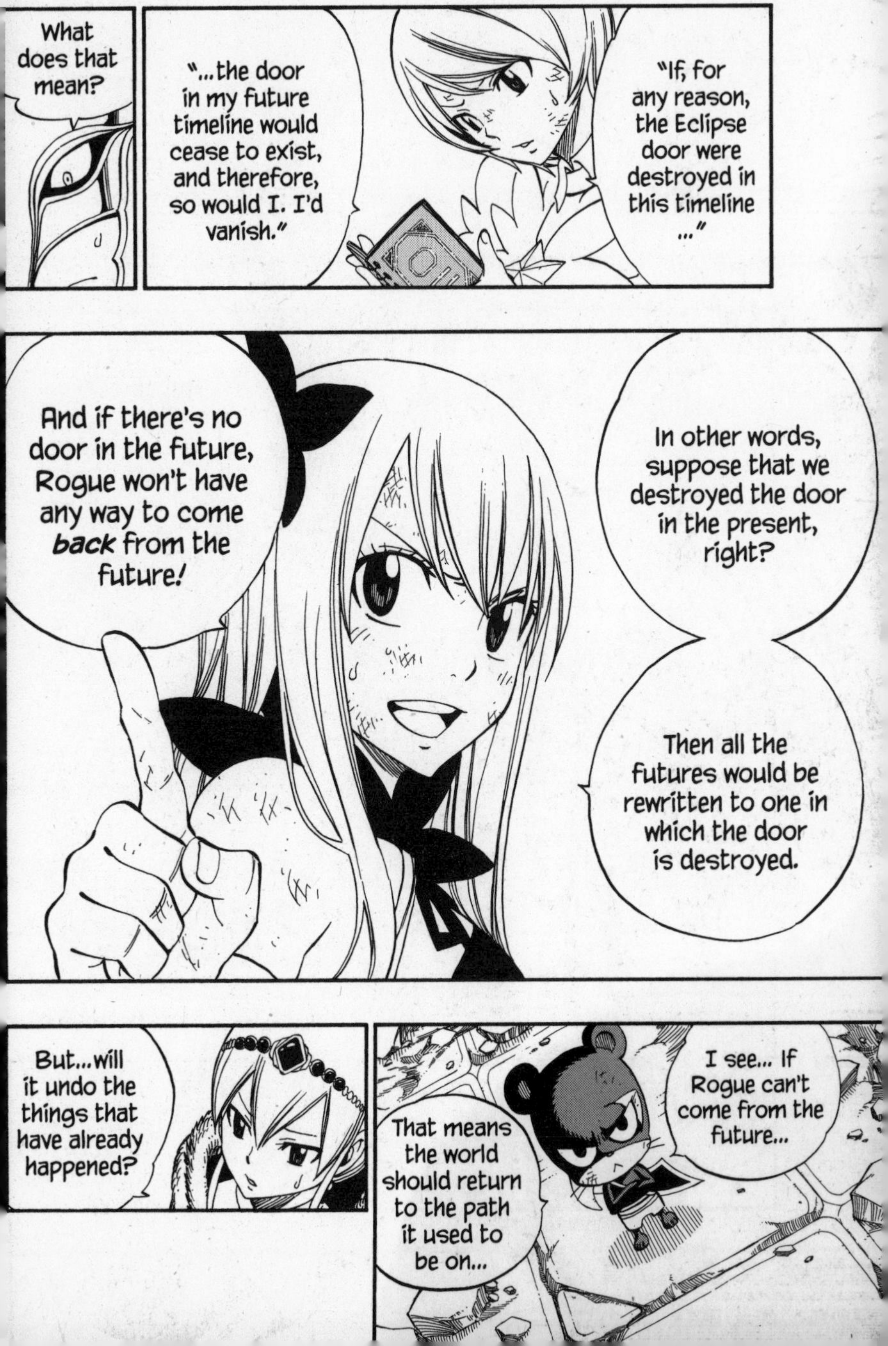
"If, for any reason, the Eclipse door were destroyed in this timeline ..."
"...the door in my future timeline would cease to exist, and therefore, so would I. I'd vanish."
What does that mean?
In other words, suppose that we destroyed the door in the present, right?
Then all the futures would be rewritten to one in which the door is destroyed.
And if there's no door in the future, Rogue won't have any way to come *back* from the future!
I see... If Rogue can't come from the future...
That means the world should return to the path it used to be on...
But...will it undo the things that have already happened?

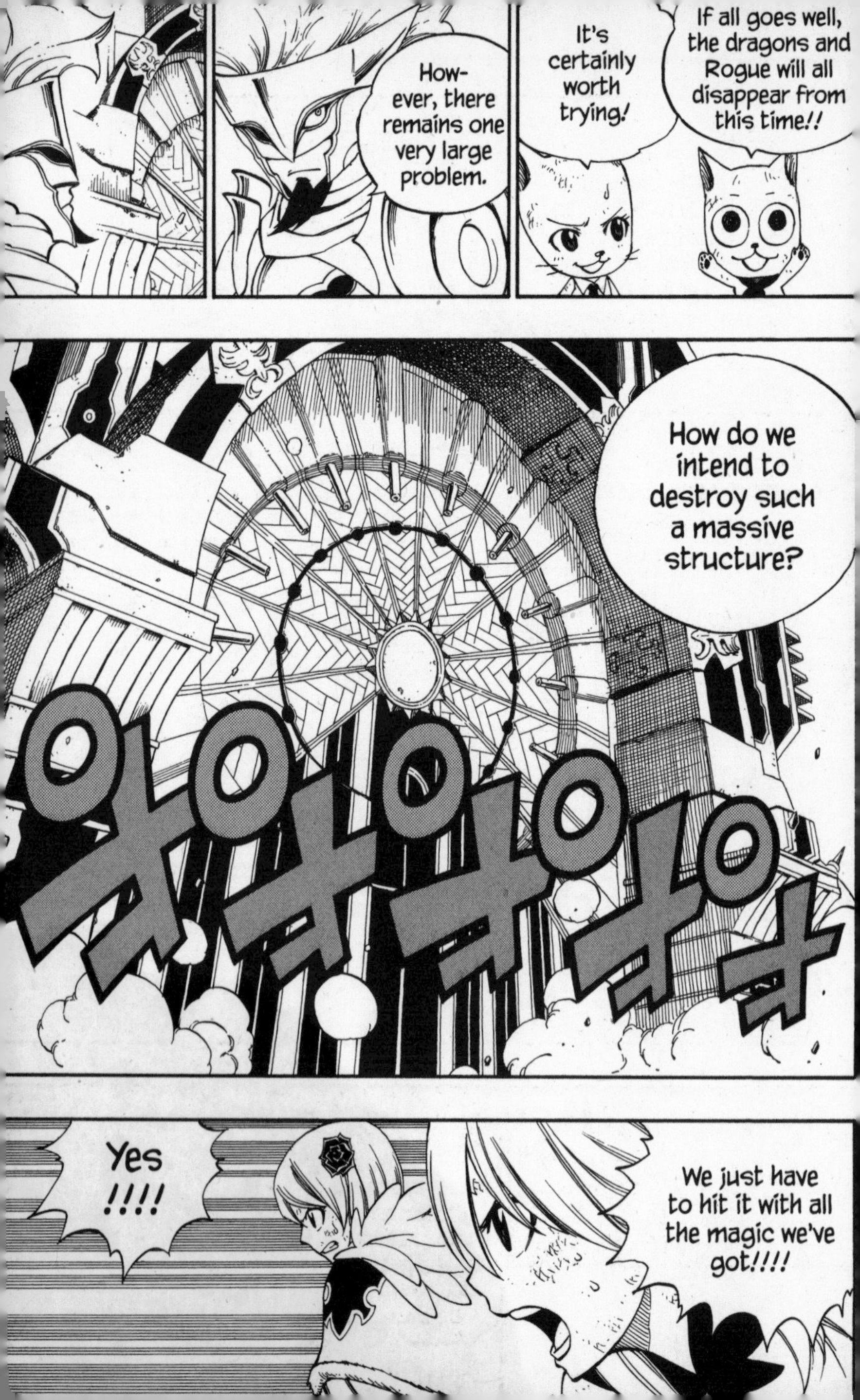
If all goes well, the dragons and Rogue will all disappear from this time!!
It's certainly worth trying!
How-ever, there remains one very large problem.
How do we intend to destroy such a massive structure?
We just have to hit it with all the magic we've got!!!!
Yes !!!!

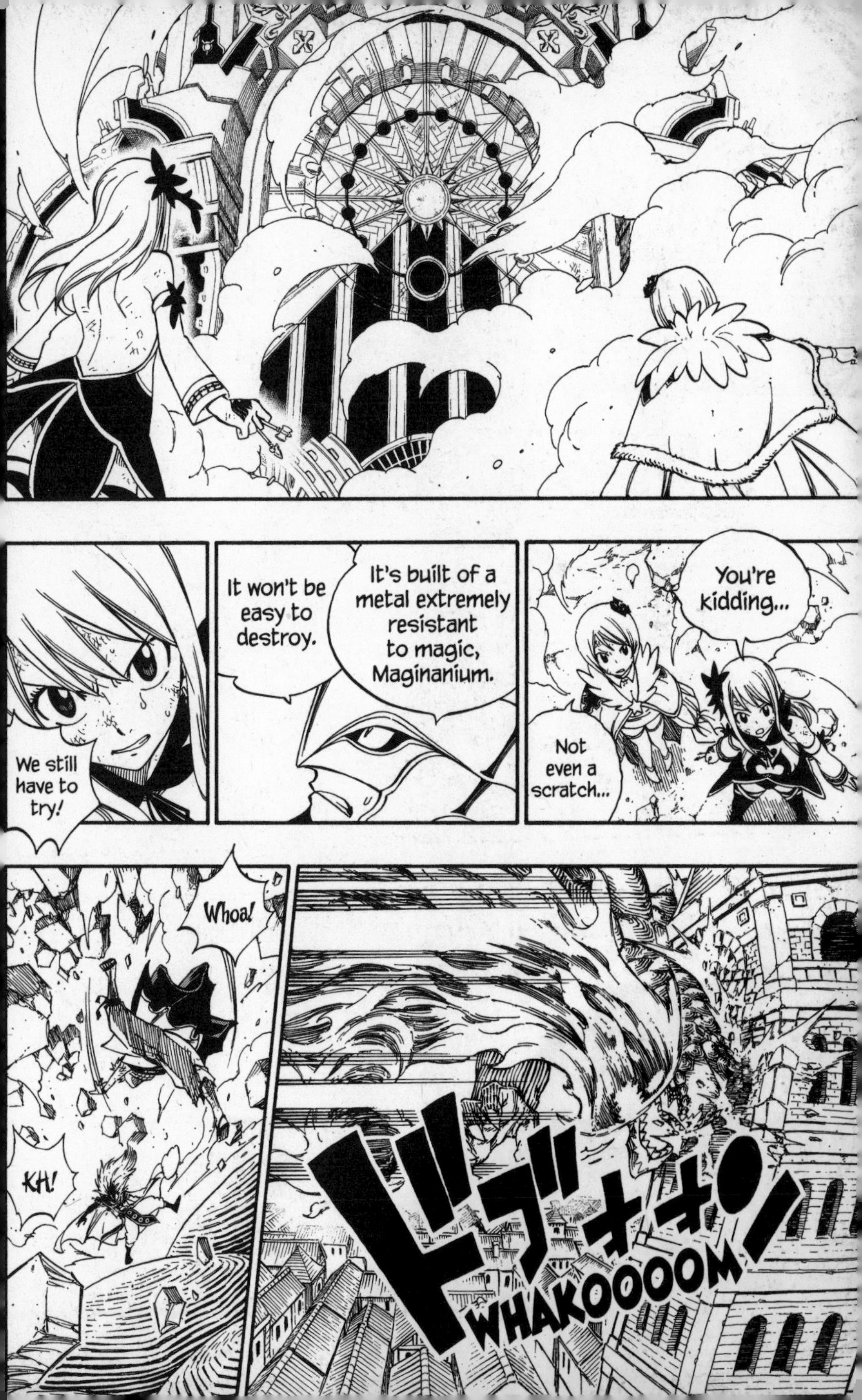
You're kidding...
Not even a scratch...
It's built of a metal extremely resistant to magic, Maginanium.
It won't be easy to destroy.
We still have to try!
WHAKOOOOM
Whoa!
KH!

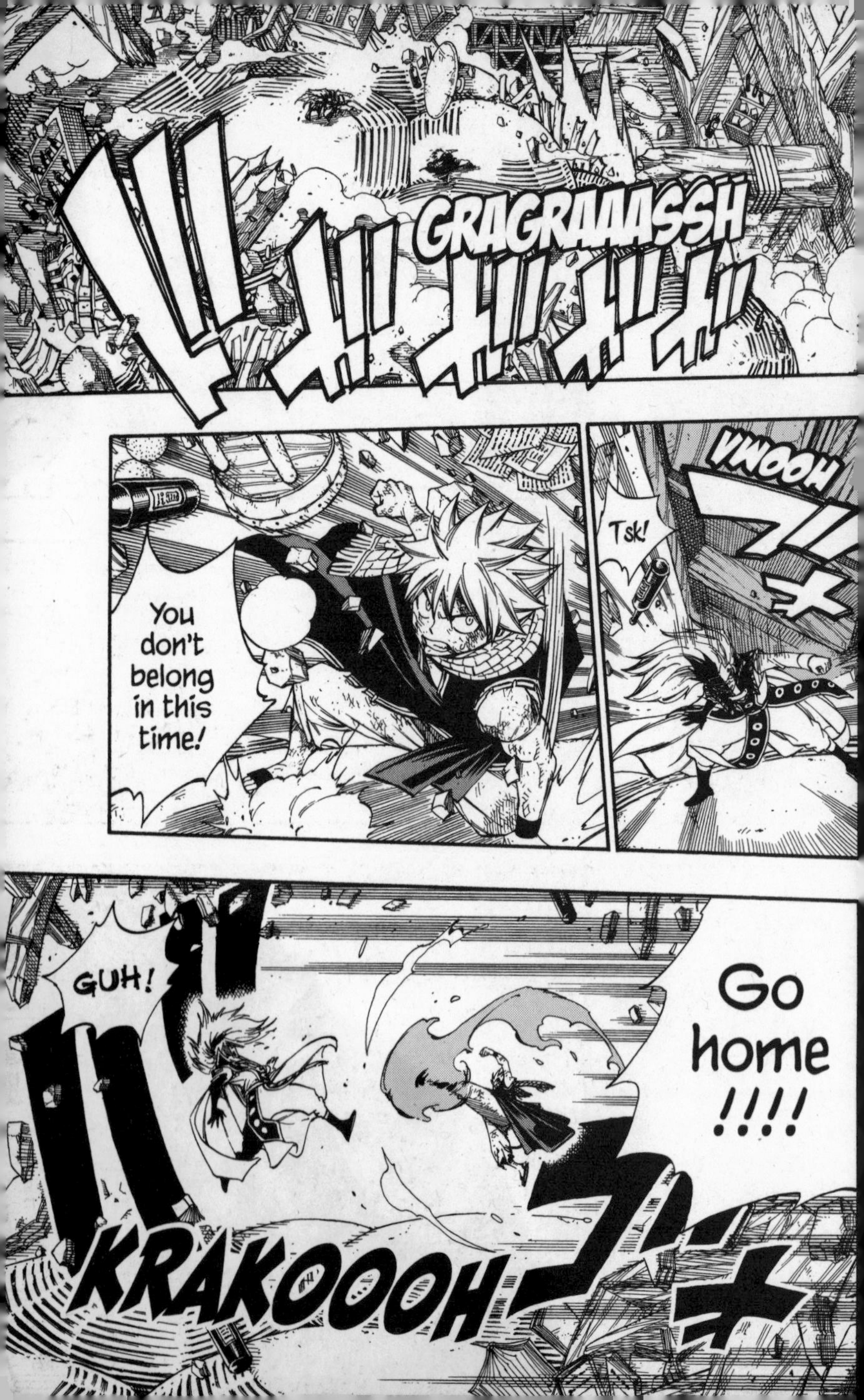
GRAGRAAASSH
VWOOH
Tsk!
You don't belong in this time!
Go home !!!!
GUH!
KRAKOOOH

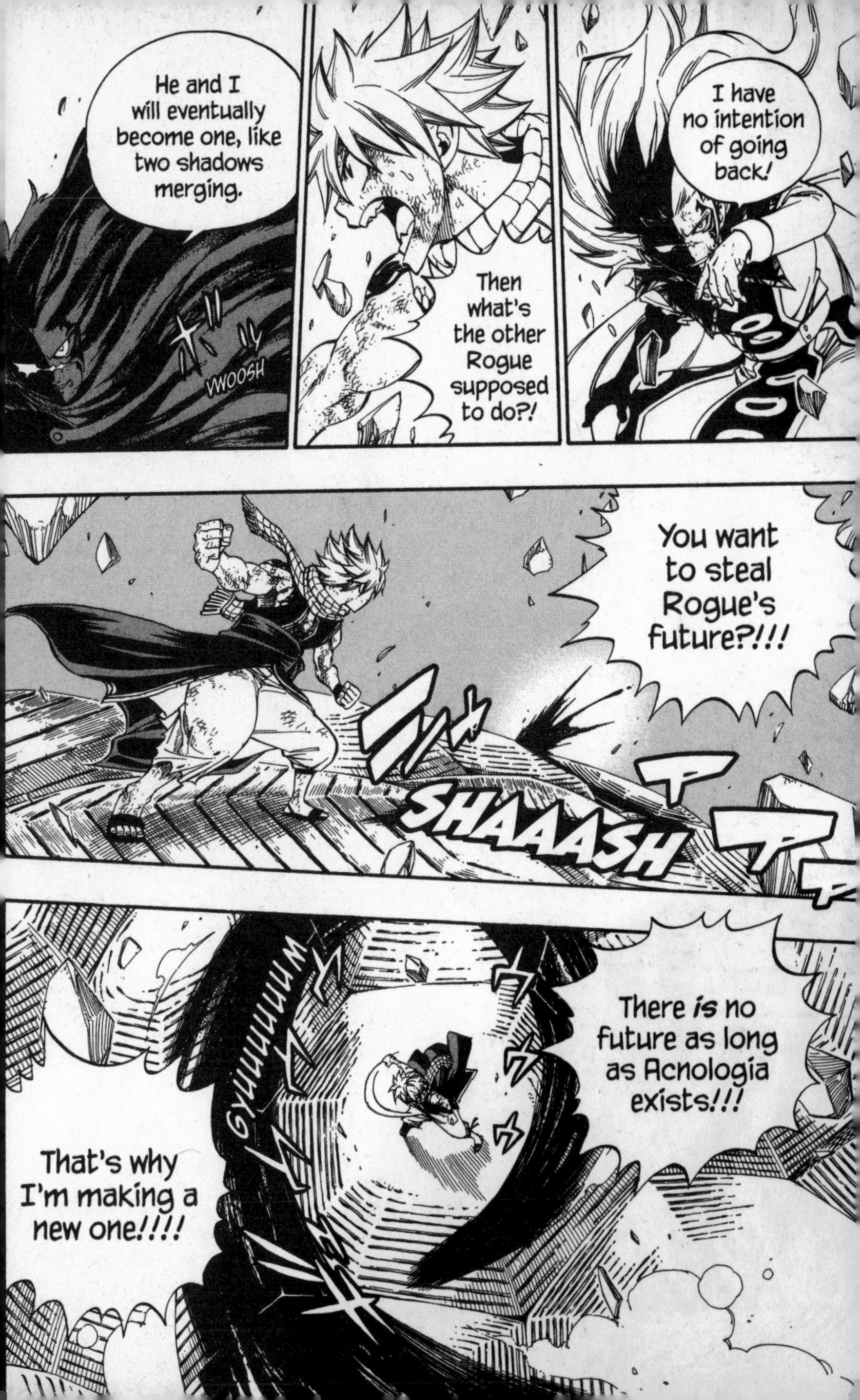

I have no intention of going back!
Then what's the other Rogue supposed to do?!
He and I will eventually become one, like two shadows merging.
VWOOSH
You want to steal Rogue's future?!!!
SHAAASH
There *is* no future as long as Acnologia exists!!!
GYUUUUUUN
That's why I'm making a new one!!!!

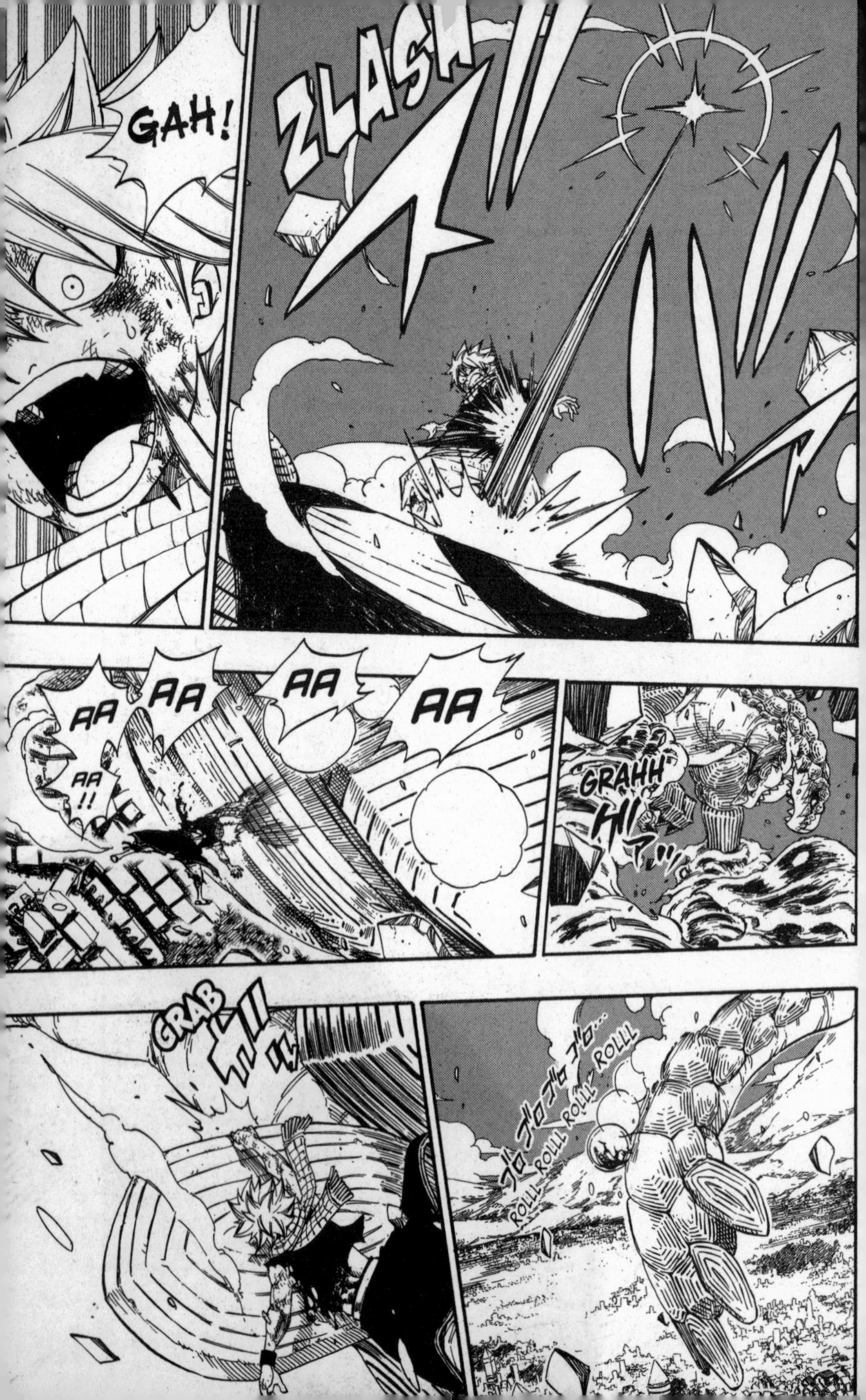

ZLASH
GAH!
GRAHH
AA
AA
AA
AA
AA!!
ゴロゴロゴロ...
ROLLL ROLLL ROLLL ROLLL
GRAB

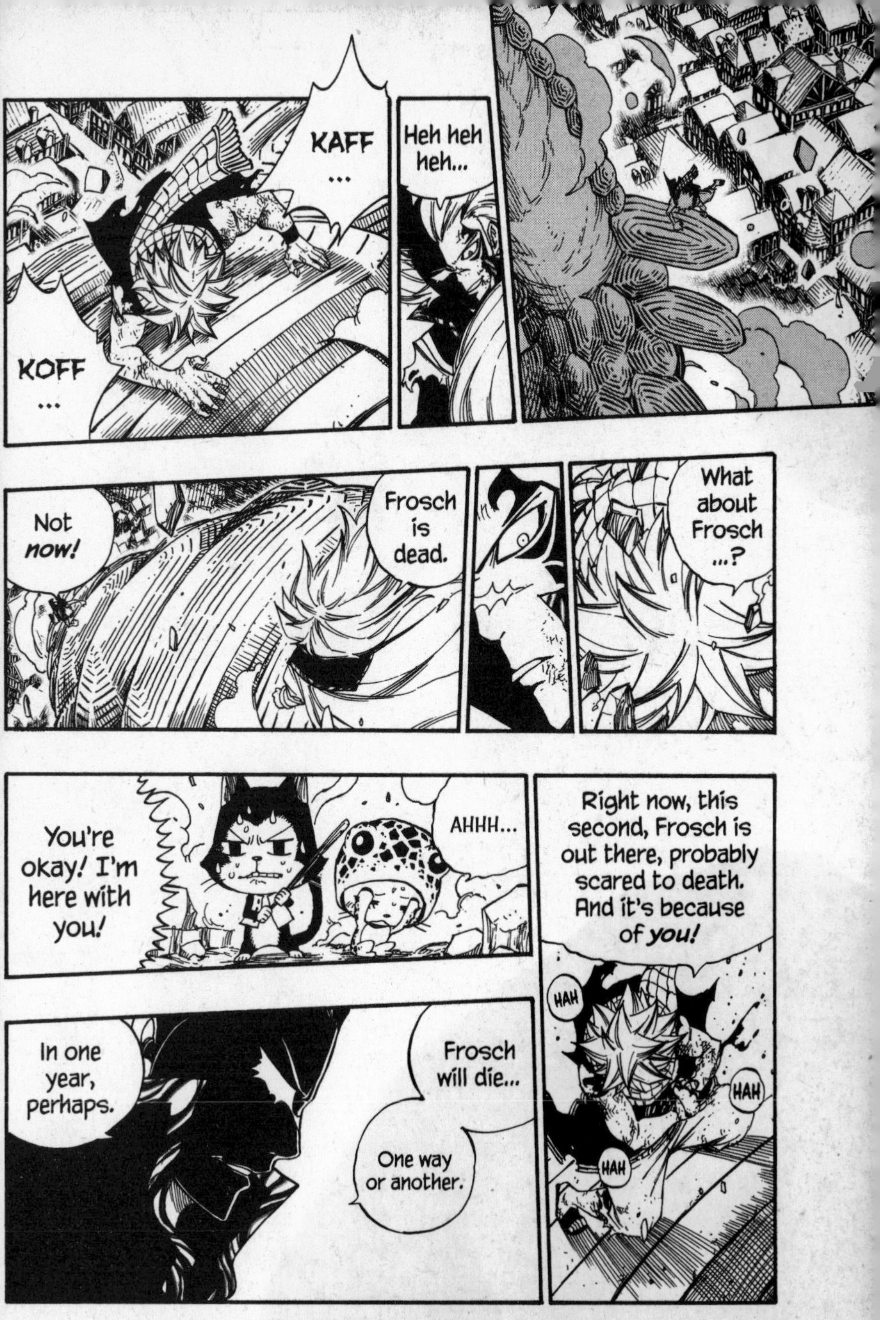
Heh heh heh...
KAFF ...
KOFF ...
What about Frosch ...?
Frosch is dead.
Not *now!*
Right now, this second, Frosch is out there, probably scared to death. And it's because of *you!*
HAH
HAH
HAH
AHHH...
You're okay! I'm here with you!
Frosch will die...
In one year, perhaps.
One way or another.

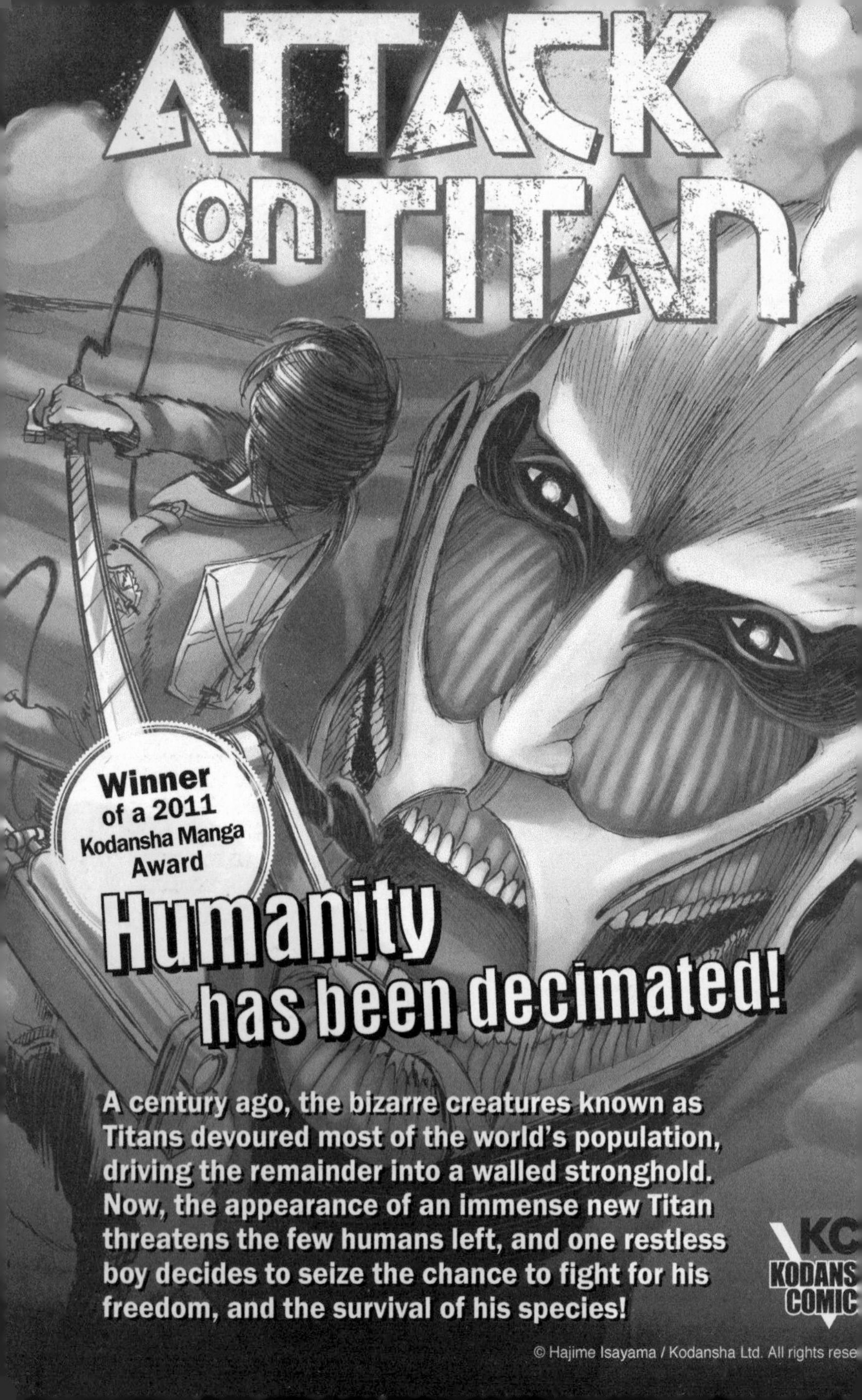

ATTACK on TITAN

Winner of a 2011 Kodansha Manga Award

Humanity has been decimated!

A century ago, the bizarre creatures known as Titans devoured most of the world's population, driving the remainder into a walled stronghold. Now, the appearance of an immense new Titan threatens the few humans left, and one restless boy decides to seize the chance to fight for his freedom, and the survival of his species!

KC
KODANS
COMIC

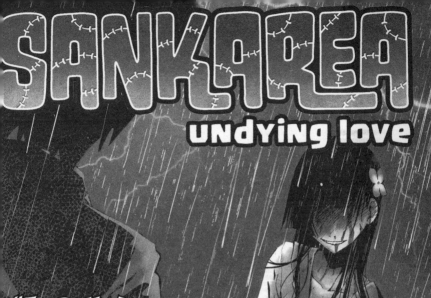

SANKAREA
undying love

"I ONLY LIKE ZOMBIE GIRLS."

Chihiro has an unusual connection to zombie movies. He doesn't feel bad for the survivors – he wants to comfort the undead girls they slaughter! When his pet passes away, he brews a resurrection potion. He's discovered by local heiress Sanka Rea, and she serves as his first test subject!

Fairy Tail volume 39 is a work of fiction. Names, characters, places, and incidents are the products of the author's imagination or are used fictitiously. Any resemblance to actual events, locales, or persons, living or dead, is entirely coincidental.

A Kodansha Comics Trade Paperback Original.

Published in the United States by Kodansha Comics, an imprint of Kodansha USA Publishing, LLC, New York.

Publication rights for this English edition arranged through Kodansha Ltd., Tokyo.

First published in Japan in 2013 by Kodansha Ltd., Tokyo
ISBN 978-1-61262-416-7

Printed in the United States of America.

www.kodanshacomics.com

9 8 7 6 5 4 3 2 1

Translation: William Flanagan
Lettering: AndWorld Design
Editing: Ben Applegate

TOMARE!

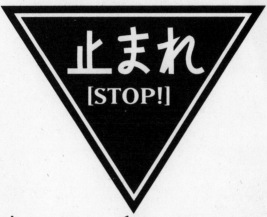

止まれ
[STOP!]

You're going the wrong way!

Manga is a completely different type of reading experience.

To start at the *beginning,* go to the *end!*

That's right! Authentic manga is read the traditional Japanese way—from right to left, exactly the *opposite* of how American books are read. It's easy to follow: Just go to the other end of the book and read each pa̶g̶e̶—a̶n̶d̶ e̶a̶c̶h̶ p̶a̶n̶e̶l̶—f̶r̶o̶m̶ r̶i̶g̶h̶t̶ side to left side, starting at the top ̶.̶.̶.̶.̶.̶.̶.̶.̶.̶.̶.̶.̶.̶.̶.̶.̶.̶ manga as it was meant to be!